The Comprehension Approach to Foreign Language Instruction

Harris Winitz, Editor
University of Missouri—Kansas City

Newbury House Publishers, Inc. / Rowley / Massachusetts / 01969
ROWLEY • LONDON • TOKYO

1981

Library of Congress Cataloging in Publication Data
Main entry under title:

The Comprehension approach to foreign language instruction.

1. Languages, Modern--Study and teaching--Addresses,
essays, lectures. I. Winitz, Harris, 1933–
PB36.C57   418'.007   80-20928
ISBN 0-88377-181-0

Cover design by Carol Eldridge.
Cover art by Syd Baker.

NEWBURY HOUSE PUBLISHERS, INC.

Language Science
Language Teaching
Language Learning

ROWLEY, MASSACHUSETTS 01969
ROWLEY • LONDON • TOKYO

First printing: November 1981

Printed in the U.S.A.   5   4   3

DEDICATION

Valerian Postovsky at work

Valerian Postovsky
1918–1977

Steeped in the tradition of the audio-lingual and grammar translation methodologies, Valerian Postovsky dared to push the past aside. He did what many find impossible to do late in their academic careers. He challenged his own educational experiences and biases, and began to develop an alternate learning strategy.

Vladivostok, Russia was Val's birthplace; the year was 1918. When he was two his family immigrated to China, where Val received his primary and secondary education. In 1953, after being awarded the bachelor's and master's degrees from the University of California at Berkeley, he joined the Defense Language Institute as an instructor of Russian and remained there with his wife Vera until his death in 1977. His doctoral dissertation, completed at Berkeley in 1970, reflects Val's first contribution to the study of language comprehension.

I met Val in 1972 after he had attained the position of Director of Slavic Languages. Our first meeting was filled with excitement. Along with my colleague James Reeds, I involved myself in an exhaustive two-day discussion of the comprehension approach and its implications for language teaching.

In the next five years Val labored indefatigably over his research. He refined his instructional system, tested scores of subjects, and produced a number of significant articles. One of his important contributions is reprinted in this volume.

Val heard the rhythmic beats of a different drummer and kept those last five years filled with activity. He had "promises to keep, and miles to go," and even death's final proclamation did not stop him. The work of this gentle and beneficent person will someday be completed, as others someday will complete our work.

Contents

The Comprehension Approach: An Introduction

Harris Winitz

Professor of Speech Science and Psychology
University of Missouri, Kansas City

If I wanted to learn a foreign language, my first inclination would be to try to understand it. I would be particularly pleased if I were able to comprehend conversations in a new language even though I might be unable to utter a single word. That comprehension should be the focal methodology in the acquisition of a foreign language is an uncommonly held tenet among foreign language instructors and among adults who wish to acquire a second language. Students and teachers of language often insist that instruction in speaking and grammatical principles should play the fundamental role in learning to master a new language. The teaching of understanding or comprehension seems to be of secondary significance. It is not clear why this is so.

Recent advances in theoretical linguistics, child language investigations, and, most importantly, preliminary experimentation in foreign language instruction, indicate the primary role of comprehension in the acquisition of language. These three areas of inquiry and the special significance each has for a comprehension-based methodology will be considered.

With the shift in the 1960s from structural grammars to transformational grammars, the enormous complexity of the human grammatical system was recognized and appreciated for the first time. Chomsky (1965) cleverly employed the phrase "tacit knowledge" to describe the knowledge a speaker-hearer has of the language he or she knows. Of particular significance for the psychological study of language was the observation that speakers can tell when an utterance is ungrammatical, but often cannot tell why. Ungrammaticality has served and continues to serve linguists well as a tool for linguistic inquiry.

An early example presented by Chomsky (1966) involved the following:

1. John is easy to please.
2. John is eager to please.
3. It is easy to please John.
4. *It is eager to please John

In (1) and (2) "John" is the grammatical subject. "John" is also the logical object in (1). Sentence (3) is a transformed version of (1). As speakers of English, we tacitly understand subject and object relationships regardless of the position of these elements in a sentence. For this reason we reject (4) as an English sentence. Rejection of (4) does not necessarily imply that we explicitly know that underlying grammatical structures for sentences (1) and (2) are different. Chomsky used the term *deep structure* to refer to the underlying structures (phrase markers) of sentences. He used the term *tacit knowledge* to refer to the native speaker's implicit understanding of the rules that are used to generate the "deep structures" of sentences.

Consider sentences (5), (6), and (7):

5. The chicken is awful to bite.
6. The chicken is awful to do the biting.
7. Biting the chicken is awful.

Sentence (5) has two meanings that are derivable from its deep structure. In sentence (5) chicken can be both agent and object, as indicated in sentences (6) and (7). As agent, it has the meaning expressed in (6), and as object, the meaning expressed in (7). Similarly, sentence (8),

8. The umpire ordered the players to stop the fighting.

can have two meanings. They are:

9. The umpire ordered the players to stop fighting among themselves.
10. The umpire ordered the players to stop the fighting of other people.

Tacit knowledge, then, is knowing without knowing why. Native speakers do not have explicit knowledge of the grammatical rules that they use to generate sentences. It is axiomatically clear that speakers do not frame sentences within the context of carefully thought out grammatical compositions. The art of making sentences would be slowed to the point that conversation as we know it could not exist if each grammatical principle had to be explicitly recovered by the speaker prior to the utterance of each sentence.

Imagine the complexity that a plural form would evoke. The simple phrase "cats and dogs" would require the retrieval of a complex phonological rule that describes when the plural is an [s], as in "cats" or a [z] as in "dogs." No native

English speaker, unless he or she has studied linguistics, knows explicitly the English affix rule for plurals. Yet, provide an English speaker with a nonsense stem, as Berko (1958) did, and he or she will not fail to provide the correct phonological unit. A "nush," for example, will always be pluralized as "nushes," and a "strup," as "strups." The [z] will always be appended to the stem "vorm," although the orthographic representation is *s* as in "vorms."

Why is it that foreign language students are asked to memorize rules? The belief is held that rules are an essential first step in language learning. Undeniably rules can be used to decipher the sentences of a strange language. This process is laborious, not always accurate, and does not guarantee that the end result will produce language fluency for the translator. Few teachers are convinced that rules alone are sufficient to learn a language. Precisely for this reason most language texts contain an extensive variety of practical exercises.

Some teachers recognize that rule learning provides an intellectual understanding of the grammatical systems of a language. However, they readily acknowledge that explicit understanding of rules cannot be equated with the tacit knowledge a native speaker uses to generate sentences. Twaddell (1948, p. 78) expressed it in the following way: "We know that the rules are only temporary substitutes for habits, and the sooner a rule is forgotten . . . the better. We want the student to get to the point where he can forget the rule and take the habit for granted . . ."

On the other hand statements of rules may not be an effective language teaching strategy. For example, consider the following rule for the progressive expression:

> It is formed by adding *-ing* to the verb stem; this main verb is preceded by the appropriate auxiliary verb(s), and denotes continued activity.

A common teaching strategy would be to follow this explanation with several paradigmatic examples using two or three common verbs. The English progressive has probably been introduced in this way countless times. Despite its apparent simplicity, the progressive is a structure that foreign students of English find interminably complex.

Note that the above rule identifies the *-ing* affix for the student. It tells the student that this surface form exists. This strategy, some grammarians might contend, alerts the student to the presence of a grammatical unit that he or she might otherwise not notice. It does not, of course, explain why it is that one cannot say "I am knowing," but can say "I am thinking."

Simple rules can be deceiving. Telling students that German has an indefinite and a definite article, which additionally are marked by gender, case, and number, would seem to be a time saver for the student. He or she would not have to spend valuable study time determining whether or not these functors exist and discovering their special role in German. However, unless additional information is given, the student will act as though the articles of English and German correlate in usage. It is recognized that students would have difficulty with the phonological shapes of the German articles even if the correlation between the usage of German and English articles were perfect; but this fact is beside the point. At the present time there are no rules that adequately describe for all instances the correct use of articles in English or German (or probably any other language).

Articles and the progressive are not the only elements for which the grammatical rules are incomplete. Almost all grammatical descriptions that are provided in introductory foreign language texts are limited in their descriptive capacity.

Once a superficial rule is introduced there is no turning back. The student wants to know "what it means" and "how it is used." The more the student is told about the rule, the more likely he or she will find the rule increasingly complex and difficult to understand. Transformational grammar provides descriptions far more detailed in many cases than those available twenty years ago. Although these grammatical descriptions are elegant, they are also incomplete, and in some instances not entirely correct. Furthermore, transformational rules are difficult to understand without a sophisticated background in theoretical linguistics. Although one can have an intellectual appreciation of transformational rules, it does not necessarily follow that one can use this knowledge in any real sense when learning a second language.

In summary, teaching rules to students is a standard teaching practice. The rules that are usually taught are surface rules which are often incomplete and inaccurate. Furthermore, because of their simplicity they may mislead the student into thinking that every example should fit the rule. After considerable experience with a language, students finally recognize that grammatical rules are only guides or outlines which they are happy to discard as they gain confidence with the language. Therefore, it is not surprising to hear students, who have achieved considerable success with a foreign language, comment that they no longer rely on the rules over which they so painfully labored. When asked the question, "At what point in your studies did you make this observation?" they often answer, "After I spent some time in the country of the language," or "After I had spent many years reading in the foreign language." Conceivably, as the student gained experience with the foreign language, he or she found it more and more useful to attend to underlying meaning. Perhaps in this way implicit understanding of grammar developed.

An alternative teaching approach is not to teach grammatical rules. This procedure has been advocated in the past, and is usually identified with certain phases of the direct method (Diller, 1978). Students are simply immersed in the language and are expected to discover the rules on their own.

It is generally recognized that children acquire the language of their community and home without explicit instruction in grammatical rules (Brown, 1973). The basic data are the phrases and sentences they hear and the correlated environmental events. From these observations, rules are formulated to account for regularity of data. These formulations are implicit, as children have no explicit knowledge of the grammatical rules they use. Not until the topic of grammar is studied in school do children realize that the academic discipline of grammar exists. Explicit grammatical knowledge is, therefore, not a prerequisite for the acquisition of language by native speakers. Would not this condition hold true for the acquisition of a second language?

The belief that adults can acquire a second language in essentially the same manner as children do has motivated language researchers to develop an instructional format that essentially reproduces the listening experiences of children. Listening comprehension is stressed. Students are given an opportunity to acquire the grammar of a second language by acquiring a fundamental understanding of the language. Initially the student hears sentences in the second language for which the meaning is clearly indicated through actions or pictures. All sentences are spoken by native speakers. Lexical items and grammatical units are carefully programmed to maximize implicit learning. The umbrella term for this instructional system is *the comprehension approach*. It differs significantly from other methods in the value placed on speaking exercises. Production drills and preplanned dialogues or artificially generated conversations are not used. Conversation is not discouraged. It simply is not taught. The belief is held that conversational fluency will develop as the result of learning to understand a language.

In Chapter One I provide a detailed description of the concept of nonlinear learning. The position I take is that the interrelationship among components of a grammatical system, the generative grammatical rules, are complex and great in number. Acquisition of a particular grammatical element requires an understanding of many, often distantly related structures. Thus it is reasoned that correct usage of a particular grammatical element cannot be acquired until a large part of the grammar of a language is understood. This position is in contrast to linear systems of training which emphasize mastery in production for each unit of language instruction. Comparisons and illustrations are drawn from the field of language disorders.

In Chapter Two Simon Belasco presents an interesting alternative to current teaching methodologies. He considers the ability of human beings "to inhibit partially" as the most serious obstacle to acquiring a second language. Belasco believes that developing "a state of expectancy" for morphophonemic (meaning in sound) cues can overcome the conditions imposed by partial inhibition.

Belasco suggests that emphasizing listening comprehension and reading comprehension not only are reasonable goals after two years of language learning but also are crucial to the communication process. In the absence of these skills, speaking and writing are reduced to verbal and spelling exercises. Belasco then outlines a program of instruction designed to take the language learner beyond nucleation, that stage of language learning when all the structural parts seem to fit together.

Current language teaching routines are questioned by Leonard Newmark in Chapter Three. In particular, he carefully considers the disadvantages of emphasizing speaking practice as a basic methodology for language learning. A student who is talking cannot be learning, he reasons, because language performance cannot exceed linguistic competence. Newmark concludes that new linguistic knowledge comes from listening to others talk. Practice in conversation benefits the student only after substantial linguistic knowledge has been acquired. At that point the student can participate in meaningful conversations in which additional linguistic knowledge can be acquired.

James Asher (Chapter Four) first presented the theory of comprehension learning in 1965 in a paper entitled "The strategy of the total physical response: An application to learning Russian." According to this system, students are taught to understand by responding to commands and by paying attention to verbal descriptions in the second language. Asher's teaching system, as well as that developed by Nord (Chapter Five) and Winitz and Reeds (see Chapter Six), draws support from the fact that children learn language by learning to comprehend the meaning of language. If children succeed so well with this approach, might not adults? The basic language learning processes for children and adults should not differ, Asher reasons.

Comprehension training does not mean that speaking is not permitted in the classroom. Speaking is not only allowed, but encouraged. However, a major difference between the comprehension approach and other methods is that comprehension is the central objective of the language exercises and lessons. It is generally believed by those who advocate the comprehension approach that conversational speech will develop out of the need and desire to speak, and after there is sufficient understanding of the language. Under normal circumstances of training it might occur in three months to one year.

In Chapter Five James Nord presents the theoretical underpinnings of the comprehension approach and offers some new and creative teaching techniques. He illustrates that comprehension is an active and dynamic instructional system. One dynamic component of learning to comprehend is anticipation, or prediction. Nord has devised several procedures that translate these concepts into teaching routines. The methods he proposes will be of interest to both researchers and teachers.

In Chapter Six I provide a review of research studies on the development of comprehension in the normally developing child. Additionally, I consider teaching practices that are currently used by language pathologists, and conclude that language disordered children, for the most part, are not given adequate preparation in language comprehension. An experiment on the acquisition of past tense markers by young children is presented in which comparisons are made between comprehension training and several other methods of training. Finally, the principle of comprehension training is extended to include foreign language teaching, and, in particular, a detailed description of self-instructional programs is provided.

Karl Diller (Chapter Seven) and James Asher (Chapter Four) propose a neurolinguistic interpretation of the several approaches to language teaching. Diller hypothesizes that the language areas of the brain and their interconnecting pathways are used differently depending upon the teaching method. According to Diller, the comprehension approach utilizes those language areas of the cortex that involve auditory decoding, semantic relations, and meaning. Asher concludes that the comprehension approach structures the right hemisphere to receive information and "prepares" the left hemisphere for the development of language.

The final stage in the development of a new methodology involves experimental assessment and evaluation. I know of no experimental investigations that provide the critical evidence for selecting one particular language teaching approach from the many now available. There is an obvious reason for this situation. The evidence that is required is beyond the scope of ordinary university research. A fairly large group of students would need to be retained over a long period of time.

Thus, it is not surprising to find that there are no critical studies that decisively dictate the superiority of one method over another. However, we know that some students are successful in acquiring a foreign language when attending classes in which traditional methodologies are used. Also, the success of the Defense Language Institute and university programs cannot be denied. The methodologies employed at the Defense Language Institute or at any other institution where there is a history of successful language teaching are eclectic: surface grammar, meaning through translation, dialogue drills, and conversational exercises. It is not clear what effect each of these methodologies contributes proportionally to successful language learning. None of these methodologies has been completely isolated so that its individual effectiveness can be assessed. There are long-range studies to be sure (Smith, 1970), but none that has been extended long enough to produce fluent or near-fluent speakers. Similarly, the comprehension approach provides no long-range studies that can document its effectiveness in teaching sophisticated language usage. Nevertheless, the data that are available provide evidence that the comprehension approach produces striking results. These data are reported in Chapter Eight by Robbins Burling, Alton Becker, Patricia B. Henry, and Joyce Tomasowa, in Chapter Nine by Valerian Postovsky, and in Chapter Ten by James Asher.

In Chapter Eight Robbins Burling and his colleagues report the impressionistic observation that, without any drill work during the first college term of training, the student's pronunciation in Bahasa Indonesia, the language of training, was "remarkably good." The authors comment that large doses of listening convey the essentials of phonology, thereby minimizing the need for deliberate instruction in pronunciation. This chapter contains important observations on the language-learning process and is, therefore, a valuable introduction for those who wish to begin programmatic development of lessons using the comprehension approach.

The findings of a carefully conducted investigation on retention are reported in Chapter Nine by Valerian Postovsky. He obtained the unexpected finding that no decay of comprehension of Russian occurred over a ten-day interval. Postovsky also found that individual differences narrowed as training continued. Judging from Postovsky's research, we may conclude that individual differences in language ability may not be as large as is generally believed. Also reported in this chapter are evaluations by students who have taken this program. This survey of students' attitudes confirms earlier reports by Asher (1977) and Winitz and Reeds (1975) that the comprehension approach is a nonthreatening, interference-reducing, training procedure.

Asher, in Chapter Ten, has written an extensive review of the many experiments directed toward an assessment of the comprehension approach. In some cases the investigations are descriptive reports of the performance of subjects in learning to understand a foreign language. In other instances experiments were conducted in which the comprehension approach was compared with other methodologies. Although the investigations involved relatively brief intervals of time, the evidence is strong that the comprehension method does the job well. Still needed, however, are projects that assess student performance over long intervals of time.

Does comprehension pretraining improve the learning of regular course materials of a first semester college foreign language class? This question was raised by Stephen S. Corbett and W. Flint Smith. Their carefully designed experimental procedure and interesting results are presented in Chapter Eleven. The subjects of this experiment were students enrolled in the first semester of a college Spanish course at Purdue University. The control subjects completed the course materials according to the standard procedures used at Purdue. The experimental students were assigned the comprehension material prior to taking the standard course materials. During the first six weeks of the course, the experimental subjects participated in a comprehension program utilizing an audiovisual format (about sixteen hours of training repeated one or more times), and then covered the regular course materials at an accelerated pace.

The comprehension experience did not improve acquisition of the standard course materials. Several interpretations of these findings are offered by the authors. One conclusion they drew was that the overlap in content between the two programs was minimal. Another related possibility is that the amount of comprehension training must be fairly large to affect transfer to college level material. Their estimate is that several hundred hours would be necessary.

Of particular interest to the teacher of foreign language is the application of the comprehension method to the classroom. The last two chapters are devoted to this topic. The authors are Janet Swaffar and Don Stephens (Chapter Twelve) and Paul García (Chapter Thirteen). Swaffar and Stephens describe a comprehension-based program conducted in a recent National Endowment for the Humanities funded experiment at the University of Texas at Austin. A detailed account of the training program is provided. In addition, the authors give their impressions of the success of the program, recommended revisions, and caveats.

The concluding chapter is authored by Paul García, a teacher with considerable experience in the various teaching methodologies. As García ably points out, a new teaching methodology should build on successes of the past. Although the comprehension approach appears radical in scope, it captures certain elements of the direct method, the audio-lingual method, and the grammar-translation method. First, it is recognized that comprehension is basic to all three. In the comprehension approach a new system of learning is not really advocated. The instructional format is to extend the teaching interval of one component of training, comprehension, while delaying instruction or experience in speaking, reading, and writing. Second, the comprehension approach is cognitive in orientation. As used here, cognitive is defined as a system that gives students the opportunity to engage in problem solving, the personal discovery of grammatical rules. Both the grammar-translation method and the direct method encourage problem solving, although the mental operations that are involved in these two learning systems are often viewed as being different. The audio-lingual method can also be used as a problem-solving activity, if used in the way Belasco suggests (Chapter Two). Implicit learning is a fundamental principle of the direct method, although the term *implicit* is anachronistically applied. Explicit learning is a basic premise of the grammar-translation method. Yet this method provides experiences that, indirectly, foster implicit learning.

Also, in Chapter Thirteen, Paul García describes in considerable detail his teaching program. Included is a precise account of the sequence of grammatical instruction. Several important pedagogical considerations are also discussed. The disadvantages of encouraging talking in the early phases of language instruction are carefully reviewed. Finally, considerable attention is given to the teaching of speaking, reading, and writing within the framework of comprehension training.

The chapters of this anthology contain both differences and similarities. However, there is a common set of beliefs that defines the comprehension approach:

1. Language rules are most easily and accurately acquired by inference. The basic data are the sentences of a language. The ease with which learning takes place depends upon the programmatic sequencing of the sentences.

2. Language acquisition is primarily an implicit process because the acquisition of linguistic knowledge is not, for the most part, under the explicit control or conscious awareness of the student. Furthermore, explicit instruction in (surface) rules may be harmful to the learning process.

3. The rules of a language are so complexly interrelated and so sufficiently detailed as to preclude errorless learning without exposure to a large part of the grammar of a language. In this regard language acquisition is viewed as nonlinear because information in later lessons provides clarification of material presented earlier.

4. Comprehension is a teaching routine whereby the student is systematically exposed to the sentences of a target language. Production exercises, grammatical drills, and practice in translation are not generally used as teaching routines, although they may occasionally be used to test comprehension.

5. Speaking will develop given sufficient comprehension training, although there is only preliminary research to support this contention.

The comprehension approach is an educational methodology which has attracted the interest of psychologists, linguists, and language teachers, primarily because it involves strategies of learning that utilize current and acceptable premises of psycholinguistic thought. Perhaps the primary reason for the development of the comprehension approach was to study second-language acquisition, not to teach foreign language. For this reason fossilization of the training procedures discussed in this volume is not a reasonable fear among its developers, who have as great an interest in the process of language acquisition as they do in the methodologies of language teaching.

Much experimentation remains to be completed, including investigation of the effect of extensive comprehension training on pronunciation skills in a second language. This anthology, then, is a statement of the current state of the art and should be recognized as such.

References

Asher, J. J. *Learning another language through actions: The complete teacher's guidebook*. Los Gatos, Calif.: Sky Oaks Productions, 1977.

Berko, J. "The child's learning of English morphology." *Word, 14,* pp. 150–177, 1958.

Brown, R. *A first language, the early stages*. Cambridge, Mass.: Harvard University Press, 1973.

Chomsky, N. *Aspects of the theory of syntax*. Cambridge, Mass.: M.I.T. Press, 1965.

———. *Current issues in linguistic theory*. The Hague: Mouton, 1966.

Diller, K. C. *The language teaching controversy*. Rowley, Mass.: Newbury House, 1978.

Smith, P. D. *A comparison of the cognitive and audiolingual approaches to foreign language instruction*. The Pennsylvania foreign language project. Philadelphia: The Center for Curriculum Development, Inc., 1970.

Twaddell, W. F. "Meanings, habits, and rules." *Education, 69,* pp. 75–81, 1948.

Winitz, H., and Reeds, J. *Comprehension and problem solving as strategies for language training*. The Hague: Mouton, 1975.

The Comprehension Approach
to Foreign Language Instruction

CHAPTER 1

Nonlinear Learning and Language Teaching

Harris Winitz

Professor of Speech Science and Psychology
University of Missouri, Kansas City

Interest in the use of developmental criteria for language teaching routines was rekindled in an article by Miller and Yoder (1974). These authors proposed that stages of linguistic growth should be given serious consideration in the design of language teaching programs.

Perhaps the most potentially useful application of developmental language data, advanced by Miller and Yoder, and a number of other writers (MacDonald and Blott, 1974; Holland, 1975; Lahey and Bloom, 1977; Leonard, 1978; Prutting, 1979) concerns the putative relationship between normal language stages and procedures for language training. The belief is generally held that children with delayed language should be taught language in a sequence of steps that closely parallels the stages of normal language development. This model of language training is called the stage process approach by Prutting (1979), who has provided an excellent summary of the several language stages through which normal children progress. Six stages stretching from the prelinguistic period to the adult level of communicative competence are presented by Prutting. Her summary is comprehensive, as it includes the interactive relationship of pragmatics, semantics, syntax, and phonology.

Developmental Model (Stage Process Model)
A detailed presentation on the relationship between language developmental levels and their application to the language delayed child is provided by Miller and Yoder (1974). They advise that the "content for language training for retarded children should be taken from the data available on language

development in normal children" (Miller and Yoder, 1974, p. 510). Two major considerations were advanced by Miller and Yoder: (a) within a stage of language development semantic concepts should be taught in order of their frequency of occurrence, and (b) the selection of utterance form (syntactic complexity) should be determined by the developmental sequence of normal children. The sequences recommended by Miller and Yoder are the traditional ones: (1) single words, (2) two- and three-word sentences, (3) short simple sentences, (4) morphological development, and so on.

The developmental model of language teaching, according to Prutting (1979), involves two procedures of training, vertical programming and horizontal programming. Vertical programming "is to add and expand behavior within the stage at which the child is already functioning" (Prutting, 1979, p. 22). Horizontal programming "is to move the child beyond the existing stage to the next stage" (Prutting, 1979, p. 22).

Prutting asserts that "The stage process model assessment procedure provides the clinician with remedial guidelines, based on complexity, for the *content* and *sequencing* of communicative behavior" (italics mine; Prutting, 1979, p. 22). This interpretation of complexity is intuitively reasonable, long held (Miller and Yoder, 1974), and difficult to challenge. According to this position the stages of normal language growth define complexity. Complexity, in turn, provides the rationale for using the language stages through which the normal speaking child progresses as an ordered sequence for language training.

Prutting's six stages of language are broadly defined permitting a good degree of flexibility within each developmental stage. It is also acknowledged that each stage is an "elaboration of a previous stage" (Prutting, 1979, p. 5), and furthermore, the "positing of stages is a process of abstracting highlights about development" (Prutting, 1979, p. 5). Taking these considerations into account, Prutting, within limits, advances the position that language training should involve an ordered sequence based on normal language stages. Her perspective of horizontal training captures the sequential aspect of the developmental model of language training, while her expression of vertical training indicates recognition of the nonsequential aspect of language training.

We shall define teaching models that are predicated on a step-by-step progression of developmental levels as linear models. Models for which this requirement is not made are referred to as nonlinear models. We will distinguish between these two models of training and provide a rationale for recommending the nonlinear model. Furthermore, the relationship between the teaching of language comprehension and the nonlinear model will be explored. Additionally, we will suggest that comprehension training is a fundamental property of nonlinear training.

Developmental Sequences as End Points

In 1969 I advanced the position that developmental profiles of articulation reflect the end points of a complex learning process (Winitz, 1969). Articulation profiles, it was stated, express only the age at which a sound is correctly uttered by the majority of children of a designated population. The position, later presented by Sander (1972), was advanced that articulation norms do not reveal the dimensions or processes of articulation learning. They do not indicate, for example, the phonological and articulatory history of a sound, nor the contributory psycho-social factors. Without such information the clinical usefulness of articulation norms appears limited.

A generally practiced procedure in articulatory assessment is to compare an individual child's production of a sound with that of his or her peers by utilizing developmental norms. A common strategy is to begin articulation training only when the articulation assessment reveals a developmental lag in sound production. For example, a child of five years of age who misarticulates the /θ/ sound would not be given clinical treatment because this sound, according to the developmental norms provided by Templin (1957), is not mastered until six years. The logic here is that the articulatory mechanism is not sufficiently mature to acquire /θ/ at age five.

An alternative position can be taken. Possibly, the processes that led to the acquisition of /θ/ at six years began many years prior to this time. Six years may simply reflect the end point of a process which has been unfolding for some time. The discrimination and perception of /θ/ the production of /θ/ and the phonological role of /θ/ (that is, the relationship of /θ/ to other sounds in a complex patterned network of sounds) no doubt began many years prior to age six. The evidence clearly supports the position that /θ/ does not simply emerge at age six. In fact, it is produced, although with less than a perfect record, many years prior to age six (Winitz, 1969; Sander, 1972).

Language forms also show a pattern of development that stretches across several age levels. An illustration from child syntax will be given. When children first demonstrate use of the progressive, for the most part in the present tense, the auxiliary is often omitted. An example is "The dog barking" for "The dog *is* barking." One explanation for the omission of the auxiliary is that it is not a salient unit of expression for the child (Brown and Fraser, 1964; Winitz and Reeds, 1975). Young children can understand the essential "meaning" of the progressive by the *ing* marker, and by environmental and linguistic context. The auxiliary is initially not critical for the understanding of simple progressive expressions.

A great amount of information must be absorbed in learning a language and only the most "important" details can be attended to initially. Information overload exists from the very beginning when learning a language, and can be experienced personally by trying to learn a foreign language by the immersion method. A common observation of students of a foreign language is that only parts of sentences and words can initially be acquired because so much must be learned almost simultaneously (Winitz and Reeds, 1975). The burden is enormous even when sentences are short, noncomplex, and contain a simple lexicon. Additionally, the pressure to speak often places one in the position of relying on partially stored fragments.[1]

Why do the auxiliaries of progressives eventually become salient? It is believed that they are acquired from experience with other structures that occur later in the developmental sequence. Possibly, the salience of auxiliaries emerges from experience with contrasts. The following are a few examples:

1. The dog is barking.   3. The rope loosened.
   The dog was barking.   The rope is loosened.

2. The dog is barking.   4. The boy eating is fat.
   Is the dog barking?   The boy is eating fat.

For the examples given above, the verb *is* is an important unit because its sentence position or its absence signals information about the *underlying* meaning of each sentence. Note that *is* acts as a contrastive marker or salient unit in a number of different sentence types, many of which are structurally more complex, appear later in development, than the present progressive.

It can be argued that until *is* correctly appears in progressives, the present progressive, as a syntactic construction, has not been acquired. Certain conceptual aspects of the progressive have, no doubt, been acquired, but the various forms of the progressive, as well as the difference between the progressive and other grammatical structures, may not yet be completely learned. Possibly, full understanding of the progressive cannot come about until late developing structures (present progressive versus question, or present progressive versus truncated relative clause, for example) are acquired. If our reasoning is correct, the development of language may involve linguistic knowledge acquired from experience with linguistic stages of varying complexity.

That complete knowledge of a grammatical structure cannot be derived easily from examples involving the structure alone, can be illustrated with a set of sentences, contributed by Belasco (1965). Consider the following sentences:

5. I am writing it to him.
   I am sending it to him.
   I am telling it to him.
   I am saying it to him.

The four verbs in (5) appear to be governed by the same rule of sentence construction. However, this is not the case for the next four sentences:

6. I am writing him to do it.
    I am sending him to do it.
    I am telling him to do it.
   *I am saying him to do it

The last sentence of (6) is ungrammatical, indicating that the verb *saying* functions in a grammatically different way from *writing, sending,* and *telling.* Grammatical understanding of these four verbs no doubt comes about from experiences that go far beyond their use in these grammatical contexts. The sentences of (5) and (6) illustrate that mastery of verb forms cannot be acquired by practice with a restricted range of sentences. Experience with many sentence types appears essential before there is linguistic understanding of the verbs of (5) and (6).

A distinguishing feature of children's language is that linguistic structures undergo reorganization and revision as linguistically similar and later appearing structures are acquired (Chomsky, 1969; Bellugi, 1967; Anisfeld and Tucker, 1967; Bowerman, 1978a). Bowerman (1978b) provides an account of prepositions and verbs that a young child initially used correctly in spontaneous speech, but almost a year later uttered incorrectly. One example is *take* for *put,* as in "After I do that I *take* them up again like that." (She reveals her thumbs after concealing them in her hands.) Another example is *let* for *make,* as in "I don't want to go to bet yet. Don't *let* me." (Her mother has told her she must go to bed.)

Two interpretations of these errors are offered by Bowerman. First, utterance errors result from the reorganization of the mental lexicon of a child. Words "not initially recognized as semantically related, moved closer together in meaning" (Bowerman, 1978b, p. 981). Second, in some cases there is incomplete semantic knowledge, but errors in usage do not occur because words are initially used in a relatively restricted sense (for example, *put* is used initially in the restricted sense of placement of objects, and *take* is used in the context of removal of objects). Other examples, in particular from the literature on extension of word meanings, can be provided which show that early used structures undergo revision, reorganization and reformulation. A number of interpretations, some similar to those provided by Bowerman, has also been given, but will not be detailed here.

Children, of course, will use words and structures in conversational speech despite the fact that the adult meaning of a grammatical or lexical unit has not been acquired. Even adults use words without having full understanding. Miller (1978, p. 1002) remarks that "Many adults know the meaning of *cancer* in the sense that they can use the word correctly in conversation and can tell you a great deal about cancers, yet would be totally unable to identify a particular instance." In this regard, developmental stages of language growth can provide a degree of distortion. There can be the appearance of adult-like mastery when, in fact, acquisition is limited and restricted.

Restrictions on learning are not well known; thus, a language teaching model based on an interpretation of developmental mastery may over-extend the range of achievement for a particular stage of development. Without guidelines detailing these restrictions, a teacher may come to expect more from a language delayed child than is achieved by the average child at a particular language stage. When these expectations are not met by a child, a conclusion frequently made is that comprehension training and/or production training has failed even though the teaching was conducted within the framework of the developmental model.

The point of view has been presented that knowledge of grammatical structures is often derived from experiences that are nonlinear in that they

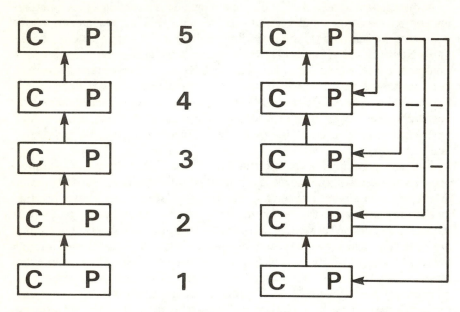

FIGURE 1.1.   An illustration of the linear (left panel) and nonlinear (right panel) models of learning

transcend several language stages. Additionally, I remarked that language stages reflect response points that are not necessarily indicative of the range and scope of language knowledge. I gave the example of the progressive and suggested that complete syntactic understanding of this grammatical structure develops after there is understanding of structures far more complex than it. The interrelationships among language structures are largely unknown and cannot be derived from developmental descriptions of linguistic stages. That is, we cannot assume that language stages and learning stages are the same. A language stage indicates a level of language knowledge. It does not indicate how and in what sequence this knowledge was obtained. Additionally, language stages are based almost entirely on expressive skills (production) and, therefore, may provide an incorrect assessment of the level of language achievement.

The contrast between a linear model and a nonlinear model of language learning can be explained by reference to Figure 1.1. The left panel of this figure represents the linear model and the right panel the nonlinear model. The numbers 1 through 5 denote hypothetical language stages; 1 is the first stage and 5 is the last stage. In the linear model, comprehension (C) and production (P) of a grammatical structure are presumed to be acquired within the same language level. The sequence of learning is termed linear because the acquisition (or elaboration) of grammatical structures within a language level is dependent only upon knowledge acquired at a previous language level. Additionally, each stage of language development, according to the linear model, is acquired in production before grammatical elements of the next level are acquired. Within this framework the influence of a later developing structure on an earlier, partially learned structure is not a consideration.

The nonlinear model is reflected in the right panel of Figure 1.1. Here it may be observed that the learning of grammatical structures depends upon C and P within each level, as well as C and P from structures much more complex and later appearing. In some cases the later developing structures may be understood but not yet produced. The relation between comprehension (or partial comprehension as the case may be) of later appearing structures and early developing structures is an important component of the nonlinear model. As described here, nonlinear learning involves the comprehension of structures in advance of a child's verbal production. As of now the interaction among linguistic structures is not well defined for the nonlinear model. We know very little about which later appearing structures will have an effect on early developing structures.

The linear model, as I interpret it, has been presented, in one form or another, as a model for language teaching by a number of writers (Guess, Sailor, and Baer, 1974; Miller and Yoder, 1974; Costello, 1977; Holland, 1975; Lahey and Bloom, 1977; Prutting, 1979). Miller and Yoder (1974, p. 521) express this approach in one of their principles of teaching as follows: "Select a single frequently occurring experience demonstrating a particular semantic function. Pair with the appropriate lexical marker, and after child demonstrates mastery, move to multiple experiences expressing the same function." Comprehension and imitation training are recommended by Miller and Yoder only as intermediate training steps. Mastery is defined by these writers as spontaneous use of the target structure. The Miller and Yoder approach exemplifies the linear training model because a single semantic function and lexical marker is selected to be trained initially as a verbal response independent of experiences with other language forms. Multiple experiences, it should be pointed out, enrich the use of a specific structure (Prutting's vertical programming). However, as indicated above, full linguistic knowledge of a structure cannot be acquired by multiple experiences that do not involve a broad enough range of linguistic information. According to the nonlinear model, experiences are broadened not so much by enrichment, but by exposure to later appearing structures.

Some suggestions for training offered by Holland (1975), and Lahey and Bloom (1977) also reflect the linear approach. Language teaching is not a major consideration in their articles on a first lexicon, but some of their teaching suggestions are of interest here. Lahey and Bloom (1977) recommend that single words should have functional value (code objects or events, etc., in the communicative sense). Following the learning of single word utterances, two-word utterances are to be taught by combination of *known forms*. This approach can be regarded as linear teaching because the stages of teaching conform in a strict one-to-one way with stages observed in language development.

An additional procedure provided by Lahey and Bloom involves *indirect teaching,* first introduced by Hahn in 1961. Indirect teaching, in contrast to *direct teaching,* is a procedure in which a particular linguistic form is incidentally acquired when the teaching has emphasized other linguistic forms and concepts. Lahey and Bloom (1977, p. 347) provide the following example: ". . . as the clinician washes she can say 'Peggy wash,' 'I wash,' and as the child washes 'X wash,' 'you wash.' " The clinician is then to observe whether or not "I" is learned. According to Lahey and Bloom, if it is used, it is to be stressed in the future. In contrast to indirect teaching, direct teaching seems to stress the acquisition of *production* for purposes of communication. Lahey and Bloom's concept of indirect teaching captures well one fundamental aspect of the non-linear learning model—that of presenting material without demanding production.

Lahey and Bloom (1977, p. 347) summarize indirect teaching by stating, "If the child learns the pronominal forms by this casual presentation, these forms can be stressed in the future." We would add that if indeed some forms are learned by casual presentation, then, possibly, almost all forms could be learned this way, which is precisely Hahn's point. In another respect, Lahey and Bloom's suggestion that forms acquired by casual presentation be stressed in the future is not in accord with the nonlinear model. The nonlinear approach would be to select additionally complex forms and teach these in a casual way also.

Comprehension and Production

A restricting influence on the use of the linear method is the insistence that mastery be defined as communication through language production. Miller and Yoder (1974) are the most specific in this regard. They recommend that input should be increased in complexity after there is demonstration of *production mastery.* Miller and Yoder (1974, pp. 522–523) state their position as follows: "First expansions of single word utterances should be of relational functions previously expressed," and ". . . the linguistic input to the child should in general be one step more advanced than the child's stage of language production as measured by MLU, except at the initial stages of single word utterance development. Input to the child would initially be single words only. . ." A feature, then, of the linear model is that the level at which input is provided is referenced by the language production of the child, and furthermore, beyond the first word stage, the input should always be one level higher.

Remarks made by Holland (1975) seem also to suggest that mastery of production is to be emphasized at each stage of language teaching. She recommends that the first lexicon (core lexicon) should contain about 35 words which are to be used to teach single word utterances, later to be combined to form two-word utterances. From her remarks it may be concluded that single words are to be used by a child as verbal productions before they are to be combined into two-word utterances. In this regard, Holland (1975, pp. 517–518) describes the activities of a model clinician. She states: "I observed a therapy session in which a gifted clinician was teaching *more*. She . . . had plans eventually to demand the word from the child." This report of Holland is significant because it emphasizes a difference between the linear and nonlinear approaches. Her report indicates that responses for a particular stage are to be taught *as production responses* before a structure within the same stage or from a more advanced stage is to be taught.

The teaching of a core lexicon is one of the major goals of the nonlinear approach (Winitz and Reeds, 1975), as it is with the linear approach. However, in the nonlinear approach production is not demanded. The training sessions center on comprehension. Speaking is not inhibited, in fact it is encouraged; it simply is not *directly* taught or *directly requested.*

In the linear and nonlinear approaches each child is actively involved in communicative interactions, but the center of focus in the nonlinear approach is on teaching meaning through *comprehension* (Winitz and Reeds, 1975).[2] The developmental sequence serves only as a guide for teaching *language comprehension.* Forms may be taught that are viewed as important for the understanding of target structures without regard to their relative placement in the developmental scale.

An example from Holland's core lexicon may be used to illustrate nonlinear teaching. She recommends that the personal pronouns "I," "me," and "you" be included in the core lexicon. Nonlinear teaching would involve planning the lessons around the understanding of these three personal pronouns, and, additionally, not demanding their production. Other personal pronouns, as they occur naturally in the free flow of conversation, would also be used. Understanding pronominal forms, in general, may be an important consideration in learning the psycholinguistic function of a particular pronoun. Similarly, the *is* of the present progressive would be taught by teaching the understanding of structures in which *is* serves as a contrast in meaning, as indicated above. A linear approach to the teaching of core pronouns or the auxiliary *is* would be to concentrate on teaching production before teaching other, more distantly related, grammatical units.

The point of view taken here is that understanding of language is the primary channel through which language is acquired (Asher, 1972; Winitz and Reeds, 1975; Krashen, 1978). A rationale for this position has been developed by these writers as well as others. In this regard a distinction is made between *forced production practice* and *spontaneous production* (indirect teaching). When comprehension is used as the method of instruction, language production is not directly taught through drills, forced imitation or modeling. Language use is encouraged, of course, by asking questions occasionally and by providing interesting and motivating communicative interactions. Within this perspective the stages of language development serve as a general guide for teaching comprehension of language. However, no emphasis is placed on teaching language production according to the stages of normal language development.

Simplification

Increasingly, there is recognition that complexity of language input to the language delayed child is an important consideration in language teaching. However, surprisingly little has been directly said about relating theories of simplification to the developmental model of language teaching. Miller and Yoder (1974), as mentioned above, recommend that the level of complexity of language input should be one level in advance of a child's developmental language level, as measured through production or language use. Their position, along with Holland (1975) and Lahey and Bloom (1977), is that input should be carefully regulated by the sequence of language stages represented by the normally developing child.

Examples provided by Holland (1975) and Lahey and Bloom (1977) indicate a fairly strict adherence to developmental sequence when teaching early language forms to children. Utterances, such as *Peggy wash* and *more throw,* are provided by these writers as examples of two-word input which are to be modeled by the child. Ungrammatical input appears to be a consequence of adapting the developmental model to clinical situations. It is not a recommended procedure of the nonlinear approach.

Summary of Linear and Nonlinear Teaching Approaches

A common set of assumptions underlies both the linear and the nonlinear approaches. There are, however, a number of major differences, which are summarized below:

1. *Linear*: The developmental language model specifies the order of input and sequence of teaching stages.

Nonlinear: The developmental language model provides a general guide for the order of input of the teaching steps.

2. *Linear Model*: Comprehension, imitation, and production are used to teach mastery of language forms in drill sessions and in communicative settings. In some instances, although not discussed above, explicit statements of grammatical rules are given. Production and conversation are encouraged through activities and communicative interactions.

Nonlinear Model: Only comprehension is formally taught. Production and conversation are encouraged through activities and communicative interactions.[3]

3. *Linear Model*: The criterion of mastery is defined as production at each developmental level.

Nonlinear Model: The criterion for mastery is comprehension or spontaneous understanding of language not necessarily restricted to a particular developmental stage.

Concluding Remarks

There is considerable overlap between these two "idealized" systems of teaching and learning. Yet there are some fundamental differences. Linear teaching is tied directly to developmental stages of language and places emphasis on language production or language output as a method of training. Comprehension of language is the central component of the nonlinear method of teaching (Asher, 1972; Winitz and Reeds, 1975). The developmental sequence provides a reference guide for teaching comprehension, but does not constrain input.

There are teaching procedures that are common to both the linear and nonlinear systems. For example, pragmatic grammars can be applied to both teaching systems. Additionally, motivational and reinforcement conditions can be applied equally well to both systems of teaching.

Simplification of input is also a common aspect of both the linear and nonlinear systems, although applied differently. In the linear system, simplified utterances closely match sentences children use at each developmental level, at least this procedure has been recommended for early developmental levels. At times ungrammatical fragments are used. In the nonlinear system the use of simplified utterances would not be constrained by the utterances children use. With both teaching systems, we would anticipate that simplification will occur automatically in the normal course of conversation between a child and a clinician.

Nonlinear teaching, of which comprehension training is the major component, has been advocated and used primarily by investigators involved in second language teaching (Asher, 1972; Asher, 1977; Winitz and Reeds, 1975; Gary, 1975; Postovsky, Chapter Nine; Burling, Becker, Henry and Tomasowa, Chapter Eight; Krashen, 1978). In this regard comprehension training has resulted in rapid acquisition of a second language when production practice has been de-emphasized and when comprehension training has been extended over long intervals of time. This procedure of teaching has not been generally recommended as a method of teaching language to children with language delay, although it is deserving of investigation. Of particular interest is the relation between the acquisition of comprehension and production when comprehension training is extended over long intervals of training that allow for exposure to a broad range of linguistic structures not directly tied to a particular developmental level, and when production is not immediately expected nor "forced" in the training process.

Notes

1. This point can be illustrated by taking a short lesson of Mandarin Chinese produced by International Linguistics, 401 West 89th St., Kansas City, Mo. 64114. The cassette tape and picture lessons may be ordered from this company free of charge.

2. In this regard it would be ideal to have language sessions structured so that two adults are always present. In this way a child may hear and watch communication taking place at a level he or she can understand.

3. Under some circumstances students might be told not to talk until they can understand adult conversation. These conditions may apply to foreign language instruction for adults who do not live in the country of the language they are learning. They may be advised that there is no real need to talk because there is no need to communicate. The entire emphasis of the training program could be placed on comprehension, including the comprehension of others who are communicating.

References

Anisfeld, M., and Tucker, G. R. "English pluralization rules of six-year-old children." *Child Development, 38,* pp. 1201–1217, 1967.

Asher, J. J. "Children's first language as a model for second language learning." *The Modern Language Journal, 56,* pp. 133–139, 1972.

———. *Learning another language through actions: The complete teacher's guidebook.* Los Gatos, Calif.: Sky Oaks Productions, 1977.

Belasco, S. "Nucleation and the audio-lingual approach." *The Modern Language Journal, 49,* pp. 482–491, 1965.

Bellugi, U. The acquisition of negation. Ph.D. dissertation, Harvard University, 1967.

Bowerman, M. "Semantic and syntactic development: A review of what, when, and how in language acquisition." In R. L. Schiefelbusch (Ed.), *Bases of language intervention.* Baltimore, Md.: University Park Press, 1978a.

———. "Systematizing semantic knowledge: Changes over time in the child's organization of word meaning." *Child Development, 49,* pp. 977–987, 1978b.

Brown, R., and Fraser, C. "The acquisition of syntax." In U. Bellugi and R. Brown (Eds.), *Monographs of the Society for Research in Child Development,* Serial No. 92, Vol. 29, pp. 43–79, 1964.

Chomsky, C. *The acquisition of syntax in children from 5 to 10.* Cambridge, Mass.: M.I.T. Press, 1969.

Costello, J. M. "Programmed instruction." *Journal of Speech and Hearing Disorders, 42,* pp. 3–28, 1977.

Gary, J. O. "Delayed oral practice in initial stages of second language learning." In M. K. Burt and H. C. Dulay (Eds.), *On TESOL 75: New directions in second language learning, teaching and bilingual education.* Washington, D.C.: TESOL, 1975.

Guess, D., Sailor, W., and Baer, D. M. "To teach language to retarded children." In R. L. Schiefelbusch and L. L. Lloyd (Eds.), *Language perspectives—acquisition, retardation and intervention.* Baltimore, Md.: University Park Press, 1974.

Hahn, E. "Indications for direct, nondirect, and indirect methods in speech correction." *Journal of Speech and Hearing Disorders, 26,* pp. 230–236, 1961.

Holland, A. L. "Language therapy for children: Some thoughts on context and content." *Journal of Speech and Hearing Disorders, 40,* pp. 514–523, 1975.

Krashen, S. "The monitor model for second-language acquisition." In R. C. Gingras (Ed.), *Second-language acquisition and foreign language instruction.* Washington, D.C.: Center for Applied Linguistics, 1978.

Lahey, M., and Bloom, L. "Planning a first lexicon: Which words to teach first." *Journal of Speech and Hearing Disorders, 42,* pp. 340–350, 1977.

Leonard, L. B. "Cognitive factors in early linguistic development." In R. L. Schiefelbusch (Ed.), *Bases of language intervention.* Baltimore, Md.: University Park Press, 1978.

MacDonald, J. D., and Blott, J. P. "Environmental language intervention: The rationale for a diagnostic and training strategy through rules, context, and generalization." *Journal of Speech and Hearing Disorders, 39,* pp. 244–256, 1974.

Miller, G. "The acquisition of word meaning." *Child Development, 49,* pp. 999–1004, 1978.

Miller, J. F., and Yoder, D. E. "An ontogenetic language teaching strategy for retarded children." In R. L. Schiefelbusch and L. L. Lloyd (Eds.), *Language perspectives—acquisition, retardation, and intervention.* Baltimore, Md.: University Park Press, 1974.

Prutting, C. A. "Process: The action of moving forward progressively from one point to another on the way to completion." *Journal of Speech and Hearing Disorders, 44,* pp. 3–30, 1979.

Sander, E. K. "When are speech sounds learned?" *Journal of Speech and Hearing Disorders, 37,* pp. 55–63, 1972.

Templin, M. C. Certain language skills in children, their development and interrelationships. *Institute of Child Welfare, Monograph Series, No. 26.* Minneapolis: University of Minnesota Press, 1957.

Winitz, H. *Articulatory acquisition and behavior.* New York: Appleton-Century-Crofts, 1969.
Winitz, H., and Reeds, J. *Comprehension and problem solving as strategies for language training.* The Hague: Mouton, 1975.

CHAPTER 2

Aital cal aprene las lengas estrangièras,
Comprehension: The Key to Second-Language Acquisition

Simon Belasco

Professor of French Linguistics
University of South Carolina

After nearly forty years of foreign language teaching, one might easily reach the conclusion that most students do not acquire a second language in the ordinary classroom situation. This does not mean, however, that a student *cannot* acquire foreign language skills after two years of high school plus two years of college foreign language training. Note that the word *training,* not *study,* is being used here deliberately.

If one examines the textbooks that have been commercially available over a forty-year period, it will be obvious that the grammatical principles contained in each of them are essentially the same: adjective agreement, forms and use of interrogative and relative pronouns, use of the indicative and subjunctive modes, sequence of tenses in adjoining clauses, and so on. There are about forty or fifty such principles, depending on how the author chooses to classify them. Of course the older texts do not have pattern drills, but the same grammatical content is patently there.

Now it requires little empirical justification to establish that the average native speaker of any language can communicate with other native speakers without utilizing many of these grammatical concepts. In fact, there is no evidence—experimental or otherwise—to indicate that it is these principles, or any other principles for that matter, that must be acquired before a language can be learned. What is more important is that certain linguistic concepts observed by these speakers are not treated in these textbooks. Nor is there any indication that their authors are even aware of them. To my knowledge no one has ever determined what elements of linguistic structure—involving the phonology, morphology, syntax, semantics, lexicon of a language—must be internalized in order to insure second language acquisition. The determination of such structure by statistical means in a Basic German or Fundamental French approach can never provide a satisfactory solution since any such approach does not recognize the problem.

Still to be isolated and identified are the elements of linguistic structure that are essential for the acquisition of any language, first or second. As Noam Chomsky (1977, p. 18) puts it, "The fundamental problem in the study of language . . . is to explain how it is possible for a person to attain knowledge of a language, knowledge that is certainly far undetermined by experience. Somehow, from the disordered flux of ordinary linguistic experience, a rich and highly articulated system of grammatical competence develops in the mind in a specific way, fairly uniformly in a given speech community despite considerable variety in care and exposure . . ."

It is common knowledge that an individual can learn one or more languages at a relatively early period of life. This is true if he or she is exposed to language used in a real, that is, a "live" linguistic setting. If exposure does take place in a normal linguistic context, the student *cannot escape* learning a language. Assuming the normal auditory and vocal apparatus, even a moron learns a first language. The number of second languages a person may learn depends on the amount of exposure, and active participation engaged in, under conditions of real communication.

When a person learns a language in an artificial, unicultural situation represented by the average classroom, success is less than remarkable. During the past forty years a lot of effort has been made to increase the amount of foreign language exposure available to high school and college students. Witness the rise and decline of the audio-lingual laboratory with the concomitant development of so-called new materials. It would be unjust to imply that audio or video techniques are of no consequence. The trouble does not lie with the hardware but with the software. In other words, the learning materials have not really changed. They are still designed to teach the forty or fifty grammatical principles that have appeared in textbooks for over a century.

Before we suggest how to make second language acquisition more effective, let us examine the conditions under which foreign language teaching is supposed to take place. This means taking a serious look at the present foreign language goals, the learning materials, the role of the teacher, the role of the students, and the physical makeup of the learning situation—not necessarily in that order.

We shall concentrate on students who take foreign language as part of their academic training, either as a required subject or as an elective. Now, as foreign language teachers, what are we supposed to do for these students over a two-year period? The goals specify that we have them understand, speak, read, and write the foreign language, and perhaps know something about its structure.

The average class contains about twenty-five students and meets three times a week for fifty minutes. If the teacher spends half the period asking questions, and the students spend the remaining half providing answers, then each student speaks on an average of one minute per period or a total of three minutes per week (Parker, 1956). Assume for the time being that the student spends no time in the language laboratory. It is inconceivable that he or she will acquire the speaking skill in 180 one-minute sessions in four fifteen-week terms for a total of three hours over a period of two years. Of course, this leaves no time for formal testing.

Let us now consider the listening skill. The chances are that the classroom teacher is not a native speaker of the language. Even if the teacher were, the student listens for half the period to the answers of classmates—replete with mistakes in pronunciation, syntax, and vocabulary. Note now that no classroom time is left for supervised reading and writing. If the teacher prepares reading and writing assignments as homework, then part of the three minutes per week contributed to oral exchange with the teacher will have to be spent on the reading selection. Still no time is allowed for correcting written exercises in class or for the discussion of structural differences that exist between English and the foreign language.

If the student does attend the language laboratory, the chances are small that the practice sessions are supervised to the extent that errors in pronunciation and syntax will be corrected, and that the student will come away with the feeling that he or she knows where mistakes were made, and that such mistakes have been remedied.

Let us return to the classroom for the moment. A language class composed of twenty-five students and a teacher is no different in physical makeup from any lecture-type situation in which students are taught facts in, for example, history, philosophy, or English literature. The role of the teacher in these situations is to impart information, and invariably he or she ends up doing most of the work. If the language teacher chooses to spend most of the class time in oral drill, much of the teacher's efforts will be remedial. He or she will be correcting mistakes. At some point, the teacher will be forced to introduce grammatical explanations. Few students can develop oral skills under these conditions.

The acquisition of skills, whether it involves typing, playing a musical instrument, or learning a foreign language, requires that the learner do not half, but most, of the work. Some science courses are taught solely in the classroom. Other science courses divide class time between the lecture hall and the laboratory. But a course in foreign language skills must be designed so that the student spend most of the time in a laboratory-type situation, and this does not mean "language laboratory" in the conventional sense. The point being made here is that the teacher must do less teaching and more guiding so that the responsibility of learning a language is shifted from the teacher to the student. This position is not an idealistic notion or hope, but is a cold and sobering fact. No amount of histrionics, theatrical talent, or motivating gimmickry on the part of the teacher will do as much good as the well-supervised activity engaged in by the student. To the point of exhaustion, I have personally expended inordinate amounts of time and energy in rapid-fire drill sessions in what must be considered a vain effort *to teach* oral skills in fifty (and even seventy-five) minute periods. There is no doubt that my oral skills—if not those of my students—benefited immeasurably from this kind of intensive drill. I had at least twenty-five minutes of practice, but each student unfortunately had only one or two minutes. The conventional classroom composed of a single teacher and twenty-five students is designed to control the flow of information from teacher to student. There is no built-in feature that will guarantee that such information will be learned.

Let us now consider the kind of foreign language materials currently in use. Since World War II, elementary foreign language textbooks have made extensive use of dialogue—pattern drill techniques. The rationale of such an approach is to create a learning situation similar to that enjoyed by speakers learning their native tongue. Each lesson contains one or more dialogues. The dialogue is deliberately "seeded" with linguistic structure and is presented in the form of a conversation, which is printed in a textbook and recorded on tape by native speakers of the language.[1]

The student learns the dialogue in steps by first listening to, then repeating, and finally reading and even memorizing the dialogue. The order of the steps may vary from teacher to teacher, but the net result is very much the same. The object is to have the student internalize the linguistic structure from simulated "natural" exposure. To aid in the internalization process, the student practices oral drills modeled on the structure seeded in the dialogue. These drills are designed to develop correct verbal "habits" through imitation, repetition, and manipulation of recurring portions of speech in one or more structural frames.[2] Ideally, the drills are of two types: (1) assimilation drills involving (a) simple repetition, (b) simple substitution, (c) progressive substitution; and (2) testing drills which are subclassified as (a) simple correlation, (b) progressive correlation, (c) transformation. The assimilation drills are designed to help the student internalize the linguistic structure. The testing drills indicate to what extent the assimilation process has been successful. In the event of low class achievement, the assimilation-testing drill sequences are repeated until performance has attained a satisfactory level. It goes without saying that the time factor does not permit a programmed step-by-step presentation of the materials needed to insure satisfactory performance for the entire class.

I have described these drills elsewhere and have discussed methods of integrating them on several occasions (Belasco, 1963a; 1971a). They are of historical interest and need not be belabored here. Suffice it to say, the use of dialogues and pattern practice *can* be helpful in the internalization process but not to the extent implied by the format of textbooks designed to teach the forty or fifty grammatical principles via the dialogue-drill route. To make a most charitable criticism, such expectations are over-ambitious.

As we have already pointed out, the characteristics of a linguistic system have never been established or clearly defined for any language. Even if the student internalizes the fifty grammatical principles—or many more—what does this mean in terms of the phonological, syntactic, and semantic features *actually needed* to acquire linguistic competence in a second language? The assumption that current materials reflect an effective pedagogical sample of the "real" language is unrealistic and self-defeating. One or more techniques must be formulated to effect linguistic internalization despite the fact that the characteristics of a typical linguistic system have yet to be defined.

Let us recapitulate what we have been saying up to this point. Considering the present conditions under which language teaching is conducted: (1) it is unreasonable to assume that understanding, speaking, reading, and writing foreign language to any significant degree can be achieved at the end of two years; (2) existing language materials are not structured to accomplish such goals; (3) the teacher is playing the role of a purveyor of information rather than that of a trained guide; (4) the student is more observer than principal participant; and (5) the ordinary classroom situation is more conducive to teaching facts than to teaching skills.

Then what skills, if any, can be feasibly acquired by the average student after two years of "training" in a foreign language at the college level? The answer is *listening comprehension* and *reading comprehension.* These are not unreasonable goals. Does this mean that speaking and writing should be eliminated from foreign language programs? Such a notion is of course absurd. What is needed is a decided *shift in emphasis* in teaching the skills. No one is going to learn how *to understand* normal, daily conversational French, German, or any other language by just listening to contrived textbook dialogues. Even after many years of formal "study," one has only to see and hear a foreign film for the first time to establish this as a fact. In order to understand the spoken language at an effective level, it is absolutely essential for one *to be trained* to listen at that level. This means spending a lot of time listening to what native speakers listen to. Contrived materials must be generously—*most generously*—supplemented by "live" materials. Effective listening is a *terminal not an immediate* objective, and the training process must make the transition from the *pre-nucleation* stage to *nucleation* and the *post-nucleation* stage in a two-year period.

The term *nucleation* as applied to language learning was first introduced by Kenneth L. Pike (1960). I (Belasco, 1965) have discussed his use of the term elsewhere, but it is worth repeating here. I quote the central theme of his argument comparing language learning to the crystallization process in chemistry. "Nucleation is involved in the first small clustering of atoms or molecules—say the first two or three dozen—into a structural pattern which will then be extensively duplicated in a repetitive pattern to form a crystal. It is difficult to get these first molecules to clump together. . . . Yet once nucleation has begun, growth may proceed with great rapidity. . . . Thus it appears that the energy barrier opposing nucleation is much greater than that opposing growth. The initial formation of starting nuclei is very difficult. The growth of these nuclei into larger units is very rapid and relatively easy and simple" (Pike, 1960, p. 291). Pike extends the analogy to language learners who have memorized many vocabulary items and grammatical rules and yet have not nucleated. "That is, though they may have many of the elements necessary for a conversation, they cannot in fact handle these. Specifically, they lack the *structure,* the 'crystallization'—which gives characteristic patterning to sentences and conversations" (Pike, 1960, p. 291). Although Pike specifically singles out the speaking skill, the analogy of nucleation applies to all the language skills.

Most students who have studied foreign language in high school come to college in a state of pre-nucleation. Their background in foreign language *is not* to be discounted by any means, however. It is a form of pre-nucleated language that has been acquired in an artificial situation. As such it can still be utilized. Unfortunately, the assumption is made at the college level that the student has reached a stage of language learning that can be developed into bona fide skills. This is the crux of the problem. The student has not yet overcome the barrier that opposes nucleation.

Dialogue memorization and pattern practice help to distinguish the number of elements that exist in the system, but they do not help the learner "clump" the elements together. In other words, it is possible to develop a high level of sophistication concerning the function of many linguistic units, but this will not insure that the learner reach into the storage bin of his or her memory, pinpoint the units, retrieve them, and then place them in structures that characterize the patterning of real sentences and conversations. To do this, the learner will have to know not only what he or she wants to say but also the form to be used in order to say it. We do not mean just a form that will permit the learner to insure that he or she is understood. That is fairly easy to do, but does not represent acquisition of the speaking skill.

Before an acceptable form can be utilized, one must have a fairly clear idea of what it sounds like in the mouth of a native speaker. That is why the degree of comprehension of the spoken language must be high before one can hope to engage in sustained conversation. Conversation is a two-way street. Even if it is possible to develop a high degree of "vocalizing," i.e., parroting stock expressions, no conversation takes place in the absence of exchange. Communication implies *receiving* as well as *sending*. It is virtually impossible to speak a first language without having first acquired auditory comprehension. This is not necessarily the case in learning a second language. Cases exist where teachers can speak a foreign language with surprising fluency yet their skill in listening is well below that of the average native speaker (Belasco, 1971b). The reason for this is not difficult to understand. Having learned mostly textbook speech, their state of expectancy for the sound of spoken utterances is limited to cultivated varieties. As soon as they are exposed to the speech of the average person on the street, their level of comprehension is considerably reduced. This is especially true when natural speech is encountered in motion pictures, radio, and television.

An example may be taken from English involving "telescoped" speech. Natural speech contains many contracted or telescoped expressions. For example, one might ask the reader: "What does *amina* mean?" The meaning, of course, becomes evident in an utterance such as: "*Amina* [ãminə] tell you right now!" The native speaker of English may be totally unaware that he or she is listening to telescoped speech when hearing it first in context. Even after becoming consciously aware of its use in a given context, the native speaker still may not realize that the telescoped version of "I am going to" is restricted to a specific structural context: *Amina* is a type of modal pre-verb. In other words, it is possible to say "amina go," "amina try," "amina fight," for *I am going to go, try,* or *fight,* but not "*amina New York," "*amina Paris," "*amina London" for *I am going to New York, Paris,* or *London.* How many language textbooks treat telescoped speech—or *morphophonemics* as it is called in linguistic analysis? The answer of course is very few, if any.

No one is going to understand the average native speaker, who uses colloquial—not textbook—speech, unless *trained to understand* the speaker (Belasco, 1967a). The language learner who learns telescoped speech along with cultivated speech will be able to understand either variety. The learner who is exposed only to cultivated speech will always have difficulty with expressions such as "Hey, djeat djet?" [dʒiyt dʒɛt] "No, djoo?" [dʒuw], translated as "Hey, did you eat yet?" "No, did you?"

It is important to emphasize here that we are not advocating that foreign language students be taught to *practice* telescoped speech. This could prove to be ludicrous—especially when heard by a native speaker. But we certainly insist that he or she be taught to *understand* telescoped speech along with cultivated speech, or the student's language learning experience will leave a lot to be desired.

Our students are currently bogged down in the pre-nucleation stage. The grammatical principles underlying the pattern drills of the average commercial audio-lingual textbook have at most perched them on top of a plateau (Belasco, 1967b). The traditional principles—even though set to sound—do not contain morphophonemic structure, nor any of the essential language structure for that matter. In this respect, language materials are too "shallow." In another respect, they are too "extensive." They represent a range too broad in scope, too diluted in terms of the elements crucial for internalization of underlying linguistic principles.

The road sloping upward to nucleation is blocked by the barrier of "inhibition" resulting from first language acquisition. Recall that I said, in a normal first language learning situation, an individual cannot escape learning his or her native tongue. If parallel language learning does not obtain at some time near the age of puberty, it becomes exceedingly difficult to have second language forms coexist with—let alone substitute for—forms acquired as a first language.

An important reason why a human being is able to learn a second language to any degree is his or her inability to *inhibit totally.* Individuals vary as to their ability to "language-inhibit." The more language-*uninhibited* a person is, the better the chances for acquiring a second language. Unlike any other creature, the human being is able to engage in a certain amount of symbol-switching without having to undergo an extensive period of retraining. For example, the reader can, on command, substitute the nonce word *gope for the word "sit" in the utterance "I tell you to sit," which will result in the nonce utterance "I tell you to *gope." In fact, the reader will be able to do this for many utterances involving such nonce words as *shiss for "beg," *peen for "jump," *plove for "stand," and so on. Of course individuals will vary as to the number of nonce word substitutions they can make. Yet no other animal can do this without undergoing an extensive retraining period. One cannot say to a dog or to an ape "O.K., all bets are off, when I say 'Sit!,' don't sit, but when I say '*Gope!,' then sit!" In other words, the animal is inhibited to the degree that it cannot "symbol-switch." But a human being is not that inhibited. He or she can do *some* symbol-switching, and, most unfortunately, it is this ability that educators, teachers, and methodologists have been exploiting ever since the idea of teaching someone a second language was conceived.

This is not to say that symbol-switching in foreign language teaching should not be used. But it should definitely not be playing the principal role that has been assigned to it over the centuries. If the degree of language-inhibition after puberty were the same as that before puberty, there would be no need for second language teaching. Since after the age of puberty, a high degree of "partial" language-inhibition does set in, the conditions for learning another language are most unfavorable. Techniques and materials relying heavily on a symbol-switching approach will do nothing to extricate the learner from the pre-nucleation stage. The learner has learned his or her first language only too well. The ability to handle familiar concepts in terms of second language forms is definitely limited. The first language forms are firmly entrenched, they are "available," and attempts to replace or parallel them with second language forms have no "vital" basis. This is also true of pre-adolescent children learning a second language by symbol-switching techniques. For them, second language learning in an artificial situation is a game. They can never be exposed to the "parallel" linguistic structure encountered by children in a natural bilingual situation. The approach that *supplements—not replaces—*symbol-switching by parallel learning can overcome the relatively high degree of partial language-inhibition that is a barrier to nucleation. This means supplementing contrived materials with "live" materials at the right time. A state of nucleation will only be reached when the essential linguistic structure has been internalized; that is, when "clumping" will have been effected.

In the post-nucleation stage, it is necessary to reduce asymptotically the amount of contrived materials to the point where dependence on such materials is nil for all practical purposes. This is the point where the learner will have achieved *mastery*. However, neither *mastery* nor even nucleation of the spoken and written skills should be part of the goals for the first two years of college foreign language training. Nucleation of the listening and reading skills *is* a feasible goal. Speaking and writing should by no means be discouraged, but training in these skills is primarily designed to aid nucleation of listening and reading. Any improvement in speaking and writing will be the result of concomitant "fallout" and is of course a desirable "plus."

Although students vary considerably in the way they learn a second language, most seem to have more difficulty with speaking and writing. They also have difficulty with listening and reading. However, the opportunities for using the speaking and writing skills—even if nucleation could be effected for these—are far fewer than for listening and reading. It is fairly simple to find accessible reading and listening sources composed in a foreign language: newspapers, books, magazines, phonograph records, tapes, radio, television, motion pictures. But how many available speakers and pen-pals exist for average college students enabling them to use their foreign language skills in situations requiring authentic conversation and written correspondence? Thus the goal of learning how *to comprehend* spoken and written foreign language materials is more practicable than learning how *to recreate* such materials artificially. Internalization of listening and reading comprehension represents genuine nucleation. The acquisition of the oral and writing skills represents at best "lightning translation" in the case of speaking and "contrived composition" in the case of writing (Belasco, 1963b).

The point has now been reached when I am ready to say something about the techniques of helping college students acquire listening and reading skills in a foreign language within a two-year period. I shall describe the role of the teacher, that of the student, and the physical facility in which nucleation can take place.

The method proposes a fifteen-week semester system divided into five three-week learning units for four semesters. Students attend three fifty-minute regular class periods each week. Unit tests are administered at the end of each of the five three-week learning units; i.e., the ninth, eighteenth, twenty-seventh, thirty-sixth, and forty-fifth sessions.

Now it must be remembered that the goals of the programs are listening and reading comprehension. All speaking and writing exercises are done to reinforce the acquisition of the first two skills. Therefore, oral pattern practice is designed not to have students engage in conversation but to have them assimilate basic structure. For the first semester, students engage in four types of activity during *each* period: listening, reading, vocalizing, and writing. To all intents and purposes, vocalizing is equivalent to oral pattern practice.

What I shall say now will come as a shock to many proponents of the audio-lingual approach. During each period students do the classwork with textbooks open. In other words, students practicing dialogues and drills will know in advance what structural principles (phonological, syntactic, semantic) the dialogues and drills are designed to internalize. They will not be compelled to infer certain generalizations about the grammar. They will practice only after they are consciously aware of what principles are involved. In other words, pattern drills will always be preceded by short structural explanations. Such explanations will treat (1) the sound structure, (2) the morphophonemic structure (predictable and nonpredictable forms arising from the accidental co-occurrence of certain constructions), and (3) the basic syntactic structure (Belasco, 1969). The student will be trained how to recognize and to pronounce reasonably all sounds and combinations of sounds, not only in isolation but also in the context of natural speech.

Thus, in a fifty-minute class period, ten minutes of class time will be spent in explanations by the teacher, ten minutes will be devoted to listening—not only to the dialogue but to a "model" class on tape performing the structural exercises the class will be expected to practice afterward, fourteen minutes of actual pattern practice, ten minutes of dictation based on the dialogue, and six minutes in a "spot" question student-teacher exchange relating to the day's activity. The textbooks are closed only during the dictation.

Whereas the listening sessions are designed to teach the student morphophonemic structure, the pattern practice teaches the basic sentence structure. The student will eventually learn that the sentences of a language are formed from one or more basic sentences of the types:

(A)   Noun   Verb
(B)   Noun   Verb   Noun v Preposition + Noun
(C)   Noun   (be)   Noun
                    Adjective
                    Adverb
                    Prepositional Phrase

Examples of each type follow:

Type A   N   V
           John speaks

Type B   N   V   N
           John speaks French

           N   V   Prep   N
           John speaks   to   Mary

           N   V   N   Prep   N
           John speaks French   to   Mary

Type C   N   be   N
           John is president

           N   be   Adj
           John is French

           N   be   Adv
           John is there

           N   be   PP
           John is in conference

N stands for noun (or pronoun), V for verb, *be* for copula (be, seem, appear, become, etc.), Prep for preposition, Adj for adjective, Adv for adverb, and PP for prepositional phrase. Thus a sentence (S) having the complex surface structure: "John told the student who was failed by the teacher not to worry," is made up of the following basic sentence types:

1. Matrix Sentence: Type B

   N_0 V N_1 Prep N_2
   S: John told something   to   someone   →

   N_0 V N_2 N_1
   John told someone something

2. Constituent Sentence: Type A (N_1:   Direct Object)

   N   V
   S: *that* Neg(ative) *the student worry*

3. Antecedent (N_2:   Indirect Object) Plus Constituent
   Sentence: Type B (Passive Transform of Relative Clause)

   N_2 N   V   N
   Antecedent/S: the student / the teacher failed the student

The Type B matrix sentence contains a direct object (N_1), which is itself a negated Type A sentence undergoing PRO(noun) deletion.

   N   V
N_1: *that* Neg *the student worry*   →   *that he*
   not worry   →   *not to worry*

The matrix sentence also contains an indirect object (N_2) in which the antecedent *the student* is modified by a relative clause, which is a passive transform of a Type B sentence.

   N_2 N   V   N
N_2: *the student / the teacher failed the student*   →
   the student / the student was failed by the teacher   →
   the student who was failed by the teacher

Since N_1 and N_2 were permuted earlier, the complex sentence reads:

——N_2————————————————————————————N_1——
   N_0 V   N   V   N   V
   John told / / the student / who was failed by the teacher / / not to worry

The "conscious" knowledge of complex sentence structure is a *terminal* objective *not an immediate* objective. Such knowledge becomes "unconscious" after nucleation takes place for the reading and listening skills.

An immediate objective for the first semester is the ability of the student to control actively the present, past, and future tenses of regular verbs and common irregular verbs. This means that rapid-fire drill is conducted during the oral practice sessions for fourteen minutes each day. Now, as has been pointed out, the conventional classroom situation is not conducive to internalizing structure—be it basic or any other kind. The problem is how to convert the classroom into a part-time orientation facility and a part-time practice/testing facility. The language laboratory is of some help but it basically does not favor "control." The answer lies in *the proper use* of a portable cassette tape-recorder. Most students own such a recorder. If not, a fairly inexpensive one may be purchased as part of required equipment. Science and engineering courses require special equipment; why not foreign languages?

The role of the teacher is to explain the rationale behind the software. The tapes contain the dialogues, all the exercises performed by model students, plus built-in student *self-pacing, self-evaluation* exercises. The role of the student is to gain control of the basic—not the complex—type A, B, C sentences in declarative, interrogative, negative, interrogative-negative, and imperative constructions during the first semester. This includes replacing a single (direct or indirect) object noun by an appropriate pronoun. Compounding of short sentences with "and," "or," and "but" is also permitted. In the classroom the teacher does not do oral drills to effect internalization of the structure, but *to test* the students' ability to handle such structure. The teacher "tests" students' ability to listen by having them identify long and short "excerpts" from all parts of the dialogue. The teacher uses dictation of the dialogue to check spelling and the handling of grammatical forms in a written context. Reading is at first limited to the vocabulary and syntactic patterns found in the dialogues, but subsequent reading selections contain all of the learned vocabulary and structure in recombined reading tests. Thus, the materials in the first semester are for the most part "contrived."

The second semester continues the procedures of the first semester with additions. The conditional mode is introduced. "If" clauses and simple dependent noun and adjectival clauses are practiced: "If John goes, so will I," "I know that John will go," "I met the man who went with John," etc. Included is the replacement of two or more object nouns by appropriate pronouns in one or more clauses. Practice also includes the conjugation and use of the present and present perfect subjunctive in dependent clauses. Short "live" materials are introduced consisting of jokes, anecdotes, and newspaper items both written and taped.

In the third semester the emphasis shifts from *contrived* to *controlled* materials. Controlled materials are transitional materials that attempt to bridge the gap between the pre-nucleation stage and liberated listening and reading. During the first year, the student has developed a "state of expectancy" for certain morphophonemic and syntactic constructions found in the context of a native speaker's daily experiences. In the second year, the listening and reading selections represent a *self-pacing, self-evaluation* teaching and testing device for understanding "live" materials. The student's cassette tape-recorder permits listening "in isolation" to recordings of newscasts, popular songs, interviews, excerpts from original plays, and so on. In the beginning, the student listens to a recording and an accompanying printed text. The text contains the foreign language script *and* the equivalent translation in English. Then the English text is gradually reduced and eliminated during subsequent selections. A short time after the English text has started to be withdrawn, the French script is asymptotically reduced.

The student spends as much time as is necessary to write down, as a dictation, that part of the listening selection which was not supported by a "crutch." In other words, he is "guessing" at the meaning of the words and the grammatical constructions—based on his interpretation of the sound pattern; i.e., the morphophonemic structure.

Once returned to the regular class, students alternately read their versions of the dictation as others try to record them on the blackboard. Pronunciation, morphophonemic patterns, spelling, and grammatical mistakes are discussed in detail by teacher and students. Thus the cognitive acquisition of grammatical principles stems from the "live" materials. The role of the teacher is that of a guide. His or her task is to have *the students explain* the discrepancies and mistakes found in the dictation. The teacher only makes explanations when none of the students can. Pattern practice is instituted only for those cases where cognitive acquisition of old or new structural principles has not been effected. After the dictation has been thoroughly dissected, each student receives a mimeographed copy of the text. Later, in isolation, the student checks his or her corrected version of the dictation against the recording and the mimeographed text.

To illustrate some of the techniques we are advocating, we shall use excerpts from *occitan,* a language that is probably unfamiliar to the reader. *Occitan* is a Romance language spoken in the southern part of France by some 11,000,000 inhabitants. It is not a dialect of French, but it does share many structural and lexical characteristics of Spanish, Italian, Catalan, and French. The principal dialects of *occitan* are *provençal, languedocien, gascon, limousin,* and *auvergnat.* The language has enjoyed literary prestige since the Middle Ages.[3]

The reason for using *occitan* is three-fold. In the first place, as an unfamiliar language it places the reader in a position similar to that of a student learning a second language. Secondly, there is enough similarity between *occitan* and the other Romance languages so that the reader who knows French, Spanish, or Italian may appreciate the situation of the student who comes to college in the pre-nucleation stage; that is, with *some knowledge* of a foreign language acquired in high school. Thirdly, *occitan* words uttered in isolation undergo extensive change in the context of normal discourse. In other words, the morphophonemic structure of *occitan* is rather complex and serves to illustrate the listening comprehension problems encountered by a student who has been trained to "speak" but not to listen.

Let us imagine that the student is taking second-year *occitan* and has been trained in the conventional audio-lingual fashion. The student has covered the so-called forty to fifty grammatical principles, and has listened to the usual amount of dialogues and practiced pattern drills based on "seeded" structures. Let us also imagine that the student is reading *La grava sul camin,* a novel by the celebrated *occitan* novelist Joan Bodon (1976).

The text that follows is written in *languedocien,* which is the standard *occitan* dialect.[4]

Sample Text for Listening

Ai paur! Darrièr la ròda de fèrre d'un vagon me soi aplatussat. Una bronzor se sarra sus l'autobahn. Diriàtz las aigas d'una granda mar. Tot còp un flac, un sarrabastal. Las bastendas de la gara fumassejan, destrantalhadas. Ai paur.

Los Alemands son partits dempuèi un brieu. Nos an daissats aquí, en plena gara, al mièg dels vagons escarmentrats. E sèm demorats aquí, totes estirats, sens gausar bolegar.

Naturally the student has had some practice in sound production but *no training in morphophonemics.* His or her "state of expectancy" is that the selected words of the sentences of the two paragraphs are pronounced as in the *first* of the two sets (columns) of phonetic transcription.

Diriàtz	[dirj<u>a</u>ts]*	[dirj<u>a</u>s]
las	[las]	[laj]
tut	[tut]	[tuk]
un	[yn]	[ym]
bastendas	[bast<u>e</u>ndɔs]	[bast<u>e</u>ndɔj]
fumassejan	[fymas<u>e</u>džɔn]	[fymas<u>e</u>džu]
los	[lus]	[luz]
son	[sun]	[sum]
dempuèi	[dempy<u>ɛ</u>j]	[demp<u>ɛ</u>j]
daissats	[dajs<u>a</u>ts]	[dajs<u>a</u>dz]
en	[en]	[em]
mièg	[mj<u>ɛ</u>tʃ]	[mj<u>ɛ</u>d]
des	[des]	[dej]
vagons	[bag<u>u</u>s]	[bag<u>u</u>z]
demorats	[demɔr<u>a</u>ts]	[demɔr<u>a</u>dz]
totes	[t<u>u</u>tes]	[t<u>u</u>tez]
sens	[sen]	[seŋ]

*Stressed vowels are underlined.

When spoken by a native speaker in the context of the sentences, however, the words are pronounced as in the second column of phonetic transcription. In other words, without consistent morphophonemic training in the first year, the "state of expectancy" for words pronounced in careful speech, or in isolation, will not help the student understand natural speech in the mouth of a native speaker. The audio-lingual method makes no systematic provision for stylistic variation. That is why students and teachers may develop a high degree of accurate "vocalizing"—if not "speaking"—ability, but a low degree of listening comprehension.

During the first year, the student should have learned that final -ats is pronounced [ats], [as] ,[adz]; that -s is pronounced [z], [j] ; that -u [ɥ] may be deleted; and that -t, -g [tʃ], -n may be respectively assimilated to [k],[d] , [m, ŋ] under specific, systematic conditions. Of course, the examples used here have been deliberately selected because they are simple and help to illustrate our point. Morphophonemics can be complex but not unteachable.

Just as no one has isolated the syntactic and semantic features that are necessary for second language internalization, neither has anyone worked out the corresponding morphophonemic principles. Nor is it essential that research in second language structural analysis be completed before students are taught to understand a foreign language. The principles can be discovered by both student and teacher in the classroom as long as "live" materials are used. The remarkable feature about such an approach is that it contains a built-in retraining program for teachers. The teacher who is a native speaker becomes intellectually aware of the morphophonemic principles that must accompany the learning of a printed text set to sound. And the non-native speaker "discovers" the cognitive techniques that improve his or her own comprehension, which thereafter are extended to the students.

A similar cognitive approach teaches the second-year student how to read. In the audio-lingual approach the student is not, strictly speaking, "taught" to read. As in the grammar-translation method, students have a vocabulary list or a dictionary and resort to the "hunt and pick" method, which is more like puzzle-solving than reading. The dictionary can be used as a supplementary tool in a cognitive bilingual approach. Placing the English text in a column on the left and the foreign language text on the right, idiomatic expressions as well as syntactic and semantic correspondences between the two languages stand out in bold relief. When the English text is encountered first, the student is put in control of the "concept." No empirical evidence exists to support the claim that in the pre-nucleation stage the student must "infer" the concept from the foreign language context. In fact, it is a waste of time to infer—rather than bilingually "match"—contexts.

Sample Text for Reading

The shadow, then, disappeared.	L'ombra, alavetz, que despareishoc.
At the end of a moment,	Au cap d'ua estona,
it reappeared in the room,	que tornèc paréisher dens la pèça,
walking stealthily,	caminant a pas de lop,
a long carbine in its left hand.	ua longa carabina dens la man esquèrra.
John perceived everything	Lo Joan qu'ac destriava tot
with perfect clarity,	dab ua perfièita claretat,
but he wasn't afraid:	mès n'avèva pas páur:
he had self-control,	la sua sang qu'èra hreda,
and his mind was clear.	lo son esperit lucid.

He remained there,	Que demorava aquiu,
glued to the window,	pegat a la hièstra,
and nothing in the world	e arren au món
could have budged him.	non l'agosse podut hèr partir.
Suddenly, he uttered a second cry,	Tot sobte que larguèc un segon crit,
this time of anger,	de colèra aqueste còp,
shaking the shutters in a rage.	en segotir raujosament los contravents.
Some dogs in the distance	Cans, au luenh,
began to howl.	que comencèn d'udolar.
The cold had become intolerable	La hred que l'èra devenguda intolerable
and he began to tremble	e que's hiquèc a tremolar
like a leaf.	coma ua huelha.[5]

The dialect of the *occitan* text is *gascon*. It differs from *languedocien* in several respects: *f* is written *h, hred* [ret] "cold," intervocalic *n* disappears *ua* (*una*) "a," initial *r* is often preceded by *a, arren* (*ren*) "nothing," intervocalic *-ll-* becomes *-r- bèra* (*bella*) "beautiful," etc. The "enunciative" *que* appears before a (non-negated) finite verb even though it does not introduce a dependent clause: *Lo Joan qu'ac destriava tot* "John perceived everything," *la sua sang qu'era hreda* "his blood was cold," *Que demorava aquiu* "He remained there," etc. Nonetheless, enough similarity with French, Spanish, and Italian exists so that with the English translation, anyone knowing one or more Romance languages can make out the meaning of the passage, determine where words and sentences end, as well as identify the structural characteristics of the language.

Students will come to the third semester with varying degrees of reading ability. They may be roughly classified according to three types. Type I reads the foreign language text and occasionally looks at the English translation. Such a student is ready for nucleation and is most uncommon after only two semesters. Type II tries to read the *occitan* text but makes extensive use of the English equivalent. Type III must read the English text first in order to grasp the concept. This student then shifts back and forth from the English to the *occitan* over and over again until he or she can understand the *occitan* passage with the English text covered; that is, without having further recourse to the English translation. The student then goes on to the next passage, proceeding in the same fashion. Most third semester students are like Type III.

In the fourth semester, the "live" listening and reading passages are expanded. Question and answer exchange based on the reading and listening passages are conducted orally and in writing in the foreign language. New structural cues are discussed as they appear. For instance in the preceding passage, the student would be required to explain that *que's hiquèc* is the third person preterit reflexive form of the verb *hicar* "to introduce" or "to put." Followed by an infinitive it means "to begin": *hicà's a trabalhar* "to begin to work." Other expressions recalled from previous selections might have been *gascon: que s'ei hicat a trabalhar; languedocien: que s'es botat a trabalhar, que s'es mes a trabalhar*—all meaning "he began to work." Short grammatical reviews could be introducd at this point involving, for instance, the function and use of the reflexive pronoun in different tenses. All of this would be tied up with old or new discrimination exercises recorded on tape. In short, all the grammar, whether new or review, arises from the reading and listening passages themselves. And everything is geared to developing a state of expectancy for new structural principles that may occur in future selections.

By the end of the fourth semester, the student will be close to nucleation in listening and reading if he or she has acquired (1) control of the "live" structure, (2) control of "live" vocabulary, (3) an awareness of differences of cultural concept, and (4) awareness of differences of cultural emphasis. Control of the first two factors will come if reading and listening has been practiced with the very materials used daily by native speakers of the language. Awareness of the last two factors comes by chance, and only if the student has been taught to anticipate "cultural contrast." For example, a British subject may not know that a speaker of American English from Pennsylvania, or from any state for that matter, does not mean he or she is a Missourian when stating "I'm from Missouri." In fact, many Americans might not be aware that this, as well as the two words *show me* or the expression *I'm from the show-me state,* all refer to a single concept, namely "You'll have to convince me before I believe what is being asserted." In other words, these expressions represent an American—not British—cultural concept that transcends the usual linguistic barriers. An American will not understand such expressions due to chance—not because he or she has not internalized a portion of linguistic structure.

Sometimes a concept may exist in both English and the target language, but the "emphasis" is different. For example, one might know the meaning of every word in an expression such as *occitan: vòls que te faga lo grand jòc o preferisses lo marc de cafè?* The reader may still have difficulty with the English translation: "Do you want me to make the big play for you, or do you prefer coffeegrounds?" In both English and *occitan,* the concept of telling one's fortune exists. But in *occitan,* the "emphasis" is being placed not on the crystal ball but on the hand waving and abracadabra, *lo grand jòc* "the big play." In addition, the emphasis is not on "tea leaves" but on *lo marc de cafè* "coffee grounds." Thus in a similar situation an American might expect "Shall I look into my crystal ball, or would you rather have me read tea leaves?" The concepts of looking into a crystal ball and looking into a cup exist for both cultures, but each language reflects a difference in emphasis. Again, the same concept can be expressed in other ways.

Both *occitan* and English have gypsies reading "the lines of the hand" *las regas de la man.* And where English speaks of "telling fortunes," *occitan* speaks of *dire la bonaventura* "telling good fortune." Cultural contrast involving differences in cultural emphasis turn out to be important factors in reading and listening comprehension. An "awareness" of such factors should take place in the nucleation stage. "Control" of such factors is characteristic of *mastery* and should subsequently take place in the post-nucleation stage.

Thus far we have been trying to adapt the conditions for nucleation to the conventional classroom situation. Such adaptation is possible with the change in the teacher's role from purveyor of information to trained guide. The student's role also changes from passive to active participant inside and outside the classroom. Ideally, however, more effective results might be obtained by shifting the emphasis from assimilating language within a two-year period to effecting nucleation of listening and reading over an indefinite period of time. This would involve a team-teaching situation stressing self-evaluation techniques and self-pacing procedures.

In this system, a team of five instructors would, for example, be in charge of 125 students. In the beginning, each instructor would have a class of twenty-five students. At the end of the first three-week learning unit, a student would be permitted to go on to the next learning unit *only if* he or she made an achievement score of 90 percent or better. Upon completing the course work for the entire year, every student would receive the grade of A since this is the grade normally given for 90 percent achievement.

Let us assign the letters A, B, C, D, and E respectively to each of the five instructors. Let us further suppose that seventy-five out of 125 students received an achievement score of 90 percent at the end of the first learning unit. Then A, B, and C with twenty-five students each would continue with the work of the second learning unit, whereas D and E would work intensively with the remaining fifty students to bring them to the 90 percent achievement level during the second three-week period. Later, let us say, out of the group of seventy-five students, only forty-two achieved 90 percent at the end of the second learning unit, and twenty out of the group of fifty students achieved 90 percent at the end of six weeks. During the third learning unit, instructors A and B would work with twenty-one students each, instructor C with thirty-three students, instructor D with twenty students, and instructor E with thirty students. Since 125 students began the course at the same time, at the end of thirty weeks (two semesters), they might be spread over the program as in Table 2.1.

Table 2.1   Spread of Students at End of Thirty Weeks

Number of the Unit (3-Week Segment)	I	II	III	IV	V	VI	VII	VIII	IX	X
Instructor	A	B	C	D	E	E	D	C	B	A
Number of students in class	1	2	4	3	2	10	18	22	33	30
			9 a.m. classes				10 a.m. classes			

This means that by the end of the thirtieth week, the instructors A, B, C, D, and E have been teaching two classes each, one at 9 a.m. and one at 10 a.m. Instructor A has one student still in the learning Unit I (first three-week unit) at 9 a.m., and thirty students in learning Unit X (tenth three-week unit) at 10 a.m.; instructor B has two students in learning Unit II and thirty-three students in learning Unit IX, and so on. The chances are good, however, that no student will still be in, for instance, Units I and II. If so, instructors A and B could share some of the students in the other learning units. In any event, no one enters the second year of foreign language training until he or she has achieved 90 percent or better in the first year. A student entering the second year of language-learning under this system will have a much better chance for success. The student advances at a pace set by his or her own capacity. Individual differences do exist for each student, and students do not learn a second language in the same way. There is no guarantee that they learn their native language in the same way. Yet they cannot fail to learn *a first language* when exposed to normal language learning conditions. In second language learning, the normal conditions turn out to be artificial. Foreign language materials, contrived as they are, can never take into account the language structure or cognitive processes that are essential for overcoming the "inhibitory" characteristics of learning a first language. Those who succeed in nucleating do so not because of the system but in spite of it—and they make up a very small percentage of the students enrolled in foreign language courses.

On the other hand, controlled listening and reading materials have built-in self-pacing and self-evaluating features—with just those phonological, syntactic, and semantic primary data that are lacking in contrived materials. With the teacher assuming the role of a guide, students the role of active participants, the classroom the aspects of a movable feast, and the materials the effectiveness of a nourishing banquet, then—and only then—will students lift themselves from "the plateau" and ascend the slope to nucleated learning.

Notes

1. For the rationale behind "seeding" procedures, see Simon Belasco, editor, *Manual and Anthology of Applied Linguistics: General Section, French, German, Italian, Russian, Spanish,* University Park, Pa.: Nittany Press, 1960; *Applied Linguistics: French, German, Italian, Russian, Spanish,* 5 vols., Boston: D.C. Heath, 1961. A revised version of the General section and the French section was published as Simon Belasco and Albert Valdman, *Applied Linguistics and the Teaching of French,* University Park, Pa.: Nittany Press, 1968.

2. Although the overall design is based on audio-lingual habit theory, the dangers of interference (wrong analogizing) in the native and target languages are discussed in S. Belasco (1963b).

3. For the works of more recent *occitan* novelists, see *Colleccion A Tots* and the *Colleccion Messatges* listed in Pèire Gougaud, *L'uèlh de la font,* Toulouse: L'Institut d'Estudis Occitans, 1977.

4. The *Alibèrt* orthography, cf. Loïs Alibèrt, *Gramatica occitana,* 2nd ed., Montpellier: Centre d'Estudis Occitans, 1976, has replaced the *graphie mistralienne* which is based on a subdialect of *provençal* and used by classical *occitanistes.*

5. Excerpt pp. 117–118) from the tale "Lo hòu de la harga" in Pèire Bec, *Contes de l'unic,* Pau: Per Noste, 1977, pp. 107–124. The English translation is by the writer of this chapter.

References

Belasco, S. "Structural drills and the refinement principle." *International Journal of American Linguistics, 29,* pp. 19–36, 1963a.

———. "The continuum: Listening and speaking." In *Reports of the Working Committees, 1963 Northeast Conference on the teaching of foreign languages,* pp. 3–21, 1963b.

———. "Nucleation and the audio-lingual approach." *The Modern Language Journal, 49,* pp. 482–491, 1965.

———. "Surface structure and deep structure in English." *Midway, 8,* pp. 111–123, 1967a.

———. "The plateau; or the case for comprehension: The 'concept' approach." *The Modern Language Journal, 51,* pp. 82–88, 1967b.

———. "Toward the acquisition of linguistic competence: From contrived to controlled materials." *The Modern Language Journal, 53,* pp. 185–205, 1969.

———. "Les structures grammaticales orales." In P. Delattre (Ed.), *Les exercices structuraux pour quoi faire?* Paris: Hachette, 1971a.

———. "The feasibility of learning a second language in an artificial unicultural situation." In Paul Pimsleur and Terence Quinn (Eds.), *The Psychology of Second Language Learning.* Cambridge, England: Cambridge University Press, 1971b.

———. "Social stratification and second language acquisition." In H. B. Altman and V. E. Hanzeli (Eds.), *Essays on the teaching of culture: A festschrift to honor H. L. Nostrand.* Detroit: Advancement Press of America, 1974.

Bodon, J. *La grava sul camin.* Nimes: L'Institut d'Estudis Occitans, 1976.

Chomsky, N. *Essays on form and interpretation.* New York: Elsevier North-Holland, 1977.

Parker, W. R. "The problem of time." *Publications of the Modern Language Association of America, 71,* pp. xviii–xix, 1956.

Pike, K. L. "Nucleation." *The Modern Language Journal, 44,* pp. 291–295, 1960.

CHAPTER 3

Participatory Observation:
How to Succeed in Language Learning

Leonard Newmark

Professor of Linguistics
University of California, San Diego

A striking deficiency of most attempts to justify a particular method of (or approach to) language teaching is that they fail to account for the success of many individual learners who have not enjoyed the putative advantages of the method proposed, nor for the failure of some individual learners who have been subjects of the favored method. In that respect, recent arguments for the comprehension approach or for Suggestology, the Silent Way, or, for that matter, older arguments for audio-lingual, direct methods (such as those of Berlitz or de Sauzé), grammar-translation, or even the grab bag called "eclectic," fail to account for the vociferous testimony of competing proponents as to the success of their own ways of teaching. And indeed, should we expect Gimbel's to pay attention to Macy's success? Why should proponents of particular approaches be concerned about the success or failure of other approaches?

The answer, I think, lies in the still primitive state of our pedagogic sciences. Given the complexity of any actual teaching situation (teaching variables, student variables, second-to-second situational variables), decisive experiments to compare the efficacy of different teaching methods or techniques continue to elude us. In real classroom experiments we are always left with nagging doubts about the role of variables that were of necessity left uncontrolled; and in well-controlled laboratory experiments we wonder about the applicability of results to the complex realities of the classroom.

Statistical arguments for the success or failure of masses of students—even in the rare cases in which careful statistics exist—will not assuage our nagging, persistent interest in the individuals who succeeded or failed in a general program where others enjoyed the opposite fortune. Instead of evading the issue by invoking slogans such as "There are exceptions to every rule" or "Some students have high language aptitudes and others don't," we can gain considerable insight by examining in clear cases the particulars of the conditions under which language learning does take place in contrast with conditions under which it does not. Such insight can then be used to revise our own approach to language teaching and to assess in a principled way the claims of adherents of various pedagogical approaches. Instead of waiting for direct experimental evidence of the superiority of one approach over another, we can put ourselves in a position in which we can judge on theoretical grounds what elements of a pedagogical approach might account for its reported success and what elements in the implementation of that approach could account for its unreported cases of failure.

First, notice that there are a large number of complex skills that *every* appropriate, normal member of a culture learns informally, in sharp contrast with the complex skills taught formally in our own educational system, for which it is characteristic that some students do well while others do badly.

In an idyll of an idealized example, imagine a hunting and gathering society which survives on the ability of its members to perform the variety of complex tasks that constitute food garnering in the society. In that society all normal boys who survive must learn the complex skill of killing animals with a spear; there is no formal school to teach spear-throwing, no one to decide how many times a given component is to be practiced before the next may be attempted. Instead, the boys in the society go out hunting with the men (while the girls go berry picking with the women):

(1) Typically, all the eligible learners succeed in acquiring the requisite skills. Contrast the bell-shaped distribution of success for students in language classes, with many learners who fail to achieve effective skills in the language.[1] It is striking that for complex and subtle social skills the culture assumes everyone of the appropriate class will master (just think of culturally determined gestures, for example), everyone in the society seems to succeed in learning; yet it is difficult to think of any deliberately taught, complex academic skill that *everyone* who has gone through the educational process will learn at an appropriate social level.

(2) There are no classrooms as such, no teachers designated as such, no pre-formed lesson plans, no formal examinations necessary for the systems to work. The learners learn from anyone (including fellow learners) they perceive as knowing more than they do; on any particular outing a given student picks up those bits and pieces he is ready to learn, out of the complex mass of skills necessary to be a good hunter; instead of formal steps marking off the acquisition of each component skill or complex of skills, the learner's progress proceeds by fits and starts, but inexorably moves him to full-fledged acceptance in the society of adults. The learner operates essentially as one of the apprentices in a shop in which the older apprentices and master craftsmen teach by example, with the younger, less experienced apprentices being given humble duties to

perform at first—which engage their attention to and participation in the process being learned.

(3) Learners have the opportunity to participate in the activity but are not held to standards of performance higher than their current level of ability allows. While differences in ability among the members of that society do exist, they are not attended to in determining who will continue to be given the opportunity to practice these skills, and thus whatever differences appear early tend to be leveled out over time.

Next consider a child in the process of learning a first or second language in the wilds (i.e., just living normally in a society that uses language). Again we notice the absence of planning and directing of the learning process by teachers, and the presence of role models performing tasks beyond the learner's own present ability to perform. Again the success rate is nearly 100 percent under these normal conditions. As in the acquisition of hunting skills, the child learning a language outside an artificial educational system serves a kind of apprenticeship to other language learners, observing what they do, participating at ever increasing levels of ability in the ordinary activities of the modeled groups. The learner's attention is directed to the language that others are using because it forms part of the total activity in which the group is participating. The contexts in which utterances are made and reactions are made to them allow the learner to understand with increasing precision their meaning. For long periods of time, especially during the earliest period, the child may not speak, but will listen attentively to others speaking and observe what they do. After a while he will try saying something himself, usually something quite short and something that he has heard repeated often in clarifying contexts. Gradually, his own utterances grow more and more ambitious and more like those of others, until at some point he becomes indistinguishable from the crowd.

But now, let us examine some cases in which language learning does not take place, even when the potential learner is exposed to the language over a protracted period of time. Why do some immigrant children acquire their parents' language natively and the language of the dominant society imperfectly if at all, while others do the opposite? In more general terms, how is it possible for an allegedly perfect language learner—the young child—*not* to learn a language spoken by his or her parents at home, while that same learner *does* learn the language of the culture in which that home is embedded? What ingredients are missing in the one learning environment that are present in the other? My contention is that those same ingredients are missing from the classroom experience of the unsuccessful student language learner and present in the experience of the successful one.

Can I learn Polish from scratch by turning on a Polish radio station and listening to the language long enough? No.[2] What is missing from the pure listening experience—the reason that mere "exposure" to the language fails, as correctly noted by its critics—is meaning. The listener who is given no clues as to the meaning of what he is hearing experiences not language but music; the listener may or may not get pleasure from and familiarity with the sounds of the language, but he cannot experience and thereby learn a language without attaching the conventional meanings to those sounds. To the extent that the learner is able to attach linguistic meanings to linguistic inputs, to that extent he is able to learn the language. And because attaching meaning to something is an experiential cognitive act, the listener must be *attending* to the string while experiencing its meaning.[3] The child who does not attend to what his parents are saying in their language, who does not participate in the activities that use that language, but who instead attends to and participates in the language activity of people outside his family, will learn the outside language rather than the one used at home. What commands the learner's attention, then, is what determines which language he learns. In all cases of successful language teaching, techniques have been found for directing the learner's attention to the instance of language (oral or written) at the same time that the learner experiences meaningfulness for it.

We cannot equate meaningfulness with the meanings of words, because, as the terms are conventionally used, the meaning of a word is an abstract and transcendent property of that word across occurrences. But learning a word requires that a particular occurrence of the word be endowed with meaning, not *the* meaning of the word, but *some* meaning. Learning the meaning of the word requires experiencing particular meaningful occurrences of the word; the degree to which a given learner's meaning for a word will be socially accurate will depend on the degree to which the contexts of the occurrences of the word have defined—in the sense of delimited—the meaning of the word and on the degree to which those contexts themselves have been defined.

For example, if a student has just entered a Spanish class on the first day of a new term, sits down, sees some well-dressed, middle-aged, dark-haired man with a clipped moustache standing behind a dais in front of the room, hears the man say (when the class quiets down) *mellamoseñorhernandez,* and pause, the student does not know whether a remark is being made to welcome the class, to tell students to open their books to page 2, to comment on the weather, to inform the students of his name, or what. But the student does guess that the remark is probably not in Swedish, nor the beginning of a recipe for making chocolate chip cookies, nor the man's mother's name, nor a command to open the window, nor a parting goodbye, because the student can give no interpretation to why the man would want to say such things in the context given. If the man now repeats his utterance (or so it seems to the learner), points to himself, goes to the board and writes "Hernandez," the student now rules out most of the alternative possibilities and guesses that the man is the teacher of the class, is speaking Spanish, and is telling them his name, the sound of which corresponds in some fashion with what is written on the board. As the man continues, performing actions and speaking in Spanish, the meaning of what is being said becomes more and more refined in the student's mind; repetitions and partial repetitions of sound sequences become associated with meanings and partial meanings in the student's understanding; and the student can be said to be learning Spanish. A variety of devices can be used to help create expression-cum-meaning correspondences in the student's mind: pictures with Spanish words written beneath them, dyad lists of Spanish words with their English translations, written dialogues with facing translations, graded readers using a large number of cognates in early pages to create contextual clues to the meanings of non-cognates, pointing to objects while saying their names, and so on. In all of these, the meaning clue is not the meaning itself, but rather a clue that may induce the learner to experience a conventional meaning for the bit of expression associated with it. If the expression bit is too long or the meaning clue too unclear to be processed by the learner at his current state of proficiency, or if the learner is not attending, the experience does not take place, and the "exposure" to language does not occur.

In both first and second language learning, the latter in both children and adults and in both child-like and adult-like settings, the learner will be judged to fail if (1) the learner is not attending to instances of the language in use, (2) inadequate provision is made to enable the learner to attach meaning to the expressions to be learned, and (3) the number and variety of expression–meaning combinations is less than required to satisfy the judge's criterion of what should constitute success. Success will be declared in the converse case: (1) if the learner is attending to instances of the language, (2) adequate provision is made to enable the learner to attach meaning to each instance, and (3) the number and variety of expression–meaning combinations is large enough to satisfy the success criterion.

It is important to appreciate this last point because so often discussion of whether a given technique or method of teaching "works" hinges on the failure to clarify the criterion of success. A teacher may report that teaching verb conjugations using flannel board with movable stem and affix morpheme patches "works." If pressed for justification, the teacher may point out that the activity of moving around the patches has kept usually passive students actively absorbed for a whole class period, and that the students perform well on tests calling on them to produce the correct verb form in response to a cue such as *tener* (*yo,* future). If such are to be the criteria of success for this teacher-judge, the methods of teaching can be aimed directly at producing the desired result (and the flannel board exercises are no worse than other devices for getting it). But as the criteria become more ambitious, and if the learner is indeed expected to be able to perform ordinary tasks in the language such as carrying on conversations and reading newspapers, so the learning activities preparing for those performances must consist of attentive perception of meaningful instances of the language, as posited above.

We can now explain why one student succeeds while another fails in learning a language or a bit of language in the same classroom, with the same teacher using the same method. Either the successful student was paying attention to the relevant language instances while the unsuccessful one was not, or the clues to meaning sufficed for the one but not the other. And we can explain why "motivation" has been considered to affect language learning: motivation may determine whether a learner in fact puts him into the kinds of situations in which language learning will take place, and whether he will pay attention when the requisite instances are presented. Note that under this interpretation, language-learning motivation is not necessary for language learning to take place: anything—including brute force—that will bring the student into the language learning environment and keep his attention will yield the learning result. Imagine, for example, an uninterested American student who hates studying foreign languages having John Rassias snap his fingers under the student's nose while teaching him Greek kinship terms. As long as the finger-snapping holds the student's interest, and as long as the association made between the Greek and English terms is clear, the student will learn; he cannot do otherwise. It has been reported that many prisoners in Nazi concentration camps learned German incredibly well by listening to their hated guards: One may pay attention to enemies as well as to friends under compelling circumstances. And it has been demonstrated by exhaustive psychological experimentation that children imitate those who control reward and punishment sanctions over them. The importance of attention-paying as a common feature in all such examples is supportive of a theory that argues for the criticalness of attention in learning.

Another noteworthy characteristic of this theory of language learning is that it does not require speaking out loud by students for them to learn a language. In the simplest *reductio* cases everyone would agree that this is possible. For example, imagine a teacher in a room with student A and student B. Turning to student A, the teacher says, "To say 'Hello' in Albanian, you say *Tungjatjeta.*" Now, the teacher says to A "*Tungjatjeta.*" If A says nothing the teacher says, "When someone says *Tungjatjeta* to you, you're supposed to say the same back to him. *Tungjatjeta.*" Perhaps now A says something approximating *Tungjatjeta,* thereby practicing saying it out loud; if not satisfied with the pronunciation, the teacher continues repeating the Albanian example to A, with repeated or refined explanations of what it means and how it is used. At some point, the teacher now turns to B and says "*Tungjatjeta.*" What I have found in numerous demonstrations of the experiment—confirmed by common experience—is that student B answers back with a pretty good approximation to *Tungjatjeta.* Asked what it means, student B answers, "Hello." Now, how could B have learned the Albanian greeting when it was A who was getting the practice in saying it? For that matter, how did A manage his first rendition of the Albanian greeting, before having the opportunity to practice it aloud? In fact, how can anyone practice anything he does not already "know"?

Without getting into the epistemological and psychological controversies involved here, it seems clear that in a common sense sense we can and do learn a great deal without doing, at least without doing overtly. A "comprehension approach" can "work," then, as long as the material presented for comprehension in fact consists of (1) sufficient (2) language instances (3) whose meaning can be inferred by students (4) who are paying attention:

(1) Sufficiency is a property that calls for a judgmental criterion. How long

does it take for someone to learn to speak a language like a native? Speaking facetiously, we might guess that it takes two years for a speaker of another language to speak like a three-year-old native speaker, thirty-four years to speak like a thirty-five-year-old native speaker, and so on (generously subtracting a year for the first-language learner's general inattentiveness to language during his first year). Since during childhood so much time is spent *not* attending to language with meaning, more reasonable estimates of time needed to reach meaningful criterion levels can be made by following an elimination process: a child of two will sleep ten to fourteen hours a day, spend many hours playing alone or out of earshot of other human beings using language, be inattentive to language being used around him, or may be unable to interpret it from the clues given, and so on—to the point that very little actual time in a day is really spent in "comprehension" environments in the language. From several convergent sources, I have estimated 300–500 as a reasonable number of hours of attention to a variety of meaningful utterances it takes for learning to speak and understand a language at the level of a four-year-old child, whether one is in fact a four-year-old child, a fourteen-year-old adolescent, or a forty-year-old adult; a level sufficient to carry on simple conversations without artificially constraining the topic. From experience with hundreds of American graduate students learning to read German or French from scratch, I estimate that 80–100 hours of such concentrated attention, on written rather than spoken language instances, suffice for a graduate student to gain a level of ability sufficient to score above 500 on the ETS Graduate Foreign Language Reading Test; which in turn seems to suffice to understand scholarly articles in the student's own field at a level adequate, for example, to write a serviceable translation. The vagueness of the criteria here reflects the vagueness of our agreement as to what constitutes a particular level of knowing a language.

The point of such estimates is that the numbers do not range from here to eternity to cover the enormous variety of student abilities, materials studied, personality of teacher, student motivation, and so on; nor are they of the enormous magnitude that some people imply is needed to accomplish the enormous task of "learning a language." Given modest, but valid, criteria of language-learning success, the time needed to learn a language can also be modest.

(2) "Language instances" is meant to exclude exposure to such things as vocabulary lists or verb paradigms or formulations in the student's own language of grammatical rules that are alleged to apply in the target language. While under some conditions such exposure may have some facilitative effect on language learning—and it has not yet been strongly demonstrated that it does—inducing the student to concentrate attention on details that he or she otherwise would ignore, clearly is neither sufficient nor necessary to learn to use a foreign language at any level of ability (Newmark and Reibel, 1968). Even linguists well versed in the grammar and lexicon of the language need the experience of language samples-in-use in order to use it themselves (Gouin,

1892, pp. 8–46); and brilliant orators and poets have always existed who have never been exposed to such artificial devices. Note that none such exist who have never been exposed to language instances in the more natural form, i.e., as language being used to say something; that is, no one has ever learned to use a language by merely learning all about it and mastering its elements in isolation from the examples in which they are embedded.

(3) That the meaning must be inferrable by the learner is a condition necessary to explain the failure of language learning in cases where we can observe the student "gaining exposure" to the language: e.g., listening to a radio program, watching and listening to a movie, memorizing a dialogue, "reading" a book in the language. As students ourselves in such situations, we know introspectively that we apparently can go through the motions of listening or reading without really listening or reading; in order to convert the apparent to the real, we must (a) concentrate on, i.e., pay attention to, what we are hearing or seeing, and (b) understand, at some level, what we hear or see. To the extent that we do understand the coded linguistic input we perceive, to that extent we register that input as language. The meaning of some inputs is so evident in particular contexts that no special mental effort need be made by the learner to attach meaning to input. The meaning of other inputs is so opaque in their contexts that no one can attach meaning to them and they add nothing to the learner's store of language. But the meaning of many inputs in their contexts is such that some students will succeed and others will fail to attach the meanings correctly to the input; as a result some students will be observed to succeed in adding and others to fail to add the same input to their linguistic store. "Good" language learners have the characteristic that they use a variety of intra- and extra-linguistic clues to attach meaning to unclear linguistic inputs, while "bad" language learners have to wait for the clear examples to come along. This may account in part for the differences noted in vocabulary size among native speakers as well as among second-language learners.

As stated earlier, the clues provided by the teacher (or language course designer) to the meanings of the linguistic inputs may take a variety of forms: embedding a new expression in a familiar context that delimits its possible meanings, "acting out" the meaning of an expression, translating the expression into a language already familiar to the student, showing (a) picture(s) related to the linguistic expression, using realia, cognates, and so forth. At present there is no known reason to insist on any of these to the exclusion of others, although proponents of one technique may insist on the superiority of certain techniques over others, on grounds of efficiency, lack of distraction from the target language, psychological immediacy, and so on.

(4) While there are of course many possible differences in ability among teachers and among students that might account for the differences in their degrees of successfulness as teachers and students, they are largely differences in their ability respectively to command and pay attention. The teacher who snaps his fingers under the student's nose while associating pictures of

vegetables to the spoken French names of those vegetables, behaves very differently from the teacher of German who in a very quiet voice speaks of his ecstasy in reading a line of poetry; both are very different from the teacher who teaches English to Dutch teenagers by analyzing the texts of rock songs they have just listened to. Yet all these teachers may well succeed by such devices in attracting, focusing, and maintaining the student's attention on the linguistic input. The student who is obstreperous and constantly interrupts class activities with irrelevant behavior, the one who looks intently into the teacher's face while daydreaming about family problems, the one who during presentation of a meaningful sentence tries to remember what the ending on the verb means, or worries that he will not remember the sentence when called on by the teacher to say it back, are making quite different mistakes. But all have in common that they are not attending to the meaning of the linguistic input presented, and *that* is the reason for their failure to learn in this instance. Bad language teachers and students do not need to change their personalities, lifestyles, talents, or beliefs in order to be effective as teachers and learners: they need only perform attention-getting and attention-giving actions, respectively, with massive amounts of meaningful language inputs.

Innovative language-teaching methods can be seen as attempts to satisfy the conditions necessary for language learning to take place. Ingenious teacher-designers in a "comprehension approach" find ways of providing satisfactory clues to the meaning of language instances—for example, sequences of single words, phrases, or sentences on a tape-recording naming a set of synchronously presented sequences of pictures—that will hold students' attention for long periods of time. Although quite different in mystique, other approaches have gained their reputations by finding other solutions to the problems of presenting language input to students in such a way as to hold their attention and attach meaning to the input. For example, the success of "silent method" classes rests on the ingenious technique of holding student attention by constantly setting language puzzles to be solved by the students and providing more and more clues until they can solve them. Exposure to the necessary language instances is laboriously arranged by eliciting closer and closer approximations of those instances from the students themselves, following techniques of "shaping," well known to experimental psychologists and elegantly described by B. F. Skinner many years ago. "Suggestology" classes employ an elaborate set of devices to get and hold student attention. To the extent that what is presented to the students while their attention is being held has the other requisite characteristics—presenting language instances and making them meaningful to the students—the method will succeed. The potential superiority of a comprehension approach over such other approaches lies in the economy of its assumptions and the simplicity of its pedagogical apparatus.

Against the common view that students learn language best when they spend a lot of time speaking it, the comprehension approach takes advantage of the logical realization that a student who is talking cannot be learning, since his performance cannot exceed his competence: All he can say at any moment is what he has already learned before. Learning cannot be by doing. New knowledge must come from the outside. Not only is speaking aloud not necessary for language learning to take place, but experiments like Postovsky's (1974) show that it can actually impede learning. Several reasons can be advanced for why this should be so: The learner who is concerned about his own impending public performance may spend the time during presentation of potential learning inputs mentally rehearsing what he already knows, in preparation for that performance, instead of attending to the new input. When he does attend to the new input, the learner may concentrate on its surface expression—economically maximizing his short-term payoff if the teacher rewards immediate echoing of the expression of the input; but in that case, the potential meaningfulness of the input is lost, and this implies, as we have seen, that the language-learning opportunity is wasted.

I am trying to teach an adult male student how to say hello in Albanian. I say "*Tungjatjeta*" and shake his hand. Now I can tell the student to repeat what I said many times so that he can "get practice in saying it," or I can continue saying it over and over to give him "practice in hearing it." If I follow the first procedure, the student is reluctant to try and asks me to repeat it myself before he proceeds. If I insist that he try, he gives an extremely inaccurate rendition—perhaps with only the initial /t/ correct—a rendition that does not improve *no matter how many times he may practice it*; if I insist that he keep practicing, the student rebels and very soon refuses to continue. If the "practice makes perfect" maxim were correct, or even the special dictum that each student must have the opportunity and be required to speak himself, we would have no explanation for the total lack of success of the teaching in this simple example. On the other hand, if I follow the second procedure and repeat the utterance over and over without letting the student say it himself, he begins to show signs of boredom and, after awhile, if I continue the inane repetition, he simply turns away and pays no attention to me. Asked now to produce the form himself, the student will do far better than in the first case, but may well have forgotten what it means and will show no inclination to continue learning the language this way. Again the dictum that language is best learned by simple exposure fails to account for the lack of success of this *reductio* case.

Another way to teach *Tungjatjeta* is for me to say it once, shaking hands, telling the student that this means "Hello" in English, or using any other device (e.g., a short skit with one person greeting another in Albanian) that will allow the student to attach meaning to the utterance; then say it again as many times as the student wishes to hear it, until he wants to say it himself and does, with me reacting to his response by returning the greeting. If he is satisfied with his performance we will go on to something else; if not, he will want to hear it again and have the opportunity to say it himself. Intuitively, we feel that this method is far superior to either of the two alternatives. But how can it be, since we see that it consists of nothing but the other two, each of which fails on its own? The answer lies in remembering that in order to learn a language one must be paying attention to linguistic inputs with meaning. In the first method, the number of inputs is simply inadequate in relation to the output I expect from the student. In the second method, I lose the student because I do not provide any motivation for him to pay attention to the inputs. In the third method, the student's attention is attracted by letting him say the utterance himself; he attends to my repetitious inputs in order to say it better himself when his turn comes to speak. Seen in this light, active student production functions in language teaching not as a learning device in its own right, but as one attention-directing device among many possible others. Its advantage over many other such devices is that it is cheap, requires no special thought or preparation by the teacher, and is highly resistant to satiation. In natural language acquisition, of both first and second languages, it is the usual device: The child *participates* in the activities of the language community in which he finds himself; that participation calls on him to produce language from time to time, and that in turn requires him to pay attention to what others say and to figure out what they mean by saying it.

Notice that this theory gives an explanation of why language inputs must in general be relatively short and repetitious. (Imagine me trying to teach Albanian to beginners by giving long lectures in the language.) When the utterance is longer than the learner can process meaningfully, he or she stops paying attention to it. If there are few repetitions, the learner is given insufficient opportunity to attach input segments to their appropriate meanings. Conversely, it has been well established with both first and second language learners that children under natural conditions learn first those items that occur frequently in easily interpretable contexts. As more and more items are learned, they themselves become part of the context for new items, accounting for the rapid acceleration in learning noted after the early stages of acquisition.

It is most instructive in this regard to notice children at the early stages of learning a foreign language in natural circumstances. In 1972 I had the opportunity to spend time in a Montessori school in Amsterdam observing (quietly) my son (Mark)—a four-year-old native speaker of English—and a four-year-old native speaker of Japanese (Yoshi) in their first four months of learning Dutch. The class was conducted entirely in Dutch, but no particular time was given to teaching the language as such. The teacher (Mevrouw Gertenbach) told me that during her nine years of teaching experience, with numerous foreign children among her students, it had never been necessary to give Dutch lessons to the foreign students (she had tried at first, but had given up when she could not get the students to respond): *All* the foreign students who stayed at the school for a school year became indistinguishable in their Dutch from the native Dutch children, and they seemed to "pick up" the language on their own. Now the most remarkable thing about Mark and Yoshi as language learners was the tiny amount of Dutch they themselves spoke during the first four months in the school. In the first week they did not say anything in Dutch. By the second week

Mark was saying *ja,* "yes," and *fraw kertn* (his rendition of his teacher's name), a feat the shyer Yoshi accomplished in the following week. During this time no amount of badgering or encouraging by the teacher could draw out more from them. By the thirteenth week both students had a small but much used productive vocabulary of formulaic phrases: *Nouw hou op!,* "Hey stop it!"; *Nee hoor,* "Well no."; *Ja hoor,* "Well yes."; Wat is DAT nouw?, "What in the world is that?!"; *Ga weg,* "Go away."; *Hand om hoog!,* "Hands up!"; *Ja meneer,* "Yes sir."; but only in activities with other children.

The two little foreigners sat in their places, joined in group physical activities, went out on the playground at recess and watched the others, but did not talk. As time went on their comprehension of the language improved enormously; by the fourth month they participated fully in classroom activities, and their speech increased moderately in frequency, length, complexity, and accuracy (in terms of their Dutch models), although they still rarely volunteered conversation not directly provoked by actions of other children. If a test of achievement based on language production had been administered at this point, neither student would have given evidence that he was in fact on his way to becoming a native-like speaker of the language within less than a year. In terms of time spent (one of the sources of my earlier estimate) the two children would hear Dutch for less than three hours a day, five days a week (when they were not absent from class); and they would never get bored "studying Dutch" in this way, even though children of this age are notorious for being unable to keep at anything for more than a few minutes at a time in formal teaching situations. It was also noteworthy that, despite the very different native languages of the two learners—one with many points of similarity with Dutch and one with very few—the only difference that would appear in their Dutch (according to the teacher) was that the shyer Japanese boy would give a first impression of knowing less than the outgoing American boy; language "interference" seemed to play no role, although cultural or personality factors might affect the superficial *judgment* of achievement by outsiders.

Why should such a learning technique produce native speakers in essentially all cases, while almost all students in language courses fall woefully short of such a goal? We have a choice of claiming either that the age of the child's brain is responsible or that characteristics of the manner of learning determine the outcome. For reasons I have alluded to elsewhere (Newmark and Reibel, 1968), I prefer the second alternative. Is it possible that the silence I noted in the two foreign children during their early exposure to Dutch was not incidental to the learning process, but essential to their becoming native-like speakers? Does it not seem reasonable to speculate that adults continue to speak foreign languages with bad accents because they are required—and require themselves—to perform too soon, before they have internalized enough input from their models to base their own speech on? Are we making students into bad language learners by forcing them to speak out loud before they have heard enough models, and then inducing them to retain their early skill levels (fossilizing them) by paying off artificially for using whatever they already know to produce long, complex utterances, before they are ready to do so naturally?

The "comprehension approach" examines the possibility that too early public utterance does interfere with language learning; and that adults can learn languages like children at least to the extent that they can both internalize auditory input directly, without the necessary mediation of the learner's native language, and acquire large grammatical and lexical inventories without overtly producing the overt phonological forms themselves that embody those inventories.

In terms of the history of language pedagogy, the comprehension approach does not introduce a totally new rationale nor a totally new set of procedures for teaching languages; as Kelly (1969) has shown convincingly, totally new ideas are hard to come by in this field. Instead, it uses an economical set of assumptions clothed in a minimum amount of mystery (unlike many of its competitors) upon which to base the design of courses. So far we do not know the limits of the approach in practice, since nothing approaching the scope of the 400 or so necessary hours of diverse input material has been produced that might be necessary before the overt performance of the students could be fairly used to test the efficacy of the method of teaching. (Remember the *mis*evaluation of method that would have arisen in the case of the two children learning Dutch, if they had been tested as early as even the fourth month—after at least some 240 hours of input.) However, from its present exploratory course implementations we can make some assessment of the approach, in terms of the general language learning theory advanced in this chapter. I shall first consider positive features and then potential deficiencies of the approach.

First, the comprehension approach courses I have examined do present linguistic input in a way that successfully commands student attention, at least for the period of time during which the presentation method forms a novelty for them. The combination of visual stimulation combined with frequent action responses (nonverbal) from students creates an attention getting and holding device that will serve for a fairly long period. We could expect it to be particularly effective during elementary stages of learning (i.e., until satiation with this form of input sets in) and with students for whom such forms of presentation are a novelty.

Second, the comprehension approach goes to great lengths to assure that students experience the meaningfulness of the linguistic input presented. In a self-instructional, individually programmed form, a course using this approach could guarantee that progress through the course could not continue unless the student had grasped some desired meaning for each input item; even in group presentation modes a sensitive teacher can take steps to achieve the same goal.

Third, since immediate correct student production is not required in the comprehension approach, the course programmer is relieved of the obligation to provide the student with mechanical drill exercises in order to increase the probability of correct student responses, or to provide explicit grammatical and phonological analyses for the student upon which the student can, theoretically, base his own productive efforts. The burden of teaching is thus placed on presentation of language samples with clues for understanding what they mean, which is just where it should be placed.

But the approach, as it has been implemented in the courses I have examined, does have potential deficiencies. First, the time and effort required to devise each program frame is large enough to make it unlikely in practice that the approach can supplant other ways of teaching languages to any great degree. If it is reasonable to expect that a student will not produce useful output until after many hours of input, the elaborateness of the presentation method militates against its use for more than a relatively small part of the language teaching. To assess this potential deficiency, we will have to wait to see whether the zealousness of its proponents will drive them to produce the massive amounts of special materials that would be needed to make the comprehension approach more than just an interesting alternative way of giving the first few weeks or months of instruction in a language.

Second, because the comprehension approach requires careful planning of each presentation item, it assumes that the course programmer can decide intelligently what items to present and in what sequence they should be presented. But in fact there is as yet no theory of language teaching that would guide those decisions. We do not know, for example, whether it is better for a student to learn thirty vocabulary items first before learning three grammatical structures into which they can be arranged, or whether those numbers should be three hundred and twelve, and seventeen, respectively, or whether intonation contrasts should be introduced before subjunctive forms of verbs are learned, or whether dative case forms have priority over forty-six new adverbs, and so on. Without such a theory, how is the programmer, deliberately designing frames whose linguistic content he predetermines, to avoid gross mistakes: How can the programmer keep from artificially distorting the linguistic input that the learner gets, in just the same way that traditional language teachers distort it? How can the conscientious programmer plan a sequence of presentation as good as the unplanned sequence that is presented in natural (in the wilds) learning of languages? Third, what happens when the novelty of the presentation form wears off for students? In this country we have witnessed the phenomenon of the fad in foreign language teaching several times over the past thirty years. In each case (the "Army" method, the language laboratory, programmed instruction, the audio-lingual method) we have watched students come to life and prosper under the new techniques, only to have them become blasé and bored as those new techniques became routine and all too familiar. That is, the attention-getting advantages of a new technique are lost when the student comes to see that technique as a tradition.

Of course, the comprehension approach need not be just one more set of faddish techniques. The principles on which it can be based are, as I have tried to show here, for the most part sound. If the approach is broadened into a general set of requirements for language courses—that language inputs be presented in such a way as to draw students' attention to their meaning and that students not be constantly required to prove what they know by producing the language themselves—it will have added an important insight to language pedagogy. If, on the other hand, it comes to be identified with particular techniques of presentation of material, it will take its place as one more interesting use of audiovisual equipment and devices in the language teaching of the second half of the twentieth century.

Notes

1.   In fairness to the classroom case it should be pointed out that the apparent superiority of socially-learned to classroom-learned skills is in part an artifact of the differences in the method of assessment: in the first case the society is enormously patient in waiting for the child to gain adult skills, and allows considerable variation in abilities to count as "skill in hunting," while in the classroom case, we give examinations and grades according to a timetable established by someone other than the learner and use fixed criteria of success that are standard for all the learners being examined.

2.   There is some evidence that such listening may facilitate learning by other means, and may even serve as a primary source of language input when the student is at a high enough level. An explanation of why such input might be effective at advanced levels is that the hearer can use contextual clues internal in the pure speech output to infer partial meanings of the unknown elements.

3.   Sometimes we may hold the memory of a sound sequence in memory without attaching meaning to it, only to make that attachment later when more information becomes available. The language learning experience takes place at the moment of attachment. The limited utility of just "hearing a language" or being "exposed" to it follow from this principle: until and unless the learner experiences the meaningfulness of what he hears, the learner has not added to his language, although he may well have added to the store of tokens to which meaning may later be attached, thus accounting for the enhancement effect that mere listening to a language has on later learning of that language.

References

Gouin, F. *The art of teaching and studying languages.* Translated by H. Swan and V. Bétes. London: George Philip & Son, 1892.

Kelly, L. G. *25 centuries of language teaching.* Rowley, Mass.: Newbury House, 1969.

Newmark, L., and Reibel, D. "Necessity and sufficiency in language learning." *International Review of Applied Linguistics, 6,* pp. 145–164, 1968. (Reprinted in M. Lester (Ed.), *Readings in applied transformational grammar.* New York: Holt, Rinehart, and Winston, 1970.)

Postovsky, V. A. "Effects of delay in oral practice at the beginning of second language learning." *The Modern Language Journal, 58,* pp. 229–239, 1974.

CHAPTER 4

The Extinction of Second-Language Learning in American Schools: An Intervention Model

James J. Asher

Professor of Psychology
San José State University

Learning another language in American schools is becoming extinct and foreign language teachers are becoming an endangered academic species.

The warning signals have come on in greater numbers and are flashing red. Consider these facts: 90 percent of U.S. colleges and universities have no language requirement for admission (Simon, 1977). And only 4 percent of all high school graduates in 1976 studied a foreign language two years or more (Simon, 1978). For those who do attempt the study of another language, 96 percent give up before achieving basic fluency (Lawson, 1971). It is possible to earn a master's or doctoral degree with no proficiency in any foreign language.

Congressman Paul Simon of Illinois was shocked to discover in his Commission on Foreign Languages and Area Studies the consequences of our underachievement in other languages. For example, most top management positions in U.S. companies operating abroad are held by foreign nationals since not enough American executives speak the languages of host countries. American technicians and executives who do work abroad often need to have interpreters regularly accompany them. Unbelievably, a recent advertising campaign by Chevrolet in South America failed because company officials did not realize that Nova—the car they were trying to sell—means "doesn't go" in Spanish.

For years after our involvement in Southeast Asia we had to rely on French experts for information on the area because there was not one American-born specialist on Vietnam, Laos, or Cambodia in an American university. When fighting erupted in Zaire, American television correspondents stayed in a hotel bar because they could not speak the local languages. They depended on local "stringers" to provide them with facts about the fighting—facts which were then flashed to the American people as authoritative information (Simon, 1978).

Finally, the State Department recognized that its foreign service officers should be fluent in the language of the country in which they serve, but Congressman Simon was astonished to find that skill in a foreign language was no longer required of applicants to the foreign service. So few Americans have language skills that the requirement had to be discontinued (Royster, 1978).

Is our underachievement in learning other languages a problem of motivation? I don't believe so, since I have yet to find one person in any audience I have addressed throughout the country who did not want to learn another language. They report a genuine desire to learn as demonstrated by enrolling in one or more language courses. But the stress they experienced was so painful that they felt compelled to escape. They experienced failure. They gave up. As a result of the traumatic experience, many believe that they are incapable of learning another language.

The mystery to be solved is this: What happens in school that generates an unbearable stress for students of all ages, including adults?

I would like to suggest several hypotheses to explain the stress; then an intervention model which has been applied successfully to reduce the stress while simultaneously accelerating the learning of language skills.

Teaching People to Talk: A Linguistic Illusion?

The first source of stress for anyone attempting to learn another language is talking in the target language. In most contemporary instructional strategies "teaching people to talk" starts immediately on the first gathering of the class.

The assumption that one person can *directly* teach another person to talk is often accepted as axiomatic—a given truth—in the catechism of linguistics. It may be heresy to propose a critical examination of such an "obvious and fundamental" truth. For example, most books, articles, and linguistic courses begin with the premise that all significant events in acquiring a language—the first or any language thereafter—begins with the infant talking. Before the infant speaks, the child's mind is a linguistic tabula rasa.

As an illustration, scan the 1977 edition of the prestigious *Harvard Educational Review,* which carried an article entitled "Trends in second-language-acquisition research." This was billed as a ". . . critical, historical overview of research on second-language acquisition with . . . special emphasis to the influence of first-language-acquisition research on studies of second-language acquisition" (Hakuta and Cancino, 1977, p. 294).

The entire article was based on the assumption—a false assumption, I believe—that the infant's speech "provides one of the most readily accessible windows into the nature of the human mind" (ibid.).

The evidence from psychologists studying infant development is that for many months before an infant begins to talk—while the child is mute except for babbling—the individual has constructed an intricate map to decode into information the noises coming from people's mouths. Infants have a sophisticated understanding of what people are saying before they can utter anything more intelligible than "mommy" or "daddy" (Bühler and Hetzer, 1935; Gesell and Thompson, 1929). For example, David, the eighteen-month-old toddler living next door to me, responded immediately and accurately the other evening when his father said, "Dave, pick up your red truck and put it on the shelf in your room."

It may be that this internalization of a sophisticated linguistic map of how the target language works *must* be achieved before the infant can talk. The map may release talk. It may make the child ready to talk.

Readiness to talk is an interesting concept because it contradicts the notion that you can *directly* teach someone else to talk. Again, studies of infant development suggest that direct intervention by adults who attempt to accelerate infant talking by coaxing, rewarding, or direct teaching will not work. Infants begin talking when they are ready—and readiness varies from child to child. Talking is like walking—unless the infant is ready, all attempts at teaching will be futile.

Readiness to talk may be biologically determined by the rate at which understanding of spoken language has been internalized. Understanding expands and expands—and at some point, talk is released. Understanding may be the essential determiner of when one is ready to talk.

Therefore, this period in infant development when one is mute but somehow internalizing an expanding comprehension of spoken language—that preverbal period before talk appears—may be the clear glass "window into the nature of the human mind." We should have been peering into that window and taking notes instead of waiting for talk to appear. While we were fidgeting with our telescope in anticipation of a significant linguistic event to begin, it had already happened.

This linguistic illusion that talk is primary in language acquisition has diverted attention away from the most crucial process in language learning—the pretalk behavior of infants. People were not looking because they had been cued to start their observations only when the infant started talking. At this point, linguistic researchers began their meticulous studies with concepts such as contrastive analysis, error analysis, performance analysis, and discourse analysis. Notice that none of those impressive procedures can be applied until the infant's babbling is transformed into speech. All of those techniques are speech dependent. But, by that time, I believe it is too late. The imprinting has already taken place. The child has internalized a linguistic map that releases the marvel of talk. We missed it.

How the infant achieves understanding. The marvel is not talking, but how the infant decoded the intricacies of the target language while silent and unable to speak.

For insight into the infant's achievement, play with this metaphor: Pretend that you are lying on your back in a huge bed with bars on both sides. You can't sit up. You can't speak. You can't even lift your head.

Creatures who seem to be eight feet tall hover around you; their elliptical faces come in and out of focus as they lean over the bars, showing a mouthful of white protrusions imbedded in their gums. As the creatures approach you, they are making noises with their mouths and taunt you with strange objects that also make peculiar sounds—rattling, jingling, and chiming noises.

Where are you? What's happening? Who are these beings? What are they trying to do?

You are, of course, an infant lying in your crib as fawning adults try to capture your attention with rattles, toys, and music boxes.

Eventually, you will comprehend the meaning of the experience—you will identify the creatures and understand the noises coming from their mouths.

The mystery is how? If we can solve that puzzle, we will simultaneously solve the problem of the most optimal procedure for learning another language.

I have thought about this puzzle for the past twenty years as I, in collaboration with colleagues, devised experiment after experiment exploring the experience of learning other languages such as Arabic, English, French, German, Hebrew, Japanese, Persian, Russian, Spanish, and Turkish. From that work, I would like to suggest a model which is one explanation for that marvelous process in which infants decipher noise into information.

Consider this: The student in a typical classroom can decode noise from an unfamiliar language into information with tools such as translating into one's native language through reading, writing, or speech. The infant has none of these tools for decoding noise into signal—for making sense from nonsense. So how does it happen?

We know from infant studies (Friedlander, 1970; McCaffrey, 1969; Moffitt, 1968, 1969) that babies are capable of making fine auditory discriminations. Within the first few months of life they are sensitive to the difference between [b] and [g] , [t] and [p] , and [i] and [a] . Infants can be selective in their attention which is sensitive enough to register the smallest change in sound that carries information. Still, this does not explain how an infant converts noise into information. It simply says that what the infant hears is not an indistinguishable garble of sound.

Still to be explained is how the infant understands what people are saying—a remarkable achievement which requires a complex figure-ground differentiation of sound. For example, the utterances the infant hears are mingled with phonemes and non-phonemes. Somehow the infant targets in on phonemes, which may be like finding in a telescope a few pinpoints of moving lights that are surrounded by millions of other moving lights.

My hypothesis is that the infant discovers meaning by decoding noise into information, when either responding to or observing others responding to commands such as:

"Look at Daddy!"   "Don't stand up in your high chair!"

"Hold my hand!"   "Come to Mommy!"

The decoding process involves synchronizing language with the infant's body movements. Simply listening to random speech is not enough. Meaning is sorted out through referents associated with actions of people, places, or things.

In what situations is decoding most apt to occur? Friedlander (1970, p. 44) has observed this: "Except in the most intimate one-to-one encounters between parent and child such as the bath, dressing, and feeding, the language environment is usually characterized by very poor signals: sloppy articulation, degraded and incomplete sentences, and extremely difficult signal/noise ratios. In some homes the radio and TV provide the only moderately clean language samples the child ever hears, and these are entirely noncontingent with respect to the baby's attention and vocalizations. . . ."

Intimate one-to-one encounters between the parent and child are almost exclusively commands uttered by the adult, such as these in a bath scene:

"Sit down!"

"Don't kick—sit down in the water!"

"That's it. Now let's put some soap on your back!"

"Don't cry! . . . I'm holding you, you're fine. Here's your duck. Look at your duck; he's enjoying the water. . . ."

In those intimate caretaking transactions in which the parent utters gentle commands to direct the infant's behavior, notice the importance of motion.

Without motion, there is no experience. For example, there is evidence that without motion we cannot see. A camera should be stationary if you want a photograph that is in focus, but people must be in motion to see. We create continual motion with shifts in our body including rapid tremors in the eye—called saccadic movements. The human eye is analogous to a staggering alcoholic who is clicking pictures with a camera which trembles unpredictably in the alcoholic's hands and yet each photograph is in clear focus.

Psychologist Roy M. Pritchard (1961) wanted to know what we would see if all movement of the body including involuntary tremors in the eye were eliminated. The ingenious procedure was this: With the subject lying on a couch, a tight-fitting contact lens was fitted to the eyeball. Mounted on the contact lens was a tiny—almost weightless—self-contained optical projector. Even though the eyeball moved with involuntary tremors the image was always projected upon one location in the retina.

When motion was eliminated to simulate the stillness of a camera, the image soon faded and disappeared. Why this happened is still a mystery that researchers continue to explore. But it seems clear that motion is essential to the construction of experiences. And experience generates facts, beliefs, reality, and truth for individuals.

It may be that language acquisition—that is, decoding the peculiar utterances the infant hears—is dependent upon a process that includes intimate parent-child transactions in which language causes motion—motor responses—that create personal experiences of reality for the child.

We know that the motion in motor skills seems to be causally related to long-term retention. Motor skills which are learned through body movements are often intact for a lifetime. For example, one can be a proficient ice skater as a child in Michigan and later move to California and not skate for twenty years.

Then one day, the person laces on ice skates and after a few warm-up trials, performs at a high level of skill.

In my research (Asher, 1981) I have demonstrated that when a second language is integrated with an individual's motions, there is rapid assimilation—that is, understanding of the target language.

The Second Source of Stress: Left Brain Input

Infants learn to understand their first language through stimulation of the right hemisphere of the brain. Children are speechless but they decode utterances they hear by motor behavior such as:

looking	eliminating
crying	handling
laughing	attempting
eating	tinkering
drinking	manipulating
touching	toying
pointing	playing

Clearly, if nature's blueprint for decoding a strange language is revealed in the remarkable achievement of cryptology by infants, then second-language instruction should begin and continue with the stimulation of the right—not the left—hemisphere of the brain.

But educators have a bias for playing to the left hemisphere in teacher activities such as:

talking	discussing
lecturing	covering
explaining	rationalizing
clarifying	intellectualizing
analyzing	

What the research shows. The discovery that the right and left hemisphere of the brain function differently may be one of the most important findings of our generation, especially for those dedicated to teaching others another language.

The research (Gazzaniga, 1967) began with simple experiments using cats. As you may know, the right and left hemispheres of the brain in animals and humans are connected by tissue called the corpus callosum.

Researchers cut the corpus callosum in cats so that there were no connections between the right and left walnut-shaped hemispheres of the brain. They wanted everything that the cat sees with the right eye to be flashed only to the right hemisphere and everything seen by the left eye to travel only into the left hemisphere. The problem is this: Each point behind the right eye has a wire-like fiber that carries information from the eye back into the brain. Some of the fibers are connected directly in a straight line into the right hemisphere and some go kitty-corner into the left. It is a puzzling bit of anatomical architecture, but part of what we and animals see with our right eye is located on one side of the brain and part of the image is projected on the other side. The left eye works the same way. Part of the image on the retina is projected to the left hemisphere and part to the right.

Those fibers going kitty-corner to the opposite hemisphere were cut, which meant that an image registered by the right eye was seen only in the right hemisphere of the brain, and, likewise, an image to the left eye was flashed only to the left brain.

Next, a Moshe Dayan-type black patch was placed over a cat's left eye so that what the animal saw with its right eye was projected only into the right hemisphere. Now the cat must solve a problem by seeing only with its right eye and right hemisphere of the brain. Visualize two swinging doors side by side. Behind one with a "V" painted on it there was food and behind the other with "Λ" there was nothing. Each time the hungry cat was released, it had to decide which door to nuzzle open for a reward of food. Of course, the door marked with a "V" that signaled food was varied randomly on each trial so that it could be on either the left or right each time the cat was released.

The result was that the cat made many mistakes before it consistently on every trial walked directly to the door with a "V." The cat had learned to make a discrimination and the learning had been recorded in the right hemisphere of the brain.

Now, what will happen if we reverse the patch to the right eye and also reverse the symbols on the doors so that the symbol "Λ" signals food hidden behind the door while "V" means no food? In cats that have not had the hemispheres of the brain divided, this task would be a difficult problem. We would expect *negative transfer*—that is, the normal cat would need more trials to learn the reversal than were needed in learning the original discrimination.

Here's what happened. The split-brain cats showed no negative transfer. The learning curve was almost identical for the reversal as for the original learning. It was as if the cat had never experienced the problem before. Literally, the left side of the brain did not know what the right had done. It was as if both sides of the brain learned the task independently.

Later, surgeons reduced the intensity of epileptic seizures in humans by cutting the corpus callosum, which then separated the right and left hemispheres of the brain. The operation worked. Patients experienced diminished epileptic seizures. A by-product was the opportunity to explore further in humans the workings of the right and left brain. The findings were spectacular and have, I believe, important implications for learning other languages.

A case history. Gazzaniga, Le Doux, and Wilson in 1977 reported the case of P. S. which illustrates the fascinating workings of each hemisphere. P. S. is a right-handed fifteen-year-old boy who experienced severe epileptic attacks at about the age of two. He developed normally until the age of ten when the seizures started again and became intractable. In January, 1976, the entire corpus callosum was surgically divided.

In one series of demonstrations after the operation, P. S. was seated a few feet from an opaque screen and instructed to fix his gaze on a dot in the center of the screen. Then a rear view projector flashed words or pictures on either the right or left side of the screen and P. S. was asked to tell what he saw. Here's what happened.

When the picture of an ordinary object, a key, was flashed on the right side of the screen, P. S. immediately said, "I saw a key." But when the object on the next trial was an apple, which appeared for an instant on the left side of the screen, P. S. reported, "I didn't see anything." Curiously, P. S. correctly named all objects projected into the left brain (those appearing on the right side of the screen), but could not name any objects that were seen by the right hemisphere (those appearing on the left side of the screen). It was as if the right hemisphere were blind.

In the next demonstration, words for common objects such as a safety pin, tire, bicycle, and playing card were flashed on either side of the screen: again, a perfect score in naming items projected into the left hemisphere and "blindness" for items flashed into the right hemisphere.

But the blindness was an illusion. The individual did see the pictures and words projected into the right hemisphere but he was not conscious of it—that is, he could not express the experience in words.

How do we know that? Even though the subject reported seeing nothing when, for instance, "apple" was flashed on the left side of the screen, when the experimenters said, "Please pick up a pencil with your left hand and write the word that just appeared on the screen," P.S. scribbled the word "apple." The researchers were astonished to discover that, even though P.S. reported seeing nothing for an item flashed to his right brain, he could write, spell, point to, or pick up the appropriate item with almost perfect accuracy.

They made the tests more complex. For example, P.S. was told, "When you see a word flashed on the screen, please say a word that is opposite. If for instance, you see 'cat,' then you would say 'dog.' If you see 'girl,' you would say 'boy.' " The results: again, "blindness" for words flashed to the right hemisphere, but he could point to the correct item from a set of four words on every trial. The same results were obtained when P.S. was asked, "This time when you see a word, give me a word that is associated. For instance, if you see 'clock,' you might say 'time.' If the word is 'porch,' you might say 'house.' " When P.S. only had to point to an associate from among three choices, there was a perfect score by either the left or right hemisphere.

They tried this variation: "P.S., when you see a word, tell me another word that rhymes. For instance, if you see 'canoe,' you would say 'new' or 'who.' " Again, if there were three choices to select from, P.S. had almost a perfect score for either hemisphere.

Clearly, the right hemisphere is mute—unable to talk—but it is processing information and can express itself if you provide a "voice box" such as touching objects, pointing to a choice from alternatives, or even spelling.

The right brain understood action verbs, because P.S. could point to a picture from a set of pictures that represented words such as "sleeping," "laughing," and "drinking." Remember, when each of those words appeared and were transmitted to the right hemisphere, P.S. reported, "I didn't see anything," yet he was able with almost perfect accuracy to point at the correct item in a set of choices.

In an infant's development of understanding, I suggested that the child decodes when the parent directs the infant's movements in caretaking situations such as dressing and feeding. I was most interested in how a split-brain patient processes commands. The directions to P.S. were, "When you see a word such as 'laugh,' please laugh. If you see 'cry,' then cry."

When the command "rub" was flashed to the right hemisphere, the subject rubbed the back of his head with his left hand.

He was asked, "What was the command?"

He said, "itch."

It appeared as if a command was received in the right brain, followed by a change in behavior. The rubbing, for example, was observed by the left hemisphere which made an interpretation. Notice that the left brain was not aware of what caused the movement in P.S., but it attempted to describe the behavior it observed.

This process was further shown in this demonstration: "P.S., assume the position of a_____" and the word "boxer" was flashed to the right hemisphere. Immediately, P.S. shifted his body into a pugilistic stance.

"P.S., what word did you see?"

Without hesitation, he said, "boxer."

Later the demonstration was repeated, but just after "boxer" was projected to the right brain, P.S. was restrained from moving. Then he was asked, "What word did you see?"

He said, "I didn't see a word."

Moments later, when he was released, he assumed the position and said, "O.K., it was boxer."

Is the left hemisphere able to understand commands? The evidence suggests, in the case of P.S., that when a command such as "laugh" is flashed to the left hemisphere, the individual often utters the word aloud, which is heard by the right hemisphere that executes the command.

Both hemispheres can recognize the correct response to a command when one is only required to point to a picture in a set of pictures, but only the right hemisphere seems able to express appropriate behavior in response to commands.

Implications for language acquisition. As an hypothesis, I believe that the infant decodes the meaning of language in the right hemisphere. The target language is deciphered when spoken commands by adults "cause" changes in the infant's motor behavior.

The infant's left hemisphere cannot speak, but for hundreds of hours it observes, observes, and observes language "causing" different actions in the infant—until it is ready for its feeble attempt to talk. Gradually, the left becomes more and more aware that, through talk, it has the power to "cause" events to happen. But throughout the child's development, the left shadows the right. The child's understanding as demonstrated in body expressions is far in advance of speaking.

I believe that nature's design continues to operate when an individual—child or adult–attempts to learn a second or third language. Therefore, it seems clear that a logical starting point for any instructional program that intends to teach another language would be to structure the content especially for the right hemisphere. But most contemporary instructional strategies do the reverse. They start by playing to the left hemisphere in exercises such as:

> *Listen and repeat after me.*
> This is left hemisphere processing by (a) translating noise into one's native language, and (b) producing talk before the student is ready. The consequence of input to the nonoptimal hemisphere is to generate stress.

> *Memorize this dialogue.*
> Again, the left hemisphere must store and retrieve talk which it is not ready to do. Long-term remembering of talk is a more complex demand than repeating a strange utterance a moment after hearing it. The result is more stress.

> *Pronounce these vocabulary items.*
> Usually, the student is pressed to talk with no distortions. Not only is the left hemisphere unable to talk, it cannot fine-tune utterances for perfect pronunciation. This is still more stress. In the infant, talk appears long after the child has sophisticated comprehension of the structure and meaning of the target language—and when talk does appear, it is not perfect. It takes many years for the child's speech to shape itself gradually in the direction of the adult speaker.

> *Read this sentence. Write your answer to this question.*
> Reading seems to be a left hemisphere activity, but writing may be a function of the right hemisphere. Exactly how these fit into a hemispheric model for learning another language is a fascinating problem for future research. Given what we now know, both reading and writing probably should be delayed until comprehension of spoken language has been thoroughly internalized.

Of course, all of the left hemispheric activities such as "listen and repeat after me" are valuable, but at a more advanced stage of training.

Playing to the right hemisphere. The optimal starting point in teaching a second language is to enter the strange language through the right hemisphere. During the past twenty years, I have explored one way to achieve this by simulating the format in adult-child caretaking transactions.

The instructional strategy is to seat a few students on either side of the instructor and request, "When I say something in the target language, listen carefully and do what I do. For example, if I say, 'Tate!' and I stand up, you stand up. Just listen and act rapidly without trying to pronounce the words yourself."

Then, with the instructor as a model, the students start responding with actions to one-word commands such as "Stand up," "Sit down," "Walk," "Stop," "Turn," and "Run." Most of the students are surprised that they can demonstrate perfect understanding with body movements in a few trials. Then the one-word sentence is expanded into:

"Stand up; point to the door; walk to the door; touch it; and open the door!"

Students are impressed that within a few minutes their comprehension can be expanded even more rapidly than infants acquiring their first language through commands.

Within a few hours, students understand grammatical constructions that are nested in the imperative, such as:

"When Maria walks to Juan and hits him on the arm, Shirou will run to the chalkboard and draw a funny picture of the instructor."

With entrance into the right hemisphere where language "causes" changes in the student's behavior, individuals can rapidly decipher the language code. As the student expands understanding of how the target language works and what it means, there is a point when the person is ready to talk. This readiness cannot be forced. It will occur spontaneously. And when talk appears, it will not be perfect. There will be many flaws, but gradually it will shape itself in the direction of the native speaker.

In comparison, a left hemispheric entrance is slow-motion learning. Each detail of production—which the student is not ready to make—is practiced before the student has internalized a holistic pattern of how the language works. By practicing surface features of production prematurely, the learning process is slowed down to a tedious, monotonous pace that extinguishes attention and retention. The consequence is stress.

The Third Source of Stress: The Reality of One's Native Language

Why bother with commands that "cause" changes in the student's behavior? Why not simply *explain* to the students what each utterance means either through translation into the native language, or pictures, or pantomime? The problem is this: If we merely tell the students, for example, that "Tate" means to stand and "Suware" means to sit down, do the students internalize the meaning of each utterance?

The answer is definitely no. The right hemisphere of the brain does not accept a translation as the genuine meaning of the noises coming from the instructor's mouth or the peculiar print in the instructor's book. The right brain does not believe in the truth of my assertion that:

"Suware!" means "Sit!"

"Tate!" means "Stand!"

"Hashire!" means "Run!"

There are two reasons for my conclusion that the right brain resists the storage of *suware* as sit, *tate* as stand, and *hashire* as run. The first is that the right hemisphere has already stored a model that is powerful and is in direct conflict with the new data presented to it. The model is the result of thousands of experiences in which:

"Sit!" means "Sit!"

"Stand!" means "Stand!"

"Run!" means "Run!"

Three basic principles of learning operate to produce the storage of a powerful model that is mutually exclusive with the new model one is attempting to store. The prior model cannot coexist in harmony with the new model.

The first principle of learning that creates a powerful prior model is *contiguity*.The spoken or printed word "Run!," for example, immediately precedes the action in oneself and others in thousands of situations.

The second principle is *frequency* of pairing between the symbol, spoken or written, and the referent. It occurs in the thousands. And the third principle is *feedback*.When the spoken or written English utterance appears, the predicted action always follows. There is a cause-effect relationship which validates the connection as the truth.

But there is another aspect that further strengthens the power of the prior model. That is the Solomon Asch Effect.

The Solomon Asch Phenomenon. Solomon Asch (1955), a psychologist at Swarthmore College, created a series of elegant experiments to explore the power of the group to influence the individual's decisions.

The task was simple. You would be invited to participate in a study in which you would join a group of people to judge visually the lengths of lines. For example, you would look at a standard line and select which line—A, B, or C— was about the same length as the standard.

What you would not know was that everyone in the group except you was a confederate of the experimenter. They had been rehearsed in the decisions they would make. Line A may have been closest in length to the standard; but what would your decision be as you waited for your turn to speak, and the first person said, "Line B is the closest in length to the standard," the next person said, "Yes, I think it's Line B," and the next individual said, "It's Line B."? Now it's your turn. What would you say?

Solomon Asch discovered that the group had a powerful influence in shaping the individual's decisions—even for an unambiguous problem such as judging the length of lines. He called the impact of the group on individuals "yielding" behavior.

Yielding—that is, conforming to group pressure—is about maximum when there are three or more people in the group besides yourself. It decreases when you have at least one other person who agrees with you, but increases again if your "partner" should find an excuse to leave the situation and you are again alone in a group that disagrees with your judgment.

Another interesting twist was this: If the group dynamics are reversed so that there is only one lone confederate in the group, then that one individual making deviant decisions becomes a target for ridicule. The group seemed unaware that its strength came from agreement among the members and their "reactions would change radically to seriousness and respect" if one is alone and everyone else in the group is a dissenter.

There is, I believe, an analogy between Solomon Asch's discovery about the impact of the group on an individual and the classroom in which an instructor is speaking a foreign language. Picture this: thirty students in a class believe strongly that:

"Sit" means "Sit."

"Stand" means "Stand."

"Run" means "Run."

There is one lone dissenter, the instructor who asserts that:

"Suware!" means "Sit."

"Tate!" means "Stand."

"Hashire!" means "Run."

Given these conditions, it is not surprising that students report difficulty in retaining for more than a few moments the strange utterances that the instructor makes by mouth or by writing on the chalkboard.

Piaget's Reality

There is still another factor that increases the difficulty a student has acquiring a second language in school. It has to do with a concept of reality as proposed by Jean Piaget, the creative Swiss psychologist.

Piaget (1955) observed that children younger than eight months have a motion picture concept of reality. People, places, and things are not solid and permanent to the infant. They are images like those on a motion picture screen. If we look behind the screen, we do not expect the backsides of the actors to protrude from the rear of the screen. Nor do we expect the actors to be standing beside the screen waiting to come on in the next episode. The images can be re-created, but once they are not on the screen, they have no spatial location.

Piaget believed that the infant's reality is similar to our experience viewing motion pictures. People, places, and things are images without solidarity and permanence. When they are out of view, they have disappeared. There is no point in looking for them behind the screen or in some other location.

Piaget based his conclusion about young children on demonstrations such as this: eight-month-old Jacqueline would laugh and reach for little bells that tinkled when Piaget gently shook them. As she reached, he placed the bells under a coverlet. Her eyes followed his fingers as he shook the coverlet and bells to make them ring. She laughed as long as she heard the noise but she did not reach for the coverlet nor try to search under it.

When he raised the coverlet, Jacqueline quickly stretched out her hand; but just as she was about to get it, he covered it again. She withdrew her hand. He repeated the experiment but this time hid the bells behind a fold in the sheet. Again, she would laugh when she heard the sound but made no attempt to reach for it.

Jacqueline did not look to find the hidden object because, according to Piaget, she could not conceive of a space that she could not see. When the bells disappeared from view, they were physically nonexistent. Incidentally, children of six or seven months are able to look behind and underneath a cover for hidden objects, as shown by their ability to grasp and remove objects such as eyeglasses.

How does the infant's reality as pictured by Piaget relate to students learning English, French, or Spanish? As a hypothesis, I believe that the reality created in that foreign language classroom is like the infant's motion picture concept of reality. The persons, places, and things created in the strange symbols coming from the instructor's mouth and in print do not have solidarity and permanency. They are not real. They are like images on a motion picture screen. They lack substance and dimensionality. The image exists only for a moment. Then it vanishes. It does not have a spatial location.

Piaget's construction of reality. There is more to the Piaget story—much more. It can explain some interesting similarities among second-language-learning approaches that seem, on the surface, to be quite different.

Children, according to Piaget, make a transition through different stages. There is an analogy, which I will attempt to show, between the development of children in Piaget's world and the development to be expected in a student who is making the transition to fluency in another language.

It is important that the child evolve through each of Piaget's stages. One cannot rush from stage to stage, nor can one bypass and zoom directly from an early stage to an advanced one.

In the first stage the child between birth and two is preverbal. The infant cannot solve problems by manipulating substitutes for persons, places, and things. Examples of substitutes are concepts, words, and numbers.

Infants cannot represent experiences, but must act upon them. This is the sensorimotor period. In this stage, the infant can only make motor responses such as:

sneeze	grasp
hiccough	cry
cough	look at

Yet with only motor responses as tools for sorting thousands of stimuli that enter the child's sense receptors, individuals under the age of two have deciphered how to guide their hands with their eyes (an elegant achievement), to recognize familiar faces, to walk, to explore, and to understand most utterances directed to them.

Notice that in this period, experience is perceptual but not conceptual. As long as a stimulus such as the little bells that fascinated Jacqueline are present, the child will react with looking, laughing, and reaching. When the stimulus is hidden, the infant's responsiveness vanishes immediately. The infant seems able to perceive but not conceive. As long as the stimulation is presented externally, the infant can deal with it, but when it is absent, there seems to be no internalized concept that the child continues to manipulate mentally.

Piaget believed that conceptualizations—the internal representations of reality—develop from motor acts. Actions are substitutes for internal representations. This Piaget called "motor recognition."

For example, Lucienne could not open a matchbox to find a hidden object, a watch chain; but if the box was opened enough she could poke her finger in the hole and fish out the chain. Piaget did this: He put the watch chain in the box and closed it almost completely.

Now Lucienne had a problem. She inspected the slit in the opening and tried unsuccessfully to poke her finger into the narrow opening. Now what? She looked and looked at the slit. Then she opened and closed her mouth, again and again. At first she opened her mouth just a bit, but then wider and wider. Then suddenly, she put her finger into the slit and pulled to enlarge the opening, and finally grasped the chain. Piaget believed that Lucienne used body movements to solve a problem that an adult would have solved with a concept.

During the sensorimotor period of development, the child creates a blueprint for the advanced construction of reality concepts such as space, time, objects, causality, and the production of symbols by talking.

Clearly Piaget's model of infant development is a gradual transition from the right to the left hemisphere of the brain. The infant begins to decode sights and sounds by looking, grasping, touching, pulling, pushing, sucking—all nonverbal motor movement. The infant in the sensorimotor months is tracing a map of how things work, including language. This mapping in the right hemisphere through direct manipulation is necessary for the more advanced construction of concepts in the left hemisphere that result in talking, thinking in logical, linear patterns, and solving problems through symbols—words, numbers, and internalized concepts.

Applications to Learning Another Language

Instructional approaches to language learning can be classified into left and right hemispheric strategies. For example, audio-lingual and translation are, in my judgment, left hemisphere instruction because they are organized from the beginning around talking, reading, and writing. The thinking is logical and linear and critical, with an attempt to teach directly at the start what would be in Piaget's model an advanced stage of development.

Other instructional approaches are right hemispheric, at least in part. These include Curran's Community Language Learning, Suggestology, the Silent

Way, the Winitz-Reeds-Nord comprehension training, and Asher's total physical response.

For example, in Community Language Learning (Curran, 1972) there is an infantile regression in which the learner can be egocentric—able to express any thought in the target language without restriction or censure—and simultaneously be dependent upon the counselor, who plays the role of a warm, protective adult responding to the infant's demands. In the first stage, the learner is completely dependent upon the "adult" who accepts verbal mistakes, clumsiness, and stumbling. Like a parent, the "adult" is pleased that the infant is trying. The grossness and gaucheness of the attempt is rewarded with acceptance, compassion, and love. Without stress or anxiety, the learner lurches and gropes through stages from complete dependency to complete self-sufficiency.

In Suggestology (Lozanov, 1975) there is also an infantile regression. Students are encouraged to be children by playing games, singing songs, reciting nursery rhymes, dancing, and listening to music. These are kindergarten activities that say to the student: "It's OK to be a kid. Let's play and do silly things, and babble in a crazy language.

The adult in us is locked in a closet while the child is released. The student even has a chance to wear a disguise. Each person is provided with a new identity—another name, occupation, family, and living environment.

The Silent Way (Gattegno, 1972) attempts to regress the student to Piaget's sensorimotor stage by presenting problems that the student solves by looking at, grasping, and manipulating objects. The student decodes the language by manipulation rather than hearing an explanation. The student constructs the patterns of the new language through direct exploration.

In Comprehension Training (Nord, 1975; Winitz and Reeds, 1975) no talk is expected from the student in the early stages of training. The individual is regressed to Piaget's preverbal infant who can look at, point to, and touch. The student hears a strange utterance, looks at four pictures, and touches one that matches. Then gradually the student explores more and more patterning of the language, but always the understanding of complex patterns depends upon the previous internalization of a simpler pattern. It has been demonstrated that even ten days after training, the retention of language patterns was 90 percent or higher (Postovsky, 1976).

All of the right hemisphere instructional strategies have some elements that are similar to Piaget's model, but I believe my approach, which I call the "total physical response," or "learning another language through actions," has even more features that fit Piaget's theory.

In my approach, the student is preverbal like the infant. At first the student does not attempt to speak in the target language. Like the infant in Piaget's scenario, the student constructs reality by direct manipulation of persons, places, and things. Vision and grasping are coordinated in directions from the instructor such as:

"Walk to the table."

"Touch the table."

"Touch the book that is on the table."

"Pick up the book and put it on the chair."

At this sensorimotor stage, problems are solved by direct physical engagement. Infantile regression is encouraged with playful and nonsensical directions such as:

"Henry, when Maria makes a funny face, hit her on the arm with your newspaper and throw her purse in the wastebasket."

Commands in the target language enable the student to decode grammatical patterns through motor behavior. This is an internalized competency grammar —a nonverbal linguistic map that is necessary for the later appearance of talking.

Notice that this competency grammar is not necessarily cognitive. The student will not be able, for example, to diagram a sentence in the target language to show the grammatical constituents. That is a more advanced skill of the left hemisphere. Rather, the student like the infant is competent in understanding the meaning of more and more sophisticated sentences involving complex grammatical constructions.

The importance of infantile regression may be illustrated in this story. One of my colleagues on a sabbatical leave visited another professor who teaches in a German university. When the American visitor apologized for his high school German, the five-year-old son of the host offered a lesson in German every morning before breakfast.

Using the pictures and sentences in his nursery books, the child tutored the adult in spoken German. Much to the surprise of the adult, he thoroughly enjoyed the experience and felt that he gained more understanding of the target language from the child and his nursery books than he did from "serious" school study with adult instructors and textbooks.

Piaget's infant construction of reality may be necessary even for adults if they want to achieve fluency in another language without stress. For example, if you tell me that

"Suware" means to sit down,

"Tate" means to stand up, and

"Kagame" means to squat,

I will have difficulty retaining those relationships because the critical left hemisphere of my brain has automatically evaluated each of your assertions as false. Your assertions conflict with a lifetime of prior experience in which

"Sit" means to sit,

"Stand" means to stand, and

"Squat" means to squat.

The new information is in severe conflict with already stored information. To bypass this conflict, it may be imperative that a reality be constructed that coexists with the previously constructed reality.

This means the truth of the relationships is demonstrated through primary experiences. For example, in our instructional approach, when the instructor utters "Suware!" the student sits down; "Tate!" and the student stands up; "Kagame!" and the individual squats. The message to the right brain with these sensorimotor directions is, "If 'suware' did not mean to sit down, why did my body sit." The sensorimotor directions construct a Piagetian reality using, in this case, Japanese as the target language. This reality coexists with another reality that was constructed using English as the target language.

Apparently it is possible to have a symbiotic relationship among many parallel realities. One is distinct from the other. They do not interfere with each other.

Even more interesting, this sensorimotor approach results in an understanding of novel sentences. That is, the student like the infant is able to understand the rearrangement of constituents into utterances they have never heard before.

Perhaps the most important test of fluency for a language skill is the creation of novel sequences. It is not enough for input to equal output. If a student can only understand *exactly* those utterances heard or read in training, the approach has low efficiency. Output from the student must be *more than* the input from the instructor. This knowledge is shown when the student responds immediately to novel sentences—ones the students have never heard directly in training.

One of the first investigations of novelty in understanding the target language was accomplished by the Kelloggs (Kellogg and Kellogg, 1933) who reared a female chimpanzee as the younger sister of 9½-month-old Don Kellogg. After months of being a member of the Kellogg family, the chimpanzee, named Gua, could understand sentences she had responded to many times, such as:

"Kiss your hand!"

"Give Donald the glass!"

But Gua could not understand if you recombined the words to produce a new arrangement as, for instance,

"Kiss Donald!"

One of the most startling discoveries was that, given the same experiences, Gua could not understand novel sentences that were a simple task for Donald. Novelty in the language of animals continues to be a topic of serious study for psychologists, but this research will not be reviewed here.

It is critical that any instructional strategy demonstrate its effectiveness by showing that the students comprehend novelty, because understanding novelty is perhaps the most important index of fluency in a language.

Demonstrations of students learning another language through infantile regression to a sensorimotor preverbal stage may be seen in four documentary motion pictures.[1]

SUMMARY

More than 95 percent of American high school students who begin the study of another language give up before experiencing the enjoyment of achieving basic fluency. The reason is stress which becomes more and more painful until the students feel compelled to escape from the school situation.

The first source of stress was an expectation of talk before students were ready. The second source of stress was instructional strategies that played to the left hemisphere of the brain, and the third source was the reality of one's native language, which generates interference with the learning of another language.

The intervention model to reduce stress is to delay talk from students until they spontaneously indicate a readiness to speak. Readiness to talk will develop gracefully if the instructional program is designed for the right rather than the left hemisphere of the brain. The split-brain research was reviewed, as was Piaget's work, to present a model for second-language learning based on how infants acquire—without stress—their first language. Infants learn through motor behavior to comprehend the target language before talking appears.

Note

1.   The films are distributed by Sky Oaks Productions, Dept. D, 19544 Sky Oaks Way, Los Gatos, California 95030.

References

Asch, S. E. "Opinions and social pressures." *Scientific American,* pp. 3–7, November 1955.

Asher, J. J. *Learning another language through actions: The complete teacher's guidebook.* (Third printing) Los Gatos, Calif.: Sky Oaks Productions, 1981.

Bühler, C., and Hetzer, H. *Testing children's development from birth to school age.* New York: Farrer and Rinehart, 1935.

Curran, C. A. *Counseling-learning: A whole-person model for education.* New York: Grune and Stratton, 1972.

Friedlander, B. Z. "Receptive language development in infancy: Issues and problems." *Merrill-Palmer Quarterly of Behavior and Development, 16* (1), pp. 7–51, 1970.

Gattegno, C. *Teaching foreign languages in schools: The silent way.* New York: Educational Solutions, Inc., 1972.

Gazzaniga, M. S. "The split brain in man." *Scientific American, 217* (2), pp. 24–29, 1967.

Gazzaniga, M. S., LeDoux, J. E., and Wilson, D. H. "Language, praxis, and the right hemisphere: Clues to some mechanisms of consciousness." *Neurology, 27,* pp. 1144–1147, 1977.

Gesell, A., and Thompson, H. "Learning and growth in identical twins: An experimental study by the method of co-twins control." *Genetic Psychology Monographs, 6,* pp. 1–124, 1929.

Hakuta, K., and Cancino, H. "Trends in second-language-acquisition research." *Harvard Educational Review, 47* (3), pp. 294–316, 1977.

Kellogg, W. N., and Kellogg, L. A. *The ape and the child.* New York: McGraw-Hill, 1933.

Lawson, J. H. "Should foreign language be eliminated from the curriculum?" In J. W. Dodge (Ed.), *The case for foreign language study.* New York: Modern Language Association Materials Center, 1971.

Lozanov, G. "The nature and history of the suggestopaedic system of teaching foreign languages and its experimental prospects." *Suggestology and Suggestopaedia, 1,* pp. 5–15, 1975.

McCaffrey, A. Speech perception in infancy. Reported as a personal communication, 1969. In B. Z. Friedlander, "Receptive language development in infancy: Issues and problems." *Merrill-Palmer Quarterly of Behavior and Development, 16* (1), pp. 7–51, 1970.

Moffitt, A. R. "Speech perception by infants." Unpublished doctoral dissertation, University of Minnesota, 1968.

Moffitt, A. R. "Speech perception by 20–24 week old infants." Paper presented at the meeting of the Society for Research in Child Development, Santa Monica, California, March, 1969.

Nord, J. R. "A case for listening comprehension." *Philologia, 7,* pp. 1–25, 1975.

Piaget, J. *The construction of reality in the child.* New York: Basic Books, 1955.

Postovsky, V. A. "The priority of aural comprehension in the language acquisition process." In G. Nickel (Ed.), *Proceedings of the Fourth International Congress of Applied Linguistics,* Vol. 3. Stuttgart, Germany: HochschulVerlag, 1976.

Pritchard, R. M. "Stabilized images on the retina." *Scientific American, 204* (73), pp. 2–8, 1961.

Royster, V. "Thinking things over." *Wall Street Journal,* 15 February 1978.

Simon, P. "Battling language chauvinism." *Change,* p. 10, November 1977.

———. "A message to foreign language teachers." *The Teacher's Edition of Bonjour,* pp. 3–4, May 1978.

Winitz, H., and Reeds, J. *Comprehension and problem solving as strategies for language training.* The Hague: Mouton, 1975.

CHAPTER 5

Three Steps Leading to Listening Fluency: A Beginning*

James R. Nord

Associate Professor of Education
Michigan State University

In recent years there has been an increasing interest in listening comprehension. Simon Belasco (1965, p. 482) has called it "the most underestimated and least understood aspect of foreign language." Yet little has actually been done to understand it or to increase its role in the language-learning process. While the audio-lingual methodology places listening first in the sequence of language skills, the listening that has taken place has been largely a *listening for speaking* rather than a *listening for understanding*.

Belasco (1971, p. 194) stated that at the end of the 1960–1961 Pennsylvania State University French Institute, he was "jolted by the realization that it is possible to develop so-called 'speaking' ability (vocalizing) and *yet be virtually incompetent in understanding* the spoken language." In practical terms, listening comprehension is of paramount significance. When speaking a language, a learner can manipulate a relatively narrow range of vocabulary at his or her own pace to express an idea, but when listening to the reply he or she no longer controls the choice of vocabulary. One must be prepared to assimilate those words which are a part of the speaker's active vocabulary and must adjust to the speaker's rate of speech. In order to handle a simple conversation, an individual must have a much broader competency in listening comprehension than in speaking; this is especially the case when conversing in a foreign language with a

---

*This chapter includes quotations from *Learning another language through actions; The complete teacher's guidebook*, by James Asher; *The metaphorical brain*, by M. A. Arbib; and *A practical guide to the teaching of French*, by Wilga Rivers. All were reprinted with the kind permission of the publishers.

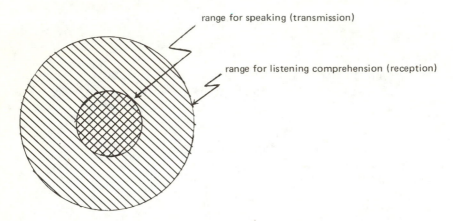

range for speaking (transmission)

range for listening comprehension (reception)

FIGURE 5.1   Normal range of receptive and expressive language ability

native speaker of that language. In terms of range of lexicon and structure, the comparable capabilities might be illustrated by the areas of two concentric circles (see Figure 5.1). Moreover, in a dynamic sense, as a learner's language skill improves, we can visualize both concentric circles enlarging simultaneously with the outer (listening comprehension) circle always embracing a far greater range than the inner (speaking) circle.

I became directly involved in the methodology of teaching listening in 1973 when I served as a consultant to the faculty teaching an intensive Russian course in Justin Morrill College at Michigan State University. The problem facing the faculty was the low level of listening comprehension achieved by the students studying Russian. This problem showed up most dramatically in students going to Russia for a summer program in Leningrad.

The experience of the CIEE Russian Language Program at Leningrad University had shown again and again that listening comprehension was the most severely limiting factor for even the best-prepared students of Russian. One group leader noted that the general lack of student interest in lectures in literature and culture was not the fault of the lecturers: "The relatively low level of the average summer Russian program participant's comprehension of spoken Russian makes it extremely difficult for any speaker to present an interesting lecture" (Donchenko, 1972, p. 1). What this problem was pointing to in terms of Figure 5.1 was the tendency of the outer circle (range for listening comprehension) to be much too tightly drawn to the inner circle (range for speaking). Whatever a student's speaking skill, the student is sorely limited if he or she cannot comprehend a much broader range of utterances.

There is also some evidence that emphasis on the inner circle (speaking) severely retards the expansion of the outer circle (listening comprehension). The requirement to respond orally imposes *listening for speaking* and results in impaired comprehension. This problem was treated in a short experiment by James Asher involving the performance of drill movements by commands in Russian. Asher (1969, p. 13) found that the students who merely performed the commands did so with a greater degree of reliability than those who first repeated the command before performing the necessary movement. He concluded that "the stress of trying to pronounce the alien utterance may retard listening fluency. . . . The optimal strategy may be serial learning in which one achieves listening fluency just before one attempts to speak." There is other experimental support for this position. In a study on the associative reaction time in language acquisition, Ley and Locascio (1972) state: "Our research suggests that one must make associations to verbal materials during learning in order that the material can be later recalled, and that some procedure such as repeatedly saying the material aloud interferes with the association process and, therefore, has a detrimental effect on learning."

There is evidence that attempting to speak before listening comprehension is acquired may cause problems in speaking. The requirement to speak before one completely comprehends brings about the detrimental effect of *task overload* (of stress and anxiety) on language learning. High anxiety has detrimental effects on speaking: there is a tendency to force the speaker back to his or her native grammatical structure or vocabulary when the speaker becomes over-anxious (and this in turn usually leads to greater anxiety). As Gaier (1952, p. 11) has expressed it: "It leads to an impairment in the ability to improvise in an unstructured and/or new situation. This results in stereotyped, habitual, and familiar approaches that may be maladaptive in the situation."

In addition to the evidence that speaking too soon is detrimental to both listening comprehension and speaking, there is also evidence that speaking is not even necessary to learn listening comprehension. The fact that receptive control can exist even without production has been recognized, as in the case of such abnormal conditions as anarthria, in which a child (because of congenitally conferred motor defects) never acquires a speaking ability in his or her language. Lenneberg (1962, p. 424) has reported in detail one such case, typical of others, in which a patient without productive skills nevertheless had acquired language in the sense that he possessed the grammatical schema necessary for decoding, i.e., for understanding. This study in particular strikes deep at those motor theories of language acquisition that attach primary importance to the roles of overt imitation and the developing of motor speech skills, and it lends support to the view that decoding as well as encoding skills are "dependent upon the *acquisition of a single set of organizing principles.*"

In an effort to develop the techniques and materials necessary to end, at least in part, our neglect of listening comprehension, the Justin Morrill College intensive Russian program at Michigan State University began a project emphasizing listening comprehension as a focal skill.[1] We were initially supported in our efforts by two major research efforts in which oral response was intentionally delayed in the early stages of language learning. The experiments by James Asher (1969, 1972) and by Valerian Postovsky (1970, 1974) led us to believe that listening comprehension was crucial; they also provided guidelines of how we might proceed in our program.

In an experiment focused on listening comprehension of German, Asher (1972) required no speaking whatsoever. Instead, he required the students to respond to oral stimuli with a movement of the body. For example, the student was told: "Go to the table and pick up the mirror." The requests started simply and were first modeled by the instructor. Later, the vocabulary and structure became more complex. Some vocabulary, particularly abstract words, were written on cards and manipulated as objects. Asher noted that after sixteen hours of instruction, the students, on their own volition, pressed the instructor to let them speak. Once listening comprehension was achieved, transfer to the speaking skill was very rapid. In regard to reading, Asher (1972, p. 136) noted:

> Although the experimental subjects far excelled the controls in listening skills, it was expected that perhaps the reverse would be true for reading skill. Since the training emphasis of the control group was reading and writing, we expected these students to have significantly higher reading comprehension scores. The results, using a 37-item reading test, showed no significant difference between groups. Surprisingly, even though the experimental subjects had no systematic training in reading, there was enough positive transfer from listening skill to make both groups quite similar in their reading achievement.

In a large and tightly controlled experiment conducted by Postovsky (1970, 1974), oral response was replaced by written response during the first four weeks of the Defense Language Institute's intensive Russian program. When written response to oral stimuli was employed to the complete exclusion of oral response, Postovsky found: (1) better overall language proficiency, (2) a high degree of transfer from writing to speaking, (3) better control of grammar structure, and (4) that the introduction of the Cyrillic alphabet prior to intensive pronunciation practice does not create a greater problem of graphic interference on speaking than the reverse sequence of presentation normally creates.

In these experiments by Asher and Postovsky, oral response was replaced in the early stages of language learning by physical (body movement) response in the case of Asher and by written response in the case of Postovsky. In both experiments the student's focus was on listening comprehension of the oral stimuli of an instructor or tape.

Two insights that were drawn from this research were:

(1) Delay of oral practice in the early stages of language learning is a key factor in reducing task overload.

(2) Proficiency in listening comprehension is readily transferable to other language skills (including speaking and reading).

But what is listening comprehension? As we pondered ways of focusing on listening comprehension in our instructional program, we could not at first find a satisfactory theoretical frame of reference. There was extensive literature on reading, writing, and even speaking—but *listening,* as common as it may appear in practice, was little treated as a theoretical subject or through experimentation.

One thing was clear; listening is not a simple skill easily learned by simple immersion in a sea of sound. People who go to a foreign country to learn the language often find themselves immersed in a sink-or-swim situation and are often disappointed that they cannot learn the language faster or better. In these situations, the people are exposed to a great amount of *listening opportunity*; but this experience is not equivalent to learning *listening comprehension* and, therefore, leads to developing listening comprehension slowly, if at all.

Ervin-Tripp (1971) tells of two young American children whose parents were deaf and did not speak. The children, whose hearing was normal, were exposed to great chunks of television speech, but they could not speak or understand English. It may be that television speech is too rapid and the sentences are too long and/or complex to permit the short-term memory to sort out the basic recurring elements. It may be that the children, like strangers in a new land, were unable to associate the sea of sound, flowing from the TV, with any meaningful parts of their lives. Recent research on normal mother-child dialogues indicates that children learning a first language are spoken to in short phrases; in many instances, one-word expressions (Broen, 1972). Short meaningful units apparently must be presented and learned so they may later be chunked into larger and larger meaningful units. Excessive exposure to a second language without meaningfulness may even be detrimental to learning the language.

Postovsky (1970, 1974) described two informal experiments conducted at the Defense Language Institute, which involved a large amount of exposure to audio training. For one project, the subjects worked largely with material devoid of lexical meaning, whereas in the other project, understanding of the foreign language messages was crucial at each step of the way. This second group developed superior oral fluency despite the fact that the emphasis was almost totally on the development of aural comprehension. The first group did not, however, achieve any degree of proficiency in any of the skills of the language; moreover, when phased into the regular Russian program, starting from the beginning, their comprehension and overall performance was inferior throughout the course. Postovsky (1970, pp. 28–29) indicates that, "One had the impression that the programmed materials (of that specific program) conditioned the students not to associate sounds of the Russian language with meaning."

It seemed to us that the building of listening comprehension through meaningful listening exercises must be as carefully researched, tried, and tested as the building of speaking ability had been attempted in the audio-lingual methodology. The evidence pointed in this direction, but we could find few guidelines for developing carefully graded listening exercises. A theoretical model for acquiring proficiency in listening comprehension had to be formulated. A preliminary model was created in 1973. In brief, the original model postulated three ascending consecutive phases through which a person might gain fluency in listening comprehension:

> In the *Decoding Phase* the student responds to oral stimuli by selecting from a series of alternative answers; there is immediate feedback as to the correctness of the response. In the *Anticipatory-Response Phase* the student is required to anticipate what is going to be said next. The *Self-Monitoring Phase* involves vigilant tasking, such as the detection of error or incongruity in the speech patterns presented; it develops a critical listening ability which the student can later use to monitor his speech (Ingram, Nord, and Dragt, 1975, p. 4).

The initial outline of the model now appears sufficiently stable and can be generalized to warrant both increased explanation and increased public scrutiny and reaction. Since the original formulation of this model (Ingram et al., 1975), each of the phases has been further refined and expanded. They have been refined in terms of theoretical comprehensiveness and expanded in terms of operational exemplars.

This chapter will be divided into three basic units. The first section will discuss in greater depth the first step of the process, the *Semantic Decoding Phase.* The second section will discuss the second step, the *Anticipatory Feed Forward Phase.* The third section will discuss the third step, the *Discrepancy Feedback Phase.* In each of these phases, the basic teaching techniques will be discussed.

STEP 1: THE SEMANTIC DECODING PHASE

I will illustrate the three steps to listening fluency by describing basic teaching techniques found useful in each phase. The examples come from experiences with languages as diverse as Chinese, Hebrew, Japanese, Russian, and Swahili, as well as English as a foreign language. Most of the illustrations in the first section refer to an experimental Russian course taught at Michigan State University in 1973–1974, but the teaching techniques themselves can be generalized to almost any language.

Until there is a basic association made between sound system and meaning system there is little hope of sound triggering meaning or meaning triggering sound. In the first three weeks of classroom instruction, students in the experimental Russian course were introduced to the meanings of Russian utterances by the strategy developed by James Asher, which he calls "Total Physical Response."[2] In its initial stage the instructor states a command and models a physical movement; the students imitate the same physical movement. Then the instructor states the command without performing the physical movement. The students are to carry out the command. Next, individual students are called upon to perform a wide variety of physical responses (in Russian) on command.

"Stand!"

"Sit down!"

"Point to the ceiling (the wall, your left ear, to where the student in the yellow shirt is sitting, etc.)!''

Besides providing a very broad framework for an introduction to the sounds and vocabulary of the target language, the Asher method of Total Physical Response can also involve complex decisions in listening comprehension:

"If the student on your left is wearing glasses, go to the board and write her surname, but if she is not wearing glasses, take out a piece of paper and write your own surname."

The Asher technique involves all students because those who are not called upon to perform a given command are nonetheless intrigued as to whether the student so designated will do it correctly. Sometimes a follow-up question is asked of students as they observe the performance of another student:

"If he understood me correctly, raise your hand!"

When used imaginatively, this technique provides the most uniformly successful method we know of to elicit successful responses from students of all degrees of language aptitude. Our experience indicates that the range of foreign language aptitude is not nearly so divergent in listening comprehension as in oral response; nowhere is this "overperformance" by lower-aptitude language learners more apparent than in total physical response drills. In our Russian classes, the Asher technique was employed intensively in the classroom during the first three weeks; subsequently it was employed only occasionally. Student comments on the course unanimously valued this method of instruction and wished there had been more physical response drills.

We then prepared comprehension exercises of our own to be used in the language laboratory. They were designed to teach the semantic decoding aspect of listening fluency. The laboratory materials (tapes and worksheets) provided: (a) choices of meaning following every utterance heard, (b) an immediate indication of whether the choice selected was correct or not, and (c) no requirement of oral response from students while in the laboratory.

Examples of the worksheets prepared for *vocabulary introduction* are illustrated in Figures 5.2 and 5.3. In Figure 5.2, an introductory technique on what we call the "stairway" form is illustrated. Upon hearing the first utterance, the student begins on the top line and guesses between two alternatives. The student's active response-choice is immediately confirmed or denied through immediate feedback technology, so that he or she "learns" the association between sound and picture. The immediate feedback technology used was *latent image.*[3] Upon hearing the second utterance, the student will most likely mark the second step of the first column if the utterance is the same. If it sounds different the student "guesses" that it is the second column. In either case the student's choice is immediately confirmed or denied by the immediate feedback technology, and the student can recheck, if necessary, to be sure he or she has made the correct guess. The binary choice for the first three audio utterances expands to three for the fourth utterance, then to four for the sixth utterance and eventually to seven. We decided not to exceed seven choices because the short-term memory capacity of adults is about seven informational units. When more

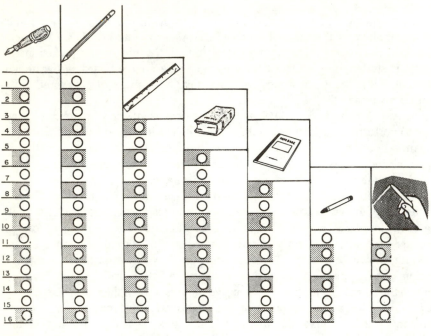

FIGURE 5.2.   The stairway form

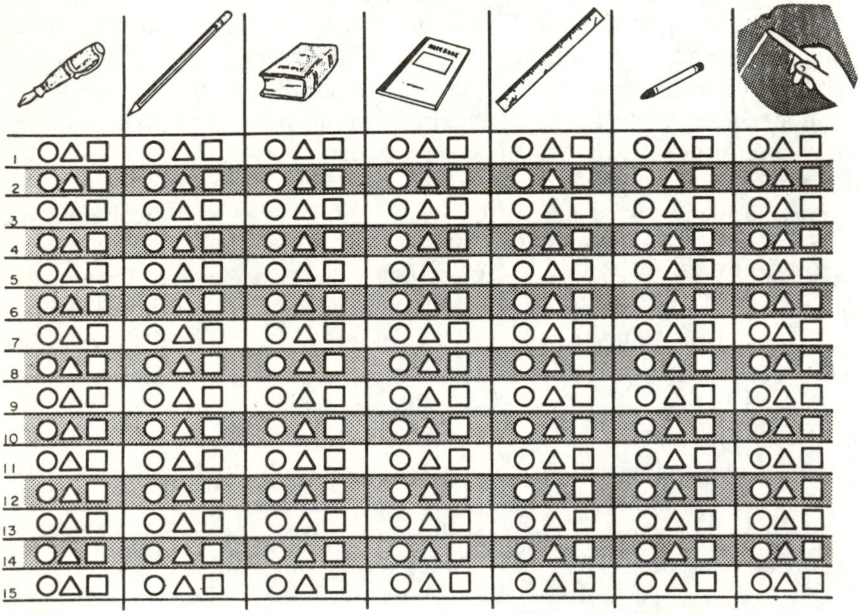

FIGURE 5.3.   The plateau form

than seven units are present, clustering or chunking of units occurs in order to reduce the number to seven or less (Miller, 1956).

We have tried to organize the units into "semantic" as well as "grammatical" categories for several reasons. Each set of seven pictures was selected to be of the same general grammatical class, i.e., nouns, adjectives, or verbs. Thus almost any meaning pictured on a sheet could be inserted within a given sentence. For example, if pictures representing the verbs: touch, drop, pick up, push, pull, and shake were on a sheet, any one of the words could be inserted in the following sentence: "_____ the red ball."

The semantic association of units and their class names was also developed. For example, one sheet may have truck, bus, car, bicycle, etc.; another sheet may have hat, gloves, pants, shirt, etc.; while a third sheet has banana, pear, apple, orange, etc. Later, after the specific names are learned, the class names would be introduced by having a single sheet which contained pictures of a car, a shirt, an apple, etc. The audio utterances would then be the class names vehicle, clothes, fruit, etc., rather than the specific name. Any particular unit could be further divided if this was found necessary or useful. For example, a set of specific types of hats such as straw, top homburg, etc., could be generated. There seems to be almost a natural clustering of around seven units per class, therefore this number was used in most groupings.

The stairway form (Figure 5.2) contains insufficient repetition to ensure good association of sound to meaning. Therefore, we provide an immediate follow-up to the stairway introductory form with a review exercise sheet, called the "plateau" form (Figure 5.3). As in the stairway form, there are seven pictures across the top (this time in a different order). There are now seven pictorial choices of which one is to be selected for each utterance. This exercise sheet actually provides three separate review exercises. First, using only the circles the student hears an utterance three times and marks the circle under the item he or she associates with the utterance. The student then moves to the second line from the top and hears another utterance three times before marking his or her choice in the appropriate circle. After completing fifteen such responses the student is at the bottom of the page and has finished the "circle drill," the drill that provides three repetitions of each utterance. The "triangle drill" and "square drill" are performed in precisely the same fashion except that each of the fifteen utterances is stated twice for the triangle drill and only once for the square drill.

The reduction in the number of presentations of the audio signal is a means of ensuring a continued challenge to the learner. We have assumed on the basis of research in achievement motivation that a certain amount of uncertainty is intrinsically motivating (McClelland, 1970).

Therefore, we recommend that the student be kept somewhat uncertain. To maintain maximum motivation, we used a heuristic which assumes that people who are 90 percent or more certain of something tend to be bored with it, while people who are less than 70 percent certain of something or some situation tend to be frustrated by it and tend to have high anxiety about it. We, therefore, deliberately tried to keep the error rate of students at somewhere between 10 and 30 percent. This level can be accomplished by manipulating the number of presentations, the form of the presentation, and the rate of speech.[4] With repeated exposure, the number of times a vocabulary item was repeated was reduced. Words were also buried in sentences in later drills. The rate of speech was manipulated so that students who were having a great deal of trouble and making many mistakes could listen to a slower tape, while those who were making few mistakes and becoming bored were given compressed speech versions of the tape. We recommend that final listening tests should be played at about 20 percent compression (Lee, 1972) (faster than normal) to insure that listening fluency has been developed to the point where normal listening is easy.

The Semantic Decoding Phase of our program began with *vocabulary introduction* exercises utilizing the formats of Figures 5.2 and 5.3. Included were the following subcategories of vocabulary: cognates, vocabulary using specific letters of the alphabet (to reinforce introduction to the orthography), parts of the body, articles of clothing, foods, vegetables, people of varying ages, verbs, telling time and colors. *Numerical exercises* provided a series of addition or subtraction problems with the answer provided in latent-image form. In such drills the students record the numbers they hear on their worksheet, perform the mathematical task requested, and then verify their answer by marking the latent-image answer provided on a worksheet. This procedure has proven to be an effective means for the rapid assimilation of Russian numbers.

A series of morphological exercises was also included in this phase. In some cases, there are clear semantic implications of morphological markers. For example, the singular and plural markers on words have strong semantic implications. On the other hand, morphological markers, such as gender, seem to have weak semantic implication and are used primarily in a grammatical sense. These exercises thus bridge the gap between phase one and phase two, but are presented here as an illustration of our basic teaching technique.

The basic technique was one of having the students listen to words, or words in sentences, and having them decide whether they were singular or plural; whether they were past, present, or future; whether they were first or third person; or whatever the inflectional marker indicated. The students were provided choices and given immediate feedback confirmation. Figure 5.4 illustrates the form used for gender marking exercises.

Vocabulary introduction, numerical exercises, and *morphological exercises* are examples of the kinds of drills that comprise the Semantic Decoding Phase of our listening comprehension exercises. Although in no sense complete, they do provide an example of the wide application to which the decoding phase of listening comprehension can be applied. During a ten-week period (one academic term), there was no required oral response of any kind in the language laboratory. Students were, however, required to make at least one decision in

	M	F	N		M	F	N
1.	—	—	—	26.	—	—	—
2.	—	—	—	27.	—	—	—
3.	—	—	—	28.	—	—	—
4.	—	—	—	29.	—	—	—
5.	—	—	—	30.	—	—	—
6.	—	—	—	31.	—	—	—
7.	—	—	—	32.	—	—	—
8.	—	—	—	33.	—	—	—
9.	—	—	—	34.	—	—	—
10.	—	—	—	35.	—	—	—
11.	—	—	—	36.	—	—	—
12.	—	—	—	37.	—	—	—
13.	—	—	—	38.	—	—	—
14.	—	—	—	39.	—	—	—
15.	—	—	—	40.	—	—	—
16.	—	—	—	41.	—	—	—
17.	—	—	—	42.	—	—	—
18.	—	—	—	43.	—	—	—
19.	—	—	—	44.	—	—	—
20.	—	—	—	45.	—	—	—
21.	—	—	—	46.	—	—	—
22.	—	—	—	47.	—	—	—
23.	—	—	—	48.	—	—	—
24.	—	—	—	49.	—	—	—
25.	—	—	—	50.	—	—	—

FIGURE 5.4.   Morphological exercise form for learning Russian gender markers

response to each and every utterance they heard; they were provided immediate confirmation or denial of the validity of their decision.

FIGURE 5.5.   Typical picture bingo form

In addition to the exercises just described, a number of other exercises have since been tried in the teaching of other languages. Bingo, for example, was found to be a popular way to practice listening comprehension for numbers. Variations in the audio sentences such as the use of additions (4 + 3) and subtractions (25 − 6), instead of giving the number label directly, helped to increase attention. From Bingo we went to *Picture Bingo* (Figure 5.5). Using the pictures previously used in the stairway and plateau sheets, we created a number of Picture Bingo card sets for a class.

The audio sentences used would be varied. At the beginning, only the word itself was used. Later, the word was used in a sentence. Still later, a more complex inferential statement about the picture was used, such as "he is man's best friend" or "he is the king of the jungle" or "he has a long, long neck." Idioms of the particular language and/or culture can be used for these exercises.

The Semantic Decoding Phase also includes reading comprehension. The introduction of reading may be delayed a short or long period depending upon

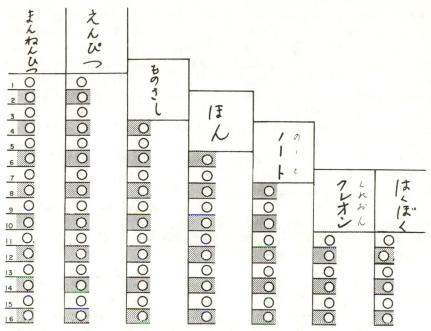

FIGURE 5.6.   Stairway form for teaching the reading of Japanese

the potentiality for graphic interference. Russian has a Cyrillic alphabet which is new to most learners. It also has a close symbol–sound correspondence. Reading was, therefore, introduced relatively soon, because little graphic interference was anticipated.

Reading was introduced through listening. One technique for doing this is to use the stairway and plateau forms, with written words replacing the pictures. Figure 5.6 illustrates this technique for Japanese. This language is used as an illustration because there is a close correspondence between the sound symbol and the written form. Japanese has both a phonetic system and an ideographic system of writing. We are illustrating here the phonetic system. The phonetic symbols are not a romanized alphabet and, therefore, graphic interference is avoided. Thus the individual can learn to "read" the common written form directly from the sound rather than having to "go through" a romanized version of the language which may cause graphic interference. The written vocabulary items that are initially taught are those previously learned by sound. Thus, the meaning is transferred from sound to writing just as in learning to read one's native language. The introduction of reading for a language that uses a roman alphabet is delayed longer because of graphic interference. For example, if reading were introduced early in the teaching of French, the written form would probably dominate the hearing pattern. Each sound would be distorted by the listener to conform to what it might sound like in English. When no reading is allowed for a period of time, the basic sound system is internalized directly and thoroughly and is distorted less when reading is taught.

For the latter two terms of the intensive Russian course, the students received cassette tape players. Besides listening to past exercises from the language laboratory and listening to the pattern drill tapes accompanying their regular textbook, students were given a large amount of listening-reading material. The material consisted of cassette recordings and dittoed transcripts with unfamiliar words provided with latent-image glosses. That is, all words that had previously been taught were unchanged. But new vocabulary that was to be learned had the English translation printed in latent image above the word. As the listener/reader came across the words he or she did not understand, the reader simply marked above it with a latent-image pen and the translation would appear. These types of exercises extended basic vocabulary and provided practice in listening and reading continuous prose.

In the Justin Morrill intensive Russian program, where this three-phase model was first applied, the Semantic Decoding Phase was emphasized. The students were able to build up an extensive, receptive vocabulary quickly. As a consequence, they appeared capable of comprehending large amounts of simple Russian. Although no speaking was required, students began to express themselves in Russian. They felt comfortable with receptive comprehension and wanted to talk. A few mistakes were noted in phonology. More were noted in certain grammatical elements, such as case endings, plural endings, and various noun-verb agreements. These errors arose, however, primarily within the Semantic Decoding Phase of training and provided further evidence for the necessity and importance of the next two phases.

Although there was no training in pronunciation, the pronunciation of the students for the most part seemed satisfactory; in fact, often better than a corresponding audio-lingual course which stresses speaking. We are not the only ones to believe that pronunciation drills can be reduced, if not eliminated, through meaningful listening exercises. Osgood (1963, p. 279) surmises that "discrimination of critical phonemic cues are developed 'incidentally' in the course of learning to behave differentially to meaningful speech units."

Listening training, however, should still be emphasized. Our techniques of listening practice will be explained in a later section.

The primacy of grammar first, vocabulary second, is mostly based upon the audio-lingual paradigm which sees overt "talking" as primary. In order to talk and express oneself, a "grammar" or logical schema is necessary. For simple understanding, a large vocabulary seems more critical. Rivers (1975, pp. 83–84) gives an excellent example of this general phenomenon.

Because of this initial tendency in listening to take the easier road of semantic decoding, students with an *extensive vocabulary* can often interpret a great deal of what they hear by sheer word recognition and logical reasoning. A person listening to a news broadcast might identify the following lexical items:

... jeune femme ... vingt-cinq ans ... avion ... Air France ... liaison Paris-Nice ... menace ... armes .. obligé ... pilote ... Marseille ... quatre heures ... série ... exigences ahurissantes ... Finalement ... aéroport ... Marseille ... brigade anti-commando ... décidé ... intervenir ... trois hommes déguisés ... stewards ... montés ... appareil ... abattu ... pirate de l'air.

With this basic information, his knowledge of similar situations, and his powers of inference, the student would probably have little difficulty deducing the following facts:

Une jeune femme de vingt-cinq ans s'est emparée d'un avion d'Air France effectuant la liaison Paris-Nice. Sous la menace de ses armes, elle a obligé le pilote à mettre le cap sur Marseille et pendant quatre heures elle a formulé une série d'exigences ahurissantes . . . Finalement, à l'aéroport de Marseille la brigade anti-commando a décidé d'intervenir: trois hommes déguisés en stewards sont montés dans l'appareil. Ils ont abattu la pirate de l'air.

This process is what Schlesinger (1968, p. 122) has called *semantic-syntactic decoding,* because the listener perceives the essential semantic cues and rapidly assigns these to such roles as actor, action, object, etc., according to his or her knowledge of the real world, and only resorts to syntactic rules when this does not work in very complex sentence structures. The generative semanticists (Lakoff, 1972) believe that logical categories and logical classes provide the natural basis for grammar and, therefore, ultimately of language use. Therefore, initial emphasis on meaning seems reasonable.

This approach fits well with Arbib's (1972, pp. 208–209) analysis of the evolution of the human brain, and the probable parallel evolution of language. Arbib stated it as follows:

Where many linguists have taken *syntax* (the grammatical rules of the language) as primary to the study of language, we would see it as secondary in the evolution of language. If we did not understand the passive construction and registered only the elementary meanings (semantics) of "apple," "eat," and "boy," our model of the world would lead us to understand their concatenation as meaning what in English we convey by "the apple was eaten by the boy," rather than "the apple ate the boy". . . we may hypothesize that syntax evolved as subtle modifiers became required to distinguish the possible meanings of long catenations of signs.

The techniques described in the Semantic Decoding Phase have been used by a number of researchers and teachers in the U.S. and in other countries. In particular, Winitz and Reeds (1975) used a technique very similar to the stairway and plateau procedures of ours. Neither knew of the other's work at the time. Mueller and Niedzielski (1968) were already using the same concept as early as 1966.

In summary, the Semantic Decoding Phase seems to be a necessary but not sufficient condition for developing listening fluency. It does develop, to a degree, the kind of listening comprehension often tested under the label of listening comprehension, but we believe it is insufficient to create the internal cognitive structures essential for the acquisition of speaking, reading, and writing. People who claim they can comprehend, but have difficulty speaking, may have ended their cognitive development at this stage. In order to develop full language competence, we believe listening fluency is required, and this involves two more phases: the Anticipatory Feed Forward Phase, and the Discrepancy Feedback Phase. These phases will be explained next.

STEP 2: ANTICIPATORY FEED FORWARD PHASE

While it seems clear that the Semantic Decoding Phase is the necessary first step in building both listening fluency and language competence, it is also becoming clear that semantic decoding is not sufficient to achieve listening fluency or language competence. A second step, the Anticipatory Feed Forward Phase, was recognized as necessary for the development of listening fluency and complete language acquisition.

It was soon obvious that the teaching procedures were not as simple nor as straightforward as those used in the Semantic Decoding Phase. Little was achieved in this phase when comprehension training was introduced at the Justin Morrill intensive Russian language program. Ingram, Nord, and Dragt (1975, p. 17) comment as follows:

> While little was developed that was explicitly addressed to the anticipatory response phase of listening comprehension, certain of the morphology drills engendered an awareness of the grammatical and lexical complements possible for given syntactic contexts. Some thought was given to drills using the so-called Cloze technique (i.e., where, say, every sixth word is left blank in a prose passage), but no exercises were actually prepared.

The goal of this phase is to teach the student to develop in his or her mind a plan or general abstract schema. In reality, there are two basic schemata which need to be built up and related to each other. There is a basic linguistic schema and a basic semantic schema. Within each, there is a contiguity which helps the observer/listener to anticipate what comes next. As Bandura (1977, p. 12) states it:

> There are certain regularities in the succession or coexistence of most environmental events. Such uniformities create expectations about what leads to what. Knowledge of conditional relations thus enables one to predict with varying accuracy what is likely to happen under given antecedent conditions.

Within the linguistic schema, there are basic noun-verb agreements, adjective-noun agreements, word order sequences, etc., required by the language structure. For example, number agreement between noun and verb must be maintained in English. The sentence "the men _____ big" requires a plural form of the verb "to be." The plural form is anticipated in this frame. Within the semantic schema, there are basic associations made between objects and events. The object "table" anticipates "chair," the object "man" has high association with "woman." Most word association games are semantic anticipation games.

Most audio-lingual methodology tends to restrict the written form until speaking is well underway. We were concerned with the acquisition of the central nervous system's cognitive structure, not a particular performance or skill. We taught reading without evoking speaking by paralleling learning to read with learning to listen.

First, the students listened to a passage they could easily comprehend aurally. Then they listened to the passage and simultaneously looked at the printed text. For this process to work well, students should look at the same word they are hearing. There must be continuous matching of the auditory sounds with the written form. This is what Don Tosti (1974) calls "vigilance tasking."

In order to achieve vigilance tasking, we utilized the Cloze technique (Taylor, 1953). This technique normally involves eliminating every sixth or seventh word in a text, and having the student fill in the empty spaces with the appropriate word. It was originally designed as a measure of text readability.

The Boy Who Painted Cats

A   long   time   ago   in   small   village

in   Japan   lived   poor   farmer   and   wife.

They   were   very   good   people.   They   had

many,   many   children   and   it   was

difficult   to   feed   them   good   food.

When   oldest   son   was   fourteen,   he   was

strong   enough   to   help   father   and   little

girls   helped   mother   almost   as   soon

as   they   could   walk.

FIGURE 5.7.   Student form of missing parts exercise

To illustrate how vigilance tasking techniques were developed, I will describe a program designed to help Japanese students learn listening fluency in English. The Japanese students were given a written sheet (see Figure 5.7). They simultaneously listened to an audio tape rendition of the same story (see Figure 5.8). Their task was to listen and to follow the text. Whenever they heard a word, but did not see a word written, they were to mark the open space with a latent-image marker. When they were correct, the hidden word was revealed by means of the latent-image imprint. When the students finished a paragraph, they marked, with the latent-image pen, in the box at the right of the paragraph to determine the number of spaces in which hidden words were placed.

It is obvious to native speakers of English that many of the articles and personal possessive pronouns were eliminated from the passage (see Figure 5.7). Native speakers do not even need to hear the audio tape to find and fill in the missing parts of this passage. Their anticipatory mechanism is so well developed that they can immediately tell which words are missing. Japanese, on the other hand, have learned to "read" English by translating it into Japanese.

The Boy Who Painted Cats

A	long	time	ago	in	(a)*	small
village	in	Japan	lived	(a)	poor	farmer
and	(his)	wife.	They	were	very	good
people.	They	had	many,	many		children
and	it	was	difficult	to	feed	them
good	food.	When	(the)	oldest	son	was
fourteen,	he	was	strong	enough	to	help
(his)	father	and	(the)	little	girls	
helped	(their)	mother	almost	as	soon	as
they	could	walk.				(7)

*Items in parentheses were written in latent image on the written sheet
given to the students and these items were pronounced in the audio
rendition of the story.

FIGURE 5.8.   Audio version of missing parts exercise

Because there are no articles in the Japanese language, a fairly accurate translation can be made without close attention to articles. As a result, the Japanese literally become functionally deaf to these elements of speech. They have great difficulty hearing them.

After listening to a paragraph once, Japanese students would often mark only three or four spaces. When they marked the box at the side, they would discover that there were seven spaces which should have been marked. This came as a shock to them, but the greater shock came when they discovered that even a second or third listening was not enough to "tune the ear in" on these elusive words. Gradually, students developed anticipatory listening habits which made it possible for them to hear more and more of the articles as time went on. This particular technique can be used very broadly in helping students focus on certain redundant features of the language. In French, the articles *le* and *la* may be focused on in this way. In Russian the case endings may be focused upon using this technique.

The cold October rains _____ . It was late in the afternoon and Doctor Stuart walked to the window. He tried _____ at the village, but the wind _____ the rain against the glass. He _____ a thing. He turned, walked to the fire and drank some more hot lemonade. He _____ no one _____ _____ for help—not tonight—especially, no one from the swamp. Doc Stuart _____ the swamp and its people. For many years he _____ their doctor. He _____ of the swamp and what heavy rains did to it. Green River _____ _____ toward the Mississippi, flooding all of the farm lands. "I _____ _____ no time to be sick," he said. "People _____ _____ me in this weather." He thought _____ . He had traveled from home to home, helping _____ and their children. Often he would travel _____ . He would get home _____ , have a cup of hot coffee, then be off to help some- one else. Here it was winter again, and he was sick, and there was no one to help _____ _____ —no one but young Doctor Hastings and old Doc Jones. No one knew _____ as he did. Surely young Doctor Hastings did not, he was just _____ . There was _____ at the door. Doc Stuart jumped _____ . "It has come," he said in a sad voice, but he had known it would come sooner or later, he had felt it _____ . He opened _____ .
There was Jason Tucker _____ .

FIGURE 5.9.   An example of a text in which parts of sentences are omitted

After the listening and reading skills have developed, the initial stages of writing instruction can begin. We wanted to focus on the anticipatory listening stage while we were engaging students in their first writing exercises, so we developed a modified form of the classic dictation exercise. We refer to it as the "fading dictation."

A cassette tape version would accompany the written text in which words or parts of words, such as the articles or the case endings, are absent. This practice goes another step toward building up anticipation of certain parts of speech. Exercises in which larger portions of the text are missing (see Figure 5.9) would follow. The prompts for writing are slowly faded away. First, the audio prompts for the missing words or phrases can be faded by lowering the volume. Second, the written text can be faded so that the student is required to write more and more of the text. The focus of these exercises is not on writing skills, but rather on building a more complete internal cognitive structure of the language through anticipatory listening.

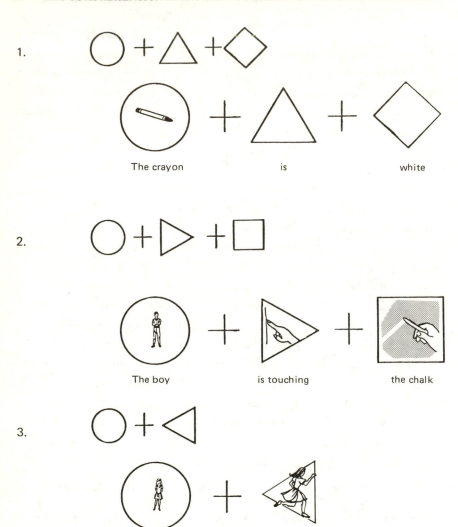

FIGURE 5.10.   Picture grammar form

These techniques were not fully satisfactory to us because they mixed language skills. We continued to look for a listening approach to Anticipatory Feed Forward that was independent of the other language skills. One technique, which seems to satisfy this requirement, is the picture grammar approach. It has two different versions. One is a picture grammar form which is illustrated in Figure 5.10. In this form, three basic "sentence types" are illustrated with pictures. What is involved is a way to learn to anticipate structural parts. For example, Figure 5.11 shows just one sentence type used to teach Japanese sentences that have a Subject–Object–Verb order. In Figure 5.11 the column of

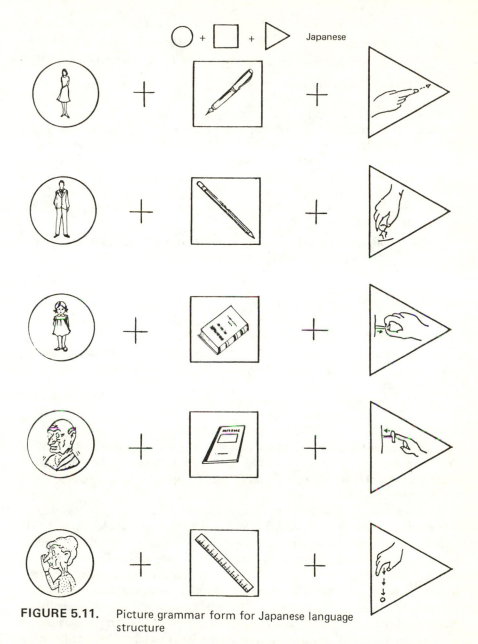

FIGURE 5.11.   Picture grammar form for Japanese language structure

circles depicts the subject or actor. The object is represented by the squares and the verb by the triangles. A person viewing this array would then be given several sentences which use the vocabulary of Figure 5.11. The student is to point to the appropriate picture as each sentence is expressed. The worksheet for this exercise is displayed in Figure 5.12.

1. The grandfather is pointing to the pencil.
2. The mother is picking up the notebook.
3. The daughter is pulling the pen.
4. The father is dropping the book.
5. The grandmother pushed the pen.
6. The father dropped the pen.

FIGURE 5.12.   Audio examples used with picture grammar form

Another technique uses picture cubes. Picture cubes are cubes with pictures on each face. The cubes are about the size of children's toy blocks (one and a half inches on each side). They can be made with heavy cardboard and tape or by modifying toy blocks. Each cube has pictures of a particular perceptual class. That is, it is either an object (noun), a property of objects (adjective), an action (verb), etc. The objects are also grouped according to categories, i.e., articles of clothing, foods. For example, a simple picture cube game could be played with four cubes as follows:

1. A noun cube contains pictures of the various members of the family: father, mother, son, daughter, grandfather, grandmother.
2. A second cube has pictures of the various actions a hand can do: pick up, drop, point to, touch, push, pull.
3. A third cube has pictures which contain objects that can be manipulated by hand: book, pen, pencil, notebook, ruler, crayon.
4. A fourth cube has different colors on each side.

A native speaker of the language can now say a wide range of sentences using the basic meanings depicted on these four blocks. A language learner might hear, for example:

"The mother picked up the blue book," or

"Grandfather dropped the brown ruler," or

"Push the book to the black mother."

The listener must listen to the sentence and anticipate each picture by holding the "total picture" in mind. He or she then manipulates each of the cubes to place the correct (corresponding) picture on the top face. All cubes need to be arranged in the proper order.

Another technique which has been tried and found useful in developing semantic anticipation is to carry on bilingual conversations (Mackey, 1971; Landis, 1978). The teacher speaks only in the target language, but the student can speak in whichever language he or she feels comfortable. Thus the teacher may speak in French, but, in the early part of training, the native language of the learner is used in response. The class can generally comprehend at least one half of the conversation. This procedure may encourage anticipation of the basic elements of the conversation. If the teacher is a native or near native speaker of French, students will always be hearing native French. They will not be spending half of the classtime listening to the poor pronunciation and grammatical misconstructions of their classmates, which is usually the case in classes in which speaking in the target language is emphasized. This type of bilingual conversation can also be used with language tutors who have a poor speaking ability in English. If the tutors can comprehend enough English to maintain a discussion, they can carry on a bilingual conversation. This way both the student and the tutor can increase their listening fluency in the new language while speaking in their own native tongue. It makes it easier on both parties, it develops the language competence through listening, and it is more interesting to both tutor and student because they can express themselves much better in their own tongue. Most importantly, they can discuss topics they are interested in, control the conversation more, and thus anticipate responses from other speakers.

Finally, we came up with a technique which is similar to looking up a name in a telephone directory. If you know what name you are looking for, if you anticipate seeing the name, you can skim quickly through the book and suddenly it appears.

This basic procedure gave rise to a number of exercises of which the following is an example. It involves telling time. A series of clocks is used (see Figure 5.13). Following the visual display of a clock, a student hears three or four different clock times spoken *rapidly*, only one of which is correct. For example, for clock number two, the student hears:

    a. "It's twelve o'clock."
    b. "It's twelve ten."
    c. "It's one o'clock."
    d. "It's two o'clock."

The student is to mark the letter (a, b, c, or d) he or she thinks is correct. Immediate feedback is provided for correct responses. In this case, the anticipation of the answer is similar to looking at the clock, thinking the time, and waiting to hear it.

Exercises of this type build up in the mind a readiness to speak. They build up an anticipation of what might be said when presented with a situation. It is a good start toward listening fluency and language competency, but it is not enough.

There are still chances for error. There are still possibilities that the cognitive map still has some flaws in it. These flaws tend to be undiscovered at this point because they may be unimportant to the receptive comprehension of the language, but they may be important when it comes to formulating an expression. For example, people who are passengers in a car may get a good orientation to the city if they pay attention, but it is not until they begin to drive that they find out they did not pay attention to some critical turns in the road. The same analogy may be true for the transfer of listening to speaking. We may find that expressive skill is not fully trained by experience in decoding and anticipatory feed forwarding.

One final phase seemed to suggest itself. When people begin to speak a new language, there is generally a class of errors that are made (Richards, 1974). By determining the errors of previous learners of a language, we can bring these errors to the attention of beginning language students and, perhaps, reduce their frequency. This is why we developed step three: *Discrepancy Feedback Phase.*

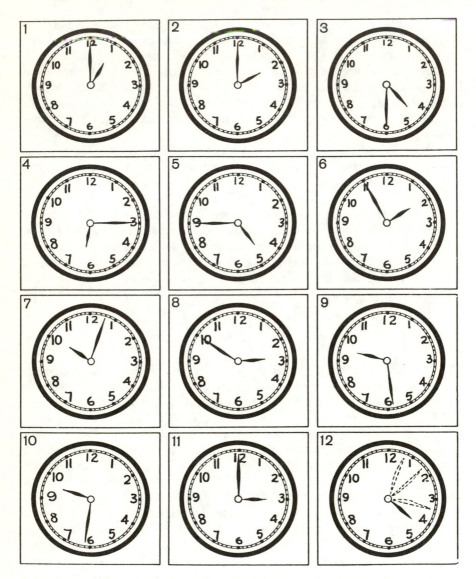

FIGURE 5.13.   Anticipatory feed forward form with clocks

STEP 3: DISCREPANCY FEEDBACK PHASE

The last phase follows the other two phases and introduces students to the discrepancy principle: the comparison of signals between what is anticipated and what is received. This phase has been referred to as the *error recognition* or *error detection* phase (Ingram et al., 1975). *Discrepancy feedback* seems to be a more accurate and inclusive term.

.The basic principle behind the *Discrepancy Feedback Phase* is the "sounds wrong" phenomenon. Whether reading a text or listening to a person speak, as native speakers (listeners) of the language we can detect discrepancies and errors because they sound wrong. We do not consciously analyze what we hear; we do not look for broken rules; we do not even differentiate between the written and spoken forms. Practice in listening has somehow built up in us an anticipation of what to expect, a monitoring device which detects whatever does not sound like we expect it to.

Many techniques previously described can be adapted to include discrepancy feedback as a part of an exercise. For example, Asher (1977, p. 23) points out:

> . . . Karen Bouldin from San Diego developed a procedure of "error detection" to increase the self-confidence of her students who were learning English.
>
> It goes this way. Not in the beginning, but as the training progressed, Bouldin would periodically utter a wrong command. For instance, with a book in her hand she would say, "Shirou, take this *glass* from my hand and put it on the table!" Instantly, students would spontaneously correct her with, "It's not a glass! It's not a glass! It's a book."

A wide range of jokes depends almost entirely upon the discrepancy detection mechanism. Puns are perhaps the most common joke format that twists receptive expectations. For example:

> Hungry girl: "Do you serve shrimps here!"
> Waiter: "Certainly; we cater to everyone."

> "Is your house warm?"
> "It ought to be. The painter gave it two coats last week."

> "What part of the car causes the most accidents?"
> "The nut that holds the wheel."

The person expects to hear one thing, but hears something else. Discrepancy signals flash, but are quickly subdued when it is recognized that the statement is not an error, but just was not expected. The joke is on the listener who was fooled, temporarily, into believing the speaker had committed an error in speech. When people understand jokes in a second language, they are well on the way to listening fluency.

In our development of self-instructional modules for teaching error recognition through independent study, we found the BABN tower mechanism (see Figure 5.14) to be quite useful, particularly when working in the purely audio area of error recognition. The name BABN comes from a technique for changing a question that has only two alternatives into a question format that has four choices. The alternatives are A and B but the choices are Both, A, B, Neither; hence the name BABN. The error recognition procedure was covered in a previous article (Nord, 1977) and will only be reviewed briefly here.

The procedure involves learning to make discriminations between correct and incorrect sequences. The first step is collecting a list of items. One set of errors commonly made by Japanese students of English is contained in *Improving Your Conversation* by Vernon Brown (1971). Also included is the correct version. It is obvious that some of these errors, while perhaps not grammatically incorrect, sound odd to a native speaker or are inappropriate for

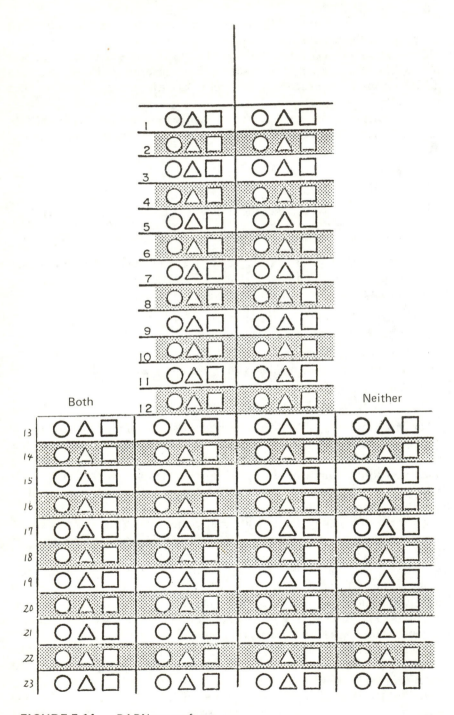

FIGURE 5.14.   BABN tower form

the meaning desired. An error is made most dramatic by placing it in contrast with the appropriate sentence. Rather than having the student simply read the correct and incorrect sentences, the student is asked to guess which sequence of each pair is correct, as he or she listens to them being spoken. Mechanically, a tape recording is made to provide the sound of the two alternative sentences. A BABN tower is impregnated with latent-image chemical to provide immediate feedback confirmation for the correct hypothesis. For example, in going through the program the student hears:

1. A. How are you?   B. How are you?
   Thank you.   Fine, thank you.

2. A. Let's discuss politics.   B. Let's discuss about politics.

3. A. What do you think about that?   B. How do you think about that?

4. A. Please once more.   B. What did you say?

5. A. It's not such a famous place.   B. It's not so famous place.

For each pair, the student chooses what he or she believes (or guesses) is the correct (or appropriate) sentence, i.e., the one that sounds right. The student marks with the latent-image pen in the correct circle and, if the student has guessed correctly, a black mark will appear. If not, no mark will appear and the student must try the other circle.

One particular error, which is incorrectly engrained in the brains of many Japanese students, is illustrated in sentence number four. The expression, "Please once more" is almost a direct translation of *Mo ichido itte Kudasai*, the Japanese expression for the occasion. It is reinforced by native speakers repeating what they have said, but it is not a native expression appropriate to the situation. Most English speaking people say B. "What did you say?" Most Japanese students will rub their latent-image markers over the circle representing A, "Please once more" until the marker goes through the paper, looking for the dot they "know" should be there. This set of pairs was repeated several times through the exercise. Personal experience has shown a marked reduction in general conversation of the expression "Please once more" and an increased use of the expression "What did you say?" by students who have gone through this error recognition exercise.

As the student proceeds down the BABN tower, the choices expand from two to four. The student is still provided only two sentences, A and B, but now must decide whether A sounds right, whether B sounds right, whether *both* sound right, or whether *neither* sounds correct. The increase in choices forces a greater degree of discrimination, increasing the likelihood of recognizing errors. In this particular format, the student listens to a total of seventy-two sentence pairs, going through the circles first, then the triangles, and finally the squares. The later pairs are spoken more rapidly and the pairs heard earlier are occasionally repeated to ensure a rapid and semi-automatic error recognition. The building of this type of self-monitoring system has proven very helpful in overcoming habitual errors common to a particular national group.

The drill just described is based upon an error analysis of actual mistakes made by Japanese learning English. Many of the errors are a result of interference from the Japanese language, and perhaps are accentuated by an early emphasis on speaking English before listening fluency is developed. There are also some intra-language patterns that create potential sources of interference for native speakers as well as for foreign language speakers.

A comparison of mistakes made by foreign language learners with those made by young children learning their native language points to some similarity between these two processes. Muskat-Tabakowska (1969) provides a few examples. The first set consists of sample utterances taken from two four-year-old English children. The second set consists of statements by adult Polish students studying English. The statements and types of errors are as follows (Muskat-Tabakowska, 1969, p. 47):

1. "She *maked* it bigger." (overgeneralization)
   "We learned him to say it." (distribution)
   "I've got a tractor *who* can move earth." (distribution)
   "Do you know what sometimes I do?" (word-order)

2. "He *leaved* the room." (overgeneralization)
   "I have *learned* him for two weeks." (distribution)
   "The film *who* was interesting." (distribution)
   "My mother asked me where was the book." (word-order)

There are other formats that can be used to add variety to the error recognition phase. Most focus attention on semantic errors. In their *Basic French*, Mueller and Niedzielski (1968) use an error recognition format with a basic true/false choice format. Using an immediate feedback chemical similar to the latent image, they expressed a number of statements and had students mark whether each statement was true or false. Another approach is to utilize a story within which each sentence is either correct, or incorrect, in grammatical or semantic form. The BABN tower technique has also been used to focus attention on accent recognition, minimal pair distinctions, intonation patterns, and so on.

Using the basic technique called vigilance tasking, several exercises in reading were developed first for the Justin Morrill intensive Russian program, and later for other language programs. The student was provided a cassette and an accompanying text which did not match the audio in all respects; an occasional word on the printed text was different from that on the cassette. By marking above each word on the text that did not coincide with the audio on the cassette, the student could tell how well he or she detected the discrepancy. Moreover, the number of discrepancies that should have been found was also indicated; that is, how many words the student should have overscored. These techniques lend themselves to teaching minimal phonemic pair distinctions.

This technique proved to be useful also in teaching spelling to native speakers (see Figure 5.15). The audio component was not needed for native speakers. A story was rewritten with an occasional word misspelled—often using the form of the common misspelling. Each student was asked to read the story, and mark

CAN YOU FIND THE MISSPELLED WORDS? READ THE FOLLOWING STORY AND WHEREVER YOU SEE
A WORD MISSPELLED, RUB GENTLY ABOVE THE WORD WITH THE LATENT IMAGE DEVELOPER PEN
AND YOU WILL SEE THE CORRECT SPELLING. AT THE END OF EACH PARAGRAPH, RUB THE BOX
IN THE LEFT MARGIN AND FIND OUT HOW MANY MISSPELLED WORDS WERE IN THE PARAGRAPH.
IF YOU DID NOT FIND THEM ALL--GO BACK AND LOOK SOME MORE. GOOD LUCK!

LAST SUMMER WE DICIDED TO ENTER THE CROSS-CHANNEL OUTBOARD MOTOR-

BOAT RACE. THERE WERE FOR OF US--DOUG, TED, PETE, AND MISELF. WE WERE

IN A SIXTEEN-FOOT MOTORBOT WITH TWO 100 HORSPOWER OUTBOARD MOTORS. THE

RASE WAS FROM LONDON TO CALAIS AND BACK TO LONDON AGAIN. IT'S A SPECIAL

RACE FOR BOT BUILDERS.

WE HAD A BAD START. AT GRAVESEND WON ENGIN DIED. WE FIXED THE

ENGINE, BUT LOST TEN MINUTES. SOON WE WER THE LAST OF 23 BOAT.

THEN CAME THE WIND. IT REALY HIT US. FROM THE NORTH SEA KAM HIGH

WAVES. THE BIG ENGINES ROARED. SOON WE PASED TWO BOATS. WE FOUGHT FOR

SPED. WE PASSED THREE BOATS. ALL OF THEM WERE IN TRUBLE AND FIGHTING

THE WAVES. WE SAW FIVE MOR BOATS RETURN TO LAND.

"WE CAN STILL WIN," SAID DOUG.

THE WIND AND SEA ROSE HIGHER. WE WERE ALMOST IN THE CHANNEL.

SUDDENLY A BIG WAVE HET US. THERE WAS A NEW SUND--SOMETHING WAS

BRAKING. WATER ROSE IN THE BOTE.

DOUG TURNED THE BOAT TOWARD LAND. BUT ONE ENGINE STOPPED.

FIGURE 5.15.   Chemically-based immediate feedback technology

above the words that he or she felt were misspelled. The correct spelling would
then appear in latent-image form. A box with the number of incorrect spellings in
each paragraph was also available to indicate how many words should have
been overscored. This particular exercise may be useful for teaching precision in
the reading of ideographs. It should then facilitate correct writing by building up
a recognition of potential errors one can make when writing.

With the completion of the Discrepancy Feedback Phase, listening fluency
will have developed to the point that speaking should develop spontaneously

and correctly, if our assumptions are correct. The practical techniques indicated are but the tip of the iceberg of what might be attempted by teachers with imagination.

SUMMARY

Listening fluency is not seen as a single, simple skill. It does not appear to be a skill learned by casually listening to the radio or television. In order to learn to understand a language rapidly and effectively, a number of requirements appear necessary. It seems necessary to develop attentive and retentive listening skills in hierarchical stages in order to develop a complete and accurate cognitive map. Carefully graded exercises need to be designed to ensure correct understanding every step along the way.

Listening fluency seems to involve at least three progressive phases. First, there is a Semantic Decoding Phase. The second listening fluency phase involves listening ahead or anticipating the next word or phrase or sentence. The third and final phase of listening fluency seems to involve discrepancy detection. After achieving listening fluency by progressing through these three stages of development, it is believed that a rather complete cognitive map will have been developed. It is also believed that a learner can then quickly achieve competence in the three other language skills. The speaking skills should come very rapidly without specific speaking instruction because the trained listening ear serves as a self-monitor. Reading is very similar to listening, and it is believed that in most cases simple reading skills can be achieved with only minimal additional training. Writing may take some additional training, but should proceed rapidly.

Notes

1.   This project was made possible by financial assistance from Justin Morrill College and the Educational Development Program at Michigan State University.
2.   This technique has been described in several articles by James J. Asher. It is also illustrated on film. One of these films, entitled *A strategy for second language learning*, is available on rental from the Instructional Media Center at Michigan State University and from Sky Oaks Productions, Dept. D, 19544 Sky Oaks Way, Los Gatos, California, 95030.
3.   For latent-image feedback technology, paper (A.B. Dick Latent Image Transfer Sheets, 97–1001) is impregnated with invisible chemical ink using a ditto machine. The images are made visible by applying another chemical (A.B. Dick Latent Image Developer, 97–3100) with a special felt-tip marker. Confirmation of the correct choice appears in the form of a large dot.
4.   Technology exists for time compressing speech, i.e., reducing the time allocated for recorded utterances. This involves electronically removing small segments into a continuous signal. The frequency of the recorded voice is not affected thereby. See, for example, F.F. Lee, "Time compression and expansion of speech by the sampling method," in the *Journal of the Audio Engineering Society, 20,* 1972, 738–742. Owing to the redundancy of human speech, recorded texts can be compressed as much as 40 to 50 percent without loss of intelligibility. Our view was that time-expanded speech would be helpful to the slower or beginning learner, while for the faster or more advanced learner compressed speech could be utilized to sustain challenge. Some compressed materials were prepared for our experiment, but they were not systematically utilized.

References

Arbib, M.A. *The metaphorical brain*. New York: Wiley-Interscience, 1972.

Asher, J.J. "The total physical response approach to second language learning." *The Modern Language Journal*, *53*, pp. 3–17, 1969.

———. "Children's first language as a model for second language learning." *The Modern Language Journal*, *56*, pp. 133–139, 1972.

———. *Learning another language through actions: The complete teacher's guidebook*. Los Gatos, Calif.: Sky Oaks Productions, 1977.

Bandura, A. *Social learning theory*. Englewood Cliffs, N.J.: Prentice-Hall, 1977.

Belasco, S. "Nucleation and the audio-lingual approach." *The Modern Language Journal*, *49*, pp. 482–491, 1965.

———. "C'est la guerre? or can cognition and verbal behavior coexist?" In R.C. Lugton (Ed.), *Language and the teacher: A series in applied linguistics*, Vol. 17: *Toward a cognitive approach to second language acquisition*. Philadelphia: Center for Curriculum Development, Inc., 1971.

Broen, P.A. "The verbal environment of the language-learning child." *American Speech and Hearing Association Monographs*, *17*, 1972.

Brown, V. *Improving your conversation*, Vol. 1. Tokyo: Meirindo Publishing Company, 1971.

Donchenko, A. Michigan State University CIEE Russian language program report. Unpublished manuscript, Michigan State University, 1972.

Ervin-Tripp, S. "An overview of theories of grammatical development." In D.I. Slobin (Ed.), *The ontogenesis of grammar*. New York: Academic Press, 1971.

Gaier, R. L. "Selected personality variables and the learning process." *Psychological Monographs, 66* (349), pp. 1–28, 1952.

Ingram, F., Nord, J., and Dragt, D. "A program for listening comprehension." *Slavic and East European Journal, 19,* pp. 1–10, 1975.

Lakoff, G. "The arbitrary basis of transformational grammar." *Language, 48,* pp. 76–87, 1972.

Landis, G. B. "Eureka! A surefire second language curriculum." *System, 6,* pp. 148–157, 1978.

Lee, F. F. "Time compression and expansion of speech by the sampling method." *Journal of the Audio Engineering Society, 20,* pp. 738–742, 1972.

Lenneberg, E. H. "Understanding language without ability to speak: A case report." *Journal of Abnormal and Social Psychology, 65,* pp. 419–425, 1962.

Ley, R., and Locascio, D. "Associated reaction time in language acquisition." Paper presented at the American Educational Research Association Annual Meeting, Chicago, April 1972.

Mackey, W. F. "Free language alternation in early childhood education." Paper presented at the Conference on Child Language, Chicago, November 1971. (ERIC Document Reproduction Service No. ED-060-755)

McClelland, D. C. "The role of educational technology in developing achievement motivation." *The affective domain: A resource book for media specialists*. Washington, D.C.: Communication Service Corporation, 1970.

Miller, G. A. "The magical number seven, plus or minus two: Some limits on our capacity for processing information." *Psychological Review, 63,* pp. 81–97, 1956.

Mueller, T. H., and Niedzielski, H. *Basic French*. Hull, Quebec: Intermedia, 1968.

Muskat-Tabakowska, E. "The notions of competence and performance in language teaching." *Language Learning, 12,* pp. 41–54, 1969.

Nord, J. R. "Error recognition as a self-monitoring skill." *System, 5,* pp. 158–164, 1977.

Osgood, C. E. "Psycholinguistics." In S. Koch (Ed.), *Psychology: A study of a science,* Vol. 6: Investigations of man as socius: Their place in psychology and the social sciences. New York: McGraw-Hill, 1963.

Postovsky, V. A. "Effects of delay in oral practice at the beginning of second language learning." Unpublished Ph.D. dissertation, University of California at Berkeley, 1970.

———. "Effects of delay in oral practice at the beginning of second language learning." *The Modern Language Journal, 58,* pp. 229–239, 1974.

Richards, J. C. *Error analysis: Perspectives on second language acquisition* London: Longman, 1974.

Rivers, W. *A practical guide to the teaching of French.* New York: Oxford University Press, 1975.

Schlesinger, I. M. *Sentence structure and the reading process.* The Hague: Mouton, 1968.

Taylor, W. L. "Cloze procedure: A new tool for measuring readability." *Journalism Quarterly, 30,* pp. 414-438, 1953.

Tosti, D. Personal communication, March 19, 1974.

Winitz, H., and Reeds, J. *Comprehension and problem solving as strategies for language training.* The Hague: Mouton, 1975.

CHAPTER 6

A Reconsideration of Comprehension and Production in Language Training*

Harris Winitz

Professor of Speech Science and Psychology
University of Missouri, Kansas City

What are the differences between the language teaching practices of today and those conducted prior to the Chomskian and Skinnerian revolutions? A representative authority of the 1950s is Helmer Myklebust, who, in a chapter published in the 1957 edition of the *Handbook of Speech Pathology,* devoted about four pages to treatment considerations. In these few pages he summarized the state of the art.

The term *inner speech* was distinguished from expressive and receptive language. Inner speech referred to the conceptual or cognitive experiences that underlie language. Receptive language referred to the recognition or understanding of language. Myklebust (1957, p. 527) expressed an interesting point in his 1957 chapter when he said,

> If expressive-language demands are made simultaneously with emphasis on receptive language, the total process and progress are confused and delayed.

Recently a similar remark was made by Wepman (1976, p. 135), motivated by his successful treatment of an aphasic patient:

> With this new concept stimulation takes the form of embellishment of thought. Removing the implied criticism of corrective therapy . . . in fact, in never asking for or trying in any way to elicit verbal expression.

Myklebust recommended expressive language training for children who did not develop language after having acquired inner and receptive language. His

---

*This chapter appeared in *Allied Health and Behavioral Sciences,* Volume 1, pp. 272–315, 1978, and is reprinted with the kind permission of the editors. Minor editorial changes and corrections of typographical errors were made by the author.

position was that expressive language will develop "reciprocally" with these two functions. In addition, he advocated "meaningful play situations" as a procedure to encourage the growth of expressive language.

In the past few years continued emphasis has been placed on the advancement of programmatic linguistics training procedures. Programmatic refers to the design of total training programs, which have as their form a basic plan of operation and several technological strategies for their achievement.

Bricker and Bricker (1974) refer to their language program as an "early language intervention system." Their program emphasizes the teaching of language within the framework of cognitive, social, and sensory motor development. Specific technological language training procedures, as discussed below, are provided within this general framework.

Hart and Risley (1976) employ the term *community-based language training.* Essentially the major emphasis here is on providing the language-deficient child with an environment that motivates the use of language with increasing frequency. Hart and Risley stress "incidental teaching," which refers to the use of language in instructional situations. However, formal language training techniques are also used, as indicated below.

Lee, Koenigsknecht, and Mulhern (1975) refer to their training program as "interactive language development teaching." In this program each child's functional capacity for language is carefully assessed. Then linguistic structures are taught through the use of stories and conversation. The sequencing of linguistic elements generally follows the order in which grammatical units are acquired by the normal speaking child.

Many other programmatic designs have been suggested which resemble to a large degree the three language teaching designs mentioned above. Each of these programs stresses careful initial testing, incidental and formal practice, and the use of developmental landmarks as goals for training. It may now be useful to outline specific technologies of language training.

Receptive Training

Receptive training is generally not ignored in most language training programs. It is often correlated or recommended to occur with sensory-motor and cognitive experiences (Bricker and Bricker, 1974; Cromer, 1974; Bloom, 1974; Miller and Yoder, 1974; Crystal, Fletcher, and Garman, 1976). However, there is no consensus with regard to how long receptive training should take place and how it is to be correlated with production training. There are two general practices that can be followed. When a clinician is convinced, through formal tests or observations, that the utterances or structures which are being trained are fully understood without contextual assistance, production practice can be initiated. A second and uncommon approach is to recognize that comprehension has been acquired and simply to continue the comprehension practice with more complex structures. This second approach will be emphasized as a preferred routine and will serve as the major theme of this chapter.

Production Training

The strategies used for production training are many and are often employed in combination with sensory-motor, cognitive, and receptive training. I will make some attempt to categorize these routines.

1. Imitation practice has been recommended by a number of investigators (Bricker and Bricker, 1974; Guess, Sailor, and Baer, 1974; Stremel and Waryas, 1974, for example). Not all investigators recommend that this technique be used in the same way. It can be used to develop elementary motor behaviors prior to receptive and productive experiences, or it can be used to elaborate upon emerging linguistic development. For example, Miller and Yoder stress "semantic" experience framed within the developmental order of linguistic structures for normal developing children, by "pairing of experience with lexical marker with imitative responses requested from the child," (Miller and Yoder, 1974, p. 521).

2. Prompting is another procedure used by many investigators to encourage production responses. A child may be asked to answer a question (Lee et al., 1975), complete a word upon hearing a sound (Hart and Risley, 1976), complete a sentence after being given the first word or the first few words (Bricker, 1972) or respond to forced alternative questioning (Crystal, Fletcher, and Garman, 1976).

3. *Conversational interaction* is a term I have invented to refer to the encouragement of spontaneous production through "dynamic" interchange of child and adult. This technique has been recommended by almost everyone who has written about language training (e.g., Muma, 1975; Bloom, 1974), in some form or another. Differences in approach reflect the theoretical framework of the investigators with regard to specific technologies. The teaching of production varies depending upon the techniques used to encourage "conversational interaction," and to what extent production is regarded as a sign of achievement.

Some investigators may regard a fourth technique as an instance of production training, namely paraphrasing or modelling. Here the clinician clarifies or elaborates upon a child's production. Later we will consider this technique within the framework of a model for comprehensive language training, since it appears to be a language comprehension rather than a language production technique. Sometimes it is recommended (Stremel and Waryas, 1974) that paraphrases be echoed, a form of imitation training.

Production, as we have defined it above through enumeration of techniques, is a procedure that directly demands the utterance of verbal responses. Often production responses are followed by reinforcing consequences, conversation, or some form of social interaction. Comprehension, as we use it here, refers only to understanding of language. Production is not demanded, although sometimes a child will indicate understanding through production.

Production and comprehension, then, refer only to the activities or processes that are employed to increase language skills. In this regard comprehension and production would be classified as performance activities through which competence can be taught.

Comprehension as an Active Process

Although comprehension and production may be distinguished as independent performance activities, there is strong theoretical support for regarding these two processes as related functions in the acquisition and use of language. In fact the current psycholinguistic position is not to regard comprehension as the passive counterpart of production.

A series of studies on ambiguous sentences indicates that subjects generally expect only one reading of an ambiguous sentence (Foss, Bever, and Silver, 1968; Carey, Mehler, and Bever, 1970). For example, the sentence, "They are visiting sailors" has two meanings, but generally only one interpretation is made by subjects, depending on whether the test sentence follows a series of sentences in which the "-ing" marks a verb or an adjective such as, "They are discussing paintings" or "They are performing monkeys" (Carey, Mehler, and Bever, 1970).

In most instances sentences or words that have the same phonetic form can be easily disambiguated by listeners because environmental and linguistic contexts generally restrict the range of grammatical and semantic meaning. Winitz, LaRiviere, and Herriman (1973) provide an example of linguistic confusion for acoustically ambiguous words. They found that when acoustically ambiguous key words or phrases were anticipated, sentential understanding was considerably reduced. Sentences such as the following were used in their investigation: "The *grocer* displayed such *green foods* as *heads* of cabbage and LET US (pronounced as [lɛrəs]) buy these items after closing the store." The four words in italics biased listeners to hear *let us,* the key word, as *lettuce.*

Anticipation unquestionably plays a heavy role in the comprehension of language. How is this prior knowledge used by the language comprehender? It has been proposed that listeners decode an incoming sentence, or portions thereof, by generating internally a putatively matching sentence (Stevens, 1972; Halle and Stevens, 1964).

This process has been described to work in the following way: First, the listener stores in immediate memory an incoming sentence; second, a sentence is generated from long-term storage; and, third, the generated sentence is compared with the received sentence. If the match is close, the linguistic and semantic components of the incoming sentence are given the interpretation of the generated sentence. If the comparator mechanism says the match is poor, additional sentences are constructed until a correct match is made.

It is believed that sentence interpretation occurs rapidly and without conscious effort. Yet there are circumstances under which we seem to have deliberate control of this process. We have all experienced the following phenomenon: We hear an unclear sentence; we ask for a repetition. The request is honored, but before the repetition is begun we have decoded the sentence.

The processes of comprehension and production may be regarded as essentially the same for mature speakers. According to the theoretical premises expressed above, production and comprehension are active processes and full knowledge of the linguistic structures of the language, as well as the circumstances under which the utterances take place, are employed in activating either system.

Acquisition of Language

It is generally recognized that cognitive development underlies the comprehension of language (see Clark, 1973b; Bowerman, 1976, 1978, for recent summaries of this literature). Although the conceptual basis for language development is of fundamentally theoretical importance, my comments will continue to be restricted to the relationship between comprehension and production of language. In particular I am interested in assessing the special roles of comprehension and production.

The most frequently asked question relating to comprehension and production pertains to the order of acquisition of these two performances. Ingram (1974) carefully constructs the several possible relationships between comprehension and production. He prefaces his argument by stating, "This chapter holds that comprehension does precede production, and that it could never be any other way" (Ingram, 1974, p. 313). Ingram (1974, p. 313) further contends:

> That *comprehension ahead of production is a linguistic universal of acquisition,* and that the empirical issues involved here are not this claim but rather the nature of comprehension and production and the gap between them.

The following comments rest heavily on Ingram's (1974) chapter and on statements contained in a monograph by Winitz and Reeds (1975). I will attempt to relate comprehension to production by initially making the assumption that comprehension precedes production, but that this relationship is often complex and difficult to assess and confirm.

Some Comprehension Must Precede Production

Ingram (1974) and Winitz and Reeds (1975) insist that some degree of comprehension must develop prior to production. The logic of this position is two-fold: (1) production implies understanding or internalization of the phonological, syntactic, semantic, and lexical systems, and (2) some level of production can occur when comprehension is not yet complete.

The channel for understanding is comprehension. When production is defined to mean a concurrent activity with comprehension training—imitation or verbalization of a motor activity, or an answer to a question—the channel for understanding continues to be comprehension.

There is no denying that memorized sentential routines can be established without their understanding, but this fact is not counter evidence to the position that to produce verbal language appropriately and consistently requires understanding of language relative to the level of production. As observed by Belasco (1965), the audio-lingual method of foreign language instruction provides students with a corpus of memorized "sentences," but there is no guarantee that meaningful production will follow. Belasco (1965, p. 483) comically noted that:

> It is true that students are capable of manipulating drills and memorizing dialogues to a very high degree of proficiency. Yet despite the ease with which they perform in this area, not many students can understand and speak the language *outside the ordinary classroom situation.*

Meaning or content has been recognized repeatedly as the primary mechanism that motivates the emergence of grammatical forms (Bloom, 1970; Brown, 1973; Bowerman, 1978). Brown (1973), for example, exhaustively catalogs the semantic domains for particles, such as *in* (containment) and *on* (support), for which meaning is the central component of acquisition.

It is now believed that production does not wait until there is full comprehension. Ingram (1974) refers to the findings on overgeneralization (Clark, 1973a, 1973b), and utilizes the theory of syntactic and semantic markers to explain the appearance of inappropriate production (such as "dada" for men in general). Similarly, Nelson's (1974) theory of functional "core" meanings can be used to explain partial comprehension and partial production. An example of partial understanding followed by inappropriate usage was told to me by a colleague of mine who reported that as a child the word "inventory" held for him the following meaning: "Father is away for two full days each year, returns late at night and is generally mad." It was not until his teenage years that he discovered the additional markers which define the adult concept of "inventory."

Anisfeld and Tucker (1967) examined the recognition of the singular-plural contrast. In one of their tasks, children were asked to choose the best (nonsense) name for a picture ((e.g. maj (singular) majex (plural)). In another task they were asked to select pictures that corresponded to a singular or plural form. Fewer errors were recorded in these conditions relative to one in which the child was presented with only one nonsense form, and was to select either a singular or plural picture. Coupled with these findings are Anisfeld and Tucker's report that children prefer a longer plural allomorph ("kren" as opposed to "k" appended to "waf," for example) to represent plural pictures ("wafkren" in preference to "wafk"). Other varieties of this technique suggested to Anisfeld and Tucker that before children fully learn the plural they learn an "extension rule" which marks plurals as longer than singulars. It is not surprising, then, to find children using nonadmissable extensions, such as [ʃuθ] (shoes) for [ʃu] (Miller and Ervin, 1964), [bukt] (books) for [buk], and [bɔkəld] (bottles) for [bɔkəl] (Smith, 1973). Admittedly, some of the above "plurals" may reflect articulatory constraints, a point we will consider shortly.

Vygotsky (1962), Menyuk (1969), Clark (1973a, 1973b), Nelson (1974), Ingram (1974), and Winitz and Reeds (1975) speculate that production may reflect only a subset of the total number of functional or grammatical features which adults use to describe a particular linguistic unit or communicative event.

As an example consider the German definite article, which is defined by gender, number, and case, and like English reflects a range of semantic dimensions relative to the indefinite article, as discussed by Brown (1973) and Maratsos (1974). The features governing the use of the definite article are not learned simultaneously. Leopold (1949, p. 79) observed irregularity in his daughter's use of this grammatical unit and commented:

> Most commonly it is *die* for all cases and genders, even in German songs, where the article seems to be the only difficulty. It is not clearly perceived on account of its lack of importance. I do not instruct her on this point.

Similarly Clark (1973b) found that the locations "in," "on," and "under" are marked differently for young children than for adults. She speculated that these prepositions are marked (+ locative), but differ along other dimensions from an adult's conceptualization.

Regardless of the theoretical orientation one takes with regard to the strategies children use to acquire concepts, lexical items, and grammatical units, it is generally agreed that linguistic growth will reflect the complexity of the concepts and the linguistic codings relative to a particular child's "cognitive" maturity (Slobin, 1971; Bloom, 1973; Clark, 1973a, for example). Given that a child's comprehension and production are not constrained by the above considerations, it does not necessarily follow that overgeneralization or over-extension provides evidence for or against comprehension preceding production or for comprehension preceding production for subsets of linguistic units.

Inappropriate production may be observed to occur because there is partial comprehension of a specific grammatical form or unit, or because of performance constraints on production, when comprehension is adequate (see Bowerman, 1978). Overgeneralizations, however, can be used, as Ingram (1974) so ably indicates, as evidence to counter claims that production begins only after there has been complete comprehension of a linguistic form or construction, or that production precedes comprehension.

The growth from partial comprehension to full comprehension may reflect a number of factors. Excluding cognitive and experiential constraints, Winitz and Reeds (1975), have lumped these factors under the category of saliency. A child, they postulate, will primarily alter the comprehension (understanding) of a particular linguistic unit when it no longer functions in a consistently meaningful way.

It has been commonly recognized that young children will omit "is" in the progressive saying "the cat eating" for "the cat is eating" even though "is" may appear in other constructions, e.g., "that is" (Brown, 1973). Omission of "is" will cause little difficulty in communication because extra-linguistic cues, in addition to a parent's understanding of a child's frame of reference, will clearly indicate meaning. At some point in a child's linguistic career the omission of "is" will cause communicative difficulty. This difficulty will cause it to become a salient grammatical unit to the child. The use of "is" is important in understanding the following pairs of sentences or segments:

The cat is eating.
Is the cat eating?

The cat eating the fish . . .
The cat is eating the fish.

The man is the agent, and the lady . . .
The man, the agent and the lady . . .

The boy pushed . . .
The boy is pushed.

It is true that for the above examples additional linguistic cues, as well as nonlinguistic cues, may often be used to indicate meaning. However, for an individual child on a particular occasion, these additional cues may not be available, or when available they may not be understood, perhaps, because they have not yet been acquired by the child. Hearing, for example, "The boy is pushed . . ." and interpreting it as "The boy pushed . . ." will cause processing difficulties, as indicated above in our discussion of "active perception." Thus, when linguistic constructions are introduced in teaching for the first time without sufficient "back-up" cues, it is not to be expected that there will be complete mastery in comprehension or production.

The development of saliency for a new linguistic unit may come about in a number of ways. A child may simply not understand a communication or a command. Or, possibly, his or her utterance will be unclear to a parent, adult, or another child.

A child will not always correct him/herself after a miscommunication. In fact, it would be surprising if that occurred. Failure in communication will simply alert a child to listen more attentively, to reassess the situation and to step up his or her "hypothesis testing." Initially, certain linguistic units, like "is," are not salient. Later, however, they become salient because they are essential elements for understanding communication, simply because communication becomes more complex. According to our perspective, then, the psychological channel for language learning is comprehension; production, when it occurs, simply contributes to the communication process, but it is not the primary channel for language acquisition.

Timing Consideration

We do not regard the process of comprehension as instantaneous. This point was made before when summarizing research on feature acquisition. However, our comments here pertain equally to specific features and to conceptual wholes. Prior to full comprehension, whether a feature or feature complex, there is postulated to be a period of recognition learning during which the particular linguistic unit is in the process of being acquired. Further, the interval over which recognition learning takes place can be short, in some instances as short as a single trial. Admittedly, one can generate a number of theoretical positions by reference to the memory literature, to explain the role of recognition learning in comprehension, but they will not be discussed here.

There are instances, cited by investigators, that seem to reflect recognition learning, in that comprehension is reported as complete for a unit or feature of a unit, and yet production is not observed. Bloom (1970) noted that during the two-word stage, utterances of the type: agent-action, agent-object, and action-object occurred, indicating that comprehension of agent-action-object had developed. Webster and Ingram (1972) observed instances of correct under-standing of personal pronouns prior to their use in spontaneous speech. Early words are reported by Nelson (1973), Huttenlocher (1974), and Sachs and Truswell (1976), to be understood before they are observed to occur in produc-tion. Winitz and Reeds (1975) observed that students learning a foreign language could identify foreign words or phrases but often could not recall a single sound.

The ability to comprehend pieces of a language without being able to recall them can be given various explanations. Huttenlocher (1974, p. 365) expresses it in the following way:

> The gap between receptive and productive language might derive from *incomplete storage of the sounds* of the words. That is, certain words might be sufficiently familiar to be recognized but not produced.

One interpretation of Huttenlocher's proposal is that a trace must be sufficiently strong before there is recall through verbal production. A second interpretation which can be made relates to the accessing or retrieval of stored information. Failure for production to emerge when there is certainty that partial or complete comprehension has been achieved may be an instance where one or more search strategies fail. Grammatical units may be in storage, but there is a restriction on their easy retrieval.

Experimental Considerations in the Testing of Comprehension

Beginning with Brown, Fraser, and Bellugi (1964), authors have commented on performance constraints as possible reasons for the lag between production and comprehension. Bloom (1970), as indicated above, was the first to note that children who produce two-word utterances know more about the underlying structure of sentences than might be inferred from a distributional analysis. Yet there has been difficulty in establishing experimental verification that compre-hension antedates production under vigorously controlled experimental condi-tions. Initially, the matter seemed to be solved by the classic study by Fraser, Bellugi, and Brown (1963). Their findings indicated that comprehension clearly preceded production for ten linguistic constructions.

In 1972 Fernald challenged the method of scoring used by Fraser et al. (1963). Each production task was scored by Fraser et al. according to minimal features that would be necessary for a correct response in the comprehension assessment. For example, whereas Fraser et al. (1963) required subjects to say *boys draw* or *boy draws* for the item to be scored correct, Fernald (1972) counted the item correct if "boy" or "boys" was used correctly, independent of the verb production. Note that for the contrast "The boy draws—The boys draw," correct comprehension could be made from the noun form alone.

With the revised scoring procedure Fernald (1972) found that the percentage of correct responses across items was 78 for production and 72 for comprehension, in contrast to 48 and 67 respectively, for Fraser et al. (1963). The revised scoring procedure of Fernald suggests a slight (but not significant) edge to production. Noteworthy is the fact that the high percentage of correct responses indicates that these particular linguistic constructions were almost completely acquired by the subject sample, which averaged three and one half years of age. In effect a ceiling was placed on their performance precluding an adequate test of a comprehension-production difference.

Another problem in the assessment of comprehension with young students is that the task may far exceed in difficulty the level of complexity that subjects use in production. For example, de Villiers and de Villiers (1973) noted that young children (those with a morpheme level, MLU, of 1.00–1.50) may not be able easily to decode sentences of the type "Make the dog bite the cat" when their output averages less than two words.

As mentioned by Baird (1972) and others, there is also the continuing problem of equating the probability of performance for the widely different tests of comprehension and production. At present there seems to be only one solution to this problem, as well as problems imposed by ceiling effects, imparting instructions to subjects, and scoring procedures. The recommendation is to classify children according to a performance level on comprehension, and then to observe production in both formal and informal (spontaneous speech) situations. Fraser et al. (1963) reported task performance for individual subjects; however, a design by Eilers and Oller (1976), initially applied to phonetic responses, appears to be excellent for this purpose.

It has long been reported that children with articulation errors evidence a deficit in discrimination (Winitz, 1969). Also it has been noted that some children demonstrate good auditory discrimination when production is impaired, motivating Locke and Kutz (1975) to conclude that production errors without associated discrimination errors is counter evidence to the claim that these two functions are related. Eilers and Oller (1976), after detailed testing, classified their children into:

$$
\begin{bmatrix} -\text{discrimination} \\ -\text{production} \end{bmatrix} \quad \begin{bmatrix} +\text{discrimination} \\ -\text{production} \end{bmatrix} \quad \begin{bmatrix} -\text{discrimination} \\ +\text{production} \end{bmatrix} \begin{bmatrix} +\text{discrimination} \\ +\text{production} \end{bmatrix}
$$

Within the framework of this paper, only group three above would be regarded as logically impossible. Instances of children's response categories falling within this group were infrequent, no doubt reflecting subject variability common to all testing situations.

The group marked $\begin{bmatrix} +\text{discrimination} \\ -\text{production} \end{bmatrix}$ is of theoretical interest not only

because it seems to demonstrate that comprehension precedes production, but because it indicates that achievement in discrimination may not always affect a change in production. In this chapter we have considered two possibilities to account for this observation. First, it may reflect a timing constraint; that is, the development of phonetic saliency is too recent to affect a change in production. Second, it may mean that the items have been salient for some time, but there is difficulty in their accessibility. Both of these issues have been raised above and will be considered again in our discussion of clinical routines for the acquirement of linguistic constructions.

The remaining two groups:

$$\begin{bmatrix} -\text{discrimination} \\ -\text{production} \end{bmatrix} \text{ and } \begin{bmatrix} +\text{discrimination} \\ +\text{production} \end{bmatrix}$$

call attention to the fact that for particular linguistic constructions comprehension may not be found to precede production simply because both skills *have not* yet been learned, or both skills *have* been learned. Therefore, in order to demonstrate that comprehension precedes production it is essential to locate that point in time, for a particular subset of children, and for a particular linguistic construction, after which learning has begun, but is not yet complete. The critical time interval will vary for children and linguistic units, as the research of Shipley, Smith, and Gleitman (1969) and Ehri (1976), among others, would suggest.

Disputations regarding the precedence of comprehension, and the interrelationships between comprehension and production cannot be resolved easily. Inherent in any testing are response biases which may be difficult to anticipate. For example, a child may use semantics or nonlinguistics cues when responding appropriately to distorted word order or to sentences in general (Wetstone and Friedlander, 1973; Clark, 1973a; Strohner and Nelson, 1974; Donaldson and McGarrigle, 1974). Therefore, the testing situation may exaggerate or underestimate performance in comprehension relative to production.

Brown (1973) reports an interesting attempt to test the comprehension of plurals with minimal pairs, such as "Give me the pencil—Give me the pencils." Brown (1973, p. 331) disappointedly commented:

> Well after they had attained criterion in spontaneous speech the children had failed to respond in a consistently correct way to the controlled inquiry.

Brown surmised that the testing situation or experimental materials may have thrown off . . . "the child's usual comprehension processing routine." Almost all would agree with Brown that the testing situation, either naturalistic or experimental, may critically determine the inferences and conclusions of serious investigative research. Differing experimental procedures led Bloom (1973) and Horgan (1976) to hold opposite positions regarding a child's understanding of syntactic order in the early one-word stage. Bloom (1973) obtained her data in naturalistic settings, observing that the order of successive one-word units was variable and, therefore, unreflective of English syntax. Horgan (1976) examined children in an experimental setting and obtained many instances of correct syntactic ordering and noted that deviate instances in ordering seemed to reflect individualistic attention to certain elements and objects. Horgan concluded that factors of focus, saliency, and interest may determine single-word ordering in the one-word stage. Her findings are in agreement with Huttenlocher (1974) who observed that children understand short contrastive sentences free of contextual or situational influences. Huttenlocher's findings were, in general, replicated by Sachs and Truswell (1976).

That an experimental design can influence one's interpretation relative to the comprehension-production issue is strengthened by a comparison of two recent studies which explore children's development of the deictic verb pairs *come/go* and *bring/take* (Clark and Garnica, 1974; Richards, 1976). The results are even more surprising in view of the differences in the subjects' ages, as we will see below. In order to test the understanding of these two verb pairs, Clark and Garnica (1974) devised a procedure that involved questioning the correctness of usage for subjects between six and nine years of age. On the other hand Richards (1976) developed a procedure in which a simulation of a conversational sequence was developed for children between the ages of four and about seven and one half years. Using animals and spatial enclosures as goals (house, barn, etc.), Clark and Garnica placed two animals outside a goal reference and one inside a goal reference. For the contrast *come/go* one item would have a bear in a small fenced garden with a dog and a rooster outside the garden. The experimenter would then say, "The dog says: Can I come into the garden? Which animal is he talking to?" In this case a correct determination would be the bear (the addressee). A speaker reference was also used for *come,* as in "Which animal can say to the dog, Come into the garden?" *Go* was similarly tested.

In contrast to Clark and Garnica's (1974) explicit testing of the subjects' linguistic knowledge of these verbs, Richards (1976) arranged for production responses by clever implementation of interesting communicative situations. For example, one segment of the *come/go* contrast was assessed in the following way. The subject, experimenter (E) and toy bear were in their respective houses. The child was instructed, "Let's play like people visiting each other. Call up E (by name) and see if she can visit you." A typical response by the child was, "Can you come to my house?" For *go,* the child would be told, "It's time for you to be home now, tell the bear what you have to do." The procedure employed by Richards (1976) produced acquisition curves which demonstrated significantly earlier development of these verb pairs than was obtained by Clark and Garnica (1974). It is possible to construe the procedures of Clark and Garnica as a comprehension task and that of Richards as a production task. Therefore a conclusion that might be drawn, but would be incorrect, is that production precedes comprehension.

Yet in one investigation, the conclusion that production precedes comprehension was offered by Chapman and Miller (1975), who examined young children's ability to understand and produce short sentences. Focusing on the correctness of word order, they tested children who were roughly between two and two and one half years of age and who had a mean length of utterance ranging from 1.53 to 3.11. In order to test word-order skills in sentences such as "The girl is carrying the dog," as well as its reversed version, "The dog is carrying the girl," Chapman and Miller (1975) included all four possible combinations of animacy for subject and object. Below, + refers to animate, − to inanimate, and S_i to sentence number.

	S_1	S_2	S_3	S_4
Subject:	+	+	−	−
Object:	+	−	+	−

Comprehension was tested by having each child select the relevant toy from among six and perform the activity stated by the examiner. For the production assessment the examiner performed an action which was to be described by the child. Some sentences were largely improbable, as instanced above, and not necessarily correlated with the animacy of the subject-object combinations. Although the subject-object relation of +animate –animate produced the highest (94) average percentage comprehension score and –animate +animate the lowest (50), as might be expected from our knowledge of children's early sentences (Brown, 1973), performance on the other two subject-object combinations was generally poor, about 65 percent.

Comprehension was actually higher than production for the +animate –animate subject-object combination. This result was especially clear for the lower aged children. Conceivably, as the authors later conceded, the children may have been responding to what they regarded as the experimenter's intent rather than to what they actually heard. This possibility is raised simply because the –animate +animate subject-object combination, which produced the highest percentage of errors, contained a set of sentences which are highly improbable and, perhaps, nongrammatical (e.g., the truck is carrying the boy). In other investigations it has been found that young children are largely insensitive to word reversals as long as meaning can be conveyed (de Villiers and de Villiers, 1972, 1973; Wetstone and Friedlander, 1973; Bushnell and Aslin, 1977).

Chapman and Miller (1975) also found that, when tested in production, correct use of the grammatical subject averaged nearly the same across all subject-object combinations of animacy. On the other hand, verb-object combinations seemed to reflect recency in short-term memory. Only two of the three elements of a subject-verb-object string, produced in correct order, was necessary to obtain a correct production score. Verb-object utterance types were the most frequent (60 percent as opposed to 22 percent for the subject-verb-object strings). It is as though the production assessment was a short-term memory task in which the subject was asked to verbalize an observed activity and was in many instances only able to recall the last part of it. This production task is decidedly less difficult than being asked to perform an activity from a verbal command, the technique used to assess comprehension. It is well known that the size of the computational lexicon will determine the level of learning, recall, and intelligibility (Miller, Heise, and Lichten, 1951).

Comparisons between comprehension and production are difficult indeed. Resolution awaits additional investigations. In the meantime it is incumbent upon those who speculate that encoding is in advance of decoding to formulate plausible reasons why a grammar of production "would not necessarily share the same linguistic competence" (Chapman and Miller, 1975, p. 369) as a grammar of comprehension. It should be remembered also that in our discussion performance constraints have been suggested to account for the advance of comprehension over production, as well as incomplete (partial) comprehension learning. However, Chapman and Miller have speculated about a different linguistic competence for the performance activities of comprehension and production.

Role of Comprehension in Semantic-Syntactic Development

With the intensity with which developmental language investigations have been pursued in the last ten years, one might expect that more would be known regarding specific communicative factors that encourage language growth. There is general consensus that parental simplification of linguistic structures encourages language growth (Snow, 1972, 1977; Broen, 1972; Philips, 1973; Fraser and Roberts, 1975; Longhurst and Stepanich, 1975), although the dynamics of the simplification process are really unknown.

Regarding communicative interaction there is the important finding by Brown and Hanlon (1970) that parents respond primarily to the "truth value" of their children's utterances. They did not find that the frequency of parental disapproval and nonsequiturs was correlated with syntactic correctness. Winitz and Reeds (1975) inferred that responding to the truth-value of children's utterances is essentially reducible to a comprehension learning experience. Inappropriate responding will cause a child to "rethink" his or her utterance. Eventually the rethinking will be reflected in production. Winitz and Reeds (1975) concluded that possibly all of the many production-type tasks (e.g., paraphrasing, questions, forced imitations, prompting) can be construed as a form of comprehension training and, therefore, all language acquisition is through the comprehension mode. Whitehurst (1977) also seems to hold this general position.

Reaching beyond the developmental literature into the rehabilitation literature, the comprehension-production issue continues to be of singular importance. There are many interesting studies in this area; however, we shall present only those which are directed to the major theme of this chapter.

Systematic use of comprehension teaching has been found to be a successful procedure for the acquirement of linguistic knowledge, even for subjects with intellectual deficits (Baer and Guess, 1971). Yet the question remains, what is the role of production training and how should it be combined with comprehension practice?

In an early investigation, Guess (1969) trained two mongoloid children to discriminate between singular and plural objects. Following this training the subjects learned to produce plural endings with minimal imitation practice. This study and others like it motivated two interesting studies with normal children by

Ruder, Smith, and Hermann (1974) and Ruder, Hermann, and Schiefelbush (1977). As can be easily guessed, the issue in training related to the order of training and interrelationship between comprehension and production.

In the first investigation Ruder et al. (1974) trained subjects to comprehend or imitate (imitate without meaning—that is, without presentation of pictorial items) Spanish nouns. Essentially there were three experimental conditions: (1) comprehension only, (2) imitation training following comprehension training, and (3) comprehension training following imitation training. Production was tested by asking for the names of the pictorially presented items. Continued comprehension training produced very few correct production responses. The other two conditions resulted in spontaneously correct production responses; however, imitation following comprehension generally resulted in a greater number of correct production responses than comprehension following imitation.

Before we conclude that effective language training should involve practice in both comprehension and imitation, it is important to note that the response criterion used in this study included articulatory proficiency as well as production. Subject responses were judged in terms of "acceptable and identifiable approximation to the Spanish label . . ." (Ruder et al., 1974, p. 21). Imitation may have proved to be effective here because the comprehension task did not require precise discrimination of phonological contrasts, simply because the inventory of training items was small.

The second Ruder et al. investigation (1977) again demonstrated that production did not improve substantially until imitation training began. In some instances the effect of imitation training was dramatic. Production was seen to improve almost spontaneously, after imitation training was initiated, in agreement with the findings of Guess (1969).

In 1965 Winitz and Preisler conducted a discrimination experiment in which the "comprehension" required was directly related to the production for children who on pretest uttered [skr] for [sr] in the context [srəb]. When the discrimination training was contrastive and related (/skr-sr/), spontaneous improvement in production was noted, in contrast to irrelevant discrimination training (/sl/-/ʃl/).

Ruder et al. (1977) suggested that their findings support Asher (1972) and Winitz and Reeds (1975) who posit that comprehension training is essential for language acquisition. They contend, however, that their findings do not support the "strong" claim made by Winitz and Reeds (1975) that comprehension training will spontaneously result in correct production responses.

The position held by Winitz and Reeds (1975) was made with regard to the learning of a natural language system where the linguistic contrasts are subtle and intricate, and where all contrasts have been made available to the subject. When tests of the comprehension–production issue are experimentally implemented, careful consideration of the range of contrastiveness needs to be made. Often a subset of comprehension tasks will not provide enough exposure to and experience of the relevant contrasts to produce precise (or correct) responses in production. However, the issue regarding the need for imitative practice still remains controversial and will be explored further in the section on language training strategies.

EXPERIMENTAL INVESTIGATION

In an effort to provide for control over the contrasts in comprehension training, a miniature experiment was conducted. The effect of four different training procedures on the acquisition (production) of past-tense markers for strong verbs was investigated. The four training procedures were imitation, comprehension, and two types of paraphrasing, elaboration with contrasts present, and elaboration without contrasts present. The purpose of this investigation was to compare training procedures when the contrast was present. A second objective was to determine whether production would develop without any direct training in production for children who have achieved normal articulatory development.

Experimental Materials

Two sets of strong verbs served as the experimental materials. One set, designated verb group a, consisted of verbs that formed the past tense by changing the vowel [ɪ] to [æ]. Included in this set were the following five verbs: drink:drank; sing:sang; sink:sank; ring:rang; swim:swam. A second set, denoted verb group b, consisted of five verbs for which the past tense is formed by changing the vowel [i] to [ɛ], and for which four of the verbs add a final [t] marker. The five verbs were: leave:left; feel:felt; sweep:swept; feed:fed; sleep:slept.

Baseline Assessment

The past tense of the following seventeen regular verbs

play	pour
cry	crawl
jump	close
bake	paint
fish	knit
bump	rest
rob	weed
fan	plant
	add

and the ten irregular verbs was assessed by presenting to each subject in random order a pictorial representation of present and past activity, simultaneously displayed (see Figure 6.1, for example). The examiner pointed to the present tense and said, "Today they _____ (e.g., "drink"); yesterday they _____ (e.g., "drank").

FIGURE 6.1.   An example of present and past activity

After this initial testing, subjects were assigned to verb group *a* or verb group *b*. To be assigned to group *a* or group *b* a subject had to have pronounced incorrectly the past tense form of all five test verbs, either *a* or *b*, but not necessarily *a* and *b*. The vowel was carefully examined in the past tense form and a subject was not included if the vowel was produced correctly regardless of the pronunciation of the other phonemes. We will later refer to this assessment as lenient scoring.

Baseline assessment is indicated in Table 6.1. This table shows that the average performance on the regular verbs falls short of the maximum possible score of seventeen. On the average, however, these findings indicate that mastery of the regular past tense inflection has essentially been accomplished. Also the findings in Table 6.1 reflect the fact that the subjects in each verb group demonstrated limited facility with the past tense inflections of the other irregular verb set.

Table 6.1   Baseline Performance: Average Correct Regular Verbs and Average Correct Non-Trained Irregular Verbs

Groups	Verb Group a [I-æ]		Verb Group b [i-ɛ]	
	Regular Verbs	[i-ɛ] Verbs	Regular Verbs	[I-æ] Verbs
Imitation	14.60	1.27	14.20	.33
	(2.39)	(1.34)	(2.34)	(.87)
Comprehension	14.00	1.00	12.40	.73
	(2.53)	(.97)	(2.82)	(1.29)
Elaboration-different	13.73	1.53	12.40	1.00
	(3.43)	(1.36)	(2.15)	(1.51)
Elaboration-same	15.33	1.07	13.13	.80
	(2.12)	(.85)	(2.60)	(1.56)

Subjects

Subjects were selected from the first grade of several elementary schools (CA = 85, SD = 4.0 months) and randomly assigned to experimental groups. Each group contained eight boys and seven girls. All subjects were white with normal intelligence (> 90 IQ) and hearing, monolingual speakers of English, and without a speech disorder or physical abnormality.

Training

All groups received training on three successive days. On each day four instances of the present and past tense form of each of the five verbs were presented. The experimental arrangement segmented the training into four instructional blocks within which each verb contrast (present and past) appeared once. In each block the ten verb contrasts appeared in random order. Thus, on each day of training each verb contrast, present and past, occurred four times on each of three days or a total of twelve times throughout the training. Each verb was elicited in the third person plural so that tense would be marked only by the vowel change. For example, for "he rings:he rang" both a vowel and an [s] mark the present, and the absence of [s] and a vowel mark the past; however, for the pair "they ring:they rang" a vowel contrast marks the difference.

Groups aa and 1b: Imitation

Subjects were presented with contrasting pictures and were instructed to repeat the examiner's sentence. On each day of training the present tense utterance for the first block was: Today they _____ (e.g., "sleep"), and the past tense utterance was: Yesterday they _____ (e.g., "slept"). On the second block the present tense was: Now they _____ , and the past tense was: They just _____ . On the third and fourth blocks the present and past utterance to be imitated was: They _____ . The examiner responded "right" to correct responses and "wrong" to incorrect responses.

Group 1a was trained on the [ɪ] - [æ] verb contrast, and group 1b was trained on the [i] - [ɛ] verb contrast. The letters a and b are used to mark the same verb contrasts for all remaining groups.

Groups 2a and 2b: Comprehension

Subjects were presented with contrasting pictures and were instructed to point to the correct picture. The examiner's utterances were identical to those for group 1; however, the subjects were instructed not to repeat the sentences. Responses were confirmed as correct or incorrect, as indicated for group 1.

Groups 3a and 3b: Elaboration—Different

Subjects were presented with contrasting pictures and were stimulated to respond to one of two pictures by the examiner's question "What happens here?" or "What happened here?" Following each child's response the examiner responded with a paraphrase, using the same phrases for block one and two as in groups 1 and 2. For blocks three and four elaborative phrases were used, such as, "The fathers feed the boys because it's faster; They slept until the alarm rang; They swim together because it's fun; They sank to the bottom of the ocean."

Groups 4a and 4b: Elaboration—Same

Training for groups 4a and 4b was identical to group 3 with the exception that only one picture was presented at a time. The subjects in this group were unable to observe simultaneously the verb contrast.

Retest and Retention

Each subject was tested following the third day of training, and after an interval of one week. This second assessment (one week later) was designated the retention test. Only one block (one instance of each present and past form) was assessed during retest. However, retention was assessed by presenting three blocks or three opportunities to recall. For both retest and retention the examiner pointed to the picture and said "They _____" and the subject was to fill in the correct word. No confirmation of correct responses was provided during these two assessments.

Results

The findings for both verb groups for the four conditions are presented in Table 6.2. Both stringent and lenient scoring was used. If all phonemes of a verb in their correct order, that is, an exact pronunciation, were uttered correctly the stringent criterion was satisfied. Only the vowel needed to be uttered correctly for the lenient criterion to be satisfied. (e.g., [slɛp] for "slept," [dræŋ] for "drank" and [fɛdəd] for "fed."

Significance between groups was assessed by the Mann-Whitney U-test. For the [ɪ]-[æ] contrast the only significant difference at retest (stringent and lenient) was between the comprehension and the elaboration-same groups (p < .05), although the scores for the comprehension group were above those of the two other groups. The comprehension and elaboration-same groups also differed significantly for the first (lenient) and third (stringent) blocks of the retention test. All differences favored the comprehension groups.

For the [i]-[ɛ] contrast, as can be observed in Table 6.2, none of the differences for this verb contrast was significant.

Discussion

The results of this miniature verb training session are largely inconclusive with regard to type of training. However, an interesting finding is that "production" practice is not essential to improvement in production, as the comprehension

Table 6.2   Retest and Retention Averages

Groups	Retest	Retention 1	Retention 2	Retention 3
		1	*2*	*3*
		[I-æ]		
Imitation				
Stringent	3.80 (1.83)	3.33 (1.89)	3.33 (2.07)	3.13 (2.06)
Lenient	3.81 (1.83)	3.33 (1.89)	3.27 (2.02)	3.20 (2.07)
Comprehension				
Stringent	4.20 (1.33)	4.00 (1.75)	4.40 (1.31)	4.40 (1.31)
Lenient	4.60 (0.61)	4.13 (1.75)	4.47 (1.31)	4.47 (1.31)
Elaboration-different				
Stringent	3.53 (1.67)	3.87 (1.63)	3.67 (1.85)	3.80 (1.76)
Lenient	3.60 (1.62)	4.07 (1.44)	4.00 (1.54)	4.00 (1.71)
Elaboration-same				
Stringent	2.67 (1.96)	2.87 (1.89)	3.00 (2.00)	2.67 (1.92)
Lenient	3.13 (1.67)	3.27 (1.65)	3.13 (2.09)	3.00 (2.00)
		[i-ɛ]		
Imitation				
Stringent	2.27 (1.44)	2.47 (1.93)	2.80 (2.04)	2.93 (2.05)
Lenient	2.60 (1.58)	2.87 (1.89)	3.27 (2.08)	3.20 (2.10)
Comprehension				
Stringent	2.07 (1.55)	1.87 (1.82)	2.33 (1.85)	2.53 (1.89)
Lenient	2.60 (1.58)	2.33 (2.08)	2.87 (2.03)	3.13 (2.12)
Elaboration-different				
Stringent	2.00 (1.46)	2.13 (1.75)	2.60 (1.96)	2.27 (1.98)
Lenient	2.53 (1.71)	2.73 (2.05)	3.07 (2.08)	2.80 (2.17)
Elaboration-same				
Stringent	2.73 (1.69)	3.00 (1.79)	3.20 (1.97)	3.20 (2.04)
Lenient	3.00 (1.63)	3.47 (1.59)	3.47 (1.82)	3.27 (2.02)

NOTE: The percentages in parentheses are the standard deviations.

group achieved the same degree of improvement without any practice in production.

All groups had an opportunity to observe the pictorial referents of the verb contrasts (nonsimultaneously for the elaboration-same groups) and in this regard were able to attach meaning to structural changes. Conceivably, the groups did not evidence degrees of difference because all subjects were given an opportunity to comprehend the meaning of the verb change.

A strict test of the effect of imitation training would be to present the items without pictorial displays. A strict test of the effect of elaboration would also involve removal of the pictures. Meaning was central to all of the four conditions and this element would need to be removed from the noncomprehension groups in order to assess the independent role of production practice.

There is at least one basic error in the design of this study which should be corrected in later investigations. The subjects were not assessed on their ability to comprehend the verb contrasts. Possibly, this study is an effort in motivation and, therefore, may not reflect language change.

Within the framework of this chapter, this study provides evidence that production need not be trained to effect a change in production. This finding confirms several previous studies, as reported above. Further, this finding is in agreement with my interpretation of the study by Ruder et al. (1974). I had speculated that when contrasts are precisely controlled, comprehension would produce a reliable shift in production.

I recommend further investigation on the comparative effect of training style, as an effort to uncover the nature of language learning as well as to obtain the most efficient language training routines.

Foreign Language Instruction

At this point I wish to describe how comprehension has been operationalized as a foreign language teaching technique. Evaluation of the success of the comprehension approach will also be made.

The teaching of comprehension has not been totally ignored by the foreign language establishment. In 1965 (p. 491) an American foreign language professor, Simon Belasco, remarked that "The most under-estimated and least understood aspect of foreign language learning today is audio-comprehension." Ten years later Professor Edward Sittler (1975, p. 5) of Germany echoed Belasco's statement, "The primacy of hearing in the language learning process has never been thoroughly investigated or (sic) scientifically tested." When Belasco's remark was published, Professor James Asher (1965) of San José State University had already begun an in-depth analysis of the role of comprehension in foreign language instruction. Asher's innovative research was anticipated by J.R. Firth, a well-known British linguist. A reference to his work was made by another British linguist and phonetician, Abercrombie (1965, pp. 188–189), who reports:

> During the war [second World War] this [the development of receptive skills] was done at the School of Oriental Studies in London under Mr. Firth. His students were taught to understand Japanese—not to talk it, to write it, or to read it. By limiting their activities to this small part of the language, they had extraordinary success with it.

I want to emphasize again that the relationship between comprehension and other language skills has not been completely ignored by foreign language teachers. However, with the exception of James Asher (1977), language experts have never emphasized that the "bulk" of language teaching should be restricted to comprehension training.

Asher (1972) proved comprehension training to be a highly successful approach. One investigation dealt with adults who had significantly poorer aptitudes in foreign language, as measured by the Modern Language Aptitude Test. With only thirty-two hours of comprehension training they were compared with college students who completed either one or two college semesters of German. The adults were markedly superior to the college students in listening skills. They scored equally well on the reading tasks, when measured against the college students who had completed the first semester in German. No comparisons in reading were made between the adults and the second-semester college students. However, it is safe to conclude that the reading skills of the adults would have been as good as that of the college students.

In another investigation (Asher, Kusudo, and de la Torre, 1974) the comprehension procedure was employed to teach Spanish to college students for three hours, one evening a week. The course lasted two college semesters or about thirty weeks, a total of ninety hours of instruction. No homework was assigned to the students. Standardized language examinations were used to test the students' progress. After just forty-five hours of instruction the average performance of the students in listening, reading, writing, and speaking was equivalent to that of college students, or high school students who had 200 hours of instruction. The results are surprising in view of the fact that no homework or study was required.

The students in the ninety-hour program were involved in some speaking and reading, but the program primarily emphasized understanding. The training involved the following percentages of skill training: 70 percent listening; 20 percent speaking, and only 10 percent reading.

Often when other people hear about the application of the comprehension method for the teaching of foreign languages, they equate it with the "conversational" method. To many the conversational method means speaking in the classroom. It also means that grammatical exercises are eliminated or greatly reduced in scope. The comprehension approach and the conversational approach, however, differ greatly.

In a recently published book entitled, *Learning Another Language Through Actions,* Asher (1977) outlines the set of procedures for teaching language comprehension. After an initial orientation period, students begin by learning to respond to commands: "Stand up," "Sit down," "Walk," "Stop," "Jump" and so forth. Each student is asked to carry out a set of commands, sometimes in unison and sometimes alone. Students eagerly carry out these commands regardless of their age. Their motivation is high because they realize that they have no difficulty in understanding the language.

As training continues sentence length is gradually increased. Asher recommends that sentences such as the following be introduced in the early lessons: "You sit down" and "You stand up." Paraphrases as well as commands are used. A student is commanded to walk to a table and the instructor says: "She walks to the table." During this phase of training, Asher introduces more verbs, such as "walk," "touch," and "pick up." The negative is also introduced, as in "Do *not* pick up the paper."

Each session, according to Asher, can last about three hours. For children the sessions should probably not exceed one hour. In the ninth class, that is, after about twenty-four hours of listening, the student learns commands such as the following:

Point to the salesman.

With your finger draw a circle around the saleswoman.

Point to the book that I am holding.

At about this time students answer questions with single-word replies. Usually the response is their name or another student's name, and "yes" and "no."

Gradually the material becomes more complex. Counting and time are taught. By the seventeenth lesson, or fifty-one hours later, the students ask the instructor questions and engage in dialogue.

Asher's program, then, begins with listening training. Students are not asked to talk until they have heard almost fifty hours of instruction, although this time interval has varied in the several experimental demonstration courses taught under the direction of Asher. Gradually the students are encouraged to talk, they are never really forced to talk, and most importantly they do not memorize sentences, as is the case with the audio-lingual method.

In 1971 James Reeds and I developed a self-instructional program that we soon realized resembled closely Asher's approach. I vividly remember saying to myself that despite the apparent differences between second language learning and first language learning, the basic processes appear to be essentially the same. Therefore, foreign language learning could be used as a device or experimental technique to study theoretical issues in native language acquisition or psycholinguistics.

Asher's students are taught to respond to the commands of their teacher, spoken in a foreign language, by making a physical response. Primary emphasis in this approach is placed on learning to make an appropriate physical action because Asher believes physical activity improves learning. In the self-instructional programs of Winitz and Reeds (1975) and Postovsky (1976; also Chapter 9 below), the student listens to words, phrases, and sentences and selects the correct picture from among three or four alternatives. The material can be presented by closed circuit television or in book form. Physical activity, in response to the commands of a classroom teacher, is not used in these programs.

An example of the first few items from a program developed by Winitz and Reeds (1975) to teach German will now be described. The first frame consists of a single item, "pencil," which appears in the upper left quadrant (see Figure 6.2). After several frames, a second word, "shirt," is added. Later three words are added (Figure 6.3). Subsequent to the presentation of single nouns, adjectives and verbs are added. In Figure 6.4 the sentence, "The lady eats the egg" is represented. Alternate foils are also given in this figure, so that there is overlap among lexical items. Winitz and Reeds (1975) believe that learning is accelerated when alternate foils reflect varying degrees of intersection. The degree of intersection is carefully programmed in order to teach the student to focus on the appropriate syntactic and semantic relationships.

The format that was just described is simple, simple to explain to students, and simple for students to use. All the student does is listen and select the correct

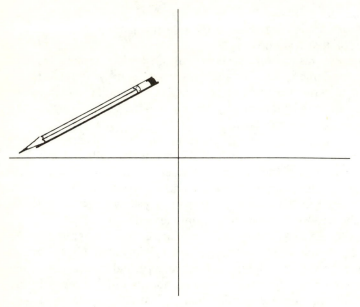

FIGURE 6.2.   The first frame of lesson one of the language program

FIGURE 6.3.   A later frame (frame 10) of the first lesson

FIGURE 6.4.   A frame appearing in lesson 21 of the language program

picture from an array of pictures. Gradually more and more complex items are added according to a linguistic sequence developed by Winitz and Reeds (1975). Stories are also used as a device to convey abstract structures.

In the multiple-choice approach students are asked to make a response. They are to look at four pictures and select the correct item. Their responses can be verified in a number of ways. The answer can be provided in the lesson book, or an instructor can indicate which picture is correct.

Recently I developed a modification of the multiple-choice procedure (Winitz, 1978). The linguistic sequence is essentially the same, but only a single picture is presented at one time. This program was developed to reduce costs involved in the multiple-choice format. Also it appeared that the multiple-choice format was not essential beyond the early lessons. Students often commented that they "know" the correct response more than 95 percent of the time. With the exception of multiple pictures being reduced to one, no other modification of the multiple-choice format was made. The linguistic sequence of "simple" to "complex" is retained. Further, students are not asked to talk until they fully understand the language.

Let's examine some of the lessons of this approach. In Figure 6.5 is a story introducing past activity. This story is introduced at the beginning of the tenth hour of instruction. The past tense sequence is represented in Figure 6.5.

The branch.

The branch breaks.

The cat falls down.

The dog chases the cat.

The cat sees a telephone pole.

The cat climbs up the telephone pole.

FIGURE 6.5.   Past tense activity
(Reproduced from H. Winitz, *The Learnables*, International Linguistics, Kansas City, Missouri, 1978.)

The dog barks.

A boy comes by.

The boy chases the dog away.

The cat climbs down
the telephone pole.

The boy pets the cat.

The boy returns home.

Figure 6.5 (continued)

see overleaf

"I found a cat on the
telephone pole."

"A dog chased the cat."

"The cat climbed up the
telephone pole."

"The cat climbed up the
telephone pole?"

"May I keep the cat?"

"Certainly. You may keep the cat."

Figure 6.5 (continued)

Past activity, represented in Figure 6.5, is easy to learn because students are asked only to understand it, not to use it in conversation or in drill practice. Only listening and understanding are involved, making learning easy and effortless. Through this activity of listening, new words and structures are absorbed in preparation for production. It is the demand for immediate production that often makes language learning distasteful and onerous.

Language learning, using the pictorial format, has received initial testing by Winitz and Reeds (1975) and Postovsky (1975). According to Winitz and Reeds (1975), students have little difficulty understanding German sentences with this approach. Speaking, as expected, was not as advanced as understanding for some eight hours of pictorial-sentence experience. Translation seemed to be easier than speaking. Students were able to translate German sentences into English, presumably because they understood the meaning of the German sentence.

A large-scale evaluation of the pictorial self-instructional program was conducted by Postovsky (1975) at the U.S. Army Defense Language Institute at Monterey, California. The language of instruction was Russian. A television monitor was used to display four pictures for each of the frames, as described above. Soldiers were instructed to select the picture that corresponded to the Russian words or sentences. Each lesson consisted of 100 frames, which were presented at a rate of about one every twenty seconds. The total listening time was about thirty minutes for each of the 100-frame lessons.

Twelve lessons, which correspond to about six hours of listening time, were developed by Dr. Postovsky. These lessons were given two weeks prior to the beginning of the conversational language course in Russian.

The soldiers learned the material easily and did not forget any of the items when tested ten days following instruction. It was a surprising finding that the soldiers retained all of the material after ten days, because they were not told that they would be retested after the initial instructional period had been concluded. Postovsky (1975; also Chapter 9 below) commented:

One of the most interesting aspects of this study relates to stability of recognition knowledge. Some loss in comprehension of learned material was anticipated . . . but did not occur.

Two other remarks of Postovsky are of interest:

In an attempt to determine the students' attitude for this mode of instruction, post-cycle questionnaires were administered at the end of the program, following the first retention test. . . . Review of these data indicates that the program provoked a very positive and often enthusiastic response. After the beginning of regular instruction, the progress of the experimental subjects in their respective classes was monitored and their performance was found to be significantly above the norm.

Finally, the last line of Postovsky's paper gives the following conclusion.

The evidence we are obtaining suggests that the second-language acquisition process can be made less strenuous and more productive by reversing the emphasis in the initial phase of instruction from intensive training in oral production to rapid development of aural comprehension.

Unfortunately in February, 1977, Dr. Postovsky's life abruptly ended at a time when he was beginning to make a significant contribution to the study of foreign language learning. His goal was to develop and test the influence of comprehension training on language mastery. In order to accomplish his goals, he was busily preparing Russian aural-comprehension lessons. Hopefully the Defense Language Institute will carry on the tradition of scientific study to which Dr. Valerian Postovsky contributed so much.

Not all share the direction that foreign language education may be taking. But more curious is the position held by Crystal, Fletcher, and Garman (1976), who advocate the application of traditional foreign language practices for teaching language-impaired individuals. They remark (Crystal et al., 1976, p. 118):

> . . . mother tongue remediation has a great deal to learn from the field of foreign-language teaching, where studies in the use and appropriateness of structural drills have been in progress for over half a century. It is however remarkable how little the remedial language professions have been influenced by this field.

They conclude by taking note of the fact that language investigators interested in rehabilitation have not made themselves aware of what "foreign language methodology has to offer." There is no evidence to indicate that traditional foreign language methodology can be effectively used with language retarded children.

LANGUAGE TRAINING STRATEGIES
FOR DELAYED LANGUAGE CHILDREN

The focal point of this chapter has been that comprehension is the basic performance skill through which language is learned. We are of the opinion that production practice is not a factor in language acquisition, yet it may well be an important component, and, perhaps, a very natural one at that, to speed the acquisition of comprehension.

Nelson (1973) made an important discovery several years ago when she found that language comprehension at fifteen months of age was impressively correlated with linguistic structure and vocabulary at two years and again at two and one half years. Nelson (1973, p. 79) comments:

> This is of considerable theoretical interest for our understanding of the process of language learning. It indicates the probable importance of covert language processing prior to language production as an organizing factor and emphasizes the need for further study of this process.

Comprehension is important not because it precedes production, but because it appears to be the basic mechanism through which the rules of a language are internalized. Nelson's finding that there is a high association between comprehension and production also suggests that there is individual variation in the ability to absorb linguistic knowledge or its requisite precursors.

Role of Production in Language Training

I take the viewpoint that all of language learning is comprehension or under-standing and that production exercises should not be utilized as a clinical or instructional routine. This position should not be interpreted to mean that children should not be encouraged or motivated to talk. Rather, the style of the language training sessions should promote and stimulate verbal communica-tion. When a child talks we should respond. When the child does not talk we should continue to talk, doing our best to pair linguistic and nonlinguistic meaning.

The training study cited above, as well as research in foreign language acquisition, suggests that production will follow when there has been complete comprehension of a specific language feature or structure. A brief interval of imitation training may increase a child's personal confidence that he or she can talk. However, giving a child the opportunity to talk may produce the same effect in a much more natural way.

There is no particular advantage to insisting on imitation practice concurrent with or following comprehension training. First, production, I believe, follows comprehension. Second, in some instances, there is only partial comprehension, simply because a grammatical construction may be understood without complete mastery of all of its elements. For example, -ing is apparently the salient element when children first learn the progressive. If production practice includes the auxiliary is, emphasis is placed on a unit which may be noticed, but is not yet comprehended. Similarly, if the articles a and the are stressed in production practice before a child's linguistic system has evolved to the point where these units are linguistically significant, mastery in production is not to be expected. Third, there may be performance constraints, restrictions on the storage and retrieval of grammatical structures, which will result in incorrect imitation.

Insistence on production mastery at each step of comprehension (e.g., Miller and Yoder, 1974; Bricker and Bricker, 1974; Hart and Risley, 1976; Crystal et al., 1976) can be referenced as a linear system. According to this principle, each stage of comprehension or apparent comprehension should be followed by proof of mastery as evidenced in production. Linear systems have proved unsatis-factory in foreign language teaching, motivating serious re-evaluation of current methodology by an increasing number of the foreign language profession. Furthermore, the evidence from child language research convincingly demon-strated that production does not follow comprehension in linear increments.

At this point one may ask the simple question: What about the child who comprehends but does not produce? If we are sufficiently confident that this situation holds for an individual, I have no substantive advice on this point. An intuitive response would be to suggest exercises that will convert the knowledge that is comprehended into production. Demanding speech when it has not occurred in the natural interplay of training would hardly seem to be a reasonable alternative. Memory exercises, that is, emphasizing retrieval of the correct linguistic form after failure, appear to share the same properties as those techniques that demand speech.

It is true that recall routines could be established, especially for learning lexical items, which might activate or develop a child's searching strategies. This approach may be appealing to some, but it is unlikely that it will be substantially beneficial for language learners, for it is unknown what the executive restrictions are that inhibit development of language production, and, if known, whether these restrictions could be lifted. Careful experimental work is required with language delayed children to know whether a failure to produce linguistic utterances is a restriction on retrieval (accessibility) when there is evidence that storage (availability) as measured by comprehension, is sufficiently strong.

As a training strategy, increased comprehension exposure for children who demonstrate linguistic inabilities in production would be our preference. After all, there are very few children classified as impaired in language who fail to produce any language utterances. The problem is not that they cannot produce, but that their production is delayed or deficient, depending upon the interpretation one wishes to make from studies that have concentrated on this issue. However, the deficiency-delay issue is not of importance here. My point is simply that production may well be constrained, but the fact that it does occur in sufficient quantity would seem to argue against a general disability in retrieval. Retrieval should continue to develop with increasing exposure and natural use of language.

Comprehension Techniques

Procedures for teaching comprehension have been outlined by Winitz and Reeds (1975). In this section I will mention two important processes: (1) simplification and (2) inappropriate responding.

Simplification has been observed to occur in the speech addressed to young children in comparison to that of older children and adults. Recently, Snow (1977) concluded that syntactic simplification is uncorrelated with the beginning of language production, as the degree of syntactic complexity of the mother remained essentially constant from near birth to about three years of age. She found, for example, that mean length of utterance (MLU), a fairly good measure of overall syntactic complexity, was about four words throughout this interval.

Since syntactic simplification was found to be constant in the first three years of life, Snow (1977) concluded that mothers may not be specifically responding to cues of attention and comprehension from their child. It should be noted that an average MLU of four may reflect a restriction on the average minimal size unit, and, therefore, averaging statistics at this age level may be inappropriate.

Snow (1977) preferred to conclude, from her analysis of the typical exchanges between a mother and child, that adjustments by mothers in style, length, and complexity of sentences indicate that mothers are primarily trying to teach conversational principles. Snow's conclusions are reasonable, yet it still can be concluded that parent-child dialogues reflect comprehension not only from the child's side but the parent's side as well. Consider one mother's questions to her child:

What else have you got in your face?
Where's your nose?
Where's your nose?
Ann's nose?

I would like to interpret these questions as a lesson in the grammar of ownership, in addition to conversational experience in turn-taking, as Snow suggests.

Inappropriate responding on the part of the adult may be deliberately used to encourage comprehension learning. Several writers have commented that inappropriate expansion, and questioning of what a child says may serve as important communicative experiences (Brown, 1973; Winitz and Reeds, 1975; Winitz, 1975) because they are used as communicative checks by parents (Bushnell and Aslin, 1977).

Bushnell and Aslin (1977) examined the deliberate use of inappropriate expansions, with a young two-year-old whose MLU was 2.26. Using questions, an adult conveyed to the child lexical, phonetic, and syntactic misinterpretations. Syntactic misinterpretations were accepted most by the child. It is our contention (Winitz and Reeds, 1975) that as the complexity of syntax grows and meaning cannot be derived without attention to it, syntactic rejection will also increase. Like simplification we regard inappropriate responding to be a procedure that encourages the development of comprehension.

Concluding Comments on the Role of Speaking Exercises in Language Training

In the mid-1960s a case was made by Chomsky (1965), McNeill (1966), Lenneberg (1967), and others that linguistic skills are largely innate. It was argued essentially that the mechanisms or properties of all natural languages are available at birth and that through language stimulation language-particular rules are acquired. The learning process was not regarded as passive, since it was often stated that the acquirement of language-particular rules comes about by an active discovery or selection process. Later research has placed greater emphasis on the facilitating properties of speech addressed to young children, which was found to be relatively simple in structure (Snow, 1972; Longhurst and Stepanich, 1975). This finding does not negate the general belief that children acquire language by making covert discoveries of the rules that govern structural arrangements. Only that the discovery process is substantially aided, if not in fact made possible, by initial exposure to sentences noncomplex in structure. Additionally, the order in which structural elements of linguistic structures are observed to occur in young children (Brown, 1973), may be of significance in understanding the learning (discovery) process.

Although the discovery process is generally believed to be an active rather than a passive process, it does not follow that "explicit awareness" is a feature of active processing. Most likely, the process of grammatical discovery by children is conducted without explicit awareness. Rules seem to be acquired without conscious knowledge of their structure.

As is generally recognized, the aim of linguistic inquiry is to make explicit the grammatical rules that guide the speaker-hearer in the construction of sentences. It is a difficult and impressive art, which, because of its complexity, demonstrates rather persuasively that the speaker-hearer does not have explicit understanding of grammatical rules, and yet is able to generate sentences according to rule.

Comprehension training, as a methodological approach, does not provide the learner with a set of explicit rules. Rather the goal of comprehension training is to bring the student into contact with a wide range of language data, systematically presented, so as to facilitate the discovery process.

There is another reason why "comprehension through discovery" may prove to be a valuable routine for teaching language to disordered language children. It can be argued that because language rules are not easily recoverable by the speaker-hearer, deliberate and explicit grammatical instruction would not be an appropriate psychological experience for learning a language. Unfortunately this hypothesis remains untestable because complete grammars are not yet available and there is no indication that they will be soon. Yet it is not uncommon to observe clinical programs that encourage the use of explicit grammatical knowledge either through imitation and/or question-and-answer routines (talking exercises) or through sentence-making routines (exercise in the formulation of sentences).

The procedural strategies involved in production practice are distinctly different from those used to teach language through comprehension. The comprehension approach stresses primarily that there be contact with language data. From this contact, given the appropriate environmental circumstances, it is believed that implicit understanding of the grammar will develop.

Several strategies (see Winitz and Reeds, 1975) are used to facilitate implicit understanding, of which simplification is one. The strategy of forced speaking (speaking exercises) is not utilized because it is believed that speaking exercises play no significant role in the discovery process. However, speaking is not discouraged. Rather it is encouraged by establishing a functional language interaction between child and teacher, and child and parent (Hubbell, 1977). Within the framework of the premises presented in this chapter it is assumed that speaking will develop as a natural by-product of instruction in comprehension provided that the latter is conducted within a facilitating and rewarding environment.

Finally there is an additional conclusion, made by Zimmerman and Rosenthal (1974) regarding observational learning, which relates to the issue of forced speaking exercises. Observational learning refers to the acquisition of (or solution to) a task by making observations of a model's behavior in contrast to a learning task involving self-generated responses. In the case of language learning, the model's behavior would be the utterance of sentences, which would provide the essential data for the mastery of underlying grammatical structures. Most interesting is Zimmerman and Rosenthal's (1974) conclusion that verbalizations on the part of children may interfere with observation and rule learning. Zimmerman and Bell (1972, p. 228) express it in the following way:

> . . . in more conceptually formidable tasks requiring induction and transformation, simple verbal description of a model's behavior would depart from and interfere with covert processes.

In one experiment Zimmerman and Bell (1972) had children learn to associate a number with the spatial position of an arrow. A clockwise turn established an ordinal relationship between spatial position and number. Overt verbal descriptions by the children, during a model's presentation of this task, interfered with acquisition. These results appear to be generalizable to language learning. Children who are instructed to verbalize "surface structure" rules, while covertly trying to master complex grammatical relationships, may be subject to an enormous amount of interference. Conceivably the rules they may be trying to verbalize may be unavailable in any conscious or deliberate form.

On the other hand, if we make the assumption that the rules can be correctly expressed by the language learner there is the possibility that they may be ill-formed because there has been exposure to a limited amount of data. The forced practice of making sentences and/or forced practice of expressing rules, then, may be a source of considerable interference in language learning. Belasco (1965) illustrates this point well with the following series of sentences:

I am writing it to him.
I am sending it to him.
I am telling it to him.
I am saying it to him.
I am writing him to do it.
I am sending him to do it.
I am telling him to do it.
*I am saying him to do it.

Incomplete exposure to sentence types can result in the second-language learner speaking the last (ungrammatical) sentence above.

Among teachers of foreign languages, a growing number are beginning to recommend the delay of oral practice or speaking as an important strategy in language learning. Gary (1975) is one individual from the foreign language discipline who, in addition to presenting experimental evidence to support this point of view, references a report by Sorensen (1967), an anthropologist who has studied Columbian and Brazilian Indian cultures. Sorensen (1967) comments that among these Indians, languages are learned well by initially emphasizing comprehension. He reports as follows:

> The Indians do not practice speaking a language that they do not know well yet. Instead, they passively learn lists of words, forms, and phrases in it and familiarize themselves with the sound of its pronunciation. The diverse and discrete phonologies of these languages and their dialects loom very prominently in the Indians' regard. They may make an occasional preliminary attempt to speak a new language in an appropriate situation, but if it does not come easily, they will not try to force it.

> An Indian, then, does not want to try to speak a language until he knows it quite well (Sorensen, 1967, pp. 679–680).

Gary (1975, p. 680) concludes:

> . . . the Indians appear to be utilizing the most effective strategy they know for learning language—delaying oral production until reaching an appropriate state of readiness.

References

Abercrombie, D. Discussant of V. F. Allen, "Preparation of dialogue and material for students of English as a foreign language." In H. B. Allen (Ed.), *Teaching English as a second language.* New York: McGraw-Hill, 1965.

Anisfeld, M., and Tucker, G. R. "English pluralization rules of six-year-old children." *Child Development, 38,* pp. 1201–1217, 1967.

Asher, J. J. "The strategy of the total physical response: An application to learning Russian." *International Review of Applied Linguistics, 3,* pp. 291–300, 1965.

———. "Children's first language as a model for second language learning." *The Modern Language Journal, 56,* pp. 133–139, 1972.

———. *Learning another language through actions: The complete teacher's guidebook.* Los Gatos, Calif.: Sky Oaks Productions, 1977.

Asher, J. J., Kusudo, J., and de la Torre, R. "Learning a second language through commands: The second field test." *The Modern Language Journal, 58,* pp. 24–32, 1974.

Baer, D. M., and Guess, D. "Receptive training of adjectival inflections in mental retardates." *Journal of Applied Behavior Analysis, 4,* pp. 129–139, 1971.

Baird, R. "On the role of chance in imitation-comprehension-production test results." *Journal of Verbal Learning and Verbal Behavior, 11,* pp. 474–477, 1972.

Belasco, S. "Nucleation and the audio-lingual approach." *The Modern Language Journal, 49,* pp. 482–491, 1965.

Bloom, L. *Language development: Form and function in emerging grammars.* Cambridge, Mass.: M.I.T. Press, 1970.

———. *One word at a time: The use of single word utterances before syntax.* The Hague: Mouton, 1973.

———. "Talking, understanding, and thinking." In R. L. Schiefelbusch and L. L. Lloyd (Eds.), *Language perspectives—acquisition, retardation, and intervention.* Baltimore: University Park Press, 1974.

Bowerman, M. "Semantic factors in the acquisition of rules for word use and sentence construction." In D. Morehead and A. Morehead (Eds.), *Normal and deficient child language.* Baltimore: University Park Press, 1976.

———. "Words and sentences: Uniformity, individual variation and shifts over time in patterns of acquisition." In F. D. Minifie and L. L. Lloyd (Eds.), *Communicative and cognitive abilities— early behavioral assessment.* Baltimore: University Park Press, 1978.

Bricker, W. A. "A systematic approach to language training." In R. L. Schiefelbusch and L. L. Lloyd (Eds.), *Language of the mentally retarded.* Baltimore: University Park Press, 1972.

Bricker, W. A., and Bricker, D. D. "An early language training strategy." In R. L. Schiefelbusch and L. L. Lloyd (Eds.), *Language perspectives—acquisition, retardation, and intervention.* Baltimore: University Park Press, 1974.

Broen, P. "The verbal environment of the language-learning child." *American Speech and Hearing Association Monographs, 17,* 1972.

Brown, R. *A first language, the early stages.* Cambridge, Mass.: Harvard University Press, 1973.

Brown, R., Fraser, C., and Bellugi, U. "Explorations in grammar evaluation." In U. Bellugi and R. Brown (Eds.), *The acquisition of language. Monographs of the Society for Research in Child Development,* Serial No. 92, Vol. 29, pp. 79–92, 1964.

Brown, R., and Hanlon, C. "Derivational complexity and order of acquisition in child speech." In J. R. Hayes (Ed.), *Cognition and the development of language.* New York: John Wiley and Sons, 1970.

Bushnell, E. W., and Aslin, R. N. "Inappropriate expansion: A demonstration of a methodology for child language research." *Journal of Child Language, 4,* pp. 115–122, 1977.

Carey, P. W., Mehler, J., and Bever, T. G. "When do we compute all the interpretations of an ambiguous sentence?" In G. B. Flores d'Arcais and W. J. M. Levelt (Eds.), *Advances in psycholinguistics.* Amsterdam: New Holland Publishing Co., 1970.

Chapman, R. S., and Miller, J. F. "Word order in early two and three word utterances: Does production precede comprehension?" *Journal of Speech and Hearing Research, 18,* pp. 355–371, 1975.

Chomsky, N. *Aspects of the theory of syntax.* Cambridge, Mass.: M.I.T. Press, 1965.

Clark, E. V. "Non-linguistic strategies and the acquisition of word meanings." *Cognition, 2,* pp. 161–182, 1973a.

———. "What's in a word? On the child's acquisition of semantics in his first language." In T. E. Moore (Ed.), *Cognitive development and the acquisition of language.* New York: Academic Press, 1973b.

Clark, E. V., and Garnica, O. K. "Is he coming or going? On the acquisition of deictic verbs." *Journal of Verbal Learning and Verbal Behavior, 13,* pp. 559–572, 1974.

Cromer, R. F. "Receptive language in the mentally retarded: Processes and diagnostic distinctions." In R. L. Schiefelbusch and L. L. Lloyd (Eds.), *Language perspectives—acquisitions, retardation, and intervention.* Baltimore: University Park Press, 1974.

Crystal, D., Fletcher, P., and Garman, M. *The grammatical analysis of language disability.* London: Edward Arnold, 1976.

de Villiers, J. G., and de Villiers, P. A. "Development of the use of word order in comprehension." *Journal of Psycholinguistic Research, 2,* pp. 331–341, 1973.

de Villiers, P. A., and de Villiers, J. G. "Early judgments of semantic and syntactic acceptability by children." *Journal of Psycholinguistic Research, 1,* pp. 299–310, 1972.

Donaldson, M., and McGarrigle, J. "Some clues to the nature of semantic development." *Journal of Child Language, 1,* pp. 185–194, 1974.

Ehri, L. E. "Comprehension and production of adjectives and seriation." *Journal of Child Language, 3,* pp. 369–384, 1976.

Eilers, R. E., and Oller, D. K. "The role of speech discrimination in developmental sound substitutions." *Journal of Child Language, 3,* pp. 319–329, 1976.

Fernald, C. E. "Control of grammar in imitation, comprehension and production: Problems of replication." *Journal of Verbal Learning and Verbal Behavior, 11,* pp. 606–613, 1972.

Foss, D. J., Bever, T. G., and Silver, M. "The comprehension and verification of ambiguous sentences." *Perception and Psychophysics, 4,* pp. 304–306, 1968.

Fraser, C., Bellugi, U., and Brown, R. "Control of grammar in imitation, comprehension and production." *Journal of Verbal Learning and Verbal Behavior, 2,* pp. 121–135, 1963.

Fraser, C., and Roberts, N. "Mother's speech to children of four different ages." *Journal of Psycholinguistic Research, 4,* pp. 9–16, 1975.

Gary, J. O. "Delayed oral practice in initial stages of second language learning." In M. K. Burt and H. C. Dulay (Eds.), *On TESOL 75: New directions in second language learning, teaching, and bilingual education.* Washington, D.C.: TESOL, 1975.

Guess, D. "A functional analysis of receptive language and productive speech: Acquisition of the plural morpheme." *Journal of Applied Behavior Analysis, 2,* pp. 55–64, 1969.

Guess, D., Sailor, W., and Baer, D. M. "To teach language to retarded children." In R. L. Schiefelbusch and L. L. Lloyd (Eds.), *Language perspectives—acquisition, retardation, and intervention.* Baltimore: University Park Press, 1974.

Halle, M., and Stevens, K. N. "Speech recognition: A model for a program for research." In J. A. Fodor and J. J. Katz (Eds.), *The structure of language: Readings in the philosophy of language.* Englewood Cliffs, N.J.: Prentice-Hall, 1964.

Hart, B., and Risley, T. R. "Community-based language training." In T. D. Tjossem (Ed.), *Intervention strategies for high risk infants and young children.* Baltimore: University Park Press, 1976.

Horgan, D. "Linguistic knowledge at early stage I: Evidence from successive single word utterances." *Papers and Reports on Child Language Development, 12,* pp. 116–126, 1976.

Hubbell, R. D. "On facilitating spontaneous talking in young children." *Journal of Speech and Hearing Disorders, 42,* pp. 216–231, 1977.

Huttenlocher, J. "The origins of language comprehension." In R. L. Solso (Ed.), *Theories in cognitive psychology.* Potomac, Md.: Lawrence, Erlbaum Associates, 1974.

Ingram, D. "The relationship between comprehension and production." In R. L. Schiefelbusch and L. L. Lloyd (Eds.), *Language perspectives—acquisition, retardation, and intervention.* Baltimore: University Park Press, 1974.

Lee, L. L., Koenigsknecht, R. S., and Mulhern, S. T. *Interactive language development teaching.* Evanston, Ill.: Northwestern University Press, 1975.

Lenneberg, E. H. *Biological foundation of language.* New York: John Wiley and Sons, 1967.

Leopold, W. F. *Speech development of a bilingual child,* Vol. 4. Evanston, Ill.: Northwestern University Press, 1949.

Locke, J. L., and Kutz, K. J. "Memory for speech and speech for memory." *Journal of Speech and Hearing Research, 18,* pp. 176–191, 1975.

Longhurst, T. M., and Stepanich, L. "Mothers' speech addressed to one-, two- and three-year-old normal children." *Child Study Journal, 5,* pp. 3–11, 1975.

Maratsos, M. P. "Preschool children's use of definite and indefinite articles." *Child Development, 45,* pp. 446–455, 1974.

McNeill, D. "Developmental psycholinguistics." In F. Smith and G. Miller (Eds.), *The genesis of language.* Cambridge, Mass.: M.I.T. Press, 1966.

Menyuk, P. *Sentences children use.* Cambridge, Mass.: M.I.T. Press, 1969.

Miller, G. A., Heise, G. A., and Lichten, W. "The intelligibility of speech as a function of context of the test materials." *Journal of Experimental Psychology, 41,* pp. 329–335, 1951.

Miller, J. F., and Yoder, D. E. "An ontogenetic language teaching strategy for retarded children." In R. L. Schiefelbusch and L. L. Lloyd (Eds.), *Language perspectives—acquisition, retardation, and intervention.* Baltimore: University Park Press, 1974.

Miller, W., and Ervin, S. "The development of grammar in child language." In U. Bellugi and R. Brown (Eds.), *The acquisition of language. Monographs of the Society for Research in Child Development,* Serial No. 92, Vol. 29, 9–34, 1964.

Muma, J. R. "The communication game: Dump or play." *Journal of Speech and Hearing Disorders, 40,* pp. 296–309, 1975.

Myklebust, H. R. "Aphasia in children—diagnosis and training." In L. E. Travis (Ed.), *Handbook of speech pathology.* New York: Appleton-Century-Crofts, 1957.

Nelson, K. "Structure and strategy in learning to talk." *Monographs of the Society for Research in Child Development*, Serial No. 149, Vol. 38, 1973.

———. "Concept, word, and sentence: Interrelationships in acquisition and development." *Psychological Review, 81*, pp. 267–285, 1974.

Philips, J. R. "Syntax and vocabulary of mothers' speech to young children: Age and sex comparisons." *Child Development, 44*, pp. 182–185, 1973.

Postovsky, V. A. "The priority of aural comprehension in the language acquisition process." In G. Nickel (Ed.), *Proceedings of the Fourth International Congress of Applied Linguistics*, Vol. 3. Stuttgart, Germany: HochschulVerlag, 1976.

Richards, M. M. "*Come* and *go* reconsidered: Children's use of deictic verbs in contrived situations." *Journal of Verbal Learning and Verbal Behavior, 15*, pp. 655–665, 1976.

Ruder, K. F., Hermann, P., and Schiefelbusch, R. L. "Effects of verbal imitation and comprehension training on verbal production." *Journal of Psycholinguistic Research, 6*, pp. 59–72, 1977.

Ruder, K. F., Smith, M., and Hermann, P. "Effects of verbal imitation and comprehension on verbal production of lexical items." In L. V. McReynolds (Ed.), *Developing systematic procedures for training children's language. American Speech and Hearing Association Monographs, 18*, pp. 15–29, 1974.

Sachs, J., and Truswell, L. "Comprehension of two-word instructions by children in the one-word stage." *Papers and Reports on Child Development, 12*, pp. 212–220, 1976.

Shipley, E. F., Smith, C. S., and Gleitman, L. R. "A study in the acquisition of language: Free responses to commands." *Language, 45*, pp. 322–342, 1969.

Sittler, E. V. "Preface." In *Die Logik des Hörens: besser Hören = besser Lernen. Schriftenreihe des Pädagogischen Instituts Düsseldorf*, Heft 26, Juni 1975.

Slobin, D. I. "Developmental psycholinguistics." In W. O. Dingwall (Ed.), *A survey of linguistic science*. Baltimore: University of Maryland, 1971.

Smith, N. V. *The acquisition of phonology*. London: Cambridge University, 1973.

Snow, C. E. "Mothers' speech to children learning language." *Child Development, 43*, pp. 549–565, 1972.

———. "The development of conversation between mothers and babies." *Journal of Child Language, 4*, pp. 1–22, 1977.

Sorensen, A. P. "Multilingualism in the northwest Amazon." *American Anthropologist, 69*, pp. 670–684, 1967.

Stevens, K. N. "Segments, features, and analysis by synthesis." In J. F. Kavanagh and I. G. Mattingly (Eds.), *Language by ear and eye, the relationships between speech and reading*. Cambridge, Mass.: M.I.T. Press, 1972.

Stremel, K., and Waryas, C. "A behavioral-psycholinguistic approach to language training." In L. V. McReynolds (Ed.), *Developing systematic procedures for training children's language. American Speech and Hearing Association Monographs, 18*, pp. 96–130, 1974.

Strohner, H., and Nelson, K. "The young child's development of sentence comprehension: Influence of event probability, non-verbal context, syntactic form, and strategies." *Child Development, 45*, pp. 567–576, 1974.

Vygotsky, L. S. *Thought and language*. Cambridge, Mass.: M.I.T. Press, 1962.

Webster, B. O., and Ingram, D. "The comprehension and production of the anaphoric pronouns, *he, she, him, her* in normal and linguistically deviant children." *Papers and Reports on Child Language Development, 4*, pp. 55–78, 1972.

Wepman, J. M. "Aphasia: Language without thought or thought without language." *Asha, 18*, pp. 131–136, 1976.

Wetstone, H. S., and Friedlander, B. Z. "The effect of word order on young children's responses to simple questions and commands." *Child Development, 44*, pp. 734–740, 1973.

Whitehurst, G. "Comprehension, selective imitation, and the CIP hypothesis." *Journal of Experimental Child Psychology, 23*, pp. 23–38, 1977.

Winitz, H. *Articulatory acquisition and behavior*. New York: Appleton-Century-Crofts, 1969.

———. *From syllable to conversation*. Baltimore: University Park Press, 1975.

Winitz, H. *The learnables*. Kansas City, Mo.: International Linguistics, 1978.

Winitz, H., LaRiviere, C., and Herriman, E. "Perception of word boundaries under conditions of lexical bias." *Phonetica, 27,* pp. 193–212, 1973.

Winitz, H., and Preisler, L. "Discrimination pretraining and sound learning." *Perceptual and Motor Skills, 20,* pp. 905–916, 1965.

Winitz, H., and Reeds, J. *Comprehension and problem solving as strategies for language training.* The Hague: Mouton, 1975.

Zimmerman, B. J., and Bell, J. A. "Observer verbalization and abstraction in vicarious rule learning, generalization, and retention." *Developmental Psychology, 7,* pp. 227–231, 1972.

Zimmerman, B. J., and Rosenthal, T. L. "Observational learning of rule-governed behavior of children." *Psychological Bulletin, 81,* pp. 29–42, 1974.

CHAPTER 7

Neurolinguistic Clues to the Essentials of a Good Language Teaching Methodology: Comprehension, Problem Solving, and Meaningful Practice

Karl C. Diller

Professor of English (Linguistics)
University of New Hampshire

What was your worst language learning experience? That is the first question I ask of students in my applied linguistics courses.

My own worst experiences were with dead languages. I majored in Classical Greek, and studied four other dead languages: Latin, Biblical Hebrew, Old English, and Modern German. I would like to insist that German, the way it was taught to me, was as dead as the others. In an eight-credit elementary course we almost never used German meaningfully, either for listening comprehension or for conversation. The exams were translations from English to German, using sentences directly out of the textbook, which made it easy to get an A. But what did that A mean in terms of competence?

This chapter will consider two questions: (1) What is missing from the grammar-translation method?, and (2) What is essential for an effective method of language teaching? There is new evidence on the answers to these questions from Winitz and Reeds's (1975) experiments teaching foreign languages through listening comprehension and from recent work on the neurolinguistic foundations of methods of teaching foreign languages. I will consider each of these questions in turn, but first let us consider some neurolinguistic evidence on the more fundamental question of what second-language learning actually entails.

"Problem Solving" as Opposed to "Speech Habits" in Second-Language Learning: Neurolinguistic Evidence

T. M. Walsh and I have argued in two previous papers that many of the differences among language teaching methods can be explained with reference to

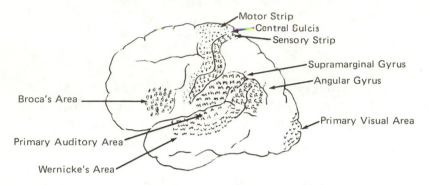

FIGURE 7.1.   Left hemisphere of the cerebral cortex

neurolinguistic facts (Walsh and Diller, 1978; Diller and Walsh, 1978). Our argument is based on the fact that there are several different specialized areas in the brain that are important for processing language, and a lesion in any one of these areas will produce its own characteristic form of language disorder.[1]

Figure 7.1 shows four major language areas:

"Speech" areas:
   Broca's area for expressive speech
   Wernicke's area for receptive speech (auditory decoding)
Meaning area:
   Supramarginal gyrus: word-object relations, semantic processing
Reading area:
   Angular gyrus: language visualization

Note the central sulcis in Figure 7.1. The motor strip on the frontal side of this gyrus controls voluntary movements for the opposite side of the body (a stroke here in the left hemisphere produces paralysis on the right side of the body). The sensory strip on the posterior side of the central sulcis processes sensations from the opposite side of the body. Language disorders from frontal lesions tend to be motor aphasias, and those from posterior lesions, sensory aphasias. *Broca's aphasia* (frontal) is characterized by effortful speech, with only a few words uttered at a time, and with special difficulty in producing sentences using the small grammatical words, but comprehension of language is relatively unimpaired as long as the grammar is not too complex. *Wernicke's aphasia,* on the other hand, is characterized by a severe comprehension deficit, but patients talk fluently, with good pronunciation in grammatical sentences that have relatively empty content. *Conduction aphasia* involves the pathway between Wernicke's and Broca's areas. Since Broca's area is intact, there is fluent speech, but since this expressive speech area is disconnected from the receptive speech area there is special difficulty with repetition.

Our argument is that different language teaching methods utilize the different

Method	Cortical Areas
Audio-lingual pattern drill of mimicking and memorizing words and sentences.	Area 22, Wernicke's Area. verbal detection and analysis of elements of language.
Empiricist-behaviorist learning theory, assumes language as speech habits.	Areas 44 + 45, Broca's Area. associated with somatic sensory-motor regions.
No emphasis placed on word-object association toward cognitive and intellectual processes.	Areas 6, 4, 3,1,2. somatic sensory-motor regions of larynx, pharynx, palate, tongue, and jaw.

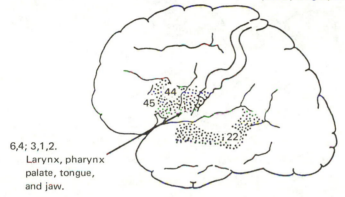

6,4; 3,1,2.
Larynx, pharynx
palate, tongue,
and jaw.

FIGURE 7.2.   Mimicry-memorization and pattern drill—extreme form
(from Walsh and Diller, 1978)

language areas and the pathways between them in different ways. An examination of the audio-lingual method[2] is especially revealing in this light. In particular, with the extreme form of the audio-lingual method, we argue that the "speech areas" of the brain (Broca's and Wernicke's areas) tend to be isolated from the areas that give language its meaning. Much mechanical speech is produced, but there is little emphasis on semantic content, word-object relations, or meaningful practice (see Figure 7.2).

There are aphasic patients whose injuries have isolated the speech areas just as we have diagrammed this isolation for the audio-lingual method (cf. Geschwind, Quadfasel, and Segarra, 1968; Haiganoosh Whitaker, 1976). The patient described by Geschwind et al., a victim of carbon monoxide poisoning, lay for several years in the hospital without ever giving any indication that she understood anything, and she never uttered spontaneous meaningful sentences. She mimicked everything that was said to her. If you asked her, "What's the weather like?," she would say "What's the weather like?" She liked to sing along

Method	Cortical areas
No speaking or writing until vocabulary and grammar are learned.	Area 22, Wernicke's Area. verbal detection and analysis of elements of language.
Follows sensory pattern of native learned speech.	Area 40. Word-object relation toward cognitive and intellectual processes.

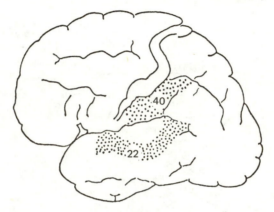

FIGURE 7.3.   Winitz and Reeds, "Rapid Acquisition of a Foreign Language by the Avoidance of Speaking"
(from Diller and Walsh, 1978)

with the radio, and one day someone noticed that she had memorized the words to new songs which had been composed after her accident. But still there was no evidence that she comprehended the meaning of any of these memorized sentences. Mechanical learning, then, is possible without understanding. This patient had speech, but not language. So we say that the audio–lingual method is a method for mastering *speech patterns,* but that it is not well designed for learning *language.*

A demonstration of the fact that language is something much more than speech habits comes from Winitz and Reeds's (1973, 1975) experiments with teaching foreign languages through listening comprehension, with complete avoidance of speaking and reading. A diagram of the Winitz and Reeds method shows that we have a strong link between Wernicke's area (Area 22: auditory decoding) and the supramarginal gyrus (Area 40: semantic relations and meaning). But Broca's area (expressive speech) and the angular gyrus (reading) are not utilized to any extent (see Figure 7.3).

With the Winitz and Reeds method, students gain large vocabularies (seventy-five words in an hour of tape) and learn to understand the foreign language without acquiring any speech habits at all!

The speech-habit theorists belong basically in the empiricist-behaviorist tradition. The chief alternative theory has been the rationalist position, which is currently held by Noam Chomsky (1965) in his theories of transformational grammar (cf. Chomsky, 1965; and discussion in Diller, 1978). For the rationalist, language universals are reflections of the complex language-processing mechanisms of the human brain, and language learners actively go about figuring out the grammars of languages that are used in their presence. Except for quotations, ritual, and clichés, almost all the sentences one hears in normal language use are new sentences which have never been heard or uttered before. Yet if these sentences are grammatical, we understand them immediately because we have internalized a generative grammar of the language. People do not generally have an explicit formulated knowledge of the rules of grammar, yet these rules are psychologically real, as seen by the fact that even small children will object to someone violating the rules of grammar to produce a grammatically anomalous sentence.

The process by which children figure out the grammar of the language around them is what we call "problem solving." This process can be seen in the regular mistakes which show that the children are operating by their own set of rules which is different from their parents' language. We all know how children over-extend the rule for the regular past tense, saying "I goed" instead of "I went." For a more specific example, my two-year-old son recently said, "Me help-you daddy night," meaning "I (want to) help daddy later." There are three characteristic mistakes in this sentence: he does not yet use the word *I*, but uses *me* in all cases; he uses *help-you* for "help" (without regard to whether he is going to help the person he is talking to); and he has taken the word *tonight* to mean "later," and pronounces it "night." These mistakes will all disappear as he figures out more about the language and moves to a more mature stage in the language learning process. The learning of a language is a problem-solving process; it is clearly not the mimicking of adult sentences.

What Is Missing in the Grammar-Translation Method?

The grammar-translation method is a slow and unnatural way to learn a language. After spending a whole semester translating Plato, I remember thinking how nice it would be to go back to the beginning of the book and just read Plato directly, without all the work of translating into English to get the meaning. When I tried, I found that I could not do it. To get the meaning, I still had to translate. My professor told me that it takes about twenty years of professional study for one to learn to read classical Greek fluently. What is missing in this method?

When we think about the grammar-translation method neurolinguistically, we can recognize that reading aloud emphasizes the link between the angular gyrus (language visualization) and Broca's area (expressive speech). Wernicke's area (auditory coding of language) is involved to a certain degree, as the ear

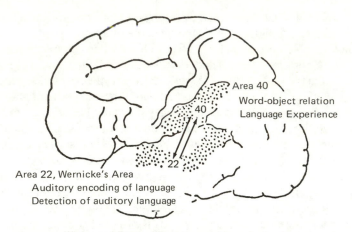

Winitz and Reeds. "Rapid acquisition of a foreign
language by the avoidance of speaking."

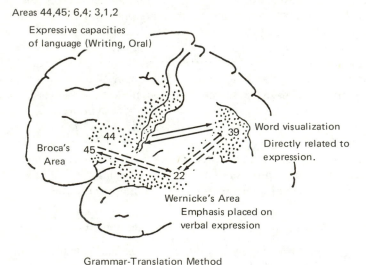

Grammar-Translation Method

FIGURE 7.4.   Comparison of Winitz and Reeds method and grammar-
translation method

(from Diller and Walsh, 1978)

hears all that is read aloud in class. It is instructive to compare our diagram for
the Winitz and Reeds method with a diagram for the grammar-translation
method, as in Figure 7.4. We see right away what is left out: It is the area for
semantic processing, for word-object relations.

With the Winitz and Reeds method, one can learn 1500 words in twenty
hours of tape. With the grammar-translation method one does not learn this

many words in a year. The Winitz and Reeds method stresses the link between the area for auditory coding and the area for meaning, and it ignores what is important for the grammar-translation method, the link between word visualization and expressive speech. In a sense the Winitz and Reeds method is almost the opposite of the grammar-translation method, and it shows very nicely what is missing in the grammar-translation method. A language taught by the grammar-translation method lacks a direct link to a network of meaning. It has no network of meaning of its own. Instead, words are linked to words in another language, and then to the meaning networks of that other language.

The Essentials of an Effective Method: Comprehension and Problem Solving

"Instead of presenting the student with a rule on a platter," says Emile de Sauzé, "We set up a few carefully chosen illustrations of that rule and we lead him to discover through skillful guidance the relationship of the new element to others previously mastered and to formulate his observations into a law governing those cases" (de Sauzé, 1929, p. 14). This is the way the direct method teaches grammar through listening comprehension and problem solving. The student's understanding of the principles of grammar, in de Sauzé's view, will "multiply his experience a thousand times" (de Sauzé, 1929, p. 4), a modest way of stating Chomsky and Humboldt's position that with grammar we make "infinite use of finite means" (Chomsky, 1965, p. 8).

The direct method of language teaching has many varieties besides de Sauzé's, and it has a long history extending well beyond the 100 years since the founding of the Berlitz schools in 1878 (see Diller, 1978, Chaps. 7, 13). There are three common characteristics of the direct methods: (1) exclusive use of the foreign language; (2) step-by-step progression from easy to difficult so that there is always accurate comprehension of each new word or construction; and (3) meaningful practice as opposed to mechanical drill. The Winitz and Reeds comprehension approach meets all these criteria, if one recognizes that meaningful practice need not be expressive. The classic direct methods of Berlitz and de Sauzé, however, involved speaking to a very high degree, with the lessons consisting mostly of a question and answer dialogue between teachers and students. In Figure 7.5, we can see how the direct method of de Sauzé involves all the language areas and pathways of the brain, and all the modes of language use including reading and writing. No wonder it is called the "multiple approach" or even the "natural method."

The question and answer dialogue with the Berlitz method would go something like this. By the second lesson, the teacher would be teaching items of clothing. Pointing to a shirt, the teacher would say, "This is a shirt. What is this?" Student: "It's a shirt." Teacher (holding up a book): "Is this a shirt?" Student: "No, it's not a shirt, it's a book." At every point the emphasis is on understanding and expressing the meaning correctly. De Sauzé would add reading and writing to this process, by asking students to write certain questions and

Method

Cortical areas

Auditory-visual information
    emphasizing word-object relation
    toward cognitive and intellectual
    processes.

Area 22, Wernicke's Area.
    verbal detection and
    analysis of elements of
    language.

Verbal comprehension combined
    with verbal expression.

Area 40, Word-object relation
    toward cognitive and intellectual
    processes.

Comprehension of written
    (visual-auditory) words and
    sentences integrated with skilled
    somatic sensory-motor regions.

Areas 44 + 45, Broca's Area.
    associated with somatic
    sensory-motor regions.

Follows neurogenetic progression
    increased by cognitive and
    intellectual skills. Individual
    differences seen within progression.

Areas 6, 4; 3, 1, 2. Somatic
    sensory-motor regions of
    the larynx, pharynx,
    palate, tongue, digits,
    hand, forearm, upper arm,
    shoulder.

Area 39, visualization of
    language in association
    with Wernicke's Area.

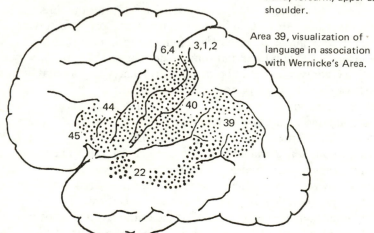

FIGURE 7.5.   The direct method of de Sauzé ("multiple approach," "natural method")

(from Walsh and Diller 1978)

answers on the blackboard, ensuring that students could write and read everything that they could understand and speak.

One can see how this "multiple approach" might work for the Berlitz schools
where each student may choose to have a tutor, or where classes are very small.
In public high schools, things are very different. Suppose that each class is fifty
minutes long, and the teacher talks at least half of that time explaining new
material (using the foreign language for the explanations) and asking questions

of the various students. Only twenty-five minutes are left for the students to talk, and if there are more than twenty-five students in the class, each student will have less than a minute of his or her own to practice talking. We can see that this "multiple approach" is actually less multiple than it might seem. On an individual basis, there is not much speaking. This point was very worrisome to linguists who thought of language as "speech habits," and in their audio-lingual method they tried to devise ways for the teacher to conduct drills by talking less, and ways for more than one student to talk at a time in choral drills of various sorts. According to the speech-habit theorists, the direct method should not work in large classes because students do not get enough practice speaking. Those linguists refused to accept the well-documented fact that the direct method works very well indeed with large classes.

The explanation for how the direct method can work for large classes comes once again from the Winitz and Reeds experiments with the teaching of German through listening comprehension, with the avoidance of speaking. As we have seen, this experiment provides a nice demonstration that language is not just "a set of speech habits," for with the comprehension approach students learn rapidly and effectively to understand languages, without gaining any speech habits at all. When we look back at de Sauzé's direct method, we see that the student in a large class must regard this method primarily as one of comprehension and problem solving, with only minimal time in the classroom for expressing one's hypotheses about the rules of the language by trying to speak. De Sauzé's direct method follows the natural hierarchy of learning in which comprehension precedes production, but it uses speech and writing to a modest extent right from the beginning to help the student in the problem-solving task of figuring out the new language.

Another method, seemingly very different, is also essentially one of comprehension and problem solving. James Asher et al. (1974), with their method of "total physical response," have shown that it is possible to teach a language very effectively entirely through the use of commands. They go from simple commands ("Stand up!," "Sit down!") to such complex commands as "Gregory, find the picture of the beautiful woman with green eyes, long black hair and wearing a sun hat that has red stripes. When you find the picture, show it to the class and describe the woman!" (Asher et al., 1974, p. 27). This method is estimated to be 70 percent listening comprehension, 20 percent speaking, and 10 percent reading and writing, at the elementary stages. Asher's statistics clearly show that the method is highly effective, and the name of the method implies that it is the "total physical response" that is the distinctive clue to its success. A closer look, however, shows us a method of comprehension and problem solving in which the commands present new material in a step-by-step progression. The total physical response may help one's memory, by giving the language a clear physical association, but most important, it is another means for meaningful response to a semantic problem set in the new language.

Let us look at a contrasting method in which listening comprehension goes wrong: the "structuro-global audiovisual method." This method is the best known French response to the empiricist-behaviorist theory of language acquisition, and is seen in such materials as *Voix et images de France* (CREDIF, 1964–1967) and *Dialog Canada I* (1974). The audiovisual method eschews all translation, and attempts to get the meaning of its dialogues across by using pictures in film strips. One might think that this would be like the Winitz and Reeds materials, and that the emphasis is on listening comprehension, but it is not. The dialogues are much too difficult to be comprehended on the first or even second hearing. In fact, each dialogue generally requires an explication by the teacher and repetition up to the point of memorization before it is well comprehended. Even then, specific items in a dialogue are not understood precisely, because of the emphasis on "global comprehension" instead of precise understanding. *Dialog Canada* says with regard to its secondary dialogues that ". . . faced with sound groups which he can't identify, the student has to learn to be satisfied at the beginning with a comprehension which is 'very global.' Equally, he has to master the feelings of frustration which will arise" (*Dialog Canada,* 1974, p. 65, my translation). This method is highly focused on the "reconditioning of behavior," and is therefore not able to deal with comprehension and problem solving in a straightforward manner. Repetition of the dialogue, with perfect pronunciation, is what is important, and global comprehension is enough. Many students are simply unable "to master the feelings of frustration which will arise" from lack of adequate comprehension, and the Public Service Commission has been trying very hard to alter and adapt this method for students who have high language aptitude scores but poor performance in class (Wesche, 1981).

We have seen with both the "audio-lingual method" and with the "structuro-global audiovisual method" that lack of emphasis on meaningful practice makes these methods deficient. That some students succeed with these methods is strong testimony to the language-learning capabilities of these human beings. Language is a symbol system in which meaning is related to acoustic (or written) signs. Relating the sound to the meaning, not just the production of the sound, is what is important. An effective language-teaching method will help the student figure out the rules that relate sound to meaning, and will code these rules in the brain in such a way that they function naturally for comprehension of the language and for expression.

Dealing with Individual Diversity:
In the larger context of "meaningful practice," comprehension and problem solving can be aided by speaking, reading, and writing.

There are instances in which generally successful methods of language teaching simply do not work well for some students.

To take an extreme and pathological example, one would probably not try the total physical response method with a quadraplegic. Nor would a profoundly deaf person be a good prospect for a listening comprehension method. Even among "normal" students, we have tremendous individual differences which mirror the language pathologies in minor ways. These differences show up when infants are learning their mother tongues: Not only are some children slower than others, they also have different strategies. Some children are very hard to understand, because they seem to try to say sentences that are much too long for their production abilities; others start with one-word utterances and build up gradually to longer sentences (cf. Peters, 1977). Language aptitude studies show that there are at least four different factors in language learning aptitude: phonetic coding, grammatical sensitivity, rote memory, and inductive language learning ability (cf. Carroll, 1963). People differ from each other on each of these abilities, and there is not a high correlation between excellence in one and excellence in another.

Suppose a student was highly able in grammatical sensitivity, rote memory, and inductive language learning ability, but was a disaster in phonetic coding ability. This student would also be a disaster with a listening comprehension method which excluded reading, writing, and speech. This is to say that reading and writing would help some people immensely in comprehension and problem solving. It might well help most people more than it would hinder them.

We need a special word about reading. The majority of people alive in the world have not learned to read, and it seems that reading is not a natural consequence of being a normal human being the way knowing a language is. On the other hand, reading comprehension practice has redeemed many a bad foreign language classroom—my German class, for example, where I read German books in the back of the room.

The main problem with reading at the elementary level is that few reading materials are organized with a step-by-step progression so that comprehension and problem solving can proceed in a natural way without reference to dictionaries and grammar books. Even with properly organized materials, however, reading comprehension will work better in conjunction with listening comprehension. Many people can read foreign languages reasonably well without having any listening comprehension at all, but few people will be truly competent at reading without also having at least moderate listening comprehension as well.

If reading and writing can help with comprehension and problem solving, what about speech? Speech, too, is an aid to solving problems of language. I asked someone at the Berlitz schools once what they did for comprehension tests. He replied that they did not need special tests, for their whole method was based on questions to the student, and they could tell by the student's responses how much had been understood. If language learning is a problem-solving process in which people make hypotheses about how the language works, then speech is the best medium for testing these hypotheses out. It gives feedback to the teacher, who can restructure the comprehension exercises appropriately.

This is not to say that speaking, reading, and writing or even listening will necessarily help in a language-learning situation. Each of these modes of language can be used to help or to hinder the language-learning process. Insofar as students fail to understand the dialogues of the structuro-global audiovisual method, for example, these listening exercises will not be very useful in contributing to language learning. Likewise, mechanical speaking or writing drills, divorced from meaning, will do relatively little to encourage learning.

Language learning, we have said, is by definition a process of problem solving in which the learners figure out how the language works on the basis of the meaningful utterances that they hear or see. Listening comprehension, with its implied problem solving, is the essential core of the meaningful practice that is required for a good method of language teaching. But a broad concept of meaningful practice which includes reading, writing, and speech along with listening comprehension, always in a step-by-step progression so that comprehension is possible, will give us the best methods.

Notes

1. For a review of the many different kinds of aphasia, with references for further reading, see Goodglass and Geschwind, 1976.

2. That is, Mimicry-Memorization, and Pattern Drill. For a critique of this method and its underlying empiricist-behaviorist theory of language learning, see Diller, 1978.

References

Asher, J., Kusudo, J., and de la Torre, R. "Learning a second language through commands: The second field test." *The Modern Language Journal, 58,* pp. 24–32, 1974.

Carroll, J. B. "Research on teaching foreign languages." In N. L. Gage (Ed.), *Handbook of research on teaching.* Chicago: Rand McNally, 1963.

Chomsky, N. *Aspects of the theory of syntax.* Cambridge, Mass.: M.I.T. Press, 1965.

CREDIF. *Voix et images de France.* Paris: Didier, 1964–1967.

de Sauzé, E. *The Cleveland plan for the teaching of modern languages with special reference to French.* Philadelphia: Winston, 1929.

Dialog Canada I. Cahier de méthodologie, niveau élémentaire, édition corrigée. Ottawa: Commission de la Fonction publique du Canada, 1974.

Diller, K. C. *The language teaching controversy.* Rowley, Mass.: Newbury House, 1978. (A revised and expanded edition of *Generative grammar, structural linguistics and language teaching,* 1971.)

———. *Individual differences and universals in language learning aptitude.* Rowley, Mass.: Newbury House, 1981.

Diller, K. C., and Walsh, T. M. " 'Living' and 'dead' languages—A neurolinguistic distinction." Paper presented to the Fifth International Congress of Applied Linguistics, 1978.

Geschwind, N., Quadfasel, F., and Segarra, J. "Isolation of the speech area." *Neuropsychologia,*
6, pp. 327–340, 1968.

Goodglass, H., and Geschwind, N. "Language disorders (aphasia)." In E. T. Carterette (Ed.),
Handbook of perception, Vol. 7: *Language and speech.* New York: Academic Press, 1976.

Peters, A. "Language learning strategies: Does the whole equal the sum of the parts?" *Language,*
53, pp. 560–573, 1977. (Reprinted in Diller, 1981.)

Twaddell, W. "Meanings, habits and rules." *Education, 69,* pp. 75–81, 1948.

Walsh, T. M., and Diller, K. C. "Neurolinguistic foundations to methods of teaching a second
language." *International Review of Applied Linguistics, 16,* pp. 1–14, 1978.

Wesche, M. "Language aptitude measures in streaming, matching students with methods, and
diagnosis of learning problems." In K. C. Diller, 1981.

Whitaker, H. "A case of isolation of the language function." In H. Whitaker and H. A. Whitaker
(Eds.), *Studies in neurolinguistics,* Vol. 2. New York: Academic Press, 1976.

Winitz, H., and Reeds, J. A. "Rapid acquisition of a foreign language (German) by the avoidance of
speaking." *International Review of Applied Linguistics, 11,* pp. 295–317, 1973.

———. *Comprehension and problem solving as strategies for language training.* The Hague:
Mouton, 1975.

CHAPTER 8

Machine-Aided Instruction in Bahasa Indonesia

Robbins Burling, Professor of Anthropology
and Linguistics, University of Michigan

Alton L. Becker, Professor of Linguistics and
Anthropology, University of Michigan

Patricia B. Henry, Instructor, Department of Foreign
Languages and Literature, Northern Illinois University

Joyce N. Tomasowa, Dosen, English Department,
Teacher Training College, Malang, Indonesia

We wish to report here on our experience at the University of Michigan with a method of machine-aided instruction in the comprehension of Bahasa Indonesia, the official language of Indonesia.[1] Our point of departure was the belief that many of the problems associated with elementary language instruction might be avoided if we would focus first upon comprehension while leaving insistence upon production for a later time. It then quickly became apparent that the more repetitive aspects of instruction could be mechanized and that this would free the instructor for more creative tasks than drill. We wanted a system of mechanization that would give students the ability to call for unlimited repetitions, without ever having to face the public embarrassment of having forgotten a word or of having to ask the teacher to repeat it again.

At the same time we recognized the dangers of student tedium and frustration when dealing for many hours with a cold and impersonal piece of hardware, and so, from the beginning, we were concerned with programming our equipment in as many different ways as possible. We hoped to make the lessons more than merely a challenge; we also wanted them to be interesting and even fun. In this chapter we will briefly describe the mechanical equipment that we have constructed, and then review a few of the ways in which we have tried to design lessons that would exploit its potentialities.

Our plan was to provide students with three things: (1) a set of earphones or a loudspeaker over which the students would hear samples of the language; (2) a series of pictures that, by illustrating objects, scenes, situations, and stories, would provide the context for the language that they have heard, and (3) a set of

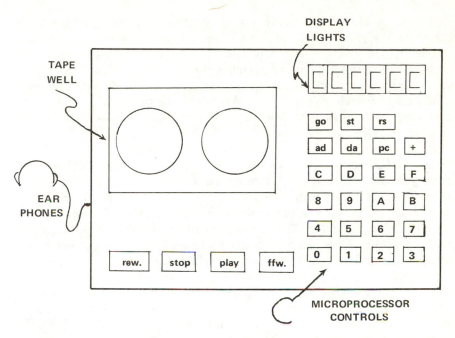

FIGURE 8.1.   Schematic description of the equipment used to present language lessons

controls with which they could respond to what they had seen and heard and by means of which they could control the equipment and determine what they would hear next.

Our pictures have been simple but entirely adequate. For the most part, we have used sketches that the least untalented member of our group drew on ditto masters. In addition to simple objects and situations, these have shown connected sequences like those familiar to our students from comic strips. These sketches are simple, but we have tried to have them reflect something of the characteristic culture of the parts of the world where Bahasa Indonesia is spoken.

Our mechanical equipment is a good deal more complex. Our present version is a self-contained unit which is about the size of a reel-to-reel tape recorder. It sits on a desk and, when necessary, it can be carried about quite easily (see Figure 8.1). At its heart are a Kim-One microprocessor and a Phi-Deck tape drive. The Kim-One is one of a number of microprocessors (genuine but minia-ture computers) that are now on the market. It is produced in considerable quantities for the competitive hobby market so it is not too expensive. It is controlled by means of a twenty-three-button "touch pad"—an array of buttons similar to those on a touch-tone telephone. The Phi-Deck is a variable speed tape-drive with a tape well which receives a standard tape cassette. The student selects the cassette of the lesson he or she wishes to study, and loads it into the tape well of the Phi-Deck. The student operates the microprocessor by means of the touch pad, and by the choice made among the buttons, demonstrates his or her understanding. The microprocessor, in turn, controls the tape drive and instructs it to play, stop, repeat, or back up. The student can work at a time of his or her own choosing. The student can select the tape of whatever lesson he or she wishes to work on, and can operate the equipment alone. While our present equipment is considerably more complex to operate than would be ideal, our goal is to produce a model that is hardly more difficult to use than a tape recorder or a pocket calculator.

As is perhaps inevitable, our first experiments have been made exciting by occasional mechanical mysteries. Until we discovered that our equipment was picking up stray electrical signals through the power line and misreading them as instructions, it had an uncanny tendency to take off on its own now and then— backing up, fast forwarding, or getting the answers out of synchronization with the frames. Once during the first term a capacitor burned out, producing a haze of alarming blue smoke, and we feared our experiment was about to come to a precipitous end. The equipment was repairable, however, and we are gradually working out its other bugs. Nevertheless, hopeful experimenters should be given fair warning that experimental equipment like ours has an eerie tendency to assume a diabolical personality of its own. During the first few weeks, mechanical failures were occasionally conducive to a certain spirited camara-derie among the students, but they could also be extraordinarily frustrating. Tinkering has steadily improved the equipment, however, and the remarkable reliability and endurance of the basic components—modern tape drives and inexpensive microprocessors—should make it possible to assemble reliable equipment without extraordinary financial outlay.

We have considered various programs that might be used to relate the student's response to the movements of the tape, but, for the moment, we have settled on a single rather simple pattern. With further development we would like to introduce more flexibility into the program but, for now, the single pattern seems quite effective. Through the earphones, the student hears a frame, consisting of an Indonesian word, phrase, sentence, or story, and then the tape stops and waits for the student to press a button on the touch pad. Typically, the student must look at one of the pictures, decide upon the relationship between what he or she has heard in the earphones and what he or she sees in the picture, and then choose a button to press. In one of the simplest types of lessons, for instance, a student has pictures of approximately nine objects, each with a number. The student hears the name for one of these objects in Bahasa Indonesia, selects the object he or she believes the word stands for, and then presses the corresponding numbered button on the touch pad. If the student presses the correct button, display lights shine with a rewarding series of "C's," but if he or she makes an error a less pleasing series of "E's" appears. The student learns immediately whether or not the correct choice has been made. When ready for another frame, the student presses the "+" button, and then hears another sample. If the student has made an error on his or her last try, the tape will back up and repeat the frame so the student must try again and, indeed, must keep trying until he or she finally hits upon the correct answer. When, after one or more errors, the student finally makes the right choice, the machine backs up two frames and plays the frame that immediately preceded the one on which the error was made. The mistake suggests the need for a bit of additional practice, and the risk of backing up encourages the student to try, as best he or she can, to develop a working hypothesis that will enable the student to make educated rather than random guesses. The threat of a repeat is not enough to be terribly discouraging, but if students persist in making too many mistakes they can back up slowly through the lesson, for they will move back one frame each time they have made, and then corrected, a mistake. No one can work through a tape without thinking about what he or she is doing. If the student's mind wanders the equipment stops and waits patiently for the student to begin again.

If the student correctly answers the frame preceding the one which he or she originally got wrong, the tape will advance once again to the frame on which the original mistake was made. This is supposed to give the student a chance for a final check of the example and a chance to consolidate his or her understanding of it. Thus, whenever a mistake is made, the student must, at a minimum, hear that frame two more times, once immediately, and once after the interval of at least one other frame. The student must get the frame right both times to proceed. As long as the student makes no mistakes he or she will move ahead step by step through the sequence of frames. In order to allow the student to hear a frame a second or third (or nth) time, without having to make a mistake, we have programmed the equipment so that one of the touch pad buttons will call for a simple repeat of the last frame played.

In our first experiments we omitted the step in which the student has to press the "+" button to continue. In that version the equipment played another frame as soon as the student pushed a single button—a new frame if it was the correct choice, otherwise a repeat. However, volunteers who tried the equipment sometimes felt rushed. After giving an answer they wanted a chance to stop and think about what they had heard, and to make sure that they had grasped the significance of their guess. They sometimes needed a pause either to consolidate their correct response in their mind or to stop and puzzle out the reason for their mistake. In actual practice with our present equipment, students often choose an answer and immediately tap the "+" button to go on, but the possibility for a pause is built into the program and on some occasions it seems essential.

GUESSING

From the start, we have hoped to construct lessons that would encourage the students to guess, to form hypotheses, and then to check their guesses by trying them out. In that way, we felt, they would gradually build up a feeling for the design of the language they were hearing. There is a very important—but far too often forgotten—principle of learning that we have tried to capture with our lessons; the principle that says we learn at least some things best by making mistakes. Fear of mistakes may be one of the chief impediments in conventional language classes, a fear that even careful teachers easily engender. When fear and anxiety capture the mind and blot out the meaning of an error one probably learns little from it. For most people, making errors in private is tolerable. Our program, in this regard, makes for a context in which one can learn from errors. Furthermore, it actually encourages a strategy of hypothesis testing by presenting problems, not just data to be memorized. The fact that errors in the hypotheses bring a series of E's in the display and a repeat of the material being learned is not intended as a punishment; it is simply an indication to the student that his or her hypothesis needs to be modified.

This forming and modification of hypotheses can become quite complex, since the problem of how to understand the sentences of a lesson can sometimes be "solved" in more than one way. For example, the language being presented in a lesson varies in accordance with the context of the pictures, but variation sometimes takes place simultaneously in several different ways (see Conclusions, below). As a result, there is no way the student can know beforehand what the crucial cue is, and he or she cannot confidently correlate the linguistic and contextual variables. The student has to guess. In this case a "mistake" can tell the learner more than a "correct" lucky guess. Students seem to grasp this point quickly. One said she didn't learn anything from one lesson; asked why, she said thoughtfully, "because I didn't make any mistakes."

By concentrating upon comprehension, we felt we could let students bypass some of the drearier aspects of early language learning. In particular, the need for focusing attention upon the excruciating irregularities of the language would be minimized as would the need to manipulate pronunciation, vocabulary, and syntax all at the same time when none of them is known at all well. We also felt that our equipment would give students extensive exposure to the language as spoken by native speakers while sharply reducing their exposure to the corrupting influence of the inevitable mispronunciations and syntactical errors of their classmates, such as always occur in conventional language classes. When using the equipment, a few students, not all, seem at times to want to vocalize. They mumble repetitions of what they have just heard, and we have not discouraged them from doing so, but before requiring students to say anything at all, we have wanted to give them many hours of experience hearing the language as native speakers use it. We have hoped that this experience would do more to encourage passable pronunciation than the most intensive, and tedious, of drills.

For all these reasons, we had high hopes that our equipment would allow a relatively rapid, and a relatively pleasant, path through the early stages of language learning. At the same time, we were concerned about the impersonality of a machine of wires and metal. We were afraid that students might become frustrated and bored by its cold and metallic personality, and that they would resent the absence of a live human teacher. Our equipment is endlessly patient, and it will repeat, without complaint, as often as a student desires repetition. But this mechanical patience is balanced by a certain mechanical insensitivity (although spiced with a certain electronic capriciousness), and in the remainder of this chapter we suggest the efforts we have made to overcome its inevitable limitations, and to introduce whatever flexibility our equipment allows, by designing lessons that would be as varied and as interesting as we could devise.

All our lessons incorporate some instructions to the student. The instructions tell the student about the pattern of the lesson and, in a few cases, they explain difficult points about the language. It seems easier for the students when these instructions are on the tape rather than in a separate sheaf of paper. The instructions tell the student which picture to turn to, and whether the frames he or she is about to hear are to be matched with numbered pictures, judged as true or false, or responded to in some other fashion. In the beginning, of course, these instructions have to be in English but, later, we shift as many as possible to Bahasa Indonesia. Even in the course of a single tape, we often change the pattern of expected responses, and in such cases one frame is devoted to instructions that tell the student about the new pattern or picture. Usually we want students to be able to pause briefly after the instructions so that they can find the correct picture or make certain that they understand what is expected, and our convention is to have the student press "Zero" as the "answer" to an instruction frame. The student then presses "+" when ready to proceed to the next example.

One of the unfortunate rigidities of our present equipment is that it has no way of distinguishing an instruction frame from the frames that consist of language samples. This means that if a student makes an error on the first frame after mid-lesson instructions are given, the machine will repeat that frame until the student gets it right and then go back to the instruction frame and play that again. This can be annoying, although it does not appear to be a serious problem as long as mid-lesson instructions are brief. With a more elaborate machine program it should be possible to eliminate repetitions of the instructions.

THE LESSONS

One obvious lesson pattern is the one already referred to, in which each of a series of numbered pictures represents a different word, phrase, or sentence. The student simply selects the picture that illustrates the frame he or she has just heard. The easiest words to present in this manner, of course, are names of picturable objects, and the pattern provides a quick and rather efficient way of offering first exposure to a new set of such words. Sixteen of the twenty buttons on our equipment allow a maximum of sixteen alternative responses, and it would be possible to program two-digit responses which would permit a far larger range of alternatives. We have felt, however, that too large a range would put an impossible burden upon a student who gets confused to the point of resorting to random guessing. With too many possible responses, stumbling upon the correct answer would become an interminable chore, and, in practice, we have limited ourselves to no more than nine to twelve alternative choices. We give the student a dittoed sheet with numbered pictures and then, in successive frames on the tape, we introduce the corresponding words or phrases. In order to minimize the need for too much aimless guessing we have adopted the practice of having the first occurrence of each new word or phrase appear in numerical order, but we intersperse these first occurrences with a review of words already covered. Thus the initial sequence of answers to a series of frames might be something like this: 1, 2, 3, 2, 1, 3, 4, 1, 4, 3, 5, . . . etc. Each time the student hears a totally new word, he or she will know that it is the next word in sequence. In principle, a student with total recall would never need to make a mistake. Of course every student does make mistakes and the equipment then automatically provides the student with repetitions and extra practice.

A sequence of about fifty frames, with each word repeated five or six times in scattered frames, can be covered within fifteen or twenty minutes and, by the time the student has finished, he or she will have the words well enough in mind to be able to recognize them in sentences, though it will certainly be necessary to hear them again in the course of the next several lessons if they are to become securely fixed in the student's memory.

While words for picturable objects are the most obvious candidates for introduction in this manner, many other types of words are quite possible. Phrases such as "the child runs," "the child sits," "the child eats," etc., can be matched with pictures of a child doing these things, while pictures of colored objects can be matched to phrases such as "the red book," "the blue book," "the black book," etc., and in this way some verbs and adjectives can be introduced. We introduced numbers by including them in phrases that referred to pictures of varying numbers of cats and coconuts.

Our very first lesson was based upon a variant of this pattern. We gave students an array of nine pictures, each of which included either one person or three persons and each of which had an empty word balloon of the kind used to enclose dialogue in comic strips. The individuals in the pictures were pointing either to themselves or to someone else, and students heard sentences with such meanings as "I am Tati," "This is Mr. Sulaiman," "That is Bambang," etc. The students had to match the sentences with the proper pictures, and in this way the students quickly learned the words for "I," "this," and "that," as well as the names of the characters who would appear in subsequent lessons.

It is a relatively easy task to design lessons of this sort and they can quickly expose students to a set of new words and give them practice in recognizing these words in a context that the picture provides, but this is probably the least imaginative of the lesson patterns we have devised, and even though students seem quite willing to work with a certain number of lessons of this form, we would fear their impatience if we offered them no variety.

One variation that changes little but that does give context to words is to provide a single picture with several numbered objects that are related in a single scene. The lesson can proceed in the same manner, but the student has the satisfaction of seeing objects in relation to one another. For an early lesson, for example, we drew a simple street scene in which such objects as a house, a school, a banana, a banana tree, a coconut, etc., were numbered so that students could select the objects named in successive frames on the tape.

More variety can be introduced by providing a number of sentences that describe a single scene. The sentences can use words that, for the most part, have already been introduced, and the easiest pattern is to ask the student to judge whether the sentences that they hear are "true" or "false" in regard to the scene that they see in the picture. Our convention has been to have them press button "one" if they believe the sentence to be true, and button "two" if they believe it to be false. Sometimes, instead of asking students to respond to sentences as either true or false, we have asked questions that require a "yes" or "no" answer but we have used the same conventions: one means "yes" and two means "no." True-false sentences and yes-no questions provide an obvious point at which to introduce negatives and various forms of questions. Whether the answer is "true," "false," "yes," or "no," every sentence heard is fully grammatical and spoken by a native speaker of the language, but the student's conscious attention is always focused upon the meaning of the sentence rather than upon its structure. This, of course, is where the attention of native speakers is focused and, insofar as possible, we believe it is desirable to direct the attention of our students to meaning, and minimize their conscious attention to phonology and syntax.

Numbers might be introduced along with many sorts of objects and events, but one area with which numbers have a natural affinity is currency. We have several lessons that include money, and one of the earliest is introduced soon after numbers appear for the first time. It is designed both to help consolidate the student's control of the numbers and to introduce the Indonesian monetary system. The pictures for this lesson show schematic coins and bills. These are labeled with appropriate numbers of rupiahs. The student hears the total number of rupiahs associated with one group of coins and bills and selects the number of the appropriate picture. Since one Indonesian rupiah is a very small amount of money, this is a natural point for the introduction of large numbers, and later lessons that include prices of objects provide additional practice.

Spatial relationships are easy to introduce. People and objects can be shown in the pictures as "in," "on," "by," "near to," or "far from" other people and objects, and the words describing these relationships can be quickly grasped. Time relationships, and events that occur through time, are somewhat more difficult to convey with the still pictures we have used, but the task has not proved to be impossible. Quite early in our lessons, we begin to use sequences of pictures that illustrate simple stories. One sequence of nine pictures, for instance, shows, successively, a woman going to the market, meeting another woman who is selling fish and a man who is selling fruit, inquiring how to find still other market people, and, finally, bargaining briefly over the price and buying some fruit. The student hears sentences that describe what is going on in each of the pictures, and these sentences include words that show the time relationships within the story.

Some of the sentences in these lessons give the words that one of the characters in the story is using. We indicate this event by an empty "word balloon." Other sentences describe what one of the characters is thinking, and we indicate this by a balloon containing a picture of the thought. Following the well-known comic strip convention, we connect a "thought balloon" to the character by a line of small bubbles. Variety and flexibility are increased when more than a single sentence can be associated with each picture. The first picture of the marketing sequence, for instance, has Mrs. Sulaiman heading toward the bazaar and thinking about coconuts, fish, and chili peppers. Sentences associated with this picture include the Indonesian equivalents for "Mrs. Sulaiman is going to the bazaar," and "Mrs. Sulaiman wants to buy fish, coconuts, and chili peppers."

Sequences of pictures that tell a story can introduce some words that show time relationships, but we also introduce specific words along with calendars and pictures of clocks. From a reference day circled on a calendar, we can count backward to "yesterday" and "last week" and forward to "tomorrow," and "next month." We can ask students to judge the truth or falsity of statements such as "three days ago it was Monday" or "three years from now it will be 1981." With simple clock faces we can indicate that at 11:30 "It is not yet noon," and that at 12:30 "Noon is already past." A sequence of pictures suggesting the time of the day by means of the sun's position in the sky can relate events to culturally recognized periods of the day. Films or video tapes might show time sequence and motion more graphically and explicitly, but they would add so many complexities to our methods that we doubt whether the results would be worth the effort.

A language cannot be learned without some sort of context, and all our early lessons, as well as the majority of those that come later, have one or more pictures to provide a convenient context. The pictures allow us to avoid, almost entirely, translations into English. Of course we cannot prevent students from doing some translations of their own, but the pressure of the lessons is always toward direct association between the language that is heard and the objects and events that are pictured. Even very simple pictures, moreover, can convey some sense of the foreign setting in which the language is used. From the beginning we use pictures that show typical Indonesian clothing, houses, shops, and trees, and we have illustrated events such as the rice harvest and food preparation in order to lend an Indonesian flavor to the lessons.

For a few of our lessons we have duplicated illustrations and photographs that show Indonesian scenes. These have an advantage over the sketches since their realism can define the social situation more precisely and, in that way, govern the language more closely. Often, however, it is easier to produce a sketch that corresponds to the lesson one wants to construct than to construct a lesson that will fit the photograph at hand.

In some cases we have combined one or more pictures with a rather long initial passage and the passage may even include a good many previously unknown words. We have, for example, a picture of people working in a rice field. Some are cutting the rice, others are collecting it in bundles at the side of the field or carrying it away on a shoulder pole. The student first hears a rather lengthy passage that describes the scene. The student is warned that the passage will contain a number of unfamiliar words, but is asked to guess their meaning and not to worry if he or she cannot, at first, understand everything. After hearing the passage through, the student turns to a slightly different version of the same picture. Here, several objects shown in the picture are numbered and even shown in detailed insets in the margins. The student is then given practice learning these unfamiliar words. Having first encountered the words in the context of a picture and a short narrative, and having already tried to guess their meaning, the drill required to learn them comes as a way of giving substance to the earlier full context, and the words seem less isolated and independent.

As we proceed, it becomes possible to develop a few lessons that have no pictures at all. These begin to give students experience with listening to and understanding the language without the help of visual hints. We give students stories of gradually increasing length and difficulty. These stories use many words with which the student is already familiar, but now and then new words are included that require a bit of judicious guessing. Sometimes we divide the story into several separate frames, each frame to be "answered" with a simple "Zero." This provides no test of the student's understanding, but it does allow the student a pause to think over what he or she has heard or even to repeat a part of the story one or more times if he or she feels that repetitions would help. The student can take as much time working through the story as he or she wishes, but need not fear mistakes. When finished, the student will have to demonstrate his or her understanding of the story in some way. The student may have to respond to yes–no questions or judge statements as true or false, and, to give variety to the lessons, we sometimes use multiple-choice questions as well. For instance, we sometimes give an incomplete sentence and then three alternative phrases that might complete it. All three are grammatically correct, but only one of them corresponds to the meaning of the story that has been heard. The student must select the correct phrase and press the correct button before going on to another example.

In a few cases we have translated words within the lessons and we have sometimes given the students a written text as support for what they hear on the tape. In the earliest lesson of this type thirteen sentences of a story are first read as a block. The story describes the arrival of two people at a train station, their visit to a restaurant in the station, their meeting with others, and their snack of cake and tea. The story includes several unfamiliar words that make the passage a difficult one for students, but we give them the written text (there is no picture with this lesson) so they can look at the text and at least associate the sounds with the letters. After hearing the text through once it is repeated one sentence at a time, and the unfamiliar words are defined by the speaker on the tape. The student hears the following explanation: "The Indonesian word *berarti* means, in English, 'means.' (pause) The phrase *berarti dalam Bahasa Inggeris* means 'means in English.' For example: *'Beli' berarti dalam Bahasa Inggeris 'buy.'* That is, *Beli* means 'buy' in English. We will use this phrase, *berarti dalam Bahasa Inggeris,* to explain new words." After this, new words from the story are translated by means of this expression in Bahasa Indonesia. Thus, while having the story explained, the student is also introduced to part of the basic Indonesian vocabulary for talking about language. The sentences of this lesson are numbered from one to thirteen, and, when going through the lesson sentence by sentence, the number is given as each new sentence is reached. At first the sentences are labeled in English as "Sentence one," "Sentence two," etc., but as soon as the students can be expected to feel comfortable with the format, they hear, instead, such phrases as *Kalimat lima* (Sentence five). Gradually, as the instructions as well as the examples shift to Indonesian, the students are weaned away from English. After some help with each sentence, the student hears questions about the story and he or she must respond correctly before going on. In this way the student is drawn through the story and given experience with the new words.

We see few limits to the linguistic complexities that could, in principle, be introduced by our technique. The limits lie, instead, in the tolerance of the students for this mechanized approach to language instruction, and in their inevitably growing desire to communicate more actively and to engage in conversations of their own. Nevertheless, we have been encouraged to find that students seem quite content to work with the equipment for periods of an hour or more and to put in several hours a week with this method. In the course of an hour with the equipment they certainly hear more Indonesian spoken than they would hear during an hour in a more conventional classroom, and everything they hear is spoken by a native speaker. Students are never corrupted by exposure to the inevitably distorted language of other learners.

In addition to their time with the equipment, the students spent two hours a week in class. One of these hours was left free for discussion of problems that arose while working through the mechanized lessons. During our first time through we felt it was essential to have this time available, so as to make sure students did not feel they had been abandoned. The lessons were discussed to whatever extent the students desired. The instructor brought in no lessons, and the students soon learned that they could structure the class themselves. When a word or grammatical process was puzzling, even after the taped lesson was finished, the student could ask for as much explanation as he or she wanted, but nothing new was introduced in this hour. A good part of these periods was spent discussing the process of language learning, what worked and what did not. Since several class members were linguists and concerned with the nature of language learning, these discussions were often spirited.

In the other "live" hour, we deliberately tried to move as far from the mechanical and structural nature of the mechanized lessons as we could. As an antidote to any dangers of overmechanization, we took a literary approach. An Indonesian or Malay proverb, chant, verse, song, mantra, joke—some short but evocative bit of language was written on the board, discussed word by word, and then urged upon the students for memorization. Something to show off with when someone asked them to say something in Bahasa Indonesia, perhaps. But also something real, usually old and fascinating, to engage their scholarly minds.

A short sample is this section of an old Malay mantra used to revive people who have fainted:

Mari, Kuh, kemari!	Here, Soul, come here!
Mari, Semangat, kemari,	Here, Spirit, come here,
Mari, Kecil, kemari,	Here, Little, come here,
Mari, Burung, kemari,	Here, Bird, come here,
Mari, Halua, kemari.	Here, Delicate, come here.

Here is an imperative rhetorical strategy (repeated, with variation, five times), some culturally important vocabulary, and the opportunity for a short stroll into the Malay/Indonesian world. Here, getting away from the mechanized lessons, we pointed instead at the more poetic, less translatable qualities of the language.

CONCLUSIONS

In the spring of 1978 we were still in our first year of experimentation with this method, but it may nevertheless be of interest to report some preliminary and admittedly impressionistic reactions of our students. As the official language of the fifth most populous nation of the world, Bahasa Indonesia is hardly a minor language, but it must be acknowledged that students who study it are unlikely to constitute an average cross-section of the American student body. Only those with specific motivation, such as the imminence of a trip to Indonesia or special association with the people from the country, are likely to sign up for a course in a language as exotic to Americans as Bahasa Indonesia. Nevertheless, we have a few students whose memories of more conventional forms of language instruction are distinctly unhappy, and they tell us that they find our methods to be mercifully lacking in threats. Worries about making foolish mistakes pose no problem. We have been careful not to look over the shoulders of our students as they have used the equipment, for, except as it affects our ideas about how to construct more balanced lessons, we do not care how many mistakes they make or how many times they need to repeat.

When, toward the end of the first term, we finally began to ask students to speak the language they had been hearing, we were gratified to find that, with no drill whatsoever, their pronunciation was remarkably good. It seems that simply by hearing large quantities of the language, students become sensitized to the phonology, and when they start to speak themselves they have a sense of what sounds right and what does not sound right. Little in the way of deliberate instruction in pronunciation seems necessary.

Another interesting—and unexpected—phenomenon that seemed to reflect a deep principle of language learning emerged. Speed of response sometimes *decreased* as understanding set in. A student might be able to respond correctly and speedily to sentences by rote memory of particular cues, but at the point of comprehension the student might slow down as he or she began to think through the phenomenon being listened to. We first observed this behavior when one of us (Burling), who had never studied Bahasa Indonesia, went through a tentative lesson to try it out, with another one of us playing the role of the machine. He responded quickly for a while but then abruptly slowed down. "Why," the rest of us asked, "did you slow down?" "Because I'm understanding the sentences and thinking them through instead of responding by rote memory." It was a moment of epiphany for us all—the realization that speed of response can be a poor and even misleading measure of ability in a language. The experience also underscores the importance, in language-learning research, of one of the researchers being a real learner who can experience the lessons and provide insights that no teacher can ever have alone. Only a learner can show what happens on the other side of the lessons. It was because one of us was able to experience the role of learner that we discovered that slowing down can be a sign of understanding.

Some subtle artistry is needed when constructing lessons that are difficult enough to be interesting but not so difficult as to seem impossible. A few of our lessons have, indeed, struck students as tediously repetitious. Others have seemed formidably difficult. We hope we are gradually getting a better sense of the ideal pacing, and ultimately we would like to have optional review sections that would let students make some of their own decisions about how much practice they need. Even now, of course, students are free to go back and review earlier lessons as much or as little as they please, and this does allow some flexibility and some adaptation to individual preferences and needs.

We have aimed for a level of difficulty in which students would have to make a few guesses, and would have to expect to make a few mistakes, but where each mistake would tell the student something about the way the language works. We have not wanted students to become bogged down in hopeless complexities, and, in the hope of avoiding too much frustration, we have provided them with transcripts of the lessons. These show each individual frame and its correct answer. Whenever they wish, students can look up the frame in the transcript, see the examples written out, and find the correct answer. This has allowed them to get past a few particularly difficult points. We have asked the students whether they would like even more guidance. Would they, for instance, prefer to have the problems of each lesson explained before starting so that they could move through it more quickly? Our students have given a decisive "No" as their answer to this question. They insisted that it was more fun and, in the long run, more useful to try to guess at the words and figure out the grammatical patterns themselves. Perhaps the students had simply been persuaded by our own arguments, for we had told them exactly what we hoped to accomplish and why we had designed the lessons in that way, but at least they were easily persuaded. Their interest in guessing their way through the lessons confirms our initial presumption: that language instruction can be made more interesting by being presented as a series of problems. Thoughtful guessing and the trying out of hypotheses can then draw students into an ever deepening knowledge of the language.

One other student reaction may be worth passing on. We have asked them for their subjective reports on the strategies they use for understanding sentences.

More than we would have expected, they report listening primarily for words—for lexical items. Pronunciation poses hardly any problem at all. The sounds of Bahasa Indonesia come through clearly on our tapes and, while a few of these are unfamiliar to English speakers, they seem to be readily accepted and distinguished from one another. Even the fairly elaborate phonological assimilation that occurs between the roots and prefixes passes with little problem. Indeed, it passes almost without notice. More surprisingly, grammatical patterns recede into the background of consciousness more quickly than we had expected. The fact that words sometimes occur in an unfamiliar order seems to make very little difference to the students. Numeral classifiers that change with the item counted, and equational sentences that lack a verb, are accepted without qualm.

What students really focus upon are the words of the sentence and the meanings of these words. They have to decide what words occur in each sentence they hear and they have to decide what these words mean. If they hear the words "tree," "cat," "in," and "two" when looking at a series of pictures, only one of which has two cats sitting in a tree, they seem to care very little about what order these words appear in. Recognizing the words and knowing their individual meanings is enough to allow one to select the right picture. This may seem to represent a pitifully imperfect and incomplete understanding of the sentence, but it corresponds rather well to the subjective feeling that naive speakers have toward their own native language. Most people who are innocent of linguistics look upon language as if it consists primarily of an inventory of meaningful words. The pronunciation of these words is little thought about, for one's native pronunciation tends to be simply accepted as the natural way to speak. Even syntax, for the untrained native speaker, reduces largely to "what sounds right." Most people have only limited (and often violently distorted) conscious ideas about the grammar of their language, but they get along fine by producing sequences of words that "sound right." A conscious knowledge of grammar is hardly necessary for the practical use of language, and too much conscious attention to formal grammatical rules may actually slow up the learners of a new language who have many other things to worry about as they try to speak and understand.

The strategy of focusing on words when working through the lessons presents a rather double-edged sword to the lesson designer. We failed to appreciate the significance of this strategy at first, and as a result we did not introduce enough new vocabulary in the early lessons. It now seems obvious that when we revise the lessons we should use a much more varied vocabulary from the very beginning. At the same time, the use of a more varied vocabulary presents difficulties of its own. If we ask for a choice between "two cats in a tree" and "three dogs in a field," for example, the student need distinguish only one of the pairs (two/three, cat/dog, tree/field) in order to get the right answer. Asking students to choose between "two cats in a tree," "three cats in a tree," and "four cats in a tree," on the other hand, narrows their attention to a specific set of items but risks a terrible tedium. In other words, using a large number of words provides a large number of cues, and it becomes difficult to focus on one specific group of words and to be sure that the students have a clear enough idea of their meaning to allow them to be easily used in later lessons. Our students have managed to use the lessons to understand more and more of the language, but they can sometimes work through a lesson without quite understanding how they have done so, and this can erode the credibility of the method for them. Multiple cues may reduce the number of errors a student makes in going through a given lesson, and this reduces the chances for problem solving and, ultimately, for learning.

The lessons that employ one complex picture, about which the students make yes–no, or true–false judgments, are less liable to this sort of problem than are those that require the students to match what they hear to one of several pictures. The problem with one-picture lessons comes in the limited range of responses available to the students. To some extent students may guess their way through the lesson without being forced to understand exactly what they are hearing since, with only two possible answers, they know the correct answer as soon as they make a bad guess, whether or not they have understood the sentence. As a way of offering more alternatives, we have occasionally made use of a multiple-choice format in which students choose a word or phrase from a short list that we provide, only one of which will accurately complete a sentence or answer a question. With this format we enter into a grayish region of semi-production. While this can be seen as running counter to our strategy of teaching only comprehension at first, it may also provide a useful way of beginning the transition to production. If, as seems to be the case, the recognition of words and their meanings is central to the comprehension of a language, it may also be the case that the need to produce the language is the basic motivation for paying attention to such things as word order and syntactical detail.

One way of dealing with the problem of multiple word-cues is to present the material in a way that will require the students to make progressively more educated guesses. Easily-pictured items can be presented first to build up a basic recognition vocabulary. Next, the student can be asked to judge sentences as true or false of a pictured scene. Thus "dog," "cat," etc., can first be taught separately, and then "the dog is in the field," "the cat is not in the tree," etc., can be presented as part of a true–false lesson. This can help to consolidate the meanings of the words in the students' minds by giving them a broader linguistic and situational context. Once these words are fairly easily understood, it becomes profitable to ask the students to choose which picture the sentence they have heard stands for—whether it is the picture of two cats in a tree or of three dogs in a field, etc. By that time it is less likely that the students will be able to ignore some words in favor of others; it is difficult to ignore words that are already known.

In the end, of course, we want our students to be able to speak Bahasa Indonesia with understandable phonology and with accurate syntax, but phonological and syntactical drills are a deadly part of many introductory language classes. If we can devise a method of instruction that minimizes such drill and that allows a sense of phonology and syntax to be absorbed unconsciously while the student focuses attention upon that part of the language where native speakers have always focused their attention—the lexicon—we may make language instruction considerably more efficient, and we will certainly make it far more pleasant.

Note

1.   Our project has received both the moral and financial support of a large number of individuals and institutions. The Center for South and Southeast Asian Studies at the University of Michigan and the Center for Research on Learning and Teaching, also at Michigan, both contributed crucial financial help that allowed us to get started, but the largest part of our financial support has come from grant number GOO-77-01121 from the Office of Education, Department of Health, Education, and Welfare. We could not possibly have proceeded without the hospitable cooperation of the University of Michigan Language Laboratory and of its Director, Erwin M. Hamson, or without the devotion and ingenuity of its technicians, Barry Legien and Kerry Sandford, and the patience of the Studio Engineer, James Bixler. The Indonesian students of Michigan's Linguistics Department, Stephanus and Katerina Djawani, Liberty Sihombing, Nangsari Ahmad, and H. Bambang Kaswanti Poerwo, not only recorded our lessons but helped to correct our linguistic mistakes. We also owe much to the patience and skill of Kathy Tilden and Linda Wilson who did much of the detailed work of organizing the final transcripts and tapes. Finally, we are much indebted to the members of the first experimental class in Indonesian who, with great patience and high good will, tried out our equipment for the first time during the academic year 1977–1978: Christine Brannick, James Clarkson, William Clinton Driver, Ira Fisher, Suzanne Grahn, Sally Lawler, Wayne Listing, and Eleanor McLaughlin.

Before beginning our own work, we knew about and had profited greatly from the excellent work with Russian of V. A. Postovsky at Monterey, but it was only after we were well launched in the design of our own lessons that we began to discover a number of other workers who had been thinking along lines parallel to our own. The most profitable way of understanding the similarities and differences among our various efforts will be to compare the chapters of this book. We wish to thank James J. Asher and Janet Swaffar for their helpful and uncompromising comments on an earlier draft of this chapter.

CHAPTER 9

The Priority of Aural Comprehension in the Language Acquisition Process*

*Valerian A. Postovsky***

Former Director, Slavic Languages
Defense Language Institute, Monterey, California

During the past decade advances in technology and methodology of research have made it possible to study, or at least to begin to understand, complex processes involved in human learning and memory. At the very least, it has become clear that the orthodox, neobehavioristic view of learning as a serial, associative process, based on a conditioned-response analogy, has given way to a more dynamic concept in which learning is viewed as a hierarchical construct of coding processes in the central nervous system, and the learner is conceived as an active processor of input data, and selector and controller of output (Lashley, 1951; Melton and Martin, 1972).

Since this theoretical orientation deals with the organization and function of human memory, it forces attention to critical questions about what it is that is being learned and how it is stored and retrieved. Obviously, any information that tends to answer these questions will have important consequences in education in general, and in foreign language teaching in particular. In this chapter an

*Chapter 9 is the original, unpublished paper presented by Dr. Valerian Postovsky at the Fourth International Congress of Applied Linguistics held in Stuttgart, Germany, 1975. A shorter version of this paper appeared in the *Proceedings of the Fourth International Congress of Applied Linguistics,* Vol. 3 (ISBN 3-8107-5001-8), edited by Gerhard Nickel, Stuttgart: HochschulVerlag, 1976. The shorter version contains minor editorial changes made by Dr. Postovsky at the time he prepared this paper for publication. This chapter reflects those changes. Gratitude is expressed to Professor Nickel and HochschulVerlag for granting permission for the reprinting of this paper.

**The views of the author do not purport to reflect the position of the Department of the Army or the Department of Defense.

attempt will be made to analyze the problem of second-language learning. Both theoretical consideration and some empirical evidence will be presented leading to a proposal for specific changes in methodology of foreign language teaching. The main topic under consideration, as the title suggests, will be priority of aural comprehension in the language acquisition process.

Traditionally in the field of foreign language teaching both teachers and learners have tended to underestimate the complexity of the learning task. This tendency can be traced directly to such common sense notions as "learning by doing" and "practice makes perfect" and to the position assumed by behavioristic psychology that language learning can be described by the imitation-repetition and analogy paradigm.

However, it is logically indefensible to assume that the second language acquisition process begins with imitation of verbal responses. Applying the new concept of learning, we can show that imitation of a foreign utterance is impossible without the use of processing devices that have been established in the human brain by prior learning. Imitation, as Susan Ervin-Tripp (1970, p. 316) observed, at a minimum "requires perception, storage, organization of output, and motor output. In addition, before the storage phase there will be interpretation if the material is interpretable." She further suggests that the student's "first encounters with a second language will be handled by the apparatus of structure and process already available," i.e., that of the student's native language. Noting similar problems with imitation, Howard Cook (1965, pp. 17–18) questioned the validity of mimicry as a teaching technique. He posed the crucial question: "If the act of mimicry is made possible and functions only because of the student's native language habits, how could it be expected to provide the best means for overcoming these habits?"

Analyzing the problem of imitation in the first language acquisition process, Hebb, Lambert, and Tucker (1971, p. 218) comment:

> It is repeatedly said that language is not learned by imitation, and yet *it is evident that imitation is involved,* for the child ends up with the vocabulary, accent and other speech mannerisms of his social group. The apparent contradiction is resolved when we see that the imitation itself, the overt motor speech, *depends on the prior perceptual learning.* In this sense, the child can imitate only what is already within his competence; *in the early stages at least the imitation is more a product of learning than a mechanism of learning.*

The priority of aural comprehension in the first language acquisition process is clearly evident and well documented (Smith, Shipley, and Gleitman, 1966; Fraser, Bellugi, and Brown, 1963; Carrow, 1968; Bloom, 1970; Lee, 1970). Even a casual observation would indicate that children demonstrate comprehension of many utterances before they develop the ability to produce any intelligible speech. The prior perceptual learning, apparently, paves the way for subsequent production. We have no valid reason to believe that the sequence of events is different for second language learning. Learning to talk in a foreign language implies learning of at least two reciprocally correlated skills: (1) *processing* of auditory input, and (2) *generation* of speech output. The first skill is the auditory *receptive* ability to comprehend the spoken word. It involves development of covert processing mechanisms which decode sequentially-ordered vocal messages into meaning. The second skill is the *expressive* ability to encode thought into sequentially-ordered vocal messages. Given this difference between the two events, it would be unreasonable to assume that the receptive and expressive skills develop simultaneously, since we have ample evidence from psychoneurological research that expressive language depends on receptive processes for its development (Myklebust, 1964; Johnson and Myklebust, 1967; Guess, 1969; Baer and Guess, 1971). This would explain why disorders in auditory receptive ability create such difficulties in acquisition of linguistic competence, and conversely, why congenital disability for acquisition of motor speech skills does not prevent development of comprehension, as is evidenced by Lenneberg's (1962) case report, *Understanding Language without Ability to Speak,* and by other studies of similar cases.

When students are tasked with production of a foreign sentence, they have to *retrieve* phonological, morphological, syntactical, and lexical elements stored in their memory and control their production on all these levels simultaneously and with the speed of speech output. When this task is assigned to beginning students, they are actually asked to retrieve something they have not yet stored in their memory and for which no processing strategies have been developed. Quite naturally, and as already noted, students will make an attempt to process the foreign sentence through the only channels available to them: those of their native language. This is where we have the problem of interference in a very real sense. The problem is readily observable in most of the free generated sentences produced by students even in the advanced phases of a foreign language training program.

Another consequence of premature oral practice, closely related to the problem of interference, is the problem of short-term memory overload. Most, if not all, of the foreign language material learned by the student is of the type that needs to be habituated rather than conceptualized. Therefore, in the production-oriented approach, which is characteristic of the contemporary methodology of instruction, the student's short-term memory is constantly overloaded with FL (foreign language) material which he or she holds for active and instantaneous recall. Since the rate of presentation of new material is always greater than the rate of assimilation (that is, development of habitual control and automaticity of response), the short-term memory early in the course reaches a point of saturation, thereby causing considerable inhibition of the learning process. If we remove the requirement for premature speech production, the function of short-term memory will be greatly facilitated, for it will be left relatively free for new perceptual learning.

It follows, then, that the student should not, initially, be required to hold foreign language material for immediate recall, but only for immediate recognition. Frequent reactivation of recognition memory will make it more and more retrievable in due time. This is, perhaps, the most essential condition,

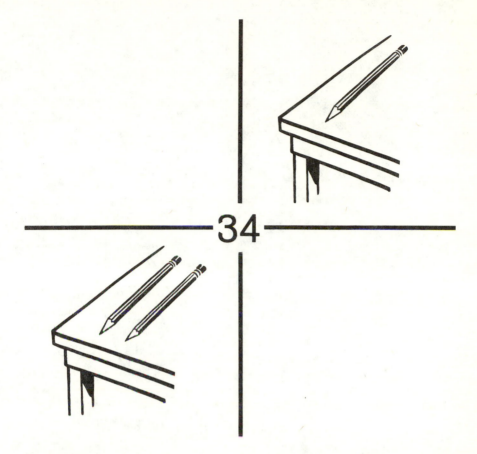

FIGURE 9.1.

which is characteristic of the specific nature of the learning task involved. When an integrated structure of language is first internalized on the recognition level, spontaneous vocal responses will follow; and then, and only then, the student is ready for oral practice.

Research in the dynamics of listening comprehension has been sporadic and often lacking in adequate experimental control. However, the picture that is emerging from several unrelated studies (Scherer, 1948, 1950, 1952; Asher, 1965, 1969; Winitz and Reeds, 1973; Ingram, Nord, and Dragt, 1974; Postovsky, 1970, 1974) tends to substantiate the theoretical position outlined above. The data from all these studies suggest with remarkable regularity that emphasis on aural comprehension training and relaxation of the requirement for oral production in the initial phase of instruction foster development of linguistic competence and produce better results than those obtained through intensive oral practice.

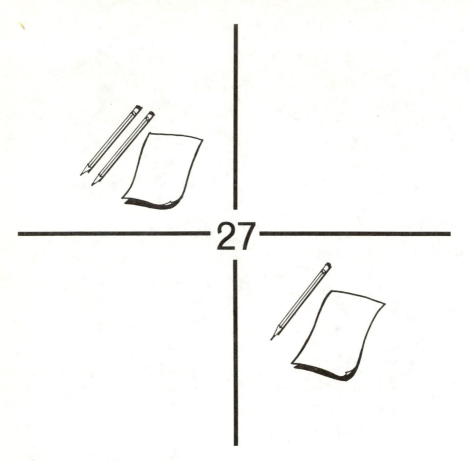

FIGURE 9.2.

At the Defense Language Institute (DLI), Presidio of Monterey, California, experimentation with comprehension-oriented methodology of instruction produced very encouraging results (Postovsky, 1970, 1974). At the present time one of the major research projects at DLI involves development of an intensive aural comprehension program for teaching Russian. The program is designed for a six-hour day with an initial delay in oral practice during the first six weeks (180 hours) of instruction. The delay in oral practice will be achieved, in part, by requiring students to respond in writing during the pre-vocal phase of instruction. It has been shown by earlier experimentation that introduction of the conventional writing system (Cyrillic alphabet) early in the course does not create significant problems in graphic interference (Postovsky, 1970, 1974). On the contrary, due to fairly regular correspondence between Russian orthography and phonology, writing practice from spoken input proved to be a valuable exercise in sound discrimination and an aid to auditory perception. For this

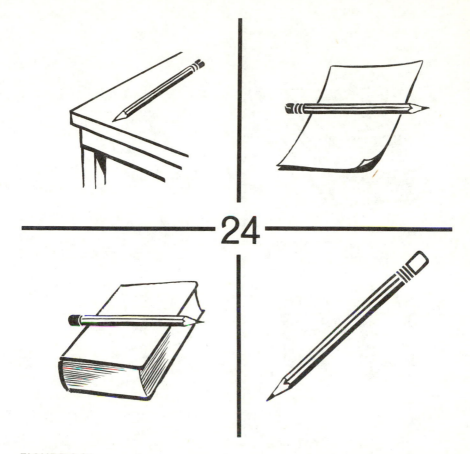

FIGURE 9.3.

reason, the two language skills, initially emphasized in the program, will be aural comprehension and transcription. It is anticipated that reading skill will develop as a corollary to writing. Students, presumably, will be able to read what they have written, although no reading aloud exercises will be conducted in the pre-vocal phase of instruction. After the writing system has been completely mastered, some reading comprehension exercises (silent reading) will be conducted. These exercises will be based on materials for which aural comprehension has already been developed. As the course progresses, reading comprehension exercises will become more complex, leading eventually to new materials with some unknown elements. In addition to the regular classroom instruction, the program includes automated media consisting of various language laboratory exercises and an audiovisual TV component.

Our experience with aural comprehension programs indicates that mere exposure of the student to the sounds of the target language is not sufficient. A program, to be successful, must satisfy at least three essential conditions: (1) the

FIGURE 9.4.

language material presented in the program must be meaningful from the very first hour of instruction; (2) the program must provide for a student response that will verify comprehension of each utterance or a short passage immediately after delivery; and (3) the program must challenge the student to guess at the meaning of unfamiliar elements on the basis of familiar elements in the linguistic environment. There are several techniques used for presenting language material in an aural comprehension course that satisfy these principal conditions, but the one we found to be most efficient is the audiovisual TV program based on Professor Winitz's model which he initially developed for teaching language-delayed children and later adapted to teaching German as a foreign language (Winitz and Reeds, 1973).

The system is based on synchronized presentation of language material and pictorial events. The student hears the utterance and then sees the picture, thus forming a direct association between the symbol and the referent. The TV screen is divided into four equal sections by vertical and horizontal lines

FIGURE 9.5.

crossing in the center of the screen. This arrangement makes it possible to project from one to four pictures simultaneously, leading the student into a multiple-choice selection procedure. Correct responses are randomly distributed throughout the program and the student's task is to select the appropriate picture corresponding to the utterance in a given frame and to mark an appropriate square on his or her answer sheet. Each unit of the program consists of 100 frames, with the total running time ranging from twenty-four to thirty minutes. The student is thus exposed to a problem-solving situation every fifteen to twenty seconds throughout the exercise.

This technique has proven to be a very useful tool for presenting language material of a concrete nature, i.e., vocabulary and structural features that lend themselves to pictorial representation. Figures 9.1–9.6, which are examples of pictures used in the language training program, demonstrate treatment of some of the grammatical concepts: plural (Figures 9.1, 9.2); location (Figures 9.3,

FIGURE 9.6.

9.4) and verb aspects (Figures 9.5, 9.6). The numbers in the centers of the figures are the frame numbers of each 100-item lesson.

In the experimental Russian program the television teaching units will be used concurrently with other media of instruction, and will normally occupy not more than two thirty-minute periods in a daily cycle. To determine the effectiveness of the program, however, twelve initial TV units were tested on two groups of students two weeks prior to their enrollment into the regular Russian course. At DLI, a new Russian class starts every month except December. This arrangement creates a very favorable experimental setting and provides ample opportunity for replication of experiments and verification of results. The first group of eleven subjects was tested in September, 1974. None of the subjects had previously studied Russian; their ages ranged between eighteen and twenty-four; and education levels varied from high school to college graduates. The program was administered in three days—four TV units per day. Thus, at the end of the third day the subjects had received approximately six hours of listening comprehension training in Russian. After each two units of the program, a short retention test was administered. Test scores on immediate retention are presented in Table 9.1.

The first twelve TV units contain 111 lexical items including verbs "to stand," "to sit," "to lie," "to read," "to write," "to see," and "to do," and numerals from one to ten. Structural complexity of sentences includes such features as accusative case denoting direct object, locative case after the prepositions "in" and "on," genitive singular after the numerals "two," "three," and "four," agreement of modifiers with nouns or pronouns in gender, number, and case, etc. Needless to say, students were not expected to produce Russian sentences, but only to understand them when spoken at a normal rate of speech.

Upon completion of the twelfth unit, subjects were tested for retention at two interval points: eighteen hours following completion of the program, and once again after a ten-day interval. The retention test contained 100 test items and was exhaustive in the sense that every lexical item and every grammatical feature presented in the program reoccurred on the test. The students' tasks were to listen to Russian sentences recorded on tape at a normal rate of speech and to write down the English translation. The test scores obtained on the retention test and the ten-day post-retention test are presented in Table 9.2. As may be observed from this table the mean test scores obtained on the retention test and the ten-day post-retention test for the group were 98.18 and 98.20 respectively.

When no difference in the level of retention was observed at the two interval points, the outcome was credited to the "test-retest" effect and to the fact that the subjects were informed that their retention of material learned will be measured after the ten-day interval. In order to control these variables, the second experiment was initiated with twelve early arrivals for the November 1974 class. The procedure was replicated except that the subjects were not informed of the ten-day post-test and the test items on the post-test were scrambled. Table 9.3 gives scores on immediate retention after each two units of the program and Table 9.4 summarizes the test and the post-test data for the second group. As reported in these tables, the mean scores for the second group were 94.45 for the retention test and 95.67 for the ten-day post-retention test.

As one can see, the outcome of the second experiment is almost identical to that of the first—both groups achieved high scores on the retention test and demonstrated remarkable stability of recognition knowledge over the ten-day period. Analysis of the data in Tables 9.2 and 9.4 also suggests no significant correlation between such variables as age, education, and language aptitude scores on the one hand, and students' performance on retention tests on the other. This outcome would seem to suggest that the test was too easy and failed to discriminate between the high and the low achievers. If this is so, then our program must be highly successful in teaching listening comprehension skills, for, as may be recalled, the test included every lexical and structural item presented in the program, and the primary objective of our study was to test effectiveness of the teaching materials and not to assess the ability of the students.

Table 9.1   Immediate Retention Test Scores, Group No. 1

Student	Test 1	Test 2	Test 3	Test 4	Test 5	Test 6
1	100	100	96.5	97.5	98	99.5
2	77	95	87	88.5	92	95.5
3	89.5	91	86	94.5	91.5	95.5
4	88.5	100	94	92.5	96	98.5
5	100	99	99	96.5	98	99.5
6	99.5	93	89	89	89	95.5
7	100	100	97	100	97.5	100
8	80.5	97.5	94	94.5	85.5	97
9	98.5	94	97.5	98	99.5	98.5
10	84	97.5	93.5	86	85.5	91
11	100	100	98	100	99.5	100
X̄ (N=11)	92.5	96.9	93.8	94.2	93.8	97.3

Table 9.2   Retention Tests for Group No. 1

Student	Age	Sex	Education	PFL*	DLAT**	Retention Test	10-Day Post-Retention Test
1	18	F	HS	SP	40	100	100
2	19	F	1 yr.	SP	22	98	—
3	18	F	HS	GM, SP	22	97	97
4	24	M	BA	GM, SP	26	95	96
5	21	M	BA	FR, GM	52	98	100
6	23	M	BA	LA, FR	28	96	96
7	21	F	BA	FR, GM	52	100	99
8	18	M	HS	FR, GM	29	99	98
9	18	M	HS	SP	25	99	98
10	23	M	HS	—	22	98	98
11	18	M	HS	FR	33	100	100
X̄ (N=11)	20.09		1.55		31.91	98.18	98.20

*Previous FL study
**Defense Language Aptitude Test

Table 9.3   Immediate Retention Test Scores, Group No. 2

Student	Test 1	Test 2	Test 3	Test 4	Test 5	Test 6
1	80	99	91.5	89	90.5	94
2	85	94.5	71.5	76.5	69	79.5
3	99	100	100	96.5	96.5	95
4	95	88.5	72.5	69	77.5	89
5	97.5	97.5	96.5	97.5	95	97
6	99	96.5	98	98.5	90	—
7	96.5	97.5	94	92.5	94	91.5
8	66.5	90.5	90.5	91.5	92	84
9	100	99	99	97.5	97.5	96.5
10	100	99	99	99.5	97	99
11	99	99	86.5	97	93	94.5
12	99	—	90	93	97.5	98.5
X̄ (N=12)	93.5	96.5	91.1	91.5	91.3	93.6

Table 9.4   Retention Tests for Group No. 2

Student	Age	Sex	Education	PFL*	DLAT**	Retention Test	10-Day Post-Retention Test
1	23	M	3 yrs.	SP	29	95	91
2	18	F	HS	SP	19	79	90
3	24	M	2 yrs.	FR, GM	37	99	98
4	19	M	1 yr.	GM	27	84	89
5	22	F	BA	FR, GM	48	98	99
6	18	F	HS	GM	36	—	97
7	20	M	2 yrs.	SP, GM	30	98	97
8	24	M	HS	—	19	93	94
9	22	M	BA	GM	30	99	99
10	23	F	BA	GM	34	99	99
11	18	F	HS	FR, GM	30	96	98
12	21	F	HS	SP, IT	21	99	97
$\overline{X}$ (N=12)	21.00		1.67		30.00	94.45	95.67

*Previous FL study
**Defense Language Aptitude Test

One of the most interesting aspects of this study relates to stability of recognition knowledge. Some loss in comprehension of learned material over the ten-day interval was anticipated but did not occur. Feedback from students suggests that mental rehearsal was one of the factors that may have contributed to this outcome. As mentioned earlier, language material presented in the program was of a concrete nature, and meaning was conveyed by way of pictures. Some students have reported that the same objects and events in real life tended to trigger recollection of Russian utterances associated with these objects and events, thus reinforcing the initial learning and making Russian utterances more meaningful. This observation supports the well-established tradition of starting a foreign language course with introduction of concrete material directly related to the immediate learning environment, but it also suggests that the choice and sequential order of recall of this material need not be necessarily regimented by the teacher.

In an attempt to determine the students' attitude for this mode of instruction, post-cycle questionnaires were administered at the end of the program, following the first retention test. Tallied results are presented in the Appendix. Review of these data indicates that the program provoked a very positive and often enthusiastic response. After the beginning of regular instruction, the progress of the experimental subjects in their respective classes was monitored and their performance was found to be significantly above the norm.

Results obtained in this preliminary investigation tend to support the notion that listening comprehension of a foreign language can be developed as a single skill, and that development of linguistic competence is facilitated when training in oral production is not attempted until considerable fluency in aural comprehension has been developed. On the basis of this and previous studies we have reasons to believe that the two skills—speech comprehension and speech production—although obviously reciprocally correlated, are not necessarily mutually reinforcing in the initial phase of instruction. This appears to be so because training in oral production requires development of total and automatic control of both lexical and structural elements presented in the program. The student's attention, therefore, is necessarily focused more on the structural details and less on the contextual meaning of the message. In comprehension training the total control of linguistic data is neither implied nor necessary. (For the alternative view, see Wilga M. Rivers, 1971.) Consequently, the student's attentional focus is shifted from preoccupation with structural details to decoding of contextual meaning. This training approach requires a different mental set on the part of the student and allows presentation of language material at a much faster rate. The evidence we are obtaining suggests that the second-language acquisition process can be made less strenuous and more productive by reversing the emphasis in the initial phase of instruction from intensive training in oral production to rapid development of aural comprehension.

APPENDIX

Post-Cycle Questionnaire (Units 1–12)

Instructions: We are interested in your opinions on each of the statements below. This is not a test of subject matter. There are no *right* or *wrong* answers. Try to put down exactly how you feel about each item. We are seeking your opinions, not compliments; so please be frank. If you want to add something or qualify any of your answers, list the item number as reference on the back of the questionnaire and then add your comments. Please write your name and SSN in the spaces provided. **YOUR OPINIONS WILL BE STRONGLY CONFIDENTIAL.** Do not hesitate to tell us exactly how you feel.

NAME: _____GROUP #1_____   SSN: _____COMPOSITE (N = 11)_____

DATE: 27 SEPTEMBER 1974   CLASS NUMBER: _____0475_____

Part A

Please apply the following scale in answering the questions below. Circle only one letter in each item.

SCALE

A. Strongly agree
B. Agree
C. Uncertain
D. Disagree
E. Strongly disagree

Statement	A	B	C	D	E
I liked this method of learning.	A [5]	B [5]	C	D [1]	E
I found it difficult to solve the grammatical problems in the sentences presented.	A	B [2]	C	D [8]	E [1]
I had a tendency to translate the Russian utterances into English while I was doing the exercises.	A	B [4]	C [2]	D [3]	E [2]
I was able to keep up with each program.	A [5]	B [6]	C	D	E
I felt the material was presented in a consistent and orderly way.	A [5]	B [4]	C [1]	D [1]	E
I found the material interesting.	A [6]	B [3]	C [2]	D	E
I felt myself to be under time pressure.	A	B	C	D [6]	E [5]
I did not feel challenged by the exercises.	A	B	C [2]	D [5]	E [4]
I think I would learn the material more quickly by studying a textbook.	A	B	C [1]	D [4]	E [6]
I found the program format and design easy to understand.	A [6]	B [4]	C [1]	D	E
I found the program boring.	A	B [1]	C [3]	D [6]	E [1]
I felt that the program was easy to follow.	A [3]	B [8]	C	D	E
I feel that this program method of instruction is superior to regular classroom instruction.	A [2]	B [5]	C [2]	D [2]	E

Part B

Circle YES or NO.

Was the TV sound track clear and audible?	[11] YES	NO
Were the TV pictures clear and descriptive?	[11] YES	NO
Were the instructions clear?	[10] YES	[1] NO
Was the OpScan Answer Sheet easy to mark?	[11] YES	NO
Were the Russian utterances clear and audible?	[11] YES	NO
Was the length of the pauses between utterances sufficient?	[11] YES	NO

I estimate that I remember. (Circle one)

A.   20% of the total vocabulary in the program presented.   0

B.   40% of the total vocabulary in the program presented.   0

C.   60% of the total vocabulary in the program presented.   0

(D)   80% of the total vocabulary in the program presented.   6

(E)   More than 80% of the total vocabulary in the program presented.   5

Post-Cycle Questionnaire (Units 1–12)

NAME: _____GROUP #2_____   SSN: ____COMPOSITE (N = 12)____

DATE: __1 NOVEMBER 1974__ CLASS NUMBER: _____0575_____

Part A

Please apply the following scale in answering the questions below. Circle only one letter in each item.

SCALE

A. Strongly agree
B. Agree
C. Uncertain
D. Disagree
E. Strongly disagree

I liked this method of learning. (1 NO RESPONSE)	9 A	2 B	C	D	E
I found it difficult to solve the grammatical problems in the sentences presented.	A	1 B	1 C	7 D	3 E
I had a tendency to translate the Russian utterances into English while I was doing the exercises.	A	1 B	C	7 D	4 E
I was able to keep up with each program.	5 A	6 B	1 C	D	E
I felt the material was presented in a consistent and orderly way.	7 A	5 B	C	D	E
I found the material interesting.	5 A	6 B	1 C	D	E
I felt myself to be under time pressure.	A	5 B	4 C	2 D	1 E
I did not feel challenged by the exercises.	1 A	B	C	11 D	E
I think I would learn the material more quickly by studying a textbook.	3 A	B	C	2 D	7 E
I found the program format and design easy to understand.	5 A	7 B	C	D	E
I found the program boring.	A	B	1 C	8 D	3 E
I felt that the program was easy to follow.	4 A	7 B	C	1 D	E
I feel that this program method of instruction is superior to regular classroom instruction.	6 A	4 B	1 C	1 D	E

Part B

Circle YES or NO.

Was the TV sound track clear and audible?	11 YES	NO 1 NR*
Were the TV pictures clear and descriptive?	11 YES	NO 1 NR
Were the instructions clear?	11 YES	NO 1 NR
Was the OpScan Answer Sheet easy to mark?	11 YES	NO 1 NR
Were the Russian utterances clear and audible?	11 YES	NO 1 NR
Was the length of the pauses between utterances sufficient?	9 YES	3 NO

*NO RESPONSE

I estimate that I remember: (Circle one)

A.   20% of the total vocabulary in the program presented.   0
B.   40% of the total vocabulary in the program presented.   0
C.   60% of the total vocabulary in the program presented.   0
(D) 80% of the total vocabulary in the program presented.   6
(E) More than 80% of the total vocabulary in the program presented.   6

References

Asher, J. J. "The strategy of the total physical response: An application to learning Russian." *International Review of Applied Linguistics, 3,* pp. 291–300, 1965.

———. "The total physical response approach to second language learning." *The Modern Language Journal, 53,* pp. 3–17, 1969.

Baer, D. M., and Guess, D. "Receptive training of adjectival inflections in mental retardates." *Journal of Applied Behavior Analysis, 4,* pp. 129–139, 1971.

Bloom, L. *Language development: Form and function in emerging grammars.* Cambridge, Mass.: M.I.T. Press, 1970.

Carrow, M. A. "The development of auditory comprehension of language structure in children." *Journal of Speech and Hearing Disorders, 33,* pp. 99–111, 1968.

Cook, H. R. "Pre-speech auditory training: Its contribution to second language teaching and motivation for continuous broadcasting." Ph.D. dissertation, Indiana University, 1965.

Ervin-Tripp, S. "Structure and process in language acquisition." *Round Table Monograph, 21,* pp. 313–344, Washington, D.C., Georgetown University, 1970.

Fraser, C., Bellugi, U., and Brown, R. "Control of grammar in imitation, comprehension, and production." *Journal of Verbal Learning and Verbal Behavior, 2,* pp. 121–135, 1963.

Guess, D. "A functional analysis of receptive language and productive speech: Acquisition of the plural morpheme." *Journal of Applied Behavioral Analysis, 2,* pp. 55–64, 1969.

Hebb, D. O., Lambert, W. E., and Tucker, G. R. "Language, thought and experience." *The Modern Language Journal, 55,* pp. 212–222, 1971.

Ingram, F., Nord, J., and Dragt, D. "Developing a programmed workbook for listening comprehension in Russian." Paper delivered at the Soviet-American Conference on the Russian Language, Amherst, Mass., October, 1974.

Johnson, D. J., and Myklebust, H. R. *Learning disabilities, educational principles and practices.* New York: Grune and Stratton, 1967.

Lashley, K. "The problem of serial order." In L. Jeffress (Ed.), *Cerebral mechanisms in behavior—The Hixon symposium.* 1951. Also available in S. Saporta (Ed.), *Psycholinguistics: A book of readings.* New York: Holt, Rinehart, and Winston, 1961.

Lee, L. L. "A screening test for syntax development." *Journal of Speech and Hearing Disorders, 35,* pp. 103–112, 1970.

Lenneberg, E. H. "Understanding language without ability to speak: A case report." *Journal of Abnormal and Social Psychology, 65,* pp. 419–425, 1962.

Melton, A., and Martin, E. (Eds.) *Coding processes in human memory.* Washington, D.C.: V. H. Winston and Sons, 1972.

Myklebust, H. *The psychology of deafness: Sensory deprivation, learning and adjustment.* (Second ed.) New York: Grune and Stratton, 1964.

Postovsky, V. A. "Effects of delay in oral practice at the beginning of second language learning." Ph.D. dissertation, University of California at Berkeley, 1970. Also available in *The Modern Language Journal, 58,* pp. 229–239, 1974.

Rivers, W. M. "Linguistic and psychological factors in speech perception and their implications for teaching materials." In P. Pimsleur and T. Quinn (Eds.), *The psychology of second language learning,* pp. 123–134. Cambridge University Press, 1971.

Scherer, G. A. C. "Reading German with eye and ear." *The Modern Language Journal, 32,* pp. 151–160, 1948.

———. "The psychology of teaching reading through listening." *German Quarterly, 23,* pp. 151–160, 1950.

———. "The importance of auditory comprehension." *German Quarterly, 25,* pp. 223–229, 1952.

Smith, C. S., Shipley, E., and Gleitman, L. "Two studies of the syntactic knowledge of young children." Paper presented at the Linguistic Colloquium, Eastern Pennsylvania Psychiatric Institute, M.I.T., 1966.

Winitz, H., and Reeds, J. A. "Rapid acquisition of a foreign language (German) by the avoidance of speaking." *International Review of Applied Linguistics, 11,* pp. 295–317, 1973.

CHAPTER 10

Comprehension Training: The Evidence from Laboratory and Classroom Studies

James J. Asher

Professor of Psychology
San José State University

Second-language instructional approaches can be classified as "explicit" or "implicit" learning (Winitz, 1978). An example of explicit learning would be an instructional format such as an audio-lingual approach that is designed directly to teach the student to talk in a second language. Implicit learning such as comprehension training (Winitz and Reeds, 1975; Nord, 1975; Swaffar and Woodruff, 1978; Asher, 1981) theorizes that speech cannot be directly taught to the student just as a parent cannot directly teach the infant to talk. No amount of coaching or coaxing by parents will accelerate the appearance of speech in the baby before the child is ready.

Readiness to talk is a developmental phenomenon in the infant which is preceded by hundreds of hours of comprehension acquisition. At some point in the infant's expanding understanding of the target language, talk is released. As far back as forty years ago, there was evidence that infants had developed a sophisticated understanding of the target language before they could utter anything intelligible (Bühler and Hetzer, 1935; Gesell and Thompson, 1929).

When speech appears, it will not be perfect. The distortions will be severely skewed, but gradually in a time period of many years, the child's speech will shape itself in the direction of the native speaker.

Explicit learning such as the audio-lingual approach is perhaps most valuable not necessarily in the beginning or even intermediate stages of learning, but at a more advanced level. The evidence is abundant that when initial and intermediate second language instruction is based on *explicit* learning, students report intense feelings of failure and disappointment (Jakobovits, 1969); attrition is high with perhaps 96 percent of the students "giving up" by Level IV (Lawson, 1971); and achievement is less than satisfactory (Carroll, 1960).

Although implicit learning through comprehension training is still in the experimental stages, the results have been promising. The approach is especially valuable for starting students in the direction of language competency while simultaneously building their confidence; which can sustain them in more advanced training which demands precision in production, either in speaking or writing.

The evidence suggests that implicit learning bypasses a dependency on one's native language to decode the target language. All instruction is exclusively in the target language. The student from the beginning experiences continual success in rapidly internalizing an expanding understanding of what the target language means and how it works. Like the infant acquiring its first language, there comes a point when talk appears spontaneously. It cannot be forced. It will appear when the student is ready. At this point, speech will not be perfect, but it can be gently and gradually shaped in the direction of the native speaker.

This transition from understanding spoken speech to production can be achieved without trauma. Rather, it has been observed to be a joyful experience.

Implicit instructional strategies tend to simulate, at least in part, the process of language acquisition that is observed in infants learning their first language. One striking feature of the infant's learning is that the left cerebral hemisphere shadows the right. The baby seems to decode the target language when utterances—usually gentle commands from adults in caretaking situations such as feeding and dressing—coincide with movements of the infant's body. The right hemisphere makes body responses when directed by utterances such as:

"Look at Daddy!"

"Give Mommy a kiss!"

"Don't spit up on your pajamas!"

In this choreography of language and body motions, the baby develops a sophisticated understanding of what is heard—and this cryptology is achieved before the baby says anything more intelligible than Mommy or Daddy (Bühler and Hetzer, 1935; Gesell and Thompson, 1929).

Furthermore, Jean Piaget (1955), the Swiss psychologist, has suggested that in this process of decoding language through infant behavior such as touching, reaching, grasping, and crying, the baby not only decodes the meaning of the strange language but also constructs reality. Unless the baby experiences language through the medium of the child's body responses, concepts are neither solid nor permanent.

Piaget has shown in his creative demonstrations with infants that the baby's initial concept of reality is like a motion picture. If we look behind the screen, we do not expect to see the protruding backside of the actor. We "know" that when the actor is off the screen, that person is not waiting in the wings to come on again. The infant initially has a motion picture of reality. People, places, and things are not solid in a three-dimensional space. Once an object or person cannot be seen, they have disappeared like the image on a motion picture screen, but they do not occupy space nearby.

For example, if you ring a bell, the eight-month-old baby will laugh and reach for the object, but if, while the baby is watching, you cover the bell with a handkerchief, the child will cease its laughter and no longer try to grasp the attractive object. It is as if once the image cannot be seen, it has vanished.

Implicit instructional strategies that play to the right hemisphere simulate one or more features of the infant's acquisition of a first language. Examples of these are Curran's Community Language Learning (1972), Lozanov's Suggestology (1975), Gattegno's Silent Way (1972), Comprehension Training by Winitz and Reeds (1975) and Nord (1975), and Asher's Total Physical Response—also called Learning Another Language Through Actions (1981). The empirical evidence for each of these approaches will be reviewed next.[1]

LOZANOV'S SUGGESTOLOGY

In this approach, there is a preverbal period of training in which the students expand their listening comprehension of the target language. Lozanov (1975) recognizes that merely explaining the meaning of utterances in a strange language is not effective. Content by itself is not enough. There is a lack of authenticity. There is a lack of believability.

The instructional model is the actor in a stage play. It is not enough for the actor to read lines from a script. There must be a performance in which the audience "believes" in the character the actor is playing. A convincing portrayal comes from the content of the dialogue integrated with appropriate intonations, gestures, facial expressions, costumes, and body movements.

The actor creates a mood of believability in the audience—a relaxation of the critical thinking in the left hemisphere and heightened sensitivity of the right hemisphere.

The actors construct a reality for the audience with their talk, behavior, props, costumes, and music. The audience can then relax their normal scepticism and enjoy the assimilation of a new experience.

This process is analogous to many features in Piaget's model of infant development which, I believe, is rich in insights for second language learning.

The evidence. Most of the research has yet to be translated from Bulgarian, but some preliminary findings are promising. For example, Velvovskiy (1975) reported that a group of twelve volunteers (university students, teachers, and engineers) in Moscow learned about 2,200 words and expressions in one month and without fatigue. Instead of rote memory in which verbal items are repeated in an attempt to imprint in the left brain, the technique was to play to the right brain with "verbal motorics" in which "kinetic acts" merge into "speech,

Table 10.1   The Impact of Peripheral Stimuli in Learning

Words Included in the Wall-Charts	Degree of Increase in the Correctly Written Words Between the Initial and 3rd Tests		Differences in the Degree of Increase Between the Two Groups
	Experimental	Control	
1. Almost	.24	.20	+.04
2. Always	.08	.00	+.08
3. Small	.31	.28	+.03
4. All	.43	.16	+.27
5. Wall	.34	.08	+.26
6. Wash	.27	.08	+.19
7. Warm	.22	.12	+.10
8. Water	.22	.12	+.10
9. Like	.22	.24	−.02
10. Nice	.20	.04	+.24
11. Write	.27	.08	+.19
12. Nine	.34	.24	+.10
13. White	.26	.08	+.18
14. Fine	.15	.20	−.05
15. Time	.19	.16	+.03
16. Wife	.17	.16	+.01
17. Name	.17	.04	+.13
18. Plate	.24	.08	+.16
19. Place	.22	.12	+.10
20. Take	.10	.04	+.06
21. Me	.17	.20	−.03
22. He	.10	.04	+.06
23. She	.04	.08	−.04
24. We	.36	.12	+.24
25. Thanks	.29	.12	+.17
26. That	.22	.32	−.10
27. There	.09	.08	+.01
28. This	.25	.08	+.17
29. How	.13	.04	+.09
30. Brown	.32	.24	+.08
31. Now	.15	.12	+.03
32. Town	.15	.40	−.25
33. Window	.27	.32	−.05
34. Yellow	.31	.24	+.07
35. Follow	.19	.20	−.01
36. Fellow	.15	.20	−.05

mimic, or other types of behavior" (p. 19). Adults are in a playful pleasing atmosphere in which they act in dramatized games. It is a kind of "infantilization."

Balevsky (1975) explored electrical activity in the brain when verbal utterances were reproduced under relaxed conditions compared with normal alertness of people. With electrodes on the left occipital-parietal area of the brain, electrical recordings were read every ten seconds with a frequency meter.

Under ordinary conditions, when eighteen students memorized the transla-tion of a German passage that had eleven sentences, electrical activity accelerated on the average by 6.3 percent. Under suggestive conditions in which theatrical intonation was used in reading and "soothing" classical music played in the background, the electrical activity increased only 1.05 percent, and yet memorization improved by 14 percent.

Similar experiments of short-term memory indicated that the relaxation of "suggestive" conditions decrease electrical activity—at least in the left occipital-parietal area—while simultaneously producing a noticeable and statistically significant increase in the efficiency of retention.

Velvovskiy (1975, p. 18) believes that "... the problem is not one of 'memorizing' but of automatically 'recollecting' whenever this becomes necessary...." He illustrated his position with this personal experience: During childbirth, a woman who was a physician by profession, "unexpectedly began repeating the foulest street cursing in the Kazakh language." Curiously, neither she nor her family spoke Kazakh, but when she was a medical student, she used to go to exotic bazaars where she heard Kazakh shouts and rejoinders that were quite incomprehensible to her. In moments of pain, "she reproduced the words she had heard in the bazaar—words she did not know and did not use" in her normal alert state.

Pashmakova (1975) hypothesized that the context that surrounds a message influences the individual's receptiveness to understanding, evaluating, and retaining the verbal stimulus. His research explored how peripheral events can affect the learning of English orthography, which is perceived to be a compli-cated task by the non-English speaker.

The research design was to hang wall-charts with thirty-six English words in the classrooms of the experimental group. "The wall-charts were hung before the lesson began and teachers were instructed not to draw the attention of the students to them and to follow the normal course of their programme" (p. 39). Neither the experimental nor the control group had training in spelling.

The results, shown in Table 10.1, were that twenty-eight of thirty-six words were reproduced better by the experimental group between the initial to the third testing while only eight in thirty-six words improved in the control group, a highly significant statistical result.

Racle (1975) reported a suggestopaedic experiment conducted in Canada to teach beginning French. The students were civil servants from typists to senior officials who ranged in age from twenty-one to fifty-four. There was an equal number of men and women.

Before the experimental training the students were given the *Modern Language Aptitude Test* (MLAT) and a pretest of skill in French. After sixty-six instructional hours, students (N = 5) who started with 60 percent profi-ciency in French achieved 87 percent; those (N = 20) with 44 percent initially, ended with 78 percent; others (N = 21) who began with 18 percent acquired 56 percent; and finally, students starting with only 5 percent achieved 42 percent. Unfortunately, the French proficiency measure was not standardized and normed so that it is not possible to compare the gains with students in more traditional classes.

As for aptitude in learning another language, those students with the highest aptitude on the MLAT started the course with a proficiency of 42 percent in French and ended with 81 percent; those with "B" level aptitude, started with 30 percent and acquired 68 percent; and students with "C" level began with 23 percent and climaxed with 56 percent.

As for student motivation, it was reported to be high, but no information was available on student attrition or the number who volunteered to continue. It should be noted that students were trained in groups of twelve and attended class one half of the day and did their customary work the other half. Therefore, we may assume that the students received their regular salary while attending class.

WINITZ AND REEDS' COMPREHENSION TRAINING

Comprehension training is a right hemisphere instructional strategy that has many features in common with Piaget's model of infant development.

First, students are silent while they decipher and internalize the working grammar of the target language. This decoding is not the usual left hemispheric tactic of translating into one's native language. Rather, the student hears the foreign utterance, then selects a picture from among a set of four pictures.

Like the young child, the student discovers how the grammar works by manipulating visual representations rather than words. For example, the program begins with the student hearing nouns such as *Frau,* then the picture of a woman. Next, *Frau* is heard again and is one choice among three other pictures. Gradually syntactic elements are expanded around the nouns to increase the grammatical complexity.

As the complexity of grammar increases, the student's attention is fine-tuned to smaller and smaller details. This is achieved by gradually narrowing choices for more and more subtle decision-making by the student.

Results. While the samples were small, comprehension training has shown promising results. For example, Reeds, Winitz, and García (1977) administered eight hours of comprehension training in German to two groups of students. The grammatic complexity included sentences with the definite article, attributive adjective and noun, and transitive and intransitive verbs in the past tense. Also, the lessons included prepositions, neuter noun plurals, and the nominative and accusative case of personal pronouns.

Group I consisted of six graduate students with no prior German. They worked seventy minutes daily and completed the fourteen lessons in two weeks. At the end, they scored 94 percent correct on the average for the grammatical features learned.

In an attempt to measure the students' understanding of novel sentences— ones they had never heard directly in the lessons—the authors at the next class meeting presented the students with three paragraphs of "new" sentences, but the information was in print. The task was challenging since the sentences were novel and in print which the students had never experienced. Their training, as you recall, was strictly listening to German utterances and selecting appropriate pictures. The result was an 80 percent score on the average when a count was made of each word correctly translated.

Group II contained thirty-two high school students enrolled in a first year German course. The comprehension training was their first exposure to German.

The high school students worked forty-five minutes a day and completed the fourteen lessons in three weeks. Like the college students, the high school students on the average had almost perfect scores of 95 percent.

On the test for understanding novel sentences in print (remember, they had no exposure to written German), their score was 70 percent on the average. As a control, sixteen college students with no prior German were asked to translate the novel sentences. Their average score was 24 percent.

The Reeds, Winitz, and García (1977) data showed extremely high retention of the semantic and grammatical features of German immediately after comprehension training, but how about long-term memory?

Using Russian as the target language, Postovsky (1976; see also Chapter 9) designed a study to assess both the short- and long-term memory of students learning to understand spoken Russian through comprehension training.

In the first study, eleven students were randomly selected from a large group who were waiting to begin their training in Russian at the Defense Language Institute, West Coast. None had previously studied Russian; their ages ranged from eighteen to twenty-four; and their educational level varied from high school to college graduates.

Each day for three consecutive days, the subjects experienced two hours in which they were silent, but listened to Russian utterances and made choices of pictures on a TV monitor.

Results of Study I. The subjects' retention was assessed (a) after each two units of the program (there were twelve units totally), (b) immediately after completing all twelve units on the third day, and (c) ten days later.

The average short-term retention after each two units of the program was extremely high ranging from 92 percent to 97 percent. Then the next day following the completion of all twelve units, the subjects listened to 100 Russian sentences that represented *every* lexical item and *every* grammatical feature in the program. The task was to write down a translation of each Russian sentence. The results were again impressive with an average score of 98 percent.

Then, the individuals were informed that they would be tested again in ten days. There was no decrement in long-term retention since the average score was again 98 percent.

Postovsky recognized that the extraordinary recall ten days later may have been an artifact of telling the subjects that they would be assessed. Would the findings hold up if the study was replicated, but the individuals did not expect a delayed assessment? This was Study II with twelve subjects.

Results of Study II. The findings were almost identical with Study I. After each two units, the average retention score ranged from 91 percent to 96 percent. The day after all units were completed, the average retention was 94 percent, and ten days later, the average score was 96 percent.

In an attempt to explain the extraordinary stability of memory over time, Postovsky interviewed the students. Many said that experiences in real life tended to arouse memories of Russian utterances they had heard so that there was a kind of involuntary mental rehearsal.

As for student attitudes toward the program, most rated the approach superior to textbooks and the traditional classroom learning. Most said they liked the program, found it interesting and challenging, and easy to follow. Most estimated that they had retained 80 percent or more of the Russian vocabulary.

The comprehension training was completed before the students entered the regular instructional program in Russian at the Defense Language Institute. Postovsky noted that the students all performed above average in their formal classes, which suggests a positive transfer-of-training from comprehension training to the traditional audio-lingual type instruction.

ASHER'S LEARNING ANOTHER LANGUAGE THROUGH ACTIONS

Like infants, students learning with this approach start their study of a second language by being silent, but performing a motor act when they are directed by utterances from the instructor.

This approach is, of course, an abstraction of infant development as students decipher the target language through body movements and internalize a working grammar which, at some point, releases talking. Perhaps "releasing" is not the most descriptive word, but talk appears when the individual is ready.

Since our approach is an abstraction of the infant's development of speech, a certain economy of time is possible. For instance, infants have only a few bodily responses they can make, such as:

hiccup	laugh
cry	look at
reach	eat
grasp	eliminate
touch	

However, students can make a hundred times as many motor responses. This difference means, I believe, that the learning stages of infants, which require hundreds of hours, can be condensed into a fraction of the time.

For instance, with two students seated on either side of the instructor in the center of the room, we can start with these directions:

"Please listen carefully to what I will say and do exactly what I do. Be silent. Don't try to pronounce the words at this time. Just listen and act with me."

Then the instructor will utter a command such as "Tate!" and everyone stands up. Then "Suware!" and, watching the instructor's behavior, everyone sits down.

The directions and motor acts start with simple one-word utterances but rapidly expand in complexity, such as "Stand up, walk to the table, and pick up the red pencil!"

Next, I will present the evidence to support this approach. First, the data for adult learning will be given, and then the data for children. We have research showing the effectiveness of the approach for the comprehension of increasing complexity of language, short- and long-term retention, and student motivation.

Japanese

In this study by Kunihira and Asher (1965) the subjects were eighty-eight volunteer English monolingual college students who had no prior exposure to Japanese. The people were randomly assigned to one of four groups with each group consisting of ten men and twelve women. Sixty-seven of the eighty-eight completed the experiment. Before the experiment, each subject was administered the *Modern Language Aptitude Test* (MLAT), and the *American College Testing Program* (ACT).

The experimental group ($N = 16$) was instructed that a voice on a tape would utter a command in Japanese. When the students heard the Japanese utterance, they were to do exactly what the instructor did. Also, the instructions were not to translate the Japanese into English, but to permit the entire body to respond as fully, automatically, and spontaneously as possible. The first command was "*tate*," and the subjects, along with the instructor, stood up. Then they heard "*aruke*" and everyone walked forward. Then "*tomare*" (stop), "*kagame*" (squat), "*maware*" (turn), "*hashire*" (run), "*tobe*" (jump) and "*suware*" (sit). Students listened and physically reacted to the one-word Japanese commands for about eight minutes. An attempt was made to randomize the commands so that this was not a serial-learning task.

After eight minutes of training, each individual was given a retention test. Twenty-four hours later they returned, and were given again individually a retention test; following this, they were given ten and a half minutes of training with utterances that were expanded to the complexity of the following examples:

"*To ni aruite ike.*" (Walk to the door.)
"*Isu ni hashitte ike.*" (Run to the chair.)
"*Tsukue ni hashitte ike.*" (Run to the desk.)

In this second training session of ten and a half minutes, people physically responded to about forty different utterances. After another retention test, the subjects were asked to return in twenty-four hours for the third training session.

In the third training session of seven and a half minutes, the complexity of the Japanese was further expanded, as these examples illustrate:

"Tsukue ni aruite itte enpitsu to hon o oke." (Walk to the desk and put down the pencil and book.)

"Kami to hon to enpitsu o totte isu ni suware." (Pick up the paper, book, and pencil, and sit on the chair.)

"Mado ni hashitte itte hon o totte tsukue ni oite isu ni suware." (Run to the window, pick up the book, put it on the desk, and then sit on the chair.)

In the third and final training period of seven and a half minutes, the people physically responded to sixteen different utterances. All the Japanese utterances on the tape were spoken at a conversational rate of transmission. Immediately after training, there was another retention test and the individuals were invited to return in two weeks for a final retention test. Here is a description of each control group:

Control group I (N = 15) listened to the same tape as did the experimental group, but they did not execute a physical response. Instead, this group sat down and watched the instructor obey each Japanese command to stand, walk, jump, etc. Control group II (N = 18) sat down, and after listening to each Japanese command on tape, they *heard* the English translation. Control group III (N = 18) sat down, and after listening to a Japanese command on tape, they silently *read* the English translation in a booklet.

Generally, in the retention tests given immediately after training, after twenty-four hours, and after two weeks, the people in the experimental group acted out their responses and the individuals in the control groups wrote their responses. The only exception was that for part of the two-week retention test, people in the experimental group wrote their responses. This procedure permitted us to evaluate whether or not writing would make any difference in the retention of the experimental group.

The retention tests were scored in terms of behavioral units. For example, if a person in the experimental group heard *"Isu ni hashitte itte hon o totte,"* the individual received one point for running, another point if the person ran to a chair, another point for running to the chair on which there was a book, and a point if the book was picked up from the chair. Therefore, for the utterance *"Isu ni hashitte itte hon o totte,"* the total possible score was four points. The same scoring procedure was used for people in the control groups except that these individuals wrote down the English translation for the Japanese.

Results. First, the control groups did *not* generally show significant statistical differences in retention among themselves.

As seen in Table 10.2, the experimental group's average retention two weeks after training was 94 percent for single-word utterances and 91 percent for short sentences. In comparison, the control groups ranged from 66 percent to 85 percent for the average retention of single Japanese utterances and 60 percent to 81 percent for short sentences.

Table 10.2   Average Retention of Single and Short Utterances Spoken in Japanese

	Experimental	Control₁	Control₂	Control₃
		Single Utterances		
Immediately after training	.90 (.14)	.78 (.17)	.92 (.10)	.64 (.26)
Two weeks later	.94 (.06)	.83 (.10)	.85 (.09)	.66 (.11)
		Short Sentences		
Immediately after training	.97 (.07)	.94 (.08)	.94 (.09)	.86 (.22)
Two weeks later	.91 (.06)	.81 (.11)	.60 (.11)	.75 (.11)

NOTE: The percentages in parentheses are the standard deviations.

Table 10.3   Average Retention of Long and Novel Utterances Spoken in Japanese

	Experimental	Control₁	Control₂	Control₃
		Long Sentences		
Immediately after training	.98 (.05)	.89 (.14)	.89 (.16)	.81 (.23)
Two weeks later	.70 (.10)	.55 (.19)	.63 (.18)	.59 (.18)
		Novel Sentences		
Immediately after training	.97 (.05)	.64 (.11)	.56 (.15)	.53 (.13)
Two weeks later	.77 (.12)	.58 (.18)	.48 (.16)	.51 (.17)

NOTE: The percentages in parentheses are the standard deviations.

Table 10.3 displays the results for the comprehension of more complex utterances. Two weeks after training the experimental group had 70 percent retention, on the average, for long sentences and 77 percent for novel sentences (which were a mixture of short and long sentences). In comparison, the control groups retained from 55 percent to 63 percent for long sentences and 48 percent to 58 percent for novel sentences.

Conclusion. As the Japanese became more complex and as utterances were recombined to create sentences the individuals had never heard before—that is, novel utterances—the comprehension of the people who deciphered the target language through body movements was almost perfect at 90 percent or better usually. Even two weeks later, their comprehension was still about 75 percent or better on the average. A sample of Americans learning to understand Japanese with right hemispheric instruction and their retention one year later may be seen in the documentary film, "Demonstration of a new strategy in language learning."[2]

Russian: The Initial Study

In the previous study, students who learned to comprehend Japanese through actions, had at least 90 percent retention immediately following training and at least 70 percent or more when tested two weeks later. They were vastly superior in retention when compared to three other approaches, especially when the Japanese utterances were more complex and novel. Novel sentences were those that were not heard directly during the training but were recombinations of familiar constituents.

In an attempt to expand the generality of our findings, the study with Japanese was replicated with Russian as the target language (Asher, 1965). College students ($N = 36$) with no prior exposure to Russian volunteered to participate and were randomly assigned to either an experimental or a control group.

As in the Japanese study, the experimental group ($N = 18$) was instructed to be silent, listen to a voice on tape which would utter a command in Russian, then do exactly what the model did. They were also instructed to act as quickly as possible after hearing a Russian command.

The control group ($N = 18$) was instructed to sit silently in their chairs, listen to the Russian commands, and imagine that they were acting along with the model. Only the model performed while the students observed the model's behavior. However, during the retention tests, after these individuals listened to a taped voice utter a Russian command, they wrote the English translation.

Results. As may be seen in Table 10.4, the students who acted along with the model during training had an average retention after two weeks of 87 percent or higher, while the students who sat and watched the model act had an average retention after two weeks of 68 percent or higher. In all comparisons, except one, the experimental group's long-term retention, either two days or two weeks following training, was statistically significant.

As with Japanese, the experimental group's higher achievement in retention was for the comprehension of more complex samples of spoken Russian such as long and novel utterances.

A SEARCH FOR AN EXPLANATION:
THE LATERALIZED BRAIN MODEL

The split-brain research by Gazzaniga (1967) and Gazzaniga, LeDoux, and Wilson (1977) suggests that the right hemisphere can express itself in actions while the left can talk. Although either hemisphere can recognize a correct answer from among a set of choices, the right brain seems to be mute yet able to generate answers through gestures and movements of the body such as pointing, touching, and grasping. The left brain provides answers by talking and writing.

The issue is this: In trying to comprehend the spoken target language, should the instructor's input be to the student's right hemisphere, and should responses from students—the output—also be from the right hemisphere? An example would be to listen to a command spoken in the target language, then obey the command along with a model by performing an action such as walking to the

Table 10.4   Average Long-Term Retention of
                  Russian Utterances

	Experimental	Control	p
Short Utterances			
48-Hour Recall	.98	.92	.05
2-Week Recall	.99	.90	.02
Long Utterances			
48-Hour Recall	.90	.83	.10
2-Week Recall	.92	.75	.001
Novel Utterances			
48-Hour Recall	.87	.75	.05
2-Week Recall	.87	.68	.005
Total			
48-Hour Recall	.92	.85	.05
2-Week Recall	.95	.81	.005

door or picking up a pencil. Our hypothesis was that input and output from the right brain is the optimal arrangement for accelerated comprehension, long-term retention, and the understanding of novel sentences.

A rival hypothesis is that the ideal would be input to and output from the left hemisphere exclusively as, for instance, when the student listens to a command in the target language, and then hears an English translation. In the retention tests, the student is expected to tell us in English what each command means.

Still another rival hypothesis is that switching from the right brain on input to the left on output is optimal—or perhaps the reverse, provide input to the left, but expect output from the right.

A detailed description of the procedure is included in an article by Asher (1969a). Essentially, the procedure was to have two college students sit one on either side of the model. Then the taped voice of a native Russian speaker would say in Russian, "Stand!" and the model together with the students would stand up. Next they heard in Russian the command, "Walk," and everyone walked forward; then "Stop," "Turn," and "Sit down." The individuals listened to an utterance in Russian and then immediately followed whatever the model did.

The first unit of training which lasted about one and a half minutes began with simple one-word commands, but after about twenty minutes of the program the complexity was increased to utterances such as these:

"Pick up the paper and pencil and put them on the chair!"

"Run to the table, put down the paper, and sit on the chair!"

"Walk to the door, pick up the pencil, put it on the table, and sit on the chair!"

There were four units in the training program each of which lasted from one and a half to seven and a half minutes. The units were spaced over a four-day period and retention tests were administered immediately following training, but also after time intervals of twenty-four hours, forty-eight hours, and two weeks.

In the retention tests, each student individually listened to a Russian utter-

Table 10.5 Average Long-Term Retention of Russian Two Weeks After Training

Groups	Single	Short	Long	Novel	Total
			Complexity of Russian Utterances		
1. Act–Act R–R	1.00	.99	.92	.87	.95
2. Observe–Act R–R	1.00	.97	.94	.92	.95
3. Observe–Write translations R–L	.95	.90	.75	.68	.81
4. Act–Write translations R–L	.94	.88	.69	.56	.76
5. Orally translate–Act L–R	.90	.83	.63	.60	.72
6. Orally translate–Orally translate L–L	.85	.69	.53	.46	.61
7. Orally translate–Write translations L–L	.77	.55	.50	.48	.55

NOTE: R–R means input to and output from the right hemisphere; L–L, left hemisphere, etc.

ance, then performed whatever the taped voice said to do. The scoring was in behavioral units for short, long, and novel utterances. For example, if the Russian utterance was "Pick up the paper and pencil and put them on the chair!," the person received one point for picking up the paper, one point for picking up the pencil, and another point if the items were then placed on the chair. Novelty was defined as a recombination of constituent parts of utterances heard in training and therefore, in this sense, the novel utterance was heard for the first time in the retention test.

Results. The results, as shown in Table 10.5, indicated that the optimal arrangement was input to and output from the right hemisphere exclusively.

In groups 1 and 2, for example, the training was directed to the right brain and the responses expected from the students also came from the right hemisphere. The retention of spoken Russian two weeks after the training was, on the average, 87 percent or higher. These individuals during training either acted with a model as directed in Russian by a voice on tape or observed a model act. However, in the retention tests, each individual performed alone in response to spoken Russian commands.

When input and output were switched either from right to left or left to right as shown in groups 3, 4, and 5 of Table 10.5, the two-week retention on the average ranged from 63 percent to 75 percent for *long* Russian utterances and 56 percent to 68 percent for *novel* Russian sentences. An example of a right to left hemispheric switch would be to observe a model act in training, but write translations in the retention tests. A left to right switch would be, for instance, to translate in training and act during the retention tests.

Finally, here is what happened when there was left brain input during the training and left brain output during the retention test at the end of two weeks:

Groups 6 and 7 showed an average retention of *long* Russian utterances that ranged from only 50 percent to 53 percent and for *novel* sentences from 46 percent to 48 percent. An example of left hemispheric input and output would be to translate orally the spoken Russian in training and during the retention tests.

The results in Table 10.5 support the conclusion that when the instructional strategy was designed exclusively for the right hemisphere, long-term retention of the target language was near the maximum of about 95 percent. If the instruction was switched from one hemisphere to the other as, for instance, using motor learning in training but requiring translation in the retention tests, then we can expect long-term retention to decrease to about 75 percent; and when the instruction is exclusively designed for the left hemisphere, then long-term retention will decrease to about 50 percent.

Is the Right Hemisphere Ideal for Comprehension Training?

Previous experiments with Russian suggested that when the right hemisphere could express itself in a motor response, significantly more comprehension was evidenced than when the left hemisphere was asked to respond with translations. However, some alternate explanations were explored. For example, there are three artifacts in the motor response that could possibly simplify the task. It may be that the artifacts accounted for the increased comprehension.

The artifacts. The first possible artifact was *position,* which means that, in many instances, the location of the student in the room may give information as to the probable direction of the next command. For example, if a command in Russian is "Pick up the pencil and book," the individual may be biased to expect that the following command will have something to do with the pencil or the book or both. Students in the control group who were writing English translations may not have been as aware of position as those who were physically relocated after each Russian command.

To test the importance of position a *position-absent* group (N = 15) acted in training and in the retention tests, but after responding to a Russian command each individual returned to a neutral position. For example, if the command was "Walk to the window and put down the pencil," the person was to execute the movement, leave the pencil near the window, and return to a neutral position, sitting in a chair at one side of the room.

If position is eliminated from the motor act during retention tests, will the increased performance vanish? The answer is no, because most of the statistical tests showed no significant difference between position-present and position-absent groups.

The second possible artifact was *concurrency,* which means that a lengthy Russian command may be simplified if the individual begins to move before hearing the entire Russian utterance. For instance, consider the command, "Run to the door, pick up the flower, and sit on the chair." If one is in motion running to the door immediately after hearing that part of the utterance, then perhaps the person has simplified the problem of comprehension. When the individual acts out each constituent of the Russian utterance while simultaneously listening to the next constituent, less attention is necessary than if the student had to wait for the entire Russian utterance to be spoken before making a move.

To test the hypothesis that concurrency accounted for the superior retention of those who demonstrated proficiency through motor behavior, a *concurrency-absent* condition was designed in which individuals ($N = 21$) acted in training and in the retention tests, but each person was delayed from acting during retention tests until the *entire* Russian command had been spoken. The results were that the elimination of concurrency from the motor act produced no discernible statistical change in retention.

The third possible artifact was *cue,* which means that the location of objects in the room may signal the direction of the next command. As an illustration, if the individual has been instructed in Russian to "... put the pencil on the chair ..." then the location of the pencil in the room will give some information about future commands. Any future mention of pencil, for example, should direct the person's attention to the chair. The continual relocation of objects in the room may be valuable information, which is unavailable to those who wrote English translations during retention tests.

To test the impact of cue on retention, a *cue-absent* group ($N = 10$) was assigned to act during the training and the testing of retention. Additionally, a set of objects (paper, pencil, book, and flower) was placed at each location the person would move to during the retention tests. When cue was eliminated from the experience, there was only a negligible effect upon performance.

The final possible artifact was *sequence,* which means that given utterance J, there was a high probability that utterance K would follow. For instance, if the Russian command was "Sit!," the next would probably be "Stand!" If the command was "Run!," the next would be "Stop!" This factor became less important in later training units when the Russian commands became complex and novel.

One group for which the retention sequence was not a factor was an *act-act* group ($N = 18$) that acted during training and retention testing. For this group the order of presentation for each command was randomized, and after the execution of each command the individual was to return to a neutral position in the room. Another group for which sequence information was absent was the *act-write* group ($N = 18$) which acted during training and translated during retention. The subjects listened to a randomized order of the commands and translated them into English.

The results were that the *act-act* and *act-write* groups, for which sequential information was absent, performed alike. None of the two-tailed statistical tests was significant. However, the *sequence-absent* groups compared with *non-sequence-absent* groups evidenced a significant decrement in retention.

A note on interpretation should be added here. This design was not a pure exploration of sequence alone. The reason is this: Since the utterances were randomized it was necessary in the *act-act* group for the people to return to the neutral position after executing each command. If they had not returned after each utterance to the neutral position the task would have been most confusing. For example, suppose a Russian command was "Run to the chair, pick up the book, and walk to the door." Then if the next utterance was, "Run to the door and put down the pencil," it would be an insolvable task.

For maximum clarity it was necessary for individuals to return to a neutral position after each utterance and to have a set of objects (paper, pencil, book, and flower) in their hands and a set located at each location (the table, chair, door, and window). This meant that for the *act-act* group, sequence, position, and cue were absent. Similarly, for the *act-write* group, sequence, position, and cue were absent. The generalization at this point was that when sequence, position, and cue were eliminated from the retention test situation, there was a highly significant decrease in the performance of individuals.

The conclusion seems to be that no single component of the motor act can account for the accelerated comprehension and retention. Apparently, an important unit of analysis is the integrated experience of listening to a direction in the target language and executing the appropriate action. It is known that contextual information is an important component in learning to comprehend the sentences of a language (Bransford and Johnson, 1972).

Do Children "Naturally" Use
the Right Hemisphere in Learning Another Language?

It is a common observation that when a family moves into a foreign country, the children achieve conversational fluency while the parents often struggle for mere intelligibility. From this, it is often inferred that children have a gift for language learning which vanishes with adulthood. The "gift" could be a function of the greater elasticity of a child's brain (Penfield and Roberts, 1959), or perhaps imprinting (Hess, 1958), which is a time interval when the individual's system is receptive to learning language.

Both hypotheses could be the explanation, but a rival hypothesis is that the context in which the new language is learned favors the right hemisphere of children and the left hemisphere of adults. For example, young children are exposed to the target language in intimate caretaking situations in which their behavior is gently directed with utterances such as:

"Wash your hands before you come to the table!"

"Let me see how well you washed your hands. Oh, oh . . . let me help you. Let's try again. Come on. Follow me into the bathroom. Take my hand . . ."

Children are also exposed to the target language in play with utterances such as:

"Throw the ball to me."

"Don't step on the line."

"Walk back three steps . . . that's it . . . no, no. One more step. Now when I say 'go,' throw the ball to me!"

In caretaking transactions and in play, the language is being decoded by children through gestures and body movement. This is stimulation of the right cerebral hemisphere which is analogous to the way the children deciphered their first language.

Adults, by comparison, are static and stationary in receiving and transmitting in the new language:

"Hello, how are you?"

"It looks like it will be a bit foggy today."

"Well, it's time for me to do my shopping. Good-bye."

Clearly, for adults the most frequent exposure to the target language is a left brain exercise.

What would happen if both American children and adults had an equal chance to learn a sample of spoken Russian through the right hemisphere?

The study published in *Child Development* by Asher and Price (1967) compared different age groups in their understanding of spoken Russian through implicit learning of the right hemisphere. The children (N = 96) were drawn from the second, fourth, and eighth grades of a public school in San José, California. The adults (N = 37) were college students recruited from undergraduate psychology courses at San José State University. None of the children or adults had prior training or exposure to Russian. The subjects in each age group were randomly divided between those who would learn by acting with a model during training and acting alone in the retention tests, and those who sat, observed a model act during the training, but then, in the retention tests, acted alone. Both conditions—*act-act* and *observe-act*—can be considered right hemispheric instructional strategies.

Results. The findings for different complexities of Russian utterances, such as single, short, long or novel sentences, are presented in the histogram in Figure 10.1.

Surprisingly, the adults outperformed the children in every age group with scores that were all statistically significant. Adults performed on the average near the maximum score of about 90 percent in the comprehension of Russian, then eighth graders with about 65 percent, followed by fourth graders with approximately 55 percent, and finally second graders, who were 45 percent.

Clearly, there was an inverse relationship between age and comprehension when the instruction was directed to the right hemisphere. Contrary to the common belief in the younger child's "natural" advantage in language learning, our data suggested that when the context of language learning for both children and adults was designed for assimilation by the right hemisphere, children lagged far behind adults in understanding spoken Russian.

Do Children Have a "Natural" Advantage in Pronunciation?

When adults and children both learned to understand spoken Russian through play, the learning curve for the children lagged far behind the adults. Adults

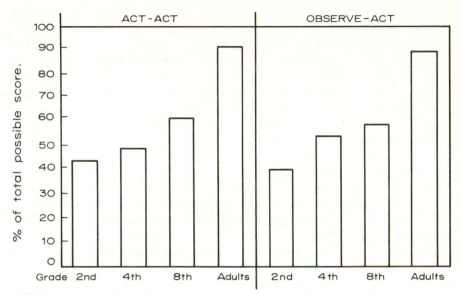

FIGURE 10.1.   Retention as measured by the total score

demonstrated accelerated comprehension, but how about pronunciation? Do children have perhaps a biological predisposition that enables them to acquire a near-native pronunciation of a second language?

In an attempt to test the hypothesis for pronunciation, Asher and García (1969) examined a group of Cuban immigrants (N = 71) between the ages of seven and nineteen most of whom had been in the United States about five years. The intent was to compare the Cuban children with American children (N = 30) in their pronunciation of English sentences. All children in both groups had learned their English in the San Francisco Bay area.

In collaboration with several linguists, the measure of English pronunciation was four sentences containing a sample of English sounds which speakers of Spanish are most apt to find difficult. Each Cuban and American child was asked to utter the following sentences:

1. I had two hot dogs and a glass of orange juice for lunch yesterday.
2. The girls were jealous because we had a better party.
3. Pat and Shirley are measuring the rug to see if it shrank.
4. It started to snow when we were about to leave for the mountains.

Before a child's pronunciation of a sentence was tape recorded, the child read and rehearsed that sentence many times until he or she felt ready to make the utterance on tape. With this procedure, the child was able to concentrate on one sentence at a time. The pronunciation of the individuals was grouped according to age, with all seven-year-old children together, all eight-year-old children together, and so forth. On the tape, the utterances of the Cuban and American children were randomly placed within each age group.

Then students in a class of American high school students (N = 19), most of whom were juniors and seniors, sat in a booth located in the language laboratory at the Blackford High School in San José, California, and listened to a replay of the sentences uttered by the Cubans and Americans. After hearing a set of four sentences uttered by a subject, the judges made a decision about the fidelity of pronunciation by checking one of the following categories:

A—indicated a native speaker
B—indicated a near-native speaker
C—indicated a slight foreign accent
D—indicated a definite foreign accent

The judges were instructed that a voice would utter four sentences after which each judge was to classify the pronunciation into one of the above four categories, A, B, C, or D.

Before starting the task, the judges listened to an illustration for each of the four categories into which pronunciation was to be classified. Then the judges listened to the subjects grouped according to age, with the nineteen-year-old subjects first, then the eighteen-year-old subjects, and so forth down to the six-year-old children. In each age group, the utterances of one to three American children, randomly positioned, also appeared along with the utterances of the Cuban immigrants. Each subject was identified on tape by initials only.

Results. The nineteen judges made 1,919 independent decisions on the pronunciation of the subjects, and in 70 percent of those decisions the judges had perfect agreement among themselves.

A near-native pronunciation was achieved by 68 percent of those children who entered the U.S.A. between one and six, 41 percent of those between six and twelve, and only 7 percent for those thirteen years or older. As to those children identified with a definite foreign accent, none was six or under, 16 percent were between seven and twelve when they entered the U.S.A., and 66 percent were thirteen years or older. The conclusion was an inverse linear relationship between age of entry into the U.S.A. and the achievement of near-native English pronunciation. *The younger the child, the greater the chances for acquiring excellent pronunciation.*

Then we wanted to know whether or not length of time in the U.S.A. was important to pronunciation skill. If a child lived in the U.S.A. one to four years, only 15 percent had a near-native speech while 55 percent had a definite accent. In comparison, for those here five to eight years, 51 percent were identified as near-native and only 10 percent had a definite accent.

So far in the analysis, both the age at which the Cuban child entered the United States and the number of years the individual lived in this country were important variables in determining fidelity of pronunciation. Next we wanted to know the interaction between these two critical variables, which may be seen in Figure 10.2.

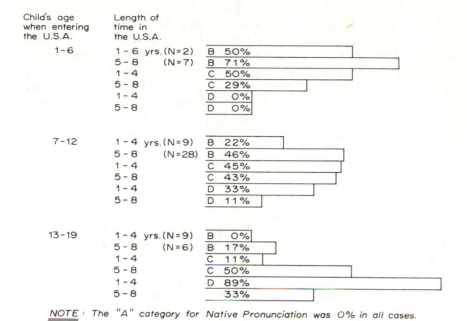

Child's age when entering the U.S.A.	Length of time in the U.S.A.		
1-6	1-6 yrs. (N=2)	B	50%
	5-8 (N=7)	B	71%
	1-4	C	50%
	5-8	C	29%
	1-4	D	0%
	5-8	D	0%
7-12	1-4 yrs. (N=9)	B	22%
	5-8 (N=28)	B	46%
	1-4	C	45%
	5-8	C	43%
	1-4	D	33%
	5-8	D	11%
13-19	1-4 yrs. (N=9)	B	0%
	5-8 (N=6)	B	17%
	1-4	C	11%
	5-8	C	50%
	1-4	D	89%
	5-8		33%

NOTE : The "A" category for Native Pronunciation was 0% in all cases.

FIGURE 10.2.   English pronunciation as a function of entry and length of time in U.S.A.

For those who lived in the United States from five to eight years and entered this country between the ages of one and six, 71 percent had a near-native pronunciation; for those who came between the ages of seven and twelve, 46 percent were near-native; and for those thirteen or older, 17 percent had a near-native pronunciation.

If the children only lived here between one and four years, near-native speech was found in 50 percent of those between the ages of one and six when they came; 22 percent of those between seven and twelve; and 0 percent of those children who entered the U.S.A. at thirteen years or older.

The conclusion was that a Cuban child had the greatest probability of achieving a near-native English pronunciation of English if the individual was six or younger when entering the new country and lived here more than five years. A child who came here at the age of thirteen or older had only a small chance of acquiring a near-native pronunciation, even if the person lived in this country five years or more.

Finally, we explored whether or not Cuban girls were better able than Cuban boys to acquire a near-native pronunciation of English. The data, which were also published in the paper by Asher and García (1969), indicated that more girls than boys had a near-native pronunciation, but the differences tended to diminish the longer the children lived in the United States. These results were generally confirmed by other investigations cited in Krashen (1975).

The data suggested that some variable within child development is a powerful determinant of pronunciation fidelity for second languages. This variable may indeed be biological. The curious puzzle is that although the probability of pronunciation fidelity is with the younger child, some older children—a small group to be sure—can also achieve an excellent pronunciation, which implies that biology does not completely determine the phenomenon. There are some important additional considerations which should be investigated. Older-aged children have a greater chance of being placed in an environment in which speech is demanded. Also they may be given formal explicit instruction in which speaking is demanded. Younger-aged subjects are rarely forced to speak and so they have an opportunity to acquire a full knowledge of the phonological rules of the target language before they do much talking. The variables of formal explicit instruction and length of comprehension experience (implicit instruction) need to be carefully examined in studies that relate age to pronunciation.

Conclusion. When the context of learning is designed so that everyone, no matter what their age, comprehends the target language through the stimulation of the right cerebral hemisphere, then the highest point on the learning curve is occupied by adults, then older children, and finally younger children. The older the child, the faster they internalize an understanding of the target language in a context of following directions to spoken commands.

For pronunciation, the relationship was reversed with this generalization: The younger the child, the higher the probability that the individual, living in a foreign country, will acquire a near-native pronunciation of the target language. The critical cut-off time seems to be puberty. After puberty, except in the rare case, it is not expected that the student will achieve a near-native pronunciation.

Of course, the generalization about pronunciation should be verified in laboratory studies where more control can be exercised over important variables such as the amount of right and left brain stimulation that can be found in implicit and explicit instruction.

What Happens When Children Experience Right Hemispheric Stimulation in School?

When the research was confined to short experiments in the laboratory, the optimal instructional design for comprehending a target language was a format that stimulated the input and output channels of the right cerebral hemisphere. Would the dramatic gains in comprehension hold when the innovative format was applied for one year in elementary school classrooms?

The experimental training program (Asher, 1977) had the following features when the target language was Spanish:

First, the students were treated as actors in a stage play in which the instructor was the director. To communicate the meaning of the Spanish utterances, there was no direct translation into English. Rather, the instructor would utter a command in Spanish such as "Stand up!" and then, as a model, the instructor with a student on either side would stand up. Next, she would say "Sit down!" and she, together with the students on either side, would sit down. Other commands in the first series were: "Walk," "Turn," "Jump," "Run," and "Stop."

Once the instructor had modeled a series of commands for a few trials, she sat down and spoke Spanish to direct the movements of individual students. Then in the next series, the commands were expanded to: "Walk to the chair," "Run to the table," "Walk to the door," "Touch the door," and so forth.

In addition to the expansion of constituents into more and more complex grammatical patterns, the second feature was to increase the student's flexibility in understanding the constituents when they were recombined to create novel and unfamiliar sentences never heard before in training. For example, the student may have seen a demonstration through modeling of: "Sit on the chair" and "Walk to the table." To achieve flexibility of understanding, the instructor uttered a recombination of familiar elements to produce an unfamiliar sentence such as, "Sit on the table." The expectation was that there would be immediate understanding of the novel sentence. In recombining constituents, an attempt was made to produce unusual sentences as, for instance, "Run to Maria, take her purse, and throw it out the window!"

A third feature was deliberately to delay spoken language from students until the twelfth hour of training. At this point, the instructor invited volunteers to reverse roles and utter Spanish commands to direct the behavior of the instructor and other students. From this time on, role reversal became a regular part of each class.

Since children's first language was the model for instruction, there was a wide tolerance for student errors in production—either speaking or writing. As an encouragement to talk in the beginning stages, students were not interrupted with corrections, so long as their speech was intelligible to a native listener. Eventually, as their confidence increased, they were corrected for more perfect production.

Reading and writing were accomplished through transfer. Once students could respond with an immediate and appropriate action to spoken commands, they were also able to demonstrate by their actions that they understood commands written on the chalkboard by the instructor. Later, they could write commands.

The children in the comparison classes experienced a modified audio-lingual approach in which they would hear a Spanish utterance from the instructor and then repeat it. Meaning was communicated by pictures or translation into English. The comparison class also had formal instruction in reading and writing, emphasizing Spanish grammar.

Results. In the initial statistical processing of data with planned comparisons using analysis of variance, most of the findings favored the experimental classes (Asher, 1977). In the conclusions to be presented, the probability is .95 or higher when evaluated by Bayesian statistics that each statement is true.

FIGURE 10.3.   From the *Spanish Picture Test*

Study 1. The first measure was the *Spanish Picture Test for Listening* in which the students looked at a picture such as the one shown in Figure 10.3, listened to a Spanish sentence about the picture, and judged whether the sentence was true, false, or incomprehensible.

For a total possible score of 70, the range of adjusted split-half reliabilities among the fifteen groups was .68 to .93 with a median of .84. Each item on the test matched vocabulary or grammatical features that both experimental and control subjects had experienced in training.

With the exception of fifth graders, all students in the experimental classes with only twenty hours of training excelled in understanding spoken Spanish, as compared with a class of ninth graders who had 100 hours of audio-lingual instruction.

Secondly, the analysis showed that, compared with the ninth graders just mentioned, three-fourths of the experimental sixth graders had a gain of 15 percent or more in listening skill, while the gain for the seventh and eighth graders was 20 percent or more.

The next measure was the *Spanish Picture Test for Reading* which was identical in content to the *Spanish Picture Test for Listening,* except that students read each sentence and then judged whether the sentence was true, false, or incomprehensible for a total possible score of 70. The range of adjusted split-half reliability coefficients was .74 to .93 with a median of .88.

After twenty hours of motor training, the seventh and eighth graders performed best in reading, followed by the sixth graders and then the fifth graders. Again, with the exception of fifth graders, all students in the experimental classes with only twenty hours of training excelled in reading Spanish over the comparison class of ninth graders who had 100 hours of audio-lingual instruction. Three-fourths of the experimental sixth graders gained 25 percent or more in reading when compared with the ninth graders who had 100 audio-lingual hours of training, while the gains for three-fourths of the experimental seventh/eighth graders was 50 percent or more.

Study 2. Although the experimental students made substantial gains in listening and reading, we felt that the *Spanish Picture Test* was too easy since it involved only true and false type responses. What would happen, we speculated, if the students had to create a story in Spanish? This seemed to be a more demanding measure of skill in producing written Spanish.

The task was to write in twenty minutes a short story in Spanish based on a cartoon with three frames of a boy running away from a table and chair, picking up a flower, and sitting at the table holding the flower. The interrater reliability for scoring the stories for two classes selected at random was .96 and .92.

After forty hours of training, all experimental students in the sixth, seventh, and eighth grades who completed the task were significantly better than a comparison class of sixth graders with forty hours of audio-lingual training. Three-fourths of the sixth, seventh, and eighth graders with action-oriented training had gains of 40 percent or more in writing skill as compared with the control group.

In fairness to the audio-lingual method, the gigantic gains in writing a short story may have been a function of action-oriented pictures used to stimulate the children's thinking. Therefore, we tried to sample writing skill with two other measures. For the first measure, the directions were: "... write as many Spanish orders or sentences as you can recall. Write everything you can remember in Spanish. You will get three points for each thought you put down on paper. See how many Spanish orders or sentences you can list in fifteen minutes. Put down anything you can recall in Spanish. Don't repeat the same words over and over. Use all the vocabulary you have. If you run out of paper, raise your hand and I'll give you more. Ready? Go!" The interrater reliability for scoring from three classes selected at random was .80, .97, and .97. The salient finding was that the experimental sixth graders surpassed with statistical significance both the experimental fifth graders and the control sixth graders. Three-fourths of the sixth graders in the experimental group had a gain of 30 percent or more.

The second measure was perhaps the best indicator of fluency of thinking in the target language because it required the production of novel thoughts in Spanish. The directions were to recombine what was heard in training to produce novel utterances. For instance: "... make up new orders or sentences —ones you have not heard in class. The wilder and crazier, the better. For example, if the normal sentences that you learned were: "*El niño juega al fútbol*" or "*El pájaro está en el árbol*" you may recombine these to produce a new sentence as: "*El niño juega en el árbol,*" and this is the type of sentence I want you to write, but the wilder and crazier it is, the better. Let your imagination run wild and produce as many new orders or sentences as you can in fifteen minutes. You will get three points for each idea you write down. Ready? Go!" The interrater reliability for scoring was .93 and .97 for two classes selected at random.

The key finding was that the experimental fifth and sixth graders surpassed the performance of control children who had a comparable number of audio-lingual instructional hours. Three-fourths of the sixth graders had an 80 percent gain or more when compared with matched children in the control class. The gain for the experimental fifth graders was about 40 percent or more.

Conclusions. When the instruction encourages implicit learning designed to stimulate the right hemisphere, children in elementary school classes learning Spanish achieved significant gains in comprehension. The children were especially outstanding for flexibility of thinking in Spanish as judged by their ability to write novel sentences. They also demonstrated flexibility in speaking Spanish as may be seen in a documentary motion picture entitled, "Children Learning Another Language: An Innovative Approach."[2]

Adults Learning Spanish in School:
The Influence of Right Hemisphere Stimulation

The experiments with Japanese and Russian were confined to language samples of less than one hour. The right hemispheric instructional strategy was expanded to a one-year program (Asher, Kusudo, and de la Torre, 1974) in an attempt to answer these questions:

First, can the entire grammatical code of the target language be internalized with a format in which students physically respond to commands? Critics have been skeptical that this is possible, although I have offered many examples showing how any grammatical feature can be nested into the imperative.

For instance, the *future tense* can be nested into a command such as, "When Luke walks to the window, Marie *will* write Luke's name on the chalkboard." The *past tense* can be incorporated into the command structure. As an illustration, say: "Abner, run to the chalkboard." After Abner has completed the action, say: "Josephine, if Abner *ran* to the chalkboard, run after him and hit him with your book." As to the *present tense*, these were nested in the imperative as, for example, "When James *walks* to the window, Shirou will write James' name on the chalkboard."

In developing the content for this one-year experimental program, we discovered that with imagination, any grammatical feature in Spanish can be imbedded in the imperative. For instance, Ramiro García used this simple innovation to differentiate the familiar from the formal in the second person pronoun. The directions to the students were: "When I put on my glasses, I am someone such as your teacher, your friend's father, or a shopkeeper. Therefore, utter a direction to me with the formal *usted*. But when I take my glasses off, I'm your best friend, a schoolmate, or your younger brother. Therefore, use the more intimate *tú* form."

For more illustrations, see Asher (1981), Woodruff (1976, 1978) and the motion picture we produced which is a step-by-step documentary of this experimental program. The title is, "A Motivational Strategy for Second Language Learning."[2]

The second question was to determine whether or not comprehension in a target language can be achieved without using the student's native language. One risk in using translation is interference—a noise generated by internal "cross talk" from one language to the other. Furthermore, our theoretical position, following Piaget's model of infant development, is that to internalize the voice of the instructor as a representative of authentic language, one must construct a reality in that target language. That construction of reality comes from a direct exploration and manipulation of persons, places, and things rather than merely being told it. Translation is telling the student about reality rather than designing situations in which the student constructs reality through motor behavior such as touching, grasping, throwing, looking, and crying.

The third question was the magnitude of positive transfer-of-training from listening comprehension to speaking, reading, and writing. Transfer-of-training is a crucial index of the instruction's effectiveness because it means a substantial saving in instructional time.

Undergraduate college students, mostly psychology majors, enrolled in an experimental course for people without prior training in Spanish. The students (N = 27) received college credit for attending the class three hours one evening per week for two consecutive semesters.

Each student in the experimental course was given the long form of the *Modern Language Aptitude Test* (MLAT). The average was 114.4 (with a standard deviation of 31.3), a score similar to the average language aptitude score of college men and women on the MLAT test. After testing, the subjects were assigned at random to two separate groups, and each group met on a different evening once each week.

Unfortunately, because of time limitations, no pretests were administered to the comparison group. An ideal procedure would be to use standardized pretests with established norms for all groups so that baselines can be determined for prior language skills and aptitude.

Listening training. The students sat in a semi-circle around the instructor. The students adjacent to her were asked to be silent, listen carefully to each command in Spanish, and do exactly what the instructor did. The students were encouraged to respond rapidly without hesitation and to make a distinct, robust response with their bodies. For example, if the command was "Corran!" the students were to run with gusto. A distinct response was an unambiguous signal that the student understood the command. The first routine involved commands in Spanish as, "Stand up!," "Walk!," "Stop!," "Turn!," "Walk!," "Stop!," "Turn!," "Sit down!"

The instructor spoke the commands and acted together with two students on either side of her for several times until individual students indicated that they were ready to perform without the instructor as a model. Each repetition of the routine was not an exact duplication because we did not want memorization of a fixed sequence of behavior.

The next step was to invite other members of the group to perform individually. Experiments have shown (Asher, 1969b) that retention is increased when individuals perform alone in response to spoken commands.

In the next routine, the commands were expanded to: "Walk to the door!," "Walk to the window!," "Walk to the table!" Then "point" and "touch" were introduced. At this juncture in training, the students had acquired enough elements so that novel sequences of increased length could be used as commands: "Eugene, stand up, walk to Claudine and touch her." "Claudine, walk to Norman, and touch his chair." The students were delighted because they realized they understood Spanish utterances they had never heard before. Also the use of playful, zany, and bizarre commands maintained a high interest level in the students. Here are three samples:

"When Henry runs to the chalkboard and draws a funny picture of Molly, Molly will throw her purse at Henry."

"Henry, would you prefer to serve a cold drink to Molly, or would you rather have Eugene kick you in the leg?"

"Rosemary, dance with Samuel, and stick your tongue out at Hilda. Hilda, run to Rosemary, hit her on the arm, pull her to her chair and you dance with Samuel!"

Production. After about ten hours of training in listening comprehension, the students were invited, but not pressured, to reverse roles with the instructor. Those students who felt ready to try speaking, uttered commands in Spanish to the instructor, who performed as directed by the students.

From this time on, about 20 percent of class time was role reversal in which the students spoke Spanish to command the instructor or peers, and later on there were skits created by the students and performed in Spanish, and still later in training there was problem solving in which students, presented with an unexpected difficulty while in a Latin country, had to talk their way through to a solution.

Reading and writing. There was no systematic training in reading and writing. For a few minutes at the end of each class meeting, the instructor wrote on the chalkboard any structure or vocabulary item requested by the students. These items in Spanish, with no English translations, were almost always utterances the students had heard during class. As the instructor wrote on the chalkboard, the students wrote in their notebooks.

Results (midway through training). The midpoint in training represented about forty-five hours of instruction in which the class time was 70 percent listening training through commands, 20 percent speaking, and 10 percent reading and writing with no homework assignments. At this point the perform-ance of three control groups was compared with that of the experimental group. The first comparison group involved high school students with one year of Spanish, the second consisted of college students finishing their first semester of Spanish, and the third, college students completing their second semester of Spanish.

Proficiency was tested by answering ten true-false questions from a story told in Spanish (Asher, 1972). Vocabulary items were those common to students. In each of the four groups, the sentences in the story were different from those used in the various training programs.

Listening and reading skill for stories. First, the experimental group with *forty-five hours of training* and no homework assignments had a significantly higher level of comprehension for stories than high school students (N = 14) with 200 classroom hours of instruction and regular homework assignments.

The second finding was that the group learning to comprehend Spanish through motor behavior had significantly better comprehension when compared with college students (N = 44) who had *seventy-five hours of audio-lingual training* in Spanish. The experimental subjects also excelled in reading skills for stories. This result is surprising because the comparison group did systematic exercises in reading and writing from a textbook. However, for the students receiving motor training, practice in this skill involved a negligible amount of time.

The third finding was rather extraordinary. The experimental group had a higher level of listening skill for stories than students finishing the second semester of Spanish, which is *150 hours of classroom instruction* not including homework. It was surprising too that the reading skills of the second semester students did not surpass the experimental group.

The transitivity factor. It may be argued that an artifact of measurement accounts for the striking differences between groups. Since the stories were developed especially for this project, there may have been an unintentional bias in favor of the experimental training.

One test of the bias hypothesis is to compare the beginning and advanced college students for transitivity. For instance, if the stories were a reasonable measure, the second-semester college students should perform with higher listening and reading skill than first-semester college students. Transitivity was confirmed since the advanced students performed significantly better in both listening and reading.

Standard proficiency tests. Midway through training, the experimental group took the *Pimsleur Spanish Proficiency Tests—Form A* (first level). Since the Pimsleur tests were designed for students in the typical audio-lingual

Table 10.6   Mean and Median Percentile Rank of Experimental Subjects on the Pimsleur Spanish Proficiency Tests, Form A (First Level)

	N	Mean	Median
Listening	18	.70	.70
Reading	17	.85	.85
Writing	16	.76	.74
Speaking	15	Good[a]	Good[b]

[a]raw score of 70   [b]raw score of 71

Table 10.7   Mean and Median Percentile Rank of Experimental Subjects on the Pimsleur Spanish Proficiency Tests, Form C (Second Level)

	N	Mean	Median
Listening	16	.49	.55
Reading	16	.69	.66
Writing	17	.67	.60
Speaking	17	Fair[a]	Good[b]

[a]raw score of 66   [b]raw score of 68

program, they may, therefore, underestimate the skills acquired by the experimental subjects.

As seen in Table 10.6, the average student performance in the experimental group was the 70th percentile rank for listening, the 85th percentile rank for reading, and the 76th percentile rank for writing. Speaking skill is assessed on the Pimsleur in three categories of "good," "fair," or "poor." The average student in the experimental group was in the "good" category.

Results (at the end of training). After *ninety hours of training,* proficiency was assessed with the *Pimsleur Spanish Proficiency Tests—Form C* (second level). This measurement was stringent because: (a) it was designed exclusively for audio-lingual training, and (b) it was meant for students who had completed the second level which is 150 hours of college instruction. Nevertheless, as may be seen in Table 10.7, the experimental group performed beyond the 50th percentile rank for listening comprehension and beyond the 65th percentile rank in reading and writing. In speaking, the students were rated between "fair" and "good."

Adults Learning German in School: The Influence of Right Hemisphere Stimulation

I first explored the application of learning German through actions in 1972; then later in 1978, Janet King Swaffar and Margaret S. Woodruff followed up with a more extensive training program at the University of Texas at Austin, which involved several hundred students.

In my initial study (Asher, 1972) the students (N = 11) were enrolled in a non-credit course in beginning German at Cabrillo Junior College in Aptos, California. The adults, who ranged in age from seventeen to sixty, met twice a week for two hours per evening.

Like the experimental training in Japanese, the students were instructed to be silent, to listen carefully to each German utterance, and to act immediately

Table 10.8   Comparison of Experimental Class
(32 Hours Instruction) and Audio-Lingual Class
(40 Hours Instruction)

Tests	Mean		Standard Deviation		t	p
	E	AL	E	AL		
Listening	.83	.75	.08	.08	2.65	.01
Story	.88	.51	.08	.19	6.27	.001
Reading	.84	.84	.10	.09	0.12	NS

NOTE: NS means not statistically significant.

along with the instructor. The training procedure and results are shown in a 16 mm color motion picture entitled, "Strategy for Second Language Learning."[2]

The commands began with one-word utterances such as "Stand!," "Walk!," "Stop!," "Turn!," and "Sit!," but within thirty minutes the utterances were expanded to the following level of complexity:

"Point to the table!"
"Touch the chair!"
"Go to the wall!"
"Pick up the money under the picture!"
"Point to the screwdriver on the chair!"

Results. By the end of thirty-two hours of training the students had assimilated approximately 500 vocabulary items.

The experimental group was compared with students completing their first college course in German and another class of students who were finishing their second college course in German.

As may be seen in Table 10.8, the experimental group had significantly better listening comprehension compared with those finishing their first college course for (a) an "easy" measure consisting of a fifty-eight-item test, and for (b) a "difficult" measure involving listening to a story with rather complicated syntax. In reading, both groups were about the same with average scores of 84 percent. It should be noted that the vocabulary in all measures was included in the instructional programs of both groups.

Surprisingly, on the "difficult" measure of listening the experimental class with only *thirty-two hours of training* surpassed the audio-lingual students who were completing their second college course in German with about *eighty hours of instruction.* On the average, the students learning to understand German through motor behavior had 88 percent comprehension, while the second semester audio-lingual students had only 68 percent.

Conclusion. With only thirty-two hours of training with instruction designed to stimulate the right cerebral hemisphere:

(1)   Comprehension of spoken German surpassed audio-lingual students who had either forty or eighty hours of instruction.

(2) There was a large magnitude of positive transfer-of-learning from comprehension to reading. (Although no data were collected to assess speaking skill, the gains were substantial after sixty hours of training as may be seen in the documentary film, "Strategy for Second Language Learning."[2])

(3) The students who were interviewed after the comprehension instruction said that they were ready—even eager—to talk in German. As the comprehension training progressed, students indicated a readiness to memorize fine details of German grammar.

The University of Texas Study. The motivation for this study as explained by Swaffar and Woodruff (1978) was that between 1970 and 1975 an average of 45 percent of University of Texas students enrolled in the beginning language courses at the Austin campus dropped their German studies after the first semester. "With the exception of Spanish, a 5 to 10 percent annual decrease in foreign language study has been a national phenomenon since 1968" (Swaffar and Woodruff, 1978, p. 27).

In an attempt to reduce attrition and improve student attitudes toward the study of a foreign language, the following innovation was introduced:

During the first four weeks of training in beginning German, twenty-three classes consisting of 398 students were silent, but acted when directed by spoken commands from the instructor. After two weeks of learning to comprehend spoken German through actions, students were encouraged to speak spontaneously on a voluntary basis. Except for a five-minute question and answer period at the close of each hour, German was the exclusive language of instruction.

Since this was a novel approach to foreign language instruction, it was necessary to persuade twenty-two teaching assistants, seven faculty members, and approximately 400 students to participate. This was accomplished with a documentary film[2] produced by Asher which showed other college students learning German through actions.

In the fifth week of instruction, a transition was made to reading using *Deutsch 2000*. After seventeen weeks of comprehension training in which students were acquiring skill in understanding spoken German and in reading German, individuals spontaneously expressed a readiness to memorize principal parts of verbs, the rules of German word order and idiomatic prepositional phrases.

Results. As for results, in prior years, using the traditional explicit learning, only 55 percent of first-semester students elected to continue their study into the second semester, but after a switch to implicit learning through comprehension training, 78 percent of first-semester students decided to continue their study of German.

As for student attitudes, the Harvard University Survey (Jakobovits, 1969) showed that one third to one half of the students in required foreign language courses with explicit instruction had no intrinsic interest in the language they were taking. A survey at the University of Illinois (Jakobovits, 1969) found that

". . . 76 percent disapprove of the foreign language requirement and 40 percent feel that foreign language study in college has actually been detrimental to them." In comparison, 76 percent to 84 percent of the University of Texas students learning German through implicit instruction said that their interest in Germany and the German language had increased. Eighty percent to 84 percent said that the course gave them a feeling for contrasts and similarities in German and American culture.

As for student achievement, 59 percent of the first-semester students and 78 percent of the second-semester students felt that they could now read German and grasp the main ideas, at least most of the time.

After the first semester, 31 percent said they felt able to understand spoken German in everyday usage (a high level expectation given the small number of instructional hours) and this proportion increased to 48 percent following the second semester.

For an objective assessment of student achievement, the classes that experienced implicit instruction were administered the listening comprehension and reading measures of *The Modern Language Association*. The results were that after one year in the innovative program, the University of Texas students scored on the average at the 70th percentile rank in listening comprehension and the 68th percentile rank, on the average, in reading German. Both scores were substantially above the expected 50th percentile rank for the national norms.

Learning to comprehend German through actions also improved the students' overall evaluation of the faculty from 64 percent on the average in previous years to 84 percent for first-semester students and from 78 percent to 88 percent on the average for second-semester students.

The research program is continuing with support from the National Endowment for the Humanities. The intent is to develop further materials for high school and college students, then to assess the impact on learning and student motivation.

CONCLUDING REMARKS

Talking is a gift that is unique to the human species. This precious gift is perhaps the most significant behavior in human development. Hence, there is a temptation to conclude that in learning another language the logical starting point is asking students to demonstrate the gift of talking.

The neglected fact is that the biological gift of talking does not appear suddenly at birth. Furthermore, talking cannot be directly taught to the infant. Neither coaching nor coaxing by parents will make the infant talk. The infant must first internalize a working understanding of the target language. The infant must experience thousands of hours of "natural" comprehension training before it is ready for its feeble attempt to speak.

That natural comprehension training (which Winitz, 1978, calls "implicit learning") is accomplished, we suggested, through thousands of transactions in which parents gently direct the infant in intimate caretaking situations such as eating, bathing, and dressing.

As infants decode the target language, their comprehension becomes more and more sophisticated through the stimulation of the right cerebral hemisphere, which is mute but can express itself in motor behavior such as laughing, crying, reaching, grasping, and pointing.

As the infant's map of the target language expands in the right hemisphere, there comes a point when the left cerebral hemisphere is ready to try its wobbly attempt at talk. Of course, the talk will not be perfect, but gradually in time—years later—the child's speech will approximate the native adult speaker.

That's the model we have proposed. Clearly, the evidence supports the model in controlled laboratory experiments and in classroom studies conducted in many languages including English, German, Japanese, Russian, and Spanish. The model seems to hold for both children and adults. It also explains why children living in a foreign country outperform their parents in acquiring the new language.

Simply, when the instruction is designed to play to the right cerebral hemisphere, starting with comprehension, the gift of talking will eventually appear—and the process of language acquisition, from beginning to end, will be intrinsically pleasurable.

Notes

1.   In our review of the literature, there were no empirical studies available for the Curran or Gattegno approaches.

2.   The film distributor is Sky Oaks Productions, Dept. D, 19544 Sky Oaks Way, Los Gatos, California 95030.

References

Asher, J. J. "The strategy of the total physical response: An application to learning Russian." *International Review of Applied Linguistics, 3,* pp. 291–300, 1965.

———. "The total physical response approach to second language learning." *The Modern Language Journal, 53,* pp. 3–17, 1969a.

———. "The total physical response technique of learning." *Journal of Special Education, 3,* pp. 253–262, 1969b.

———. "Children's first language as a model for second language learning." *The Modern Language Journal, 56,* pp. 133–139, 1972.

———. "Children learning another language: A developmental hypothesis." *Child Development, 48,* pp. 1040–1048, 1977.

———. *Learning another language through actions: The complete teacher's guidebook* (Third printing). Los Gatos, Calif.: Sky Oaks Productions, 1981.

Asher, J. J., and Garcia, R. "The optimal age to learn a foreign language." *The Modern Language Journal, 53,* pp. 334–341, 1969.

Asher, J. J., Kusudo, J., and de la Torre, R. "Learning a second language through commands: The second field test." *The Modern Language Journal, 58,* pp. 24–32, 1974.

Asher, J. J., and Price, B. S. "The learning strategy of the total physical response: Some age differences." *Child Development, 38,* pp. 1219–1227, 1967.

Balevsky, P. "EEG changes in the process of memorization under ordinary and suggestive conditions." *Suggestology and Suggestopaedia, 1,* pp. 26–36, 1975.

Bransford, J. D., and Johnson, M. K. "Contextual prerequisites for understanding: Some investigations of comprehension and recall." *Journal of Verbal Learning and Verbal Behavior, 11,* pp. 717–726, 1972.

Bühler, C., and Hetzer, H. *Testing children's development from birth to school age.* New York: Farrer and Rinehart, 1935.

Carroll, J. B. "Wanted: A research basis for educational policy on foreign language teaching." *Harvard Educational Review, 30,* pp. 128–140, 1960.

Curran, C. A. *Counseling-learning: A whole-person model for education.* New York: Grune and Stratton, 1972.

Gattegno, C. *Teaching foreign languages in schools: The silent way.* New York: Educational Solutions, Inc., 1972.

Gazzaniga, M. S. "The split brain in man." *Scientific American, 217* (2), pp. 24–29, 1967.

Gazzaniga, M. S., Le Doux, J. E., and Wilson, D. H. "Language, praxis, and the right hemisphere: Clues to some mechanisms of consciousness." *Neurology, 27,* pp. 1144–1147, 1977.

Gesell, A., and Thompson, H. "Learning and growth in identical twins: An experimental study by the method of co-twins control." *Genetic Psychology Monographs, 6,* pp. 1–124, 1929.

Hess, E. H. "Imprinting in animals." *Scientific American, 46,* pp. 3–7, 1958.

Jakobovits, L. A. "Research findings and foreign language requirements in colleges and universities." *Foreign Language Annals, 2,* pp. 436–456, 1969.

Krashen, S. D. "The critical period for language acquisition and its possible bases." In D. Aaronson and R. W. Rieber (Eds.), *Developmental psycholinguistics and communication disorders. New York Academy of Science, 263,* pp. 211–224, 1975.

Kunihira, S., and Asher, J. J. "The strategy of the total physical response: An application to learning Japanese." *International Review of Applied Linguistics, 3,* pp. 277–289, 1965.

Lawson, J. H. "Should foreign language be eliminated from the curriculum?" In J. W. Dodge (Ed.), *The case for foreign language study.* New York: Modern Language Association Materials Center, 1971.

Lozanov, G. "The nature and history of the suggestopaedic system of teaching foreign languages and its experimental prospects." *Suggestology and Suggestopaedia, 1,* pp. 5–15, 1975.

Nord, J. R. "A case for listening comprehension." *Philologia, 7,* pp. 1–25, 1975.

Pashmakova, K. "The peripheral stimuli in learning English orthography." *Suggestology and Suggestopaedia, 1,* pp. 37–44, 1975.

Penfield, W., and Roberts, L. *Speech and brain mechanisms.* Princeton, N.J.: Princeton University Press, 1959.

Piaget, J. *The construction of reality in the child.* New York: Basic Books, 1955.

Postovsky, V. A. "The priority of aural comprehension in the language acquisition process." In G. Nickel (Ed.), *Proceedings of the Fourth International Congress of Applied Linguistics,* Vol. 3. Stuttgart, Germany: HochschulVerlag, 1976.

Racle, G. "A suggestopaedic experiment in Canada." *Suggestology and Suggestopaedia, 1,* pp. 45–51, 1975.

Reeds, J. A., Winitz, H., and Garcia, P. A. "A test of reading following comprehension training." *International Review of Applied Linguistics in Language Teaching, 15,* pp. 307–319, 1977.

Swaffar, J. K., and Woodruff, M. S. "Language for comprehension: Focus on reading, a report on the University of Texas German program." *The Modern Language Journal, 62,* pp. 27–32, 1978.

Velvovskiy, I. Z. "The ideas and method of G. Lozanov in the eyes of a psychotherapeutist-psychohygienist. *Suggestology and Suggestopaedia, 1,* pp. 16–21, 1975.

Winitz, H. "Comprehension and language learning." In C. H. Blatchford and J. Schacter (Eds.), *On TESOL '78, policies, programs, practices.* Washington, D.C.: Teachers of English to Speakers of Other Languages, 1978.

Winitz, H., and Reeds, J. *Comprehension and problem solving as strategies for language training.* The Hague: Mouton, 1975.

Woodruff, M. "Integration of the total physical response strategy into a first-year German program: From obeying commands to creative writing." Paper presented at the Spring Conference of the Texas Chapters of the American Association of Teachers of German, April 3, 1976. Mimeographed. 23 pp. Available from ERIC Document Reproduction Service. Ed 126688 FL 007722. (A revised version entitled "An experimental first-year German program incorporating the total physical response strategy" may be obtained at cost from the author: University of Texas, Austin, Texas.)

———. "Comprehension and communication, fine: But what do you do about grammar?" 1978. Mimeographed. (Available from the author: University of Texas, Austin, Texas.)

CHAPTER 11

Listening Comprehension as a Base for a Multiskill Approach to Beginning Spanish: The Purdue Experiment

Stephen S. Corbett

Assistant Professor of Spanish
Texas Tech University

W. Flint Smith

Associate Professor of Spanish
Purdue University

Relatively recent research has indicated that large amounts of listening practice before speaking or reading may prepare the learner to acquire a second language with a greater efficiency than if he or she were taught all the skills simultaneously (Asher, 1966, 1969, 1972, 1974; Maistegui and Kestleman, 1973; Postovsky, 1974; Winitz and Reeds, 1973, 1975; Winitz, 1973; Gary, 1978). The findings in favor of a preparatory training period in listening comprehension, coupled with an interest in developing the receptive skills—listening and reading—in the foreign language curriculum at Purdue, motivated the authors to engage in an experimental study which employed a listening comprehension approach called OHR (Optimized Habit Reinforcement) and its corresponding materials, *The Learnables* (Winitz, 1978). This chapter describes the Purdue field study of the Winitz strategy—rechristened OIR ("To hear" in Spanish) by the investigators.

DESIGN

The study was carried out during the spring semester, 1978. Achievement and interest-motivation of students enrolled in first-semester Spanish employing OIR for the initial six weeks of the course were compared with that of similar students who studied from the beginning under a conventional, cognitive-oriented approach. Specifically, the purpose of the investigation was to determine what effects an intensive, six-week period of listening comprehension practice might have as an advanced organizer in the development of the reading

Pretests	Treatment	Criterion
O_1 O_2 O_3	X_C	O_4 O_5 O_6 O_7 O_8 O_9 O_{10}
O_1 O_2 O_3	X_{OIR}	O_4 O_5 O_6 O_7 O_8 O_9 O_{10}

1 - aptitude	4 - 7 - course examinations
2 - intelligence	8, 9 - composite, standardized
3, 10 - interest-attitude	achievement tests

FIGURE 11.1.   Experimental arrangements

skill and the ability to understand basic vocabulary and grammatical structure, in addition to inculcating listening comprehension itself. In summary, the following research hypotheses were of interest:

(1) Students who learn under a strategy designed to promote listening comprehension and transfer during the initial stages of a beginning curriculum in Spanish would achieve more on criterion measures of listening comprehension, grammatical sensitivity, vocabulary recognition, and sight readings than those instructed with a cognitive-oriented approach.

(2) Students would maintain a more positive attitude toward language learning when their study is initiated with a listening comprehension than would those who began study where attention to listening, reading, and speaking proceeded simultaneously.

A Pretest-Post-test Control Group Design (Campbell and Stanley, 1966) was employed in the study. Randomization of the subjects among the OIR and control groups was accomplished through computer registration procedures. The experimental arrangements are summarized in Figure 11.1.

Ten classes of Beginning Spanish were included in the experiment: Five were composed of students with no previous study of Spanish and five with varying degrees of previous experience. The two groups of five sections each were assigned randomly under the treatment conditions. The final sample totaled 178 students (74 OIR, 104 Control), as indicated in Table 11.1. After attrition the control group was composed of thirty-three inexperienced students—three sections (hereafter referred to as C_i) and seventy-one experienced—three sections (denoted C_e). The corresponding OIR groups contained twenty inexperienced students—two sections (O_i), and fifty-four experienced—two sections, (O_e). A Chi-square test did not indicate any systematic pattern of attrition between the two treatment conditions for either the experienced or inexperienced groups.

Table 11.1   Sample and Attrition

| | Experienced | | Inexperienced | |
	OIR	Control	OIR	Control
Original sample	58	85	31	45
Drops				
Before Exam I*	4	8	7	7
After Exam I	0	2	4	5
No consent**	0	4	0	0
Final sample	54	71	20	33
Chi-square $_{(df)}$	$4.706_{(3)}$ nsd		$.745_{(2)}$ nsd	

*Most dropped during the first two weeks of the semester.

**Includes students who would not consent to have their data and records used in the study.

The majority of students who enroll in Beginning Spanish at Purdue are in the Schools of Humanities, Social Science and Education (HSSE), or Science, which require, respectively, proficiency equivalent to the third or fourth semester of a foreign language for graduation. A closer examination of the biographical characteristics of the sample in Table 11.2 will enable the reader to determine to what extent the subjects in this study resemble other populations of interest. Chi-square tests revealed only one instance of a significant difference ($p<.05$) between the treatment groups on the selected descriptors—the school in which the experienced subjects were studying. The C_e group included a larger proportion of students in Science.

Three pre-experiment measures were administered in order to determine if the respective groups would demonstrate homogeneity of variance in language aptitude, intelligence, and interest-motivation as follows (Table 11.3): The *Modern Language Aptitude Test,* short form (*MLAT,* Carroll and Sapon, 1959), given during the first week of classes, revealed no significant differences between the groups although the mean of O_i was considerably higher than that of its counterpart. In a like manner, there were no significant differences between groups on the *Scholastic Aptitude Test-Composite (SAT-C)* nor on a survey of interest and motivation adapted from Pimsleur et al. (1963). Scores from *SAT-C* were obtained from student files during the run of the experiment; data relevant to the latter were gathered from a questionnaire completed by all students in week one of the semester.

Several achievement tests were employed as dependent variables in the study, all in multiple-choice format. The principal criterion measures were three fifty-minute course examinations, and a two-hour final. Two of the course examinations and the comprehensive final covered material presented in the basic text and were composed of four parts each: (1) a section via audiotape to measure the student's ability to comprehend vocabulary and grammatical structures presented aurally; (2) a section to evaluate knowledge of the discrete

Table 11.2   Biographical Characteristics

	Experienced			Inexperienced		
	OIR	Control	Chi-Square	OIR	Control	Chi-Square
Sex			$.417_{(1)}$			$.011_{(1)}$
Male	22	35		14	19	
Female	33	39		13	19	
Total	55	74		27	38	
School			$6.092*_{(2)}$			$1.981_{(2)}$
HSSE	32	27		13	17	
Science	10	24		5	3	
Others	13	22		9	17	
Total	55	73		27	37	
Semester			$4.325_{(3)}$			$7.261_{(3)}$
1–2	36	39		14	11	
3–4	14	18		9	11	
5–6	5	10		3	12	
7 and above	0	4		0	3	
Total	55	71		26	37	
Age			$2.289_{(2)}$			$3.127_{(2)}$
17–21	55	71		26	39	
22–30	3	9		3	6	
31 and above	0	1		2	0	
Total	58	81		31	45	
Previous Spanish			$1.087_{(2)}$			No statistic
None	0	0		27	38	
1 yr.	12	20		0	0	
2 yr.	27	38		0	0	
3 yrs. or more	16	16		0	0	
Total	55	74		27	38	
Previous other languages			$.009_{(2)}$			$1.036_{(2)}$
None	49	68		15	19	
1–2 yrs.	7	10		9	11	
3 yrs. or more	2	3		7	15	
Total	58	81		31	45	

*significant at .05 level

elements of grammar and structure; (3) several items to measure recognition of vocabulary presented in a question-answer format, or as rejoinders; and (4) sight readings—short passages of unfamiliar content to test reading through cognate recognition, sensitivity to sentence structure, and inductive reasoning based on context. The remaining course exam, based on materials presented on videotapes viewed weekly by all students in the beginning curriculum, consisted of two parts, one testing vocabulary, the other content.[1] All four examinations had been constructed systematically by taking into account the course

Table 11.3   Difference Between Groups on Pretest Measures*

Pretests	Experienced			Inexperienced		
	OIR	Control	$F_{(df)}$	OIR	Control	$F_{(df)}$
SAT-Math	N = 52	N = 72		N = 26	N = 32	
	X 49.52	X 50.39	< 1	X 48.23	X 50.41	< 1
	SD 9.94	SD 9.69		SD 10.36	SD 11.64	
SAT-Verbal	X 42.92	X 44.71	$1.45_{(1,122)}$	X 45.77	X 44.19	< 1
	SD 8.93	SD 7.52		SD 8.75	SD 9.93	
SAT-Composite	X 92.44	X 95.10	< 1	X 94.00	X 94.59	< 1
	SD 16.53	SD 15.02		SD 16.44	SD 17.45	
MLAT	N = 51	N = 67		N = 26	N = 32	
	X 51.45	X 50.42	< 1	X 50.33	X 44.48	$2.68_{(1,56)}$
	SD 14.89	SD 13.59		SD 12.30	SD 14.59	
Interest-attitude	N = 55	N = 71		N = 29	N = 35	
	X 63.35	X 63.08	< 1	X 63.48	X 64.97	< 1
	SD 15.48	SD 14.21		SD 16.13	SD 14.18	

*Variable N's reflect data from students present during testing sessions.

objectives and the relative importance of the topics to be taught. Each had been item-analyzed and revised on a regular basis for a number of years; all demonstrated Kuder-Richardson-20 estimates of internal consistency in excess of .90.

Additional criterion measures of achievement included: (1) the composite score of eight additional sight readings passages completed by all students at a rate of approximately one per week over the course of the semester; and (2) selected items from the *Pimsleur Proficiency Test, Spanish, Reading Comprehension,*[2] form A (1967). The sight readings were short passages like those found on the three major examinations. In a manner similar to other course evaluations, the individual sight readings had undergone periodic item-analysis and revision, and demonstrated a median Kuder-Richardson-20 of .49. Items from the *Pimsleur* instrument which corresponded to the scope and content of the material covered in the course were administered during the last week of the semester; the corresponding KR-20 was found to be .87.

Lastly, the affective domain was assessed through a survey of interest-attitude at the beginning and again at the end of the study and via a questionnaire administered to the experimental groups immediately upon completion of OIR, and again at the end of the sixteen-week semester.

To control for the possible effects of teaching experience and other aspects of the teacher variable, two instructors were assigned both a control and an OIR group which had not previously studied Spanish. However, scheduling conflicts prevented the implementation of a crossed design with the experienced students. The above drawback proved to be inconsequential, however, for when attrition produced n's of ten or less in both sections of O_i and two of the C_i, it became necessary to eliminate the instructor as an independent variable by pooling the classes on the experience dimension.

Teacher characteristics and their respective assignment to the treatment conditions are summarized below. All were female teaching assistants. Three instructors (A, B, and C) taught the inexperienced groups, two of whom were assigned both a section of the OIR and the control treatments, with the third teaching only a control section. Instructors B and C had but one previous semester of experience. Previous foreign residency was limited to eight and five months, respectively. Instructor A, married to a Spaniard, had taught four semesters in the beginning language curriculum and spent two and a half years in foreign residency.

In addition to instructor A, who taught both experienced and inexperienced groups, three instructors (D, E, and F) worked with students who had previous experience in Spanish. Instructor D taught both OIR and control strategies, while A, E, and F were assigned to either one or the other. The OIR instructors (A, D) had four and one semesters of teaching experience, respectively, while those instructing the control groups (D, E, and F) demonstrated between one and twelve semesters in teaching beginning Spanish at Purdue. Instructor F had also taught three years in high school. Time in Spanish-speaking countries ranged from three months to two and a half years for the OIR instructors, and from one to two and a half years for the control. Instructor E had near native fluency in the target language. The inclusion of all sections of first-semester Spanish in the study represents an attempt to counterbalance the potential effects due to the nonrandom assignment of instructors to the two treatment conditions.

MATERIALS

The major portion of the instructional materials, summarized by groups in Table 11.4, were common to both the OIR and control groups but applied in a different time frame as explained below. They included a basic textbook, a set of supplemental worksheets and tutorial tapes, a reader, various sight reading exercises taken from Spanish periodical literature and adapted to accord with the sequence of structure and syntax in the textbook, and *Zarabanda* (1972), a Spanish language "soap opera" on videotape accompanied by a manual containing a partial script of the dialogue, practice exercises, and essential vocabulary. The combined materials contained a vocabulary base of some 1,200 words and expressions.

The OIR groups worked with *The Learnables* (Winitz, 1978), twenty twenty-minute to half-hour audio-cassettes and twenty workbooks each containing two lessons apiece and corresponding pictorial referents for the words and sentences voiced on the audiotapes. The forty audiovisual lessons are designed to teach the student to recognize audially the sounds of Spanish as they correspond to a vocabulary of 1,500 words, and to provide inductive learning of basic syntax while relating all of the above to cartoon-like representations of objects, actions, and simple events. Each tape-guided lesson lasts from fifteen to thirty minutes and builds from simple vocabulary to simple sentences of generally no more than eight or nine items. Only after the learner has had an opportunity to develop a working vocabulary and to understand well all base structures, are more complex sentences presented. At the end of each lesson the student obtains feedback on his or her progress via a ten-item, multiple-choice, self-quiz presented in the same format. The voices heard on the OIR tapes are those of both male and female native speakers from different Spanish regions of the world.

A number of supplementary materials were developed by the investigators for periodic review and day-by-day evaluation of progress among the OIR students. The review items included true-false and multiple-choice exercises used jointly with pictorial frames selected at random from the OIR workbooks and the scripts for the self-quizzes. In contrast, the daily evaluations were a series of three-minute, ten-item, multiple-choice quizzes patterned after *The Learnables'* self-tests and consisted of black and white 35mm slides of three recombined pictures from the OIR workbooks, and an accompanying tape with auditory cues in the form of a word, phrase, or short sentence.

PROCEDURES

The overall course objectives were identical for both the OIR and control groups with the exception of the former's six-week period of listening comprehension training: (1) To learn to read and comprehend Spanish language materials on sight; (2) To learn to listen to and understand Spanish when presented via media or used in classroom instruction; (3) To learn to recognize fundamental grammatical relationships and elementary syntax; (4) To learn a practical speaking vocabulary to ask for and give information in a basic content.[3] Regardless of treatment condition or experience, all classes met four times each week, for fifty minutes a session, three days in a classroom, and once in a supervised, large-group language laboratory equiped with an Advent projection system for large-screen viewing of video materials.

The principal differences between the two treatment conditions were as follows: The OIR group (1) spent the first six weeks of the semester working with listening comprehension materials, and (2) then covered the regular course materials at an accelerated pace—in ten weeks instead of sixteen. These circumstances, the relationship of *Zarabanda* to both treatment conditions, and the differential moments when evaluations were undertaken for both control and experimental populations are summarized in Figure 11.2.

The relative sequencing of major grammatical structures and their distribution over the semester for both the experimental and the control groups can be seen in the Appendix where also can be inferred the relative content of each major course exam.

OIR

The first two days of the semester the OIR group completed short elementary exercises centered about the sound-symbol relationships in Spanish to allow registration and class attendance to stabilize. On the third day students began to

Table 11.4   Summary of Treatment Conditions

	Control	OIR
Materials	TEXT: *Beginning Spanish, A Cultural Approach*, Third Ed. (Armitage and Meiden, 1972) WORKSHEETS: A series of exercises (completion, question-answer, multiple-choice) to supplement the text and tutorial tapes. (Smith, n.d.) TUTORIAL TAPES: A series of supplemental lessons in an audio-tutorial format which offer explanations of grammar, practice, and self quizzes. (Smith, n.d.) READER: *Primeras lecturas en español* (Castillo y Castillo, 1973) SIGHT READINGS: Selections from Spanish periodical literature with accompanying multiple-choice questions. (Smith, n.d.) VIDEOTAPE DRAMA: *Zarabanda* (British Broadcasting Corporation, 1972)	Same as for Control with the following additions and exceptions: LISTENING COMPREHENSION AUDIO-VISUAL LESSONS: *The Learnables*, Spanish (Winitz, 1978) READER: The reader was not required.
Student preparation	Assignments composed of tutorial tapes, reading selections from the text, content questions, and/or written grammar exercises.	Same as for Control except for first six weeks of the semester, during which time students studied via the units of *The Learnables* (OIR).

Table 11.4 (continued)

	Control	OIR
Classroom and laboratory procedures	Three class meetings and one supervised laboratory session of fifty minutes each per week. Instructors followed lesson plans which included exercises to review, clarify, and expand upon concepts introduced on the tutorial tapes and in the text. Lab session used to view episodes of videotape drama, *Zarabanda*, and to complete sight reading exercises.	Same class and lab meetings for Control. Identical procedures during last ten weeks for both class and laboratory sessions. During the first six weeks class sessions consisted of the presentation of a new OIR lesson, as well as quizzes and review exercises over previous OIR lessons; lab sessions were for the viewing of the weekly episode of *Zarabanda*, and the completion of the succeeding OIR lesson.
Pace	Predetermined by the course syllabus. Approximately one to one and a half lessons each week.	Predetermined by the course syllabus. First six weeks, students completed one OIR lesson each class session. Intensive pace followed for last ten weeks with regular course materials; approximately two to two and a half lessons each week.
Evaluation	Standardized quizzes given in class at the discretion of the instructor. Departmental examinations administered to entire class as scheduled on syllabus. Distribution of examination grades determined by curve.	Quizzes and departmental examinations during last ten weeks identical to Control. First six weeks students took daily quizzes over review and current OIR lessons and weekly quizzes over *Zarabanda* episodes.

	Week 1	Week 2	Week 6	Week 10	Week 13	Week 14	Week 15	Week 16
			Exam I		Exam II	Reader	*Zarabanda*	Final
Control	------------X			------------·X	----- X	------·X	-----·X	
	xxxxxxxxxxxxxxxxxxxxxxxxxxxxxxxx							
OIR	XXXXXXXXXXXXX	-------X		------------X		·----- X	-----X	
			Exam I			Exam II	*Zarabanda*	Final

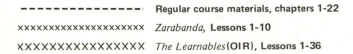

--------------· Regular course materials, chapters 1-22

xxxxxxxxxxxxxxxxxxxxx *Zarabanda*, **Lessons 1-10**

XXXXXXXXXXXXXXXX *The Learnables*(OIR), **Lessons 1-36**

FIGURE 11.2.   Differential arrangements and pace of the treatment groups

work directly with the OIR syllabus. Workbooks were distributed and students heard broadcast over a common classroom speaker the corresponding tape which directed them to view the pictures on each page, frame by frame, and to associate the words or phrases in Spanish with the referential meaning depicted by each visual. The teacher remained a passive observer while students worked through each lesson, stopping the tape only where necessary to clear up ambiguities. On the fourth day and in each session thereafter for the remainder of the six-week listening period (save review days) the class procedure was as follows: (1) A ten-item, multiple-choice quiz over past OIR lessons was administered via investigator-prepared tapes and slides. (2) Students received additional feedback on the most recent lesson studied using items from the accompanying OIR self-quiz. (3) Twenty-five minutes of class were spent with workbooks listening to the first half and part of the second of the subsequent unit (the remainder of which was assigned as homework).

The OIR groups also attended a weekly laboratory session to view the current program from *Zarabanda*; however, unlike their control counterparts who used a portion of the lab hours to practice sight-reading exercises, during the first six weeks of the semester the OIR students used the time to listen and respond to additional OIR lessons. Homework for OIR students during the first six weeks of the experimental treatment consisted of a minimum one-time review of *Zarabanda* and all OIR lessons of the week. The tapes, workbooks, and videotapes were available in an independent study, library laboratory ten hours per day; the videotape drama could also be viewed at least twice weekly on campus cable television.

During the listening comprehension stage of the study, the OIR subjects were not required to write or speak anything in the foreign language nor to read it except for occasional short phrases from *Zarabanda* which appeared in print format on the television screen in the group laboratory sessions. Throughout, the teachers and the instructions which accompanied OIR cautioned the students to refrain from attempting to repeat or write what they heard spoken on the tapes, the rationale being that any attempt to speak the language before understanding it might lead to improper pronunciation, and that reading would follow automatically if the language were first understood well through the ear.

At the end of the sixth week the OIR students had completed all but four lessons of *The Learnables*[4] and began the study of the regular textual materials at an accelerated pace. The OIR treatment from that point on consisted of identical methods, activities, and materials as the control save for the deletion of five sight-reading exercises and the reader, a procedure which provided additional time for the OIR group to "catch up" to the regular course pace.

Control

The content of the sixteen-week course for the control groups consisted of the grammatical structures and vocabulary in the first twenty-two chapters of the basic textbook, the reader, and the first ten episodes of *Zarabanda*. Students were provided with a syllabus which listed day-by-day homework assignments and supplemental audio-tutorial tapes. Classroom activities were controlled by providing the instructors with lesson plans to guide the exercises for each unit: dictation, transformation and structural drills, guided composition, question-answer exercises (with students sometimes doing the asking), and oral translation of short phrases from English to Spanish. Classtime was made available to go over homework or to clarify audio-tutorials materials. Except for brief, periodic explanation or clarification of grammatical concepts, class management and interaction were carried out largely in the target language. The prescribed weekly laboratory session included a sight reading exercise and viewing plus a quiz on an episode from *Zarabanda*.

Students in both the experimental and control groups were evaluated continually throughout the semester. Instructors selected at their discretion ten to twelve unit quizzes from among the standardized series which had been provided for the semester in the control groups. Departmental examinations were administered to all students in the respective treatments on the same day. OIR students took examinations and quizzes identical to the control; however, by definition, not until after the six-week intensive listening period. Through the sixth week, the OIR groups took quizzes over the OIR lessons, as well as the standardized quizzes over the videotape series. Thereafter they too were administered a sampling of departmental quizzes from the regular textual materials. All of the aforementioned contributed proportionally to the students' final course grades.

Finally, in an attempt to control further the instructor variable, a weekly meeting was held between the investigators and all teachers regardless of treatment condition to encourage keeping pace with and adherence to the syllabus and standardized lesson plans, and to air problems that had been recognized by either party.

ANALYSIS AND RESULTS

A single-classification analysis of variance (ANOVA) was selected to test the hypotheses following statistical routines described by Winer (1971). ANOVA was considered an appropriate procedure due to the initial homogeneous nature of the treatment groups as determined by various pretests and biographical descriptors (Tables 11.1 and 11.2). All frequency data from the end-of-term questionnaires for OIR were converted to percents and evaluated by inspection.

Achievement

Table 11.5 reports the results of the ANOVA for the two sets of treatment groups. Among the experienced, the control group scored higher than the OIR students on all of the selected criterion measures. Significant differences emerged as follows: Exam I, Listening Comprehension ($p<.05$), Structure ($p<.01$), and Composite ($p<.05$); Exam II, Vocabulary ($p<.05$); Final Exam, Sight-Reading ($p<.05$); and *Zarabanda,* Composite ($p<.05$) and Content ($p<.05$).

Tests on the data for the inexperienced groups revealed only one significant difference—the listening comprehension subtest from Exam I ($p<.05$) in favor of the control group. The OIR students outscored the control on Exam I, Sight-Reading, and Exam II, Structure, Sight-Reading, and Composite although not significantly. Alternatively, the control group achieved higher (although not significantly) than the OIR students on all of the remaining criterion measures including the Final Exam, *Zarabanda,* and *Pimsleur Reading Test.*

Figures 11.3 and 11.4 allow inspection of the proportional differences between the treatment groups as they developed over the course of the semester on both dimensions of the experience factor. The plots reveal trends as follows: (1) In most cases both treatment groups, regardless of experience, scored higher on Exam II than on Exam I; (2) Without exception all groups scored lower on the Final Exam. Figure 11.3 reveals that the experienced OIR group increased its Composite score between Exam I and Exam II to a greater degree than did the control counterpart. The largest contribution to the OIR increase came from the subtest Structure. In Figure 11.4 one observes that after Exam I the inexperienced OIR group was able to gain more proportionally than its control counterpart, and outscore it on Exam II Composite, owing to increases in all four subtests but particularly Structure. Similar trends among the experienced and inexperienced students were observed between the treatment groups for *Zarabanda* and the *Pimsleur Reading Test.*

Interest-Attitude

The ANOVA for the interest-attitude measure was based upon the post-test minus the pretest score. The results, summarized in Table 11.6, indicate that, regardless of strategy, the mean scores for all groups suffered a decline on the post-test of interest-motivation. There was, however, no significant difference between the treatment conditions for either experienced or inexperienced learners with regard to change in affective orientation.

Inspection of data from questions taken from two administrations of the questionnaire (Table 11.7) revealed that the OIR students felt unsure how much their listening comprehension had improved during the first six weeks of the semester. They were somewhat positively inclined with respect to how interesting and enjoyable were the OIR materials (question 5), and thought in retrospect that listening was a reasonably good way to begin to learn Spanish (question 6). They were ambivalent in their judgments about the length of the listening period (question 7), however, and unable to perceive any transfer from the OIR approach to their ability to read (question 8). All students were less confident about whether or not OIR had influenced their understanding of *Zarabanda* (question 9), but thought that the televised materials had enhanced to some degree their ability to read (question 10).

Discussion

The results which favored the control treatment on the majority of the criterion measures have several plausible explanations.

First, it is possible that the differences were due to the superiority of an explicit, multiskill approach, for even with six weeks of intensive training in listening comprehension, the OIR groups failed to score higher than the control on a single listening subtest. The strength of this argument is reduced, however, when one notes that the significant advantage of the control groups in listening disappeared by Exam II. Similarly, the gain that the experienced control group demonstrated in vocabulary between Exam I and Exam II disappeared by the Final, as did the small but nonsignificant increase on the structure subtest among the inexperienced students. In short, some cumulative effect was apparently at work, although its parameters are not altogether clear. On the one hand, the cognitive strategies with which the control students were instructed may have been more consonant with either their previous study of Spanish (in the case of the experienced students alone) or their expectation of how a foreign language should be taught vis à vis other school learning; that is, the explicit approach may have proven to be a more efficient means for the experienced students to reorganize previous learning and an equally efficacious advance organizer for the uninitiated. On the other hand, having a textbook early in the instructional sequence may have affected the treatment groups differentially: owing to (1) the concrete nature of the readings and explanations, (2) the reinforcement inherent in the exercises which were read, written, and discussed in class, and (3) their relative facility of review when compared to *The Learnables* which, by definition, has no printed text. The contribution of the textbook is further apparent when one notes that the OIR groups began to achieve more on a par with the control once they too had access to a reference tool beginning in

236   THE COMPREHENSION APPROACH TO FOREIGN LANGUAGE INSTRUCTION

Table 11.5   Analysis of Variance

Criterion	Items†	Experienced OIR	Experienced Control	$F_{(df)}$	Inexperienced OIR	Inexperienced Control	$F_{(df)}$
Exam I		$N=54$	$N=72$		$N=24$	$N=38$	
Listening	15	$\bar{X}$ 11.39, SD 2.84	$\bar{X}$ 12.38, SD 2.50	$4.27^*_{(1,124)}$	$\bar{X}$ 9.00, SD 2.89	$\bar{X}$ 10.50, SD 2.68	$4.34^*_{(1,60)}$
Structure	30	$\bar{X}$ 20.57, SD 6.34	$\bar{X}$ 23.24, SD 4.38	$7.76^*_{(1,124)}$	$\bar{X}$ 18.33, SD 4.65	$\bar{X}$ 19.34, SD 5.41	<1
Vocabulary	15	$\bar{X}$ 11.69, SD 3.05	$\bar{X}$ 11.97, SD 2.63	<1	$\bar{X}$ 9.46, SD 3.18	$\bar{X}$ 10.34, SD 3.54	<1
Sight-reading	10	$\bar{X}$ 7.19, SD 2.11	$\bar{X}$ 7.43, SD 1.55	<1	$\bar{X}$ 7.17, SD 2.01	$\bar{X}$ 6.93, SD 1.88	<1
Composite	70	$\bar{X}$ 50.83, SD 10.77	$\bar{X}$ 55.08, SD 9.18	$5.73^*_{(1,124)}$	$\bar{X}$ 44.04, SD 9.99	$\bar{X}$ 47.08, SD 11.71	$1.10_{(1,60)}$
Exam II		$N=54$	$N=71$		$N=20$	$N=33$	
Listening	15	$\bar{X}$ 11.39, SD 2.78	$\bar{X}$ 11.94, SD 2.56	$1.33_{(1,123)}$	$\bar{X}$ 10.05, SD 3.07	$\bar{X}$ 10.39, SD 3.13	<1
Structure	25	$\bar{X}$ 19.24, SD 3.92	$\bar{X}$ 20.14, SD 3.81	$1.67_{(1,123)}$	$\bar{X}$ 18.60, SD 3.25	$\bar{X}$ 18.06, SD 4.18	<1
Vocabulary	20	$\bar{X}$ 14.93, SD 3.07	$\bar{X}$ 16.13, SD 2.86	$5.08^*_{(1,123)}$	$\bar{X}$ 13.85, SD 2.87	$\bar{X}$ 14.12, SD 3.79	<1
Sight-reading	10	$\bar{X}$ 8.04, SD 1.64	$\bar{X}$ 8.14, SD 1.40	<1	$\bar{X}$ 7.65, SD 1.66	$\bar{X}$ 7.55, SD 2.40	<1
Composite	70	$\bar{X}$ 53.61, SD 9.46	$\bar{X}$ 56.21, SD 8.93	$2.47_{(1,123)}$	$\bar{X}$ 50.15, SD 7.86	$\bar{X}$ 50.12, SD 11.24	<1

Table 11.5 (continued)

Criterion	Items[8]	Experienced			Inexperienced		
		OIR	Control	$F_{(df)}$	OIR	Control	$F_{(df)}$
Final Exam							
Listening	25	N = 53 X 18.94 SD 4.02	N = 69 X 19.65 SD 4.33	< 1	N = 20 X 15.30 SD 5.12	N = 33 X 16.24 SD 4.56	< 1
Structure	65	X 43.19 SD 10.50	X 45.36 SD 10.79	$1.24_{(1,120)}$	X 39.85 SD 9.98	X 40.12 SD 11.22	< 1
Vocabulary	40	X 29.36 SD 6.96	X 30.86 SD 6.46	$1.51_{(1,120)}$	X 25.10 SD 7.20	X 27.58 SD 7.08	$1.51_{(1,51)}$
Sight-reading	30	X 21.77 SD 3.88	X 23.43 SD 4.04	$5.24*_{(1,120)}$	X 20.10 SD 3.63	X 21.52 SD 4.58	$1.38_{(1,51)}$
Composite	160	X 113.23 SD 22.34	X 119.30 SD 22.84	$2.16_{(1,120)}$	X 100.35 SD 21.50	X 105.45 SD 24.35	< 1
Zarabanda							
Content	30	N = 54 X 23.20 SD 4.47	N = 69 X 24.97 SD 3.10	$6.69*_{(1,121)}$	N = 20 X 23.10 SD 3.99	N = 33 X 23.64 SD 3.49	< 1
Vocabulary	15	X 11.19 SD 2.77	X 11.99 SD 2.63	$2.68_{(1,121)}$	X 10.90 SD 2.29	X 11.15 SD 3.07	< 1
Composite	45	X 34.39 SD 6.55	X 36.96 SD 5.18	$5.89*_{(1,121)}$	X 34.00 SD 5.58	X 34.88 SD 6.05	< 1
Composite sight reading	100	N = 51 X 83.16 SD 12.09	N = 68 X 84.24 SD 7.45	< 1	N = 19 X 78.00 SD 8.50	N = 30 X 82.93 SD 10.57	$2.93_{(1,47)}$
Pimsleur Reading Test	27	N = 53 X 19.81 SD 5.60	N = 66 X 21.26 SD 4.81	$2.29_{(1,117)}$	N = 18 X 16.89 SD 6.99	N = 30 X 18.00 SD 5.59	< 1

*significant at .05 level

†Variation in the number of items from subtests structure and vocabulary for Exams I and II reflects more emphasis on reading and vocabulary-building during the latter portions of the course. The increase in all subtests for the Final Exam is related to its intended comprehensive nature and two-hour testing period.

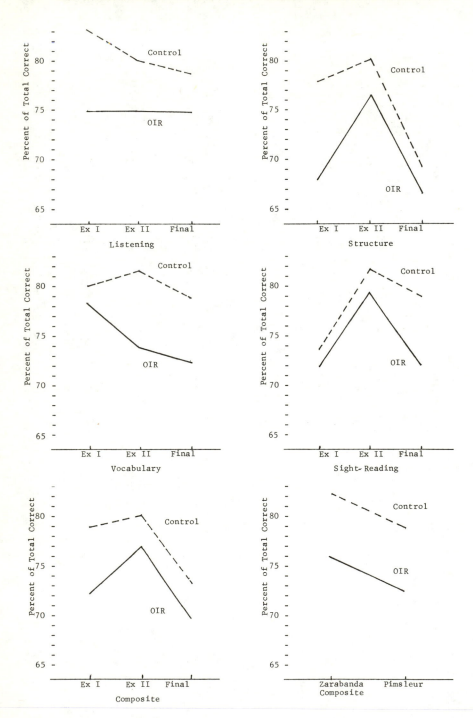

FIGURE 11.3. Proportional achievement by exam: experienced

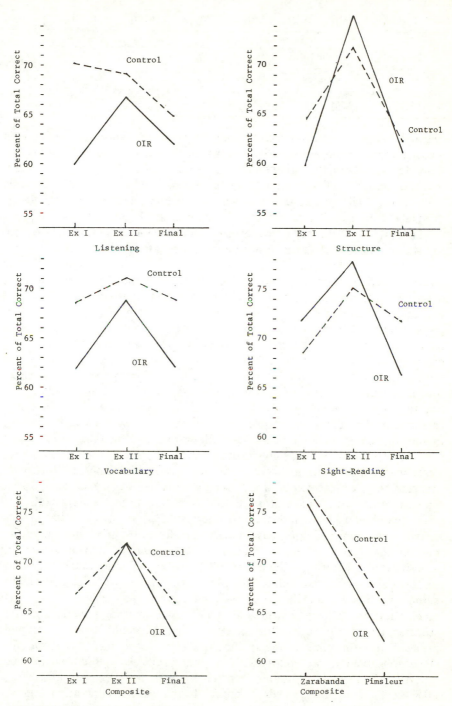

FIGURE 11.4.   Proportional achievement by exam: inexperienced

Table 11.6   Analysis of Variance: Change in Interest-Attitude

	Experienced			Inexperienced		
Criterion	OIR	Control	$F_{(df)}$	OIR	Control	$F_{(df)}$
Attitude change	N = 48 X −3.06 SD 12.23	N = 59 X −4.02 SD 9.00	< 1	N = 16 X −4.88 SD 12.44	N = 24 X −4.67 SD 9.12	< 1

the sixth week. The transition from implicit to explicit learning, coupled with acceleration and compressed assignments, may have been counterproductive, however, since from that point on the OIR students were faced with a different mode of study than that to which they had become accustomed. These events may help explain the depressed scores among the OIR experienced groups throughout the experiment and especially on Exam I.

The OIR inexperienced scores exceeded slightly those of the control on two occasions—the structure and sight-reading subtests for Exam II—but the gains were momentary and apparently a function of whatever reorganization of knowledge the textbook afforded, for they were lost on the final exam and on the other end-of-semester measures of achievement. Alternatively, the lower OIR vocabulary and sight-reading scores on the other tests may be the result of less opportunity to develop skill in reading per se. For example, the control students completed eight more practice sight-reading exercises than did their OIR counterparts; they also worked with a reader during the mid-portion of the semester while the OIR groups were in the process of trying to consolidate their intensive listening orientation through the study of grammar and reading from the text. As a result, the OIR students did not receive the same amount of practice in developing the problem-solving skills which the vocabulary and reading exercises required. Analyses of the scores from the *Pimsleur Reading Test* (1967), the composite sight-reading, and the subtest sight-reading from the three major course exams, however, revealed only one significant difference between the two treatments, a fact which leads one to speculate that some limited transfer was affected from the OIR strategy to the reading skill.

A second plausible explanation for the results of the study is that the criterion instruments did not measure skills developed by OIR students during their listening comprehension training. *The Learnables* taught contextual guessing through drawings which afforded a concrete referent to aid in ascertaining the meaning of a word or utterance. The comprehension section of the major course examinations and the *Zarabanda* quizzes presented a series of unrelated taped questions followed by three possible responses or rejoinders. The OIR students, thus, were faced with problem-solving in listening to spoken stimuli rather than the recognition of specific events developed via *The Learnables*. These observations are buttressed by data from two additional analyses reported in Table 11.8: (1) scores from ten comprehension quizzes taken by the OIR groups in comparison with a sample from a similar population studying without the OIR strategy during a subsequent semester; (2) similar attention to

Table 11.7   Analysis of Data from Questionnaire*

| | Experienced | | | | Inexperienced | | | |
| | 6th Week | | 16th Week | | 6th Week | | 16th Week | |
	Number	Percent	Number	Percent	Number	Percent	Number	Percent
1. My ability to understand spoken Spanish via The Learnables has improved progressively.								
Strongly Agree (SA)	3	.069	x		4	.166	x	
Agree (A)	18	.418	x		17	.708	x	
Uncertain (U)	14	.325	x		1	.042	x	
Disagree (D)	8	.186	x		1	.042	x	
Strongly Disagree (SD)	0	.000	x		1	.040	x	
2. I attempted to write the words and phrases that I heard spoken from The Learnables tapes.								
A great deal	4	.093	x		2	.084	x	
Quite a bit	8	.186	x		3	.123	x	
Some	9	.209	x		4	.166	x	
Not much	5	.116	x		5	.208	x	
Not at all	17	.395	x		10	.416	x	
3. I attempted to repeat aloud the words and phrases that I heard spoken from The Learnables tapes.								
A great deal	5	.116	x		0	.000	x	
Quite a bit	3	.069	x		6	.260	x	
Some	17	.395	x		10	.434	x	
Not much	9	.209	x		5	.217	x	
Not at all	9	.209	x		2	.086	x	

*variation in total respondents reflects omissions or absenteeism on days questionnaire administered

continued on page 242

Table 11.7 (continued) *

	Experienced				Inexperienced			
	6th Week		16th Week		6th Week		16th Week	
	Number	Percent	Number	Percent	Number	Percent	Number	Percent
4. Outside of class I normally listened again to each individual volume (parts 1 and 2) of *The Learnables*.								
More than 3 times	1	.024	x		1	.042	x	
Three times	3	.073	x		1	.042	x	
Twice	7	.170	x		10	.416	x	
Once	26	.634	x		12	.500	x	
Not at all	4	.097	x		0	.000	x	
5. The listening materials were enjoyable and interesting.								
Strongly Agree (SA)	0	.000	3	.057	3	.125	4	.181
Agree (A)	12	.279	23	.442	13	.541	10	.454
Uncertain (U)	14	.325	9	.173	4	.166	6	.272
Disagree (D)	13	.302	13	.250	3	.125	2	.090
Strongly Disagree (SD)	4	.093	3	.057	1	.042	0	.000
6. Listening without seeing the written word is a good way to begin to learn Spanish.								
Strongly Agree (SA)	3	.069	5	.098	3	.125	3	.136
Agree (A)	13	.302	21	.411	6	.250	11	.500
Uncertain (U)	9	.209	12	.235	6	.250	4	.181
Disagree (D)	11	.255	6	.117	5	.208	2	.090
Strongly Disagree (SD)	7	.162	7	.137	4	.166	2	.090
7. The six weeks spent on the listening materials seemed just right.								
Strongly Agree (SA)	1	.023	3	.058	1	.042	2	.090
Agree (A)	17	.404	18	.352	8	.333	4	.181

*variation in total respondents reflects omissions or absenteeism on days questionnaire administered

Table 11.7 (continued)*

	Experienced				Inexperienced			
	6th Week		16th Week		6th Week		16th Week	
	Number	Percent	Number	Percent	Number	Percent	Number	Percent
Uncertain (U)	12	.285	15	.294	7	.291	5	.227
Disagree (D)	8	.190	12	.235	7	.291	8	.363
Strongly Disagree (SD)	4	.095	3	.058	1	.042	3	.136
8. My ability to read and to understand has been enhanced by *The Learnables*.								
Strongly Agree (SA)	1	.023	3	.058	1	.042	2	.090
Agree (A)	9	.214	9	.176	7	.291	3	.136
Uncertain (U)	19	.452	30	.588	13	.541	13	.591
Disagree (D)	10	.238	9	.176	2	.084	3	.136
Strongly Disagree (SD)	3	.071	0	.000	1	.042	1	.045
9. My ability to understand the Spanish spoken in *Zarabanda* has improved progressively.								
A great deal	3	.073	5	.098	1	.042	0	.000
Quite a bit	10	.243	17	.333	3	.125	11	.500
Some	23	.560	25	.490	16	.666	10	.454
Not much	4	.097	4	.078	4	.166	1	.045
Not at all	1	.024	0	.000	0	.000	0	.000
10. My ability to read has been enhanced by *Zarabanda*.								
A great deal	4	.097	1	.020	0	.000	0	.000
Quite a bit	3	.073	15	.300	5	.208	11	.500
Some	28	.682	25	.500	11	.458	7	.318
Not much	3	.073	6	.120	7	.291	4	.181
Not at all	3	.073	3	.060	1	.042	0	.000

*variation in total respondents reflects omissions or absenteeism on days questionnaire administered

Table 11.8 Unit Quizzes

The Learnables

	Experienced					Inexperienced				
Volume†	N	OIR	N	Post-Facto	t(df)	N	OIR	N	Post-Facto	t(df)
2–3	55	X 9.73 SD .73	90	X 8.63 SD 1.33	5.62** (143)	29	X 9.55 SD .74	31	X 8.52 SD 1.03	4.36** (58)
1–5	47	X 9.89 SD .31	90	X 6.57 SD 4.22	5.37** (135)	28	X 9.79 SD .50	31	X 4.93 SD 4.33	5.81** (57)
6–7	49	X 9.29 SD .94	29	X 7.10 SD 1.86	6.80** (76)	30	X 8.93 SD 1.17	16	X 6.13 SD 1.67	6.48** (44)
8	51	X 9.57 SD .70	55	X 7.11 SD 1.44	10.96** (104)	30	X 8.87 SD 1.48	35	X 6.26 SD 1.58	6.73** (63)
9	52	X 9.17 SD .92	29	X 8.45 SD 1.70	2.44* (79)	29	X 7.83 SD 1.56	16	X 7.63 SD 1.46	.41 (43)
6–10	45	X 8.67 SD 1.15	55	X 6.07 SD 1.53	9.33** (98)	24	X 7.92 SD 1.10	35	X 6.00 SD 1.63	4.95** (57)
11–13	44	X 8.89 SD 1.13	55	X 6.82 SD 2.07	4.39** (97)	25	X 7.48 SD 1.64	18	X 5.06 SD 1.66	4.64** (41)
14	47	X 9.21 SD .95	55	X 6.35 SD 2.02	8.82** (100)	24	X 7.92 SD 1.53	18	X 6.00 SD 1.41	4.06** (40)
16–17	47	X 9.09 SD 1.02	51	X 7.06 SD 1.79	6.76** (96)	30	X 8.00 SD 1.26	52	X 5.44 SD 2.19	5.80** (30)
8	43	X 9.61 SD .66	51	X 8.29 SD 1.19	6.56** (92)	28	X 8.68 SD 1.47	52	X 6.20 SD 2.52	4.7.** (78)

seven *Zarabanda* quizzes shared by all OIR control groups during the original study. The OIR quiz results substantiate that the experimental students demonstrated learning when evaluated with criterion-related tests, for the mean scores are well above chance (3.3) and significantly higher throughout ($p<.01$) than those obtained post facto. The *Zarabanda* quiz scores, however, reveal trends similar to those observed among the major criterion measures.

Table 11.8 (continued)

Zarabanda

Volume†	Experienced					Inexperienced				
	N	OIR	N	Post-Facto	t(df)	N	OIR	N	Post-Facto	t(df)
Lesson†										
2	52	X 9.25 SD 1.06	41	X 9.24 SD .83	.05(91)	28	X 7.64 SD 1.57	35	X 8.69 SD 1.30	2.86**(61)
3	44	X 7.61 SD 1.33	68	X 7.93 SD 1.66	1.07(110)	22	X 6.96 SD 2.36	39	X 7.36 SD 1.78	.73(59)
4	51	X 8.71 SD 2.01	60	X 9.08 SD 1.18	1.19(109)	28	X 7.29 SD 2.23	33	X 7.79 SD 2.09	1.04(59)
5	46	X 8.50 SD 2.17	57	X 8.97 SD 1.09	1.41(101)	25	X 8.72 SD 1.21	36	X 8.50 SD 1.52	-.59(59)
6	47	X 7.98 SD 1.69	64	X 8.45 SD 1.67	1.45(109)	24	X 7.04 SD 2.10	34	X 7.32 SD 2.41	.51(56)
7	46	X 8.07 SD 1.78	63	X 8.60 SD 1.49	1.67(107)	23	X 5.83 SD 2.27	26	X 7.27 SD 1.93	2.35*(47)
8	35	X 8.00 SD 1.82	49	X 8.41 SD 1.77	1.21(82)	14	X 8.64 SD 1.39	26	X 8.23 SD 1.77	-.65(38)

†volumes and lessons assessed by test examination   *significant beyond .05 level   **significant beyond .01 level

Third, the results may have reflected a lack of fit between the base vocabulary from the OIR materials and the lexicon of *Beginning Spanish* which, in turn, may have biased the test scores since it was upon the latter that all course examinations had been written. A post facto comparison to that end revealed a surprisingly low correlation of words common to both sets of materials. Through Exam I, the overlap was 30 percent; the commonality increased to 35 percent by

Exam II as the OIR groups were progressively exposed to more control materials including *Zarabanda,* but the ratio remained no greater than one word in three at the end of the semester. The different topical thrust and structural content are directly related to the above. The OIR materials teach vocabulary via a modified Gouin Series—a mode of presentation linking a series of actions with appropriate utterances to describe a chain of events—usually encompassing everyday occurrences: arising, retiring, mealtime, etc. The words in OIR, thus, are as practical (*come, vaso*) or as specific (*cuchara, piyama*) as needed and are embedded in phrases that are descriptive of past, present, or future moments, and the imperative. The control materials offer socio-geographic narratives about the Hispanic world (*el clima, la instrucción*) which occasionally incorporate short dialogues as a vehicle to everyday language (*estudia, contesta*) in present and past tense. In addition, *The Learnables* do not present complete declensions and conjugations in each paradigm: *Beginning Spanish* and its exercises are very systematic in that regard. In short, the control students had an advantage in practice and inclusiveness of content from the beginning. The semester examinations thus were probably more face valid for the control groups, for while the OIR students were ultimately exposed to the same materials, they not only had less time with them, but also were unable to find in the tests the type and function of language conditioned by *The Learnables.* Said another way, the tests were task specific. Students who were trained with the OIR materials consistently performed better than the control students when the test items were taken from OIR (Table 11.8). Similarly, the OIR students did not perform as well as the control students when the tests represented the standard curriculum (Table 11.5). The critical nature of that lack of correlation was underscored further by comments from students and teachers on the end-of-semester questionnaire and in subsequent interviews with participants. Students also reported discomfort with the accelerated pace after week six, and a feeling that the receptive nature of the learning activities with the OIR materials and corresponding quizzes had lulled them into a false sense of security, despite some confidence that the listening materials were interesting and enjoyable, and a good way to begin to learn Spanish (Table 11.7, questions 5 and 6).

The relative lack of teaching experience and limited fluency with the target language among three of the instructors may have been a fourth factor working against the OIR groups, an observation substantiated by periodic classroom visitations by the investigators. Some teachers obviously felt uneasy with an approach that required only the monitoring of an audiovisual presentation during the last twenty-five minutes of each class. The clash between monitoring and their role expectancy as purveyors of knowledge may have contributed to periodic antagonism toward the OIR materials expressed during the latter portion of the course. The teachers' anxiety over the consequences of an accelerated pace may have served as a halo effect which affected student attitude as well, the combined results of which may have contributed to lower achievement among the experimental groups. Finally, the severe winter of 1978 closed the university briefly during week three of the study. Thereafter, anticipation of an extended spring-break to combat an energy crisis occasioned a marked absenteeism in all classes. Inattendance is thought to have been more damaging to the experimental groups, however, owing to the lack of a textbook or tape script in print format which could be studied intensively, off campus, prior to exams.

In summary, various factors appeared to work in disfavor toward the OIR strategy: (1) the lack of ready reference materials early in the semester; (2) a relatively small overlap in common vocabulary and grammar between OIR and the continuation materials; (3) marginal face and criterion-related validity; (4) the receptive nature of learning defined by the OIR materials themselves; and (5) both teacher and student inattention to task. Nevertheless, the occasional moments of student interest and the fact that the OIR groups seemed to be progressing toward a level of achievement consonant with that of the control in the mid-portion of the semester make desirable further investigation with an intensive listening approach as an integral part of a beginning curriculum in Spanish. Recommendations for modifications to that end are offered below.

(1) Teachers need to be instructed in detail as to how *The Learnables* will correlate with other materials. The film *A Motivational Strategy for Language Learning*[5] exemplifies how the study of a second language can be accelerated through a listening approach; similarly, it provides a basis for teachers to relate the rationale of a listening-first strategy to students who question the validity of such a process in learning a foreign tongue.

(2) The vocabulary and grammar in *The Learnables* need to be integrated systematically with subsequent curricula whether or not the strategy during the continuation period of study is to accelerate learning. Students need help to transfer to other contents the grammatical and syntactic relationships which they have acquired through listening. Thus, some overt instruction in word order, person and tense markers, and concordance seems to be needed from the first moment to help the learner consolidate concepts acquired inductively. Similar attention to vocabulary—synonyms, antonyms, definitions, and word families—should help the student extend the lexicon from *The Learnables* to new and varied situations.

(3) The OIR strategy needs to be supplemented with other types of listening comprehension activities to allow for more active participation by all. An adjustment to that end might incorporate exercises that require the students to write, draw, or act out what they hear spoken in the target language following techniques suggested by Kalivoda et al. (1971) and Allen and Valette (1977). This variation could modify to some degree the receptive mode of student response which the OIR strategy seems to foster, counteract inattention caused by materials that are presented in an unvarying format, and give the students more opportunity to respond in some overt manner. Given the reasonably close phonetic fit between English and Spanish sounds and orthography, allowing some writing—both word and phrase dictation or composition—would seem to

provide at least two additional advantages: (1) facilitate student review and out-of-class study of the materials; and (2) reduce anxiety among students accustomed to the printed word as a reinforcer.

(4) Some control over the distribution of time with which experienced students use OIR lessons seems desirable for, presumably, they will have already a reasonably well-developed cognitive base to listen with understanding. Thus, the primary challenge for the experienced is one of learning new contexts and vocabulary rather than developing receptivity; they should be able to work through *The Learnables* at a quickened pace. Conversely, the inexperienced students, by definition, need more time to develop recognition skills and an expectancy for successive elements, a circumstance that requires a lengthening of their listening comprehension training. Speech compressor-expanders and time-altered speech would seem to offer a possible advantage to both groups, allowing the experienced to speed through or review those portions of the materials that had been understood and learned elsewhere, while providing the inexperienced an opportunity to slow auditory input perceptibly (Huberman and Medish, 1974). In either case, the speech compressor-expander accomplishes the change in rate without varying the pitch or intelligibility of the original (Harvey, 1978). Alternatively, one could simply be selective about which OIR lessons are presented to students with previous Spanish, and lengthen through duplication or additional OIR lessons the total listening comprehension time for the beginner.

(5) If the low overlap in vocabulary and structures between *The Learnables* and the control materials used herein is typical of the relationship between OIR and other commonly used beginning textbooks for Spanish, then it seems obvious that there should be some lengthening of student contact hours with the OIR lessons, regardless of degree of experience—either through week-by-week integration into a given curriculum, and/or longer contact with the OIR materials themselves—thereby ensuring a sharing and building of a common vocabulary and structure from the start. Investigators who would pursue the question, however, are advised to examine the vocabulary carefully a priori in order to determine how much overlap exists and what kind of integration or lengthening might be feasible. Correspondingly, student interest and assiduity should be enhanced, as well as their achievement, to the extent that there is an apparent correlation between the base vocabulary of *The Learnables* and other sets of materials. For that reason, the testing and evaluation techniques chosen to provide feedback are of prime importance.

(6) Tests for listening comprehension beyond recombination quizzes and self tests are an important extension of the OIR approach. Specifically, the course examinations that evaluate learning during and after the OIR portion of a curriculum should incorporate pictorial referents as an aid to determining comprehension through contextual guessing, an essential element in the global skill of listening and a talent fostered in the OIR strategy. To ignore it through paper and pencil testing of discrete elements of grammar or the matching of

single words or phrases in a multiple-choice format denies that comprehension is based upon multiple clues and many contexts. Finally, unit and course examinations might test the speaking skills—pronunciation, control of vocabulary in reflective, guided, and extemporaneous speech—as much as to assess transfer from one skill to another so as to motivate attention to the listening task.

CONCLUSION

The research reported herein is an attempt to understand the use of an intensive listening experience as the foundation for further study within an *existing* curriculum in foreign languages at the university level. The results indicated that a listening approach based upon OIR followed by an acceleration of the regular course materials was not an efficient use of the listening strategy in the scope and sequence delineated by the first-semester syllabus in Spanish at Purdue. The listening-first strategy might have had success if the curricular boundaries, their management, and materials had been adjusted to exploit the potential which instruction in listening comprehension can bring to the learner (see Benson and Hjelt, 1978). To that end, additional research with *The Learnables* as a fundamental organizer for learning seems clearly warranted.

Notes

1. Representative item types included the following:
    Listening comprehension (Exam I)
    > *¿Cuántos habitantes tiene el país?*   (heard twice)
    > a. *Es una nación*
    > b. *Muchos*
    > c. *Son mexicanos*

    Structure (Exam I)
    > *Me gusta* _____ .
    > a. *leo*
    > b. *lee*
    > c. *leen*
    > d. *leer*

    Vocabulary (Exam II)
    > *En algunas calles no hay mucho espacio* _____ las casas.
    > a. *delante de*
    > b. *entre*
    > c. *alrededor de*
    > d. All of the above

    Sight Reading, proverb (Final Exam)
    > *"En abril, aguas mil"* quiere decir . . .
    > a. *El mes de abril trae mucha lluvia.*
    > b. *En abril se bebe mucha agua porque el clima es seco.*
    > c. *El otoño empieza con tormentas pero termina con tranquilidad.*
    > d. *Es cuando se mueren algunos árboles por falta de sol.*

    Examples of longer sight-readings are available from the authors upon request.

Zarabanda
   ¿Qué hace Ramiro?
   a. *Es comerciante*
   b. *Es estudiante*
   c. *Es ingeniero*
   d. *Es mecánico*

2. Items 1–5, 8–17, 19–28, 30–31, 33.

3. The students were not evaluated on their ability to speak Spanish; however, a considerable amount of time was devoted to reflective or guided speech as a motivational strategy throughout the control treatment and after week six in OIR.

4. Lessons 37 through 40 were omitted owing to a pressing time schedule aggravated by inclement weather which closed the university for three days.

5. Sky Oaks Productions, Dept. D1, 19544 Sky Oaks Way, Los Gatos, California 95030.

References

Allen, E. D., and Valette, R. M. *Classroom techniques: Foreign language and English as a second language.* New York: Harcourt, Brace, Jovanovich, 1977.

Asher, J. "The learning strategy of the total physical response." *The Modern Language Journal, 50,* pp. 79–84, 1966.

———. "The total physical response approach to second language learning." *The Modern Language Journal, 53,* pp. 3–17, 1969.

———. "Children's first language as a model for second language learning." *The Modern Language Journal, 56,* pp. 133–139, 1972.

———. "Learning a second language through commands." *The Modern Language Journal, 58,* pp. 24–32, 1974.

Benson, P. C., and Hjelt, C. "Listening competence: A prerequisite to communication." *The Modern Language Journal, 67,* pp. 85–89, 1978.

Campbell, D. T., and Stanley, J. C. *Experimental and quasi-experimental designs for research.* Chicago: Rand McNally, 1966.

Carroll, J. B., and Sapon, S. M. *Modern language aptitude test.* New York: The Psychological Corporation, 1959.

Gary, J. O. "Why speak if you don't need to? The case for a listening approach to beginning foreign language learning." In W. C. Ritchie (Ed.), *Second language acquisition research: Issues and implications.* New York: Academic Press, 1978.

Harvey, T. E. "The matter with listening comprehension isn't the ear: Hardware and software." *NALLD Journal, 13,* pp. 8–16, 1978.

Huberman, G., and Medish, V. "A multi-channel approach to language teaching." *Foreign Language Annals, 7,* pp. 674–680, 1974.

Kalivoda, T. B., Morain, G., and Elkins, R. "The audio-motor unit: A listening strategy that works." *Foreign Language Annals, 4,* pp. 392–400, 1971.

Maistegui, S. M., and Kestlemen, R. "A language teaching strategy for listening comprehension." Paper presented at the Annual TESOL Conference, May, 1973.

Pimsleur, P. *Spanish proficiency test: Reading,* Form L. New York: Harcourt, Brace and World, 1967.

Pimsleur, P., Sutherland, D. M., and McIntyre, R. D. *Under-achievement in foreign language learning.* (Final Report, Contract OE2-14-004) Washington, D.C.: U.S. Office of Education, 1963.

Postovsky, V. A. "Effects of delay in oral practice at the beginning of second language learning." *The Modern Language Journal, 58,* pp. 229–239, 1974.

Winer, B. J. *Statistical principles in experimental design.* (Second ed.) New York: McGraw-Hill, 1971.

Winitz, H. *The Learnables: Spanish.* Kansas City, Mo.: International Linguistics Corporation, 1978.

———. "Problem solving and the delaying of speech as strategies in the teaching of language." *Asha, 15,* pp. 583–586, 1973.

Winitz, H., and Reeds, J. *Comprehension and problem solving as strategies for language training.* The Hague: Mouton, 1975.

———. "Rapid acquisition of a foreign language (German) by the avoidance of speaking." *International Review of Applied Linguistics, 11,* pp. 295–317, 1973.

Zarabanda (Videotape drama). British Broadcasting Corporation, 1972.

APPENDIX
Summary of Grammar by Lesson/Week

Week	Lesson	Control	Lesson	Experimental	Lesson	Control
1	1–2	*Beginning Spanish* Sounds of Spanish What (Q), *gusta, falta*	1–4	*The Learnables* Simple present, *está, trae, pone;* Prepositions in, on, over, under; Determinant *el, la, otro; y, más*	Lesson:	*Zarabanda* ----
2	3–4	Naming and describing *y, pero; hay,* possessives; *se* passive; demonstratives, interrogatives; *tiene(n)*	5–12	Simple present, *come, entra, se ríe(n); quiere, tiene, puede;* gerund; *dónde;* Commands; *hay;* negation; Subject pronouns (*yo*); *él, ella;* Object pronouns *lo, le(s);* Demonstratives *este, esta;* Salutations; *con*		----
3*	4–5	*Es/está; de/en; también;* comparisons of equality and inequality	13–16	Simple present, *lleva, arroja, vuelve va, sé;* verbal phrase, infinitive; *se sienta;* familiar forms *-s, tú; Qué; pero; eso;* Imperfect, *estaba, tenía*	1	Say what you want: *quiere, prefiere*
4	6	*Ser* + adj; infinitive structure with *tener que, ir a* future, *gusta;* Simple present, regular verbs *el, ella, ellos, ellas*	17–24	Negation, commands; *sin,* Preterite, *miró, sirvió, vino;* Imperfect *era;* present progressive; *gusta; había,* Subject pronoun, *nosotros; hace* + weather *quisiéramos, gustaría*	2	Introduce self: *soy (de),* social introductions
5	7–8	Language, origin, nationality subject pronouns; *hacer; algo/nada, alguien/nadie, siempre/nunca, alguno/ninguno;* size; *sin/con*	25–32	Imperfect, preterite, commands; Reflexive pronouns; Future, *iré, dirá;* negation, location; numbers, time, geometric figures	3	Ask where something is: *es/está, hay, ir,* word order

*Week of 1978 winter blizzard

		Control		Experimental		Control
6	9	*Yo, usted(es)*; relative *que*; *creer, pensar, parecer*	33–40	Reflexive constructions, Imperfect, preterite, future, *tendré,* conditional, *sería*; location, nations; *conmigo*; object pronouns on infinitive; days, seasons	4	Say what you want to do: *querer, tener que* + inf
		*** Exam I ***				
7	10	*Nosotros*; *h -do*		Same as week 1, Control		----
8	11–12	Prepositions on, under, in, around, over, near, far, etc., stem-changing verbs, present, *puede(n), quiere(n)*		Same as weeks 2 and 3, Control	5	Review *por qué/porque, hacer*
9	13	Reflexive verbs; *-ndo, -mente*		Same as weeks 4 and 5, Control	6	Telling time; simple present; numbers
10	13–15	Reflexives; seasons and weather; direct objects *lo(s), la(s)*		Same as weeks 5 and 6, Control	7	Say what you are going to do: *ir a*; demonstrative *ser/estar* + adj
				*** Exam I ***		
11	15–16	Direct objects *me, nos*; Indirect objects *me, le(s), nos*		Same as weeks 7, 8, and 9, Control	8	Likes and dislikes: *gusta*; possessives
12	17	*Se lo(s), se la(s)*,prepositional pronouns; *gusta(n)*		Same as weeks 9, 10, and 11, Control	9	Shopping and ordering: *quisiera* Direct objects, *lo(s), la(s)*
		*** Exam II ***				
13	18–20	Concept of time, numbers, dates, days; preterite, regular verbs; ago		Same as weeks 11 and 12, Control		----
				*** Exam II ***		
14	20	Preterite, irregular verbs		Same as week 13, Control	10	Review
15	21–22	Imperfect; past tenses compared		Imperfect; past tenses compared		
16		*** Final Exam ***		*** Final Exam ***		*** *Zarabanda* Exam ***

CHAPTER 12

What Comprehension-Based Classes Look and Feel Like In Theory and Practice

Janet King Swaffar

Associate Professor of Germanic Languages
University of Texas, Austin

Don S. Stephens

Assistant Instructor
University of Texas, Austin

Any approach to foreign language teaching, whether long-established or newly developed, has to move beyond a purely theoretical stage to a position from which instructors, students, and authors of textbooks can say: "This is what is done in the classroom. These are suitable materials. This is the appropriate instructional approach." In moving from theory to practice, one usually discovers that the idealized model of the classroom never actually exists, nor will it exist in all its detail because of the myriad variables which any method can scarcely avoid: student motivation or attitude toward the foreign language being taught, teacher interpretation of the method and its implementation, external constraints such as classroom conditions, textbooks, and the like. A practical perspective is needed, however, which will convey a clear image of what classes should be like. Otherwise, methodological theory cannot be understood at the level of classroom application.

This chapter will therefore analyze a field experiment from two points of view. The first portion of the paper will discuss the theoretical model developed as a result of a National Endowment for the Humanities (NEH)-funded experiment conducted at the University of Texas at Austin, 1977–1978.[1] The second section will deal with the specific empirical indications arising from classroom observation of experimental classrooms.

THEORY: Preconditions for a Program

In discussing the concept "comprehension sequence," one is obliged to note that the components of that sequence and, hence, the sequence itself have not been established. To think in terms of comprehension preceding production is, of course, the obvious generalization which has gained credence in the foreign language profession. More important, however, are the constituents of that generalization. What is comprehension? What is production? Recent foreign language textbooks suggest a breakdown with listening and reading comprehension preceding speaking and writing. Such a hierarchy reflects the thinking of the behaviorist scheme of four skills, and locates its methodological fuzziness: the four skills are not discrete. For example, when reading aloud, is the student speaking or reading? Is there perhaps a synthesis of both? Does the student comprehend the text; and if so, at what level? Critically, or simply on the basis of content? Would that student be able to reiterate the content of the text after having read it aloud? Is summarizing a text a discrete skill or the result of complex activities, and so on, ad infinitum?[2]

Classroom observation suffices to illustrate the fallacy of assuming that the so-called four skills can be considered actual stages in foreign language learning. Increasingly, investigators of adult second-language learning are avoiding the consideration of skills or behaviors and are suggesting that students need to be provided opportunities for informal acquisition according to a comprehension-sequence concomitantly with formal study (Krashen, 1976). While rejecting a four-skills hierarchy, however, most theoreticians have yet to specify what the appropriate sequence should be and what form the formal study should take.

The learning sequence being developed at the University of Texas and Austin College was predicated on the assumption that, since language is used to convey meaning, learning a language means learning a system of meaning, not a set of behaviors. Accordingly, learners should work with language exclusively in meaningful contexts and situations. If conveying meaning is to be the focus of the second-language classroom, students in both comprehension and production phases need to think in that language. Thinking is assumed to involve not only recall and recognition, but also inference and critical evaluation.

Such a program design reflects some of the major precepts of child language learning evolved by direct methodologists like Gouin and, more recently, Asher. Practically speaking, a child discovers "meaning" through contact with concrete objects in the immediate environment. At Austin and Sherman, Texas we employ a similar, but not identical, process. Early classes work with classroom objects, parts of the body, clothing, and physical movements. Similar to the child, the *first* stage in the adult sequence is that of understanding the global meaning of a concrete situation rather than expecting detailed understanding of an abstract situation; that is, students are to comprehend the general idea of what is being said and then later are to comprehend some information in more detail by being exposed to a text or a situation again. At the same time, the language of a text, game, or situation is tied to the immediate, concrete setting, expressed in terms of physical action. After watching a teacher demonstration, a student may be asked to go to the door. At first, the student may only be aware that some motion toward the door is indicated. Later, in reviewing contrasting

Table 12.1   Outline of the Language Learning Sequence

Mental Processes	Instructional Aim	Student Task	Production Correlative
Recognition and recall	Information	Specific facts	Comprehension-based production
Inferring equivalences	Correlation or reference	What in the text is similar to x?	
Evaluative, synthetic reasoning	Problem solving	What are you going to do/say in a situation parallel to that of the text?	
Judgmental, critical thinking	Opinion, based on facts and inferences	What do you think about x?	Self-generated production

commands or instructions previously introduced, the teacher will ask the student to run, jump, walk, or hop to the door, and then the student will become aware of the differences in meaning of particular verbs by contrasting *walk* with verbs indicating other types of locomotion. There is, in this way, a movement from global (here: movement in a direction) to local (here: different concepts of locomotion).

In production of textbook materials and classroom procedures, our efforts have been focused on arranging the classroom tasks and text assignments to reflect the following premises:

1. Concrete (physical, visual) features before abstract.
2. Global meaning (general grasp or broad outline of people, places) before local meaning.

A student reading texts in a reader is asked first about general ideas and concrete information. The student acts out the story, pantomimes it or answers multiple choice or fill-in questions to confirm comprehension, then rereads the text to form opinions or to assess the author's point of view—in short, a more inferential or evaluative approach to the text.

The theoretical sequence we suggest is illustrated in the diagram presented in Table 12.1. From the first week of class, materials are structured to present a sequence of all four tasks—information, matching, problem solving, and opinion—for students to process and respond to in an atmosphere free of apprehension. To achieve our objectives, students must be encouraged to guess and play with the language. For example, students may be asked on first reading of a text simply to find and underline a sentence that describes the "main idea." During subsequent readings of the same text, the student could be asked to find sentences or words that are redundant (express the same general information), use the text as a basis for an interview with a fellow student, make a list of words belonging to the same general category, and the like. The chronology of the same text might be changed by the teacher, and the students asked to rearrange it into correct order. Finally, students might be asked to retell the text in their own words or to give their opinions about the text or what they would do in similar situations; but activities like these are thwarted if students fear punishment for errors in production.

One can see that it is fairly easy to describe what does *not* happen in the ideal comprehension-based class. Formal recitation, for example, is avoided because we believe it promotes stiffness, since it focuses on structure rather than meaning and use. Familiar forms of recitation, such as pattern drill and choral response techniques for pronunciation practices, vocabulary learning, and structure practice, though perhaps useful in courses with other aims (those stressing mental discipline or mastery of English grammar, for example), are inappropriate given our objectives. Likewise, elaborate descriptions and explanations in English of vocabulary, grammar, or student assignments, are not made.

Ideally, the average hour will consist of 90 percent German with occasional use of an English word for confirmation purposes and a question-and-answer session for three or four minutes at the close of the class hour, using English if the students wish.

What the teacher does do in class is, quite simply, to speak German and set the stage for the situation, matching or opinion games, and problem solving, around which the course is oriented. Tasks are designed so that a given piece of material is presented in a sequence (Table 12.1) from comprehension (at the recognition and recall level) to self-generated production (at the evaluative level) arising from problem solving. We attach particular value to problem solving in a foreign language because this activity necessitates student synthesis of higher-order thinking processes with language production (Bloom, Engelhart, Furst, Hill, and Krathwohl, 1956).

In the sequence we envision, teachers' role would be characterized as follows:

(1)   A relaxed personal demeanor which encourages playfulness with the language, spontaneity, and student experimentation.

(2)   Thorough introduction of new material to be assigned for the next day. This is particularly important in a comprehension-based course, since it is not considered desirable for students to experience apprehension or frustration about what is expected of them. Introducing the assignment involves introducing strategies for meaningful reading and, as such, must be considered an essential part of classroom learning. Since any reading text is abstracted from immediate reality, the teacher can reduce student frustration by presenting meaningful features of the assignment in a concrete way. Thus, in order to introduce, for example, the concept of singular versus plural, the teacher might bring to class a number of balls, and point out to the class: "*Hier ist ein Ball. Hier sind zwei Bälle. Hier sind viele Bälle.*" After doing this with a few other objects, the teacher might write the sentences on the board, pointing out morphological changes and the changes implied by verb-subject agreement. For

homework that night, students would read over the German grammatical descriptions and examples illustrating the description and would then have to find examples of plural nouns (or verbs, or both) in a text.

(3)   Practical commitment to the information, reference, problem solving, and opinion sequence. In a classroom situation where students are unable to provide opinions, teachers will reverse the sequence and go back to matching kinds of questions or written exercises in the form of asking students to draw pictures, find data in the text that matches an assertion on the part of the teacher, and the like. Suppose, for example, the information in a text disclosed that Nancy was not making enough money to make ends meet. If a student could not answer an opinion-type question like "What would you have done if you were Nancy?" the teacher would go back to the text, ask the student or the class to pinpoint what Nancy did do, ask them to infer what she didn't do by giving hints (i.e., "What about her boss? Did she ask for a raise? Why not?" etc.), and finally come back to the point where the original question could be asked again. The same behaviors should be consistent in assignments. Since no comprehension sequence textbooks exist at the present time, teachers adapting traditional textbooks to these principles would want to begin by presenting exercises for recognition in conjunction, perhaps, with pantomimes or picture-drawing (correlation). In a subsequent assignment or in class, material would be reviewed in terms of more demanding learning; i.e., eliciting student opinions and involving them in problem-solving tasks.

(4)   A commitment to providing learners with confirmation of their progress through informal checks such as a short (three to four minute) daily quiz at some point during each class hour, preferably toward the end. This quiz can be oral or written. It should cover only material discussed in class. Since it is not based on what students are to have prepared outside of class as a rote-memory assignment, the comprehension quiz does not seem to carry the pressure of the traditional pop quiz. In contrast to tests of outside learning, the purpose of the comprehension quiz is to check the attention level of students in class and to reinforce their comprehension. In addition, the daily quiz provides evidence to students on a regular basis of their progress in comprehension of German and, later in the semester, in production of German. Typically, the form of these quizzes is short dictation, sketch drawing, true-false, completion of multiple-choice questions.

What Kind of Classroom Implementation Reflects a Comprehension Sequence?

The problem facing teachers of any comprehension-based program is that textbooks are still based on the notion of four skills—reading, writing, speaking, and listening—with reading and listening put under the rubric of comprehension, and speaking and writing under production. As has already been pointed out, these categories are misleading. We know, for example, that it is possible to teach people to speak a language who are not really able to converse in it freely, or to read and understand extensively what is read. Conversely, many students learn to read fluently without ever developing speaking ability. The function and the degree of overlap between "skills" has yet to be established, probably because knowledge of a language is not reducible to skills. Yet many, if not most, American college classrooms begin with production practice in first-year courses and focus on reading German texts in the second year as though such an overlap could be assumed. Our traditional preparation of first-year training in production skills is not necessarily the optimal transition.

In developing a different sequence we focused on learning processes rather than on behaviors or skills. Our objective was to create a comprehension sequence that could be implemented in the classroom. Our solution at this point has been to implement a program and to design materials that coordinate a range of thinking processes with optimal classroom tasks.

Stage 1: Emphasis in weeks 1–2. We used a direct approach, with materials and instructions in German, with persons, objects, and actions visually real and tangible in the classroom. The textbook reinforced the classroom situation by offering visual illustrations of classroom activities and recapitulating all instructions and games as written texts. The teacher gave instructions, descriptions of scenes and actions in German, starting out by asking students to do such things as get up and sit down, raise books and put them on the floor, and the like. Objects that were physically present in class were used, and vocabulary was introduced topically—such as classroom objects or clothing. Additionally, we strove for a one-to-one correspondence between what was in the text to be read by students and what they did in the physical environment of class. In this way, for each new vocabulary item students had an immediate, concrete reference. If they did not understand a noun or a verb on first hearing, they would understand in subsequent pointing, teaching, or acting out. Students listened in class in order to carry out instructions, identified information ("Is that a table or a chair?" would be one kind of binary question that they could be asked), gave opinions ("Can I walk on the ceiling?" yes or no), or drew pictures based on simple descriptions. Readings in these chapters were designed to be reiterations of the experiences and activities in the classroom.

Stage 2: Weeks 3–4. In the second stage, pantomime had been introduced so that the text could move from the tangible classroom environment to a greater level of fictionalization. Thus, using the vocabulary of week one, a simple text could be presented to students about a man going to a store or a girl meeting a boy in a café, and students, hearing this story read aloud by the instructor, could act it out and thereby represent their understanding in physical behavior. Although a degree of abstraction was being achieved—the written text was at least one step removed from physical reality—all participants in the class had, by virtue of the pantomime, a concrete reference for that abstraction. The teacher's job in this situation was to identify essential characters and assign roles, designate classroom objects for props, and then tell or read the story aloud. Sometimes this pantomime could be performed more than once to allow for the individual interpretations which students would give to what they were hearing. On a subsequent day, students might read the same narrative aloud while other students pantomimed. Problems in pronunciation were treated as problems in communication. If students did not understand the person reading aloud, then it became meaningful to that student to find out how to pronounce a particular German word or set of words so that fellow students would understand. The burden of correction was shared by students and the instructor. Students were encouraged to use their mistakes to build knowledge about German pronunciation rather than to view them as sources of embarrassment or frustration.

Stage 3: Weeks 5–6. Improvisation (progressively more spontaneous production) was possible. Situations removed from the classroom (restaurants, shopping, hobbies, etc.) were introduced, thereby expanding the concrete activity to include increasingly fictionalized settings. Games centering on chronological sequence, guessing, and simulation of texts reflected, within the classroom setting, increasing semantic abstraction.[3]

At this stage, students were doing an admixture of pantomime and minimal production. For example, in a lesson introducing foods, students utilized menus from which to make orders in a series of restaurant situations such as an extremely expensive restaurant, a country inn (*Gaststätte*) or a fast-food place (*Imbißstube*). The situation determined the type of gestures, the tone of voice, and the selections students made. Students needed props at this stage, such as model interviews or typical German menus. We viewed this as the beginning of problem-solving production, however, because such speech was spontaneous and goal-directed. At this stage small-group work was initiated. Students prepared skits and the teacher directed the project, acting as a consultant to the various groups, and editing their scripts.

Stage 4: Week 7 and thereafter. Concomitantly with stages two and three, indeed, as early as the fourth week, students could begin reading more than reiterations of what happened in class, pantomimes, instructions, and the like. They could begin reading texts of discursive and journalistic nature without each textual detail needing concrete realization. Importantly, these texts presented information related to the content of the texts presented earlier. We found that as long as students had a familiar frame of reference for what they were reading, they were able to read with considerable facility. Love stories, reports of contemporary political events, discussions of leisure activities, fairy tales and fables, etc. were quickly understood, because students were already familiar with their genre and typical presuppositions. On the other hand, texts that reflected German wartime experiences or post-war response to occupation, although interesting and worthwhile literature, were not read with as much ease by American students. They lacked the framework that personal experience provides to associate detail with implication.

Grammar: Focus on Comprehension

Grammar descriptions and exercises were a component of our materials. Most widely-recognized proposals for natural-sequence courses have avoided formal presentation of grammar in the beginning stages (Postovsky, 1974; Winitz and Reeds, 1975; Asher, 1977). They have demonstrated that students begin to understand second languages quickly and may even speak and write intelligibly without the benefit of any explicit grammatical descriptions and exercises. Since children who acquire a second language learn the grammar implicitly and without explicit treatments, the necessity for formal grammar treatment in second-language courses is not self-evident.

We argue that while a language learner in natural situations evidently assimilates a large number of facts about the language and how it works, the classroom cannot provide adult learners with large enough samples of usage upon which they can develop their own hypotheses about the language. Without guidance, their notion of the language's structure will be inadequate. This does not imply, however, that traditional, morphology-based, production grammars coincide with the aims of comprehension-based instruction.

Since our objective was to present grammar for comprehension and not as a prescription for immediate production, we relied on concrete examples, illustrations, and textual diagrams rather than charts, tables, or drills. For example, we presented German prepositional phrases through student actions by pointing out the difference between sitting on a table (*Er sitzt auf dem Tisch*), sitting down on the table (*Er setzt sich auf den Tisch*), and going under a table (*Er geht unter den Tisch*).

This stresses syntactic rather than morphological features of the language. Sample sentences were drawn exclusively from the students' German readings and textbook instructions. Synthetic or fabricated examples were not used since our primary objective was to present grammar in terms of meaningful communication. In the first chapter, for example, students were asked to identify sentences as statements, commands, or questions, or to find verbs in sentences with dependent or independent clauses. We posited such focus as more relevant for comprehension of global meaning than is initial emphasis on the details of genders and cases of nouns.

From our point of view, then, it follows that grammar descriptions and exercises foster the growth of comprehension at the outset of language experience, provided they are designed and carried out in ways that are consistent with the aims of comprehension-based instruction. The adult's major advantage over the child in learning a new language is the ability to apply synthetic concepts which already exist in the adult's mother tongue. By minimizing grammar, comprehension-sequence courses may have also eliminated this advantage. The problem, if comprehension-based courses are to capitalize on the adult's ability to perform and apply synthetic ideas, is not whether paradigm treatment of grammar is essential—it evidently is not—but instead, whether explicit treatment of grammar is beneficial, and if so, what kind of treatment maximizes the benefits.

Three points must be emphasized in our particular view of grammar. First, *grammar is presented in terms of comprehension of particular forms and structures before demands for production of these same forms and structures are made.* Grammar presentations have traditionally been thought of as prescriptions for production. We think of grammar primarily as an instrument for comprehension of German, and only later as an aid in intelligible production. Physical demonstration and picture-matching exercises are later followed by diagrammatic illustrations in the class text to assist in comprehension assignments that use actual German texts rather than exercises manufactured to illustrate a grammar point. Students are encouraged, for example, to notice changes in articles and adjectives as aids in making sense out of the written text or spoken utterance, but are not required to memorize adjective endings at the outset.

Second, *errors are natural.* This points to the production phase of the sequence and relies heavily on child language acquisition theory. In the program described here, we anticipate student errors and they are viewed as a part of the language learning process. Although we assume error reduction takes place through comprehension practice in the language prior to production of spoken or written responses, we also know that this reduction will not be complete either for comprehension or production. Aggressive pedagogical battles designed to correct individual instances of production errors lower motivation, produce anxiety, and increase the reluctance to speak. Only a small percentage of the average class seems to respond positively to this type of correction. Asher (1977, p. 2) sums up the problem as follows:

> Few students—less than 5%—are able to endure the *stressful* nature of formal school training in languages. The task is to invent or discover instructional strategies that reduce the initial stress that students experience. The goal is to invent an instructional strategy that has enough motivational power to persuade 75% of students who start language study, instead of the current 15%, to continue into the third year of language training . . . [where] the probability is extremely high that they will continue for advanced work.

Moreover, a number of studies indicate that positive identification with the language and the culture that the language represents will be a key factor in command of that language (Jacobsen and Imhoff, 1974; Politzer and Hoover, 1974; Tang, 1974).

Third, *grammar presentation should be based on meaningful communication.* Practically speaking, the traditional Latin grammar model presents all grammatical features as equal when, in fact, they are not. They begin with treatment of smaller elements, like the forms of individual word classes, the "parts of speech," and then move to successively larger units, concluding with explanations of sentences. These grammars are morphology-based; syntax is treated as a function of morphology. Consequently, teaching elementary German is often referred to as teaching "*der, die, das,*" which is indicative of the degree of intellectual stimulation that can be anticipated from such a course.

The theoretical approach to foreign language learning outlined here was reflected in the sequence of instruction developed in the University of Texas/Austin College program: *concrete before abstract; global before local; comprehension before production; errors are natural.* Just as the facts of

German grammar are presented in a sequence that differs from most previous models, our instructional sequence was also designed to present opportunities for comprehension in clear stages. This is not the same thing as saying that we are doing something utterly new. While many of our methods depart from recent practice in American classrooms, they are not really original. Particular techniques may, indeed, be more or less consistent with practices in other approaches. For example, much of what happens in the first few weeks of class reflects features of the Asher (1977) program. Aspects of the direct method, such as extensive cartoon illustrations, are incorporated. Our approach to language teaching incorporates features of the so-called spiral syllabus, making use of rereading materials or reviewing features of the language in terms of increasingly detailed or demanding kinds of tasks. In short, we are not promoting the idea of newness or originality. We are suggesting a particular sequence of materials and activities to accomplish the aim of learning German through stages of comprehension, which, in turn, serve as a basis for language production.

PRACTICE

In the field experiment at the University of Texas, we strove to develop comprehension sequence materials that would foster language learning for most beginning students. Two approaches to foreign language learning were involved in the nine-month experiment: (1) a four-skills approach (the "control group"—consisting of 10 teachers, 272 students, and 15 classes during the two semesters); and (2) a comprehension-based approach (the "experimental group"—consisting of 8 teachers, 273 students, and 17 classes during the two semesters).

Classroom Visitation

Classroom visitations were conducted throughout the year by a single observer,[4] who visited both the comprehension sequence and the four-skills classes. Each of the classes was visited twice, on the average, during the course of each semester. The observer was not a participant in either track, and it was hoped that through his extensive contact with both programs and the exercising of a consistent observational technique, a reasonable degree of reliability could be achieved. It should also be mentioned that the precepts of the Flanders' Interaction Scale (Moskowitz, 1968) were reflected in the running commentaries, particularly as they related to the question of student- and teacher-initiated activities in a classroom. No attempt was made to use the Flanders' Matrix, however, since our concern was to identify instructional differences characteristic of two methodological approaches. In this sense, what teachers and students did was viewed as only one variable within the broader assessment of the newly introduced comprehension-sequence approach.

The observation technique used was a running record of:

(1)   Time allotted per classroom activity and identification of that activity (for example, short drills of verbs using the dative for the four skills; for the natural sequence, student pantomimes of a story read aloud).

(2)   A brief description of the activity and its objectives (in the foregoing example for the four-skills class, the reinforcement of the use of the dative with given German verbs; in the natural sequence class, the use of equivalence techniques, matching the spoken word with a concrete type of action or object).

(3)   Individual student or class reaction to the activities in terms of understanding, as well as the actual performance of the activity (Could students generalize from their use of the dative case in the drill situation? Were students in the comprehension situation easily able to encode the spoken text? Was any degree of spontaneity characteristic of the activity?).

Characterization of the Comprehension-Based Track

The comprehension-sequence program was in the process of developing both materials and techniques that would implement the theoretical scheme described in the first half of this chapter: second-language learning focused on cognitive processes ranging from so-called lower- to higher-order reasoning. In our case, methodological stages are more accurately categories of emphasis:

(1)   Information—recall and recognition of vocabulary and structures.

(2)   Correlation—the ability to synthesize recognition with production to a limited extent, and the matching of sounds or words on the printed page to actions or corresponding sounds and words.

(3)   Development of critical thinking—the information should be presented so that it can be evaluated by students in terms of their experiences; i.e., student opinions about different cultures, or identification of a text's point of view, method of argumentation, or organizational principles.

Stage 1: Information emphasis (recognition and recall). During the first two weeks of the sequence, extensive use was made of Asher's total physical response method to teach vocabulary and attune students to the foreign language through direct correspondences between language and concrete objects. Textbook materials presented a large number of vocabulary items: over 500 new words were introduced within this two-week period, which were related by a unifying topic such as "classroom objects," "clothing," "travel," and the like. Students played games designed to teach and demonstrate recognition and response to the new vocabulary. For example, a teacher might describe a wastebasket or a piece of chalk, and students would have to guess what was being described by either pointing to the object or saying the word if they wanted to.

Students were not required to produce the language in written or spoken form. They were taught the German alphabet in the second week and played listening comprehension games in German such as matching the alphabet letters of dictation to pictures or vocabulary items. Illustrative diagrams of grammar concepts were also used, whereby students might contrast the form of statements, questions, or commands. The grammar exercises emphasized syntactic concepts. However, morphological contrasts such as singular and plural forms of verbs and nouns were also presented as essential markers for distinguishing meaning.

Games played an important role in classes at this stage. For example, a figure would be described by the teacher, and the students would draw: "The head is a large 'O.' The eyes are two large letter 'A's with umlauts for eyebrows. The nose is a large 'Z.' The mouth is like a 'W' . . ." Such a game reinforced not only the learning of alphabet letters, but also comprehension of singular and plural forms and vocabulary in a story-like context.

By the third week, students were assigned to read texts silently and prepare "games" as class assignments. These texts consisted of five- to ten-sentence simple explanations or reiterations of what was going on in class, and thus the reading was, in our view, capable of being concretely realized in class by demonstration and pantomime. The pure command approach with oral emphasis and a focus solely on communication of action was being integrated with the more abstract task of reading. Increasingly, physical movement and concrete experience were derived from the written text rather than the written text merely recording the actions. Toward the end of the fourth week, more and more pantomimes were being used.

A consistent practice in all classes observed was review of the previous day's work in capsule form, through actions, responses to commands, pantomimes, and replaying of games. A later suggestion, which was implemented on the advice of an outside consultant, was a daily comprehension quiz to check comprehension levels and motivate students toward attention in class.[5]

Stage 2: Correlation emphasis (moving toward production: stressing contrasts and similarities in language use). In the fifth week, fictional and non-fictional texts (as contrasted with classroom oriented descriptions of activities) were introduced. These were read at home before they were discussed in class. The assignments for these texts were largely based on a word-categorization concept; for example, finding all the words in a text about travel in Germany which had to do with resort areas, or (a slightly more sophisticated variant of a correlation exercise) finding and listing all those words that had to do with the expensive resort areas and all those that had to do with inexpensive ways to travel in a foreign country. These kinds of focused-readings were to help students get the main idea of the text and were used as a primary assignment and testing tool for checking student progress in reading comprehension.

Stage 3: Development of critical thinking. The emphasis upon critical thinking began in the seventh week of the experimental program. Students were asked to conduct interviews according to an outline or model script which could be varied. For example, after having read, studied, and discussed a previous lesson on "professions," and after having read a five-page text about an American secretary working in a German firm, students then read an interview with the same secretary, consisting of usual interview-type questions: How did you get your job? What did you do on the job? How much did you earn?, etc. In the class text, students were provided with lengthy and complete answers which were derived verbatim from the previous secretary story. Using this interview as a model, students were expected to be able to answer similar questions (but in less detail) about jobs described in previously assigned job-related readings and games. Thus, they had a base of reference for answers to interview questions. If questions required a personal response, students had to invent short replies or answer from their own experience. Both written and oral versions of the interview-situation were used, although written work was done predominantly at home and oral interviews took place in groups or individually in class. Reading texts at this stage ranged from as long as one to five pages in length. They were assigned and then treated in class—usually by presenting students with typical situations they might encounter in Germany which could be compared to similar (though perhaps culturally different) situations in America. Students would then be asked yes/no or simple wh-questions, or multiple-choice written questions which would demand comparison of the two cultures or which might elicit value judgments from the students. Most of the texts were edited only slightly and came from original German sources. They dealt with subjects such as life in youth hostels or attitudes of young German students toward their school situation. By this time, the use of commands was relegated to warm-up periods at the beginning of class hours to familiarize students with current vocabulary or used simply as a tool for review.

In conjunction with reading German texts, students were provided with assignments designed to aid them in formulating opinions about the situations described. For example, a section of the text dealt with the different educational systems and problems in both the Federal Republic of Germany (BRD) and the German Democratic Republic (DDR). Students might be given a certain set of personal attitudes and then be assigned a professional goal toward which they would have to work: "You are seventeen years old, living in East Germany, and you decide you don't like school. What do you have to do to become a carpenter?" Or: "You are thirteen years old, living in West Germany, and you would like to study medicine at the university, but your grades are not good. What can you do?" A rereading assignment was a comparison between the two Germanies and among the Germanies and America. Students were asked to study a set of diagrams and derive comparisons of the two school systems by answering questions requesting specific information: "How old are BRD-students at the end of primary school? How old are DDR-students at the end of middle school? How many types of possibilities for education are there in the BRD?, In the DDR?, etc." Finally, students would be asked which system was more like the American school system, and they would have to choose between the DDR and the BRD.

While most classes had been taking dictation in the form of single words or phrases, a serious effort was made in the tenth and eleventh week for daily practice in taking dictation of sentences and paragraphs from the reading. Part of the intent of this procedure was to have students aware of the sound of the language which they read and have it correlated with the words they were able to produce and hear. We were struck by the fact that in a sequence such as this, the correlation between scores on reading comprehension quizzes dealing with matters of content or judgment and scores on dictations were very high. Although we conducted no controlled tests on this subject, one possible explanation is that both dictation and comprehension quizzes may involve similar cognitive skills. It might also be that rereading a text leads to better preparation for other kinds of examinations—dictations included.

During this phase there was increasing emphasis on reading, and unedited texts were introduced by the thirteenth and fourteenth week of the semester. Tasks and activities, which previously had been introduced through assignments asking students to select certain words or make judgments about authors' attitudes, were now reapplied as strategies for reading longer texts in order to answer very general questions. Thus, a student could be given a text on the situation of the immigrant worker living in Germany and asked simply to formulate an opinion as to whether this person was well off, shabbily treated, generally happy with his situation, or extremely disgruntled, and to point to those phrases or sentences in the text which substantiate this view. Using the same readings, students could be asked to scan a text, i.e., to look for answers to specific questions and simply ignore anything irrelevant; in this case, identifying all the instances of abusive treatment of the immigrant worker that were cited, ignoring all of the positive kinds of observations. Another written assignment technique was to ask students to reduce the text or summarize it in a few key sentences. We emphasized that the text itself should always be the model, both for vocabulary and structures used, but students were trained in simplification techniques in which they would make main clauses out of subordinate clauses and reduce sentences wherever possible or feasible to subject/verb/object or subject/verb/ prepositional phrase. In so doing, we hoped to aid their comprehension of a text as well as assist them in pinning down or identifying the main concepts of the reading assignment. A listening comprehension version of this technique was teacher dictation of several sentences from which students wrote down only subject/verb/object or subject/verb/prepositional phrase.

In the second semester, strong emphasis on the first semester reading techniques were maintained. Unedited texts with marginal glosses in the target language were used extensively during the first four weeks of the second semester. The social and political nature of most of these texts provided less reference for the students, who were unfamiliar with the events of, for example, World War II, the two Germanies, and the like. Concomitantly, there was a decrease of physical activity in the classroom, since more time was devoted simply to conceptualizing these problems rather than dramatizing them. Dictations and cloze tests were used consistently, and spoken and written production was maintained, again with emphasis on meaning and communication rather than error-free production. Speaking and writing practice was not done equally in all classes. Daily testing for listening and reading comprehension was maintained uniformly, primarily through use of multiple-choice quizzes. Speaking/writing production was tested at the teacher's discretion.

During the first semester, there was one listening and viewing lab per week which presented film excerpts, taped interviews, slide presentations, data on cognates, and related words of English and German, and, in general, materials developed to relate to the textbooks. These labs were considered a supplement or review for the other classes. Since classes met five times a week, one could consider four teacher-contact hours and one lab hour as characteristic of the first semester comprehension-sequence group. During the second semester, listening labs were held more frequently, and an inner-campus television channel replayed German videotapes for student review, in case they had not been present in the lab. These labs were accompanied by worksheets which essentially combined a variety of classroom teaching techniques—the use of dictation from reading texts, completion questions based on what had been seen or heard in films, and completion of multiple-choice questions on the content of the materials presented.[6]

Modifications of the Program

The modifications of our program and the needs which we see for the future fall into four major areas. The first of these is students. Students, we discovered, need an introduction to the learning objectives of the comprehension-sequence approach. This is, in part, simply because such an approach to language learning is new. Audio-lingual and cognitive-code books have been in existence over the past decades and have a well-established tradition. Even students who are taking a language for the first time are aware of and expect the kind of training that their friends have received in other language courses.

Beyond this, however, is a further fact: namely, the focus on reasoning processes in order to make discoveries about language, to draw inferences about meaning, to develop opinions and critical judgments, is the kind of emphasis that is not common to classroom training on a broader scale. In high school, and college as well, most classes stress recall and recognition learning and reward such learning in their testing programs. Students who criticize or make guesses may be punished by lower grades rather than rewarded for thinking for themselves.

Because of the contrast in objectives between a comprehension-based course and a traditional class, it is imperative that the new sequence is introduced to students as a kind of reversal of their usual classroom expectations, i.e., that they should feel free to be spontaneous, make jokes, have a point of view, or draw an inference with which other people, including the instructor, may or may not agree. At the same time, a new sort of evaluation procedure must be developed in this classroom, which students are aware of. Students will have to know that they are not being judged by standards of filling in blanks or the ability to answer only "who, what, where, and when" questions on readings. They must understand precisely what kinds of answers are going to be considered satisfactory by the teacher, and what sorts of learning procedures they should use in order to achieve a satisfactory or better grade in the course. Along with a clear statement about aims and objectives in the course, students must receive explicit instructions for structuring their study so that they can manage the learning procedures outlined in this chapter.

Texts

The kinds of texts selected are a key to success. For teachers who wish a compact, concise scheme for determining a broad range of textual readability, the following generalizations have proved helpful: the more "familiar" the reader is with the referents of a text, regardless of variables such as syntax or author's style, the more likely the reader will comprehend the text. By "referents," we have in mind particularly: visual scene, sequence, and agents.

1. A text providing vivid visual or scenic representations tends to be more comprehensible.
2. The actions or events of a text following chronological order, or a logical (a + b + c + ... + n) sequence, are more likely to be understood.
3. Texts about people who talk, act, or who are described are more likely to be comprehended.

If teachers are going to rely on supplementary texts or adaptation of existing texts, then these books should exhibit the criteria already cited:

1. Texts that provide a concrete discussion of events rather than analysis or speculation;
2. Texts that can be identified readily for such global features as genre, fiction, nonfiction, narration, instruction, interpretation, etc. (See Figure 12.1);
3. Texts whose materials are familiar, yet stimulating, to students.

Texts that lend themselves to comprehension-based techniques can be keyed to a meaningful typology. Students should learn to identify what kind of text they are reading, so that they can more accurately predict likely modes of reference and probable ranges of vocabulary. The distinction to be emphasized will depend largely on the particular text. A short prose text may be fictional, but is it realistic? Students can be asked to identify the text in terms of the binary pattern illustrated in Figure 12.1.[7]

Another approach to textual suitability is the use of criteria that have been developed recently and that go beyond the single problem of introduction, or rate of introduction, of new vocabulary. Criteria that evaluate syntax, concreteness, and the like, are extremely useful in helping the instructor identify whether or not beginning language students will be able to comprehend materials on the global level (Chapman, 1975).

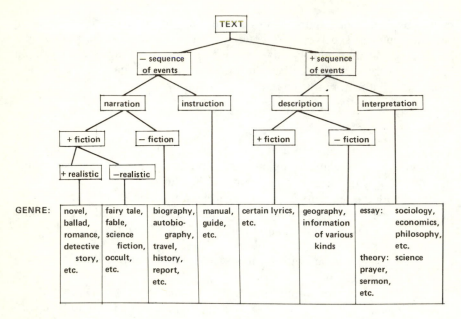

FIGURE 12.1.   Practical typology: second-language reading texts

An additional factor, which we discovered facilitates in adapting a text as well as creating texts of one's own, is the identification of the task level. Students need to know what kinds of tasks they are to perform with the texts they read and discuss. Thus, the instructor must have these student tasks in mind to pinpoint the text most suitable to a particular task. The teacher should choose certain texts or passages and avoid others depending on whether the text contains, for example, facts that can be scanned or multiple clues to its main idea sufficient for skimming. In short, whatever task is specified will make a big difference in the way the students respond to the material. Stylistically complicated texts like newspaper articles may be used at an early stage, if, for example, students are merely required to give the score of a match or specify whether a certain figure is for or against capital punishment. Reading all texts in the same manner and with the same attitude is like assuming that we really read novels and legal contracts in the same way, or that a theologian, for example, will read the Bible and the sports page with equal care, interest, and expectations. What the reader brings to a text directly influences its comprehensibility. The elusive process called "reading comprehension" or indeed, comprehension, is complex. It greatly facilitates the student's job to have objectives for comprehension clearly set out before the reading or listening task is begun—objectives that reflect the different ways people really use texts.

Another extremely useful criterion, which has been largely unexplored, is the point of reference which a text has for the student's own life. Students typically exhibit a range of interest concerning well-known historical or literary figures, such as Goethe and Schiller or Bismarck and Wagner. These figures need to be read or read about in terms relevant to previous student experience, or representative features of their works presented so that students gain a meaningful framework for knowing about the figure. The songs of Goethe, for example, are very well received among students if they hear the Schubert renditions of *Erlkönig* and *Heidenröslein* in conjunction with the written text. Similarly, sections of Schiller's *Wilhelm Tell* concerning freedom are interesting to students if they are familiar with this legend from their childhood. Simplifying or homogenizing original versions of such writing may actually diminish this interest (Honeyfield, 1977). Both linguistic and content simplification seem to lead to a reduction of communicative structure of a text. For greater reading interest, students need to begin reading unsimplified texts as early as possible. We propose that virtually unedited texts can be used almost from the beginning of a comprehension-based course, provided the readability criteria discussed here are taken into account.

An additional feature, which will be extremely important to the success either of a new kind of text or of adaptations that teachers make to their existing texts, is repetition. If texts are coordinated so that they can be reread at a later date for either more comprehensive information or perhaps for production rather than comprehensive learning, this will increase student confidence. New assignments for rereading maximize the use of texts that are unedited, and hence, probably not completely understood by most of the students, no matter how thoroughly they are treated the first time in class. This is a specific use of the "spiral" concept and is certainly in consonance with using repetition as a learning strategy.

Finally, we urge a systematic use of intensive, i.e., single paragraph, and extensive (the body of the text) reading. Such reading enables the students to bridge the gap between global understanding initially and the detailed or local understanding that they are expected to acquire in the course of the year (King, 1969).

Teacher Orientation

In the area of methodology, we found that teachers probably need the same kinds of exposure to criteria that students must be given. Even with the best of intentions, most teachers tend to be happier with passable regurgitation of specimen utterances than with critical thinking on the part of students. One problem that the comprehension-sequence faces is communicating to teachers what students ought to learn. In conducting workshops, it has been our experience that a number of people will think they understand the concepts and respond positively to the ideas, but when they provide illustrations of these concepts, it often becomes evident they have not grasped the point. For example, after reading an expository text on German schools, their idea of asking for information may be to have students leap immediately into a discussion of differences between American and German schools, a very demanding, higher-order task and one that presupposes the comprehension of the entire text. Unless teachers clearly distinguish between information and inferential, evaluative, or judgmental thinking, they and their students will be very frustrated.

Certainly there is a need for workshops where techniques that reflect thinking processes of students are illustrated and discussed. Practice in identifying the cognitive demands of a given methodology may be more useful than practice in methods per se. Various versions of Bloom's taxonomy have been with the profession for some time now, but a foreign language-teaching approach that values acquisition techniques above information retrieval is somewhat heretical in the era of the computer.

Testing

One last area of consideration is that of testing. Here again we have devised guidelines, but they are by no means the last word in the possibilities we foresee with a comprehension sequence. The first of these guidelines has already been mentioned earlier; namely, the quiz over material covered that day. This quiz we consider essential, both to motivate student attentiveness and for teacher assessment of progress during the individual class hour. For longer quizzes (thirty to forty-five minutes) we adhered strictly to the categories under which the material had been presented theretofore. Along with new variations, verbatim test items from previous lesson assignments proved to be discrete testing devices. We experimented with selections from assigned readings using slightly different questions but the same task categories—information, correlation, opinion, and problem solving. We used the material in earlier chapters for a spot check on whether or not students were, indeed, going back and reviewing materials. Since review is such an important feature of our concept, we found it easiest to encourage this by specifying that one section would appear from an earlier chapter x on a larger exam, along with more recent chapters.

In any experimental program, it is characteristic, or at least to be hoped for, that one learns. We at the University of Texas learned perhaps less from our successes than from our failures. What has been attempted in this chapter is to give a balanced view of the conclusions we were able to reach and the practices that were implemented or are now being implemented as a result of our experiences. The major things that were learned can be summed up as follows:

(1) The guiding objectives and the techniques of a comprehension-based program must be made very explicit, not only to teachers, but to students as well. Students must understand the logic behind the sequence and have some general knowledge of the research basis for the methodologies that are being employed. In practical terms, this means a good introduction in English and at least a brief classroom discussion of the methodology and its objectives.

(2) We discovered that in all our activities, but most particularly in reading, it was essential to have the task made clear at the outset. That is to say, are students reading for information; and if so, what kind of information? Are they to make inferences based on skimming the text as to what the story is about, or are

they to look at one section and reread it five or six times and generalize from that section about the author's point of view of the genre of the text?

(3) Along with making the task clear in assignments, the testing task needs to be carefully defined so that it parallels quite precisely classroom activity and classroom assignments.

(4) In our classes, the importance of fostering production became increasingly clear throughout the year. Normally in second-year classes a reading emphasis tends to mean an inhibiting of conversation and composition. While comprehension seems to provide a good base for production, production will not automatically result, in our experience, unless there are built-in props to encourage students to talk, both inside and outside of class, and to write in ways that enable them to express themselves or solve problems.

(5) The linguistic component of our program is a more radical departure from the Latin grammar model than had originally been anticipated. We discovered that, unlike the traditional Latin sequence, a comprehension-based grammar has to be language-specific. It will stress those features of a given foreign language that convey essential information. Such features will vary between, say, German and Russian or German and Swahili. Regardless of the language, however, a comprehension-based grammar must present features fostering global comprehension prior to less significant grammatical detail in a systematic way and the classroom presentation of that grammar system must correspond with an optimal comprehension sequence.

CONCLUSION

Any teaching approach that departs from entrenched traditions will not revolutionize its field overnight. It is not our objective to do so. Rather, we are interested in competitive alternatives to the status quo. The predominant approaches of recent decades have emphasized language as behavior. We believe there is a need for language instruction predicated on essentially the same processes that mature students apply in acquiring knowledge of disciplines like history, philosophy, or sociology. In predicating a language learning approach on mental processes rather than on behavior, we aspire to reach students who view learning as a holistic process. In this sense, we see comprehension-based instruction as lending renewed impetus to the centuries-old alliance of foreign language learning and humanist tradition.

Notes

1. The chapter presented was prepared pursuant in part to a grant from the National Endowment for the Humanities. However, the opinions expressed herein do not necessarily reflect the positions or policy of the National Endowment and no official endorsement by the Endowment should be inferred.

The program described here existed at the University of Texas at Austin from 1975 to 1978 and is being continued at Austin College (Sherman, Texas) under the direction of Truett Cates and at Beaver College (Glenside, Pennsylvania) under Helene C. Cohan. While the Department of

Germanic Languages at the University of Texas continued to provide nominal support for the program, the lack of active commitment and participation by faculty in classroom teaching led the director, Dr. Janet Swaffar, to temporarily discontinue the experiment. It was felt that our efforts would be better served by examining the results of our initial implementation and, on the basis of those results, refining the comprehension-based textbook under development. This book, tentatively entitled *Basis: A First Course in German,* is currently under publisher's consideration.

2.   For a more extensive discussion of this point, see G. Truett Cates and Janet K. Swaffar, "Reading a Second Language: Comprehension and Higher Order Learning Skills," *Language in Education: Theory and Practice,* No. 20 (Arlington: Center for Applied Linguistics, 1979), 1–32.

3.   Margaret Woodruff, "Activities and games for foreign language learning," 1977. Mimeographed paper (47 pp.) available from the Department of Germanic Languages (NEH grant materials), the University of Texas at Austin.

4.   Don Stephens performed the classroom visitations as part of his duties as Research Associate to the NEH grant staff.

5.   Rebecca Valette, Consultant, NEH grant project, November 10, 1977.

6.   For a detailed illustration of typical classroom techniques employed in the program, see Phyllis Manning, "From a Bird's Eye View to a Worm's Eye View: A Comprehension Based Program of Foreign Language Instruction," Proceedings of the Fourteenth Southern Conference on Language Teaching, 1978, San Antonio, Texas.

7.   G. Truett Cates, Assistant Professor, Austin College, Sherman, Texas, NEH grant participant.

References

Asher, J. J. *Learning another language through actions: The complete teacher's guidebook.* Los Gatos, Calif.: Sky Oaks Productions, 1977.

Bloom, B. S., Engelhart, M. D., Furst, E. J., Hill, W. H., and Krathwohl, D. R. *Taxonomy of educational objectives, Handbook 1: Cognitive domain.* New York: David McKay Co., 1956.

Chapman, H. "Criteria for the selection of short prose fiction to be used in Level II (intermediate) foreign language classes." Ph.D. dissertation, the University of Texas at Austin, 1975.

Honeyfield, J. "Simplification." *TESOL Quarterly, 11,* pp. 431–440, 1977.

Jacobsen, M., and Imhoff, M. "Predicting success in learning a second language." *The Modern Language Journal, 58,* pp. 329–336, 1974.

King, J. K. "A reading program for realists." *The German Quarterly, 42,* pp. 65–80, 1969.

Krashen, S. "Formal and informal linguistic environments in language acquisition and language learning." *TESOL Quarterly, 10,* pp. 157–168, 1976.

Moskowitz, G. "The effects of training foreign language teachers in interaction analysis." *Foreign Language Annals, 1,* pp. 218–235, 1968.

Politzer, R. L., and Hoover, M. R. "On the use of attitude variables in research in the teaching of a second dialect." *International Review of Applied Linguistics, 12,* pp. 43–51, 1974.

Postovsky, V. A. "Effects of delay in oral practice at the beginning of second language learning." *The Modern Language Journal, 58,* pp. 229–239, 1974.

Tang, B. T. "A psycholinguistic study of the relationship between children's ethnic-linguistic attitudes and the effectiveness of methods used in second-language reading instruction." *TESOL Quarterly, 8,* pp. 233–251, 1974.

Winitz, H., and Reeds, J. *Comprehension and problem solving as strategies for language training.* The Hague: Mouton, 1975.

CHAPTER 13

Comprehension Training in a High School Setting

Paul A. García

Southwest High School
Kansas City, Missouri

The Southwest High School German program was developed by the author for first-year classes during 1973–1978. The predominant characteristics of the course are two: comprehension training and a concurrent delay in oral response by students. Various components were introduced on an experimental basis in the five-year period; as the course came into being, therefore, no standardized or longitudinal measurements could be utilized. The degree of variables has now stabilized, and it is hoped that evaluations of the first-year course (Level One) can be made.

Southwest (by way of profile) is a comprehensive, desegregated high school, grades 9–12, with an enrollment of 1,800. It typifies urban America, displaying many—and often conflicting—needs and aspirations. Foreign languages are electives; French, German, Russian, and Spanish are offered. Departmental enrollment is about 20 percent of the student body, and continues a decade-long decline—for many reasons (including two teacher strikes in 1974 and 1977, white flight, "soft" courses, counseling) that are effectively beyond the control of the language staff. Despite these frustrating dilemmas, however, Southwest's principal, Thomas E. Kipp, has continued actively to support departmental efforts and programs because of the numerous contributions made by staff to the curriculum and the constantly challenging educational environment. In sum, although foreign language study enjoys the advantages of a sympathetic and favorable in-school administration, each new academic year produces instability and novel demands that the discipline cannot of its own overcome.

Bases, Goals, and Precepts

Elsewhere in this volume Winitz (Chapter 6) argues the case for accepting the findings of child-language experts and psycholinguists for application in foreign language teaching. There is no need to repeat the salient features of his views here, but rather let it suffice to enumerate the common bases upon which the Southwest project was founded:

1. Second-language acquisition can be nonlinearly delivered. By nonlinear is meant a nontraditional and less gradual exposure to the grammar of the language; such an approach differs from systems developed from chapter to chapter in textbooks where grammar is imparted step by step.
2. Implicit grammar learning is more advantageous to the student than explicit introduction to grammar.
3. The following objectives can be met:
   a. the student will comprehend the spoken target language;
   b. the student's (eventual) oral responses will be grammatical and creative within the constraints of a known vocabulary;
   c. the student will give evidence of a high rate of success in understanding and speaking German;
   d. the student will be taught by the use of noninhibitory techniques, thereby avoiding "learner-distress" features so common to second-language classes;
   e. the student will perform, in response to verbal stimuli, with a high retention rate.

In addition, the author also noted that several time-honored tenets of successful teaching maintained their validity; consequently, they must be considered equally essential program components:

1. The student learns by doing.
2. The student must listen to and attend class activities.
3. "Practice makes perfect."
4. The student builds and expands his or her knowledge from concrete to abstract.
5. Problem-solving techniques are viable tools for language learners.
6. Short strings of information are easily assimilated and manipulated by students.
7. Repetition can be employed by the teacher in class without students developing rejection mechanisms.

Finally, these basics, of a linguistically-oriented nature, merit inclusion:

1. Comprehension precedes production. (Passive skills come before active skills.)
2. It is not necessary for the teacher to witness speech production as proof that the student has internalized deep structure.

3. Significant (and rule-governed) oral responses by students will occur at that time when a student is ready to exhibit them, rather than at that time when the instructor thinks they are ready—a restatement of the opinion that the foreign language teacher always demands more of a student than that individual is ready to offer—and at times shouldn't.

4. Students will demonstrate at the appropriate time a transfer of training beyond listening to speaking skills, to reading and writing.

5. Students will display greater and more self-assured development in their comprehension skills, as well as in speaking activities if there exists in the classroom an atmosphere that allows and encourages a wide "threshold of error" at all times. This acceptability of varying imperfect responses with appropriate rephrasing techniques (described later) by the teacher replicates the kind of speech correction and communication activities that have been observed between parents and young children.

These psychological and linguistic considerations, implemented through activities and methods gleaned from many sources, have resulted in the Level One course described below.[1]

Program Description and Discussion

Preparations and early considerations. Before the opening day of school, the following preparations were made: first, a Level One base vocabulary was developed; this was followed by an accumulation of pictures or replicas of many of these objects. Thereupon, various techniques for implementation of the program were considered; lastly, more traditional aspects of planning were completed. With respect to the base vocabulary, the Southwest experience has shown that it is probable that an "average" Level One class can acquire between ten and twelve new lexical items per class meeting of fifty minutes, or, in the course of a school year, between 1,700 and 2,000 words. It is necessary that the lexical items chosen for presentation represent a realistic extract of the target language. To reach this goal, several conditions—those of range, frequency, spoken language, versatility, and reading language—were met. A variety of sources—several elementary textbooks, recordings, and the like—provided the first 80 percent of the vocabulary. [About 20 percent is either unpredictable (it enters into the classroom via natural circumstances) or it is formulaic. More about this aspect later.] The accumulation of pictorial tools and realia, however time-consuming the search, represents the second aspect of special preparations for the first class. I would recommend that the teacher selecting pictures secure those whose meanings will be unambiguous to students. An example of one flawed selection of the author for the word *Zahnbürste* (toothbrush) illustrates this. The picture of a youngster ready to begin brushing his teeth presented difficulties for some learners, because there was a great big smile on the boy's face. Some students wondered if the word required was "smile." Obviously, an unambiguous toothbrush by itself was easier for students than the picture chosen. The teacher relearned the lesson that in order to thwart miscomprehension, very specific pointing during the presentation of a lexical item imbedded in such a contextual representation is mandatory. The pictures collected will appear and remain displayed over a large area (175 square feet) of cork wall installed for this purpose. All pictures used are mounted on 4 by 4 inch (or larger) manila paper.

The more traditional preparations begin; the teacher adds to the base vocabulary the specific stock responses that are part of the first-year lexicon (*Bitte, Danke, Ich weiss nicht*), and amending the list so that such children's rhymes and songs as are to be used are included. Such items are introduced after their vocabulary has been learned; among the songs and rhymes used at Southwest may be mentioned the following: *"Hänschen klein," "Guten Abend, Gute Nacht," "Meister Jakob," "Mein Hut, der hat drei Ecken," "Oberammergau," "Nikolausreim,"* and *"Sauerkraut und Rüben."*[2]

It is advisable that the instructor embarking on comprehension training have an inventory available of those structures that purposely will occur during Level One. As the Southwest program developed, this group of primary grammatical features came about; it is not exclusive, however:

1. verbs (regular and irregular) in present, future, and present perfect tenses, all forms;
2. modal verbs and *möchte*;
3. nominative, dative, and accusative pronouns;
4. definite articles (very limited use of genitive forms);
5. indefinite articles (very limited use of genitive forms);
6. prepositions with the dative, dative/accusative, and accusative cases;
7. possessive adjectives;
8. noun forms with singular and (some) plural markers;
9. question words, i.e., *wo, was,* etc.;
10. declarative and interrogative statement word order;
11. imperatives—familiar and (some) polite forms;
12. some uses of *nicht* and *kein*;
13. some usage of reflexive forms;
14. some work with demonstrative forms.

This listing serves as a reference of items that occur; it is not an outline of topics to be covered. We are attempting to identify structures that will be taught students through nonlinear grammar (as defined earlier). The language is thereby taught as a means of communication rather than as an end (Lambert and Tucker, 1972; Winitz and Reeds, 1975; Adams, 1978). At Southwest the program gives German preeminence—its usage by the teacher (and eventually by the students) is for the accomplishment of specific goals (motor skills, etc.) and communicative skills. English is not used as the "real" language one falls back on in order to relay orders and move the class along "quickly." Rather, I attempt to reproduce much the same ambience of an immersion program. The props used for students represent realities with which the target language is manipulated. Participants "do things" as they hear German. For the students, language begins with simple sounds and messages; it progresses to a more difficult plane where many structural features of the language are deliberately mixed together. It is thus proper that the prospective teacher consider the rigorous linguistic and creative demands imposed on him or her by comprehension training classes.

As the first class meeting approaches, the teacher must be convinced of the value of allowing students to internalize the target language in much the same way first language is learned: various admixtures of information are taught for retention and not for immediate production; to do otherwise in the desired environment is dysfunctional. The language used in the class during this period should avoid traditionally brought-together items. A first-day (or even later) lesson on the forms of *sein* or *heissen,* for instance—"*Ich bin Dr. García, . . . Bist du Monika Rojas? . . . Heisst er Tim O'Mara?*"—cannot possibly produce maximum retention. (Included among the many reasons must be the simple proposition that the students will be attending to their new classmates' names rather than to the words surrounding the names.)

The first lesson. After students have understood the general school rules and specific classroom regulations that are expected to be met, the stage for comprehension training has been set, and one may begin. The variety of activities utilized during class are sufficiently numerous, as modern-day pedagogy calls for. At Southwest, the first practice session commences with a modest wall display of some seven to ten items in front of which the class assembles. (It is advisable to legitimize and encourage the informal desk shuffling and sitting upon tabletops by students "to get a good view" that very early on develops.) The pictures chosen for this first lesson should be as unambiguous as possible: a series of pictures published by the Ideal Corporation[3] contains items that are unmistakably discernible. A sample of possible first-day words would be the following:

Blume	(flower)
Eule	(owl)
Flugzeug	(airplane)
Kleid	(dress)
Matrose	(sailor)
Strassenbahn	(tram)
Tisch	(table)
Zähne	(teeth)

The teacher begins by rapidly and repeatedly pointing at the various items. The students silently attending will of course associate the target language utterance with the appropriate picture.

The procedure for pointing at the pictures requires some small explanation. Numerical incrementation is perceptible but gradual. The individual items are not repeated consecutively, nor does the teacher say each word once before reviewing the very first word given. Rather, two and then three items are dealt with and within a moment another one or two words are brought into use, followed by continuous and random focus on the remaining lexical items. The speed which the teacher uses helps the student to internalize the association as it produces a continuous recall. The rapidity of the spoken language further assists students, it seems; it accustoms them to fix in (memory) storage all the phonemes of an item rather than just the initial or final sound. The speed gives a definite break to the words when the factor of constant repetition is introduced. Thus the student unconsciously tends to segment the stream of sounds into their constituent words rather than into shorter units. That students hear and accept smearing and other normal speech devices is another positive (and somewhat later) feature of this technique. *Skelt,* for example, has no meaning to many students of German. Its meaning becomes apparent in the colloquial pattern "... *und [da]s Geld ... ?*"; linkages and liaisons are thereby given their rightful place at the very start of the language class. It seems that speed in presenting the picture-board items performs another service—it produces a classroom control that surely must be a self-motivated act. The students' eyes are constantly moving as they observe the teacher's pointing, providing a "game-element" not dissimilar from the time-honored shell game our students know from street life. The teacher implicitly challenges himself or herself to deliver the sounds correctly without getting tongue-tied, another aspect that students await eagerly.

We have found—as an outcome of studying the relationship of *skelt* and similar techniques to classwork—that the definite article marker can be omitted during these first stages of learning. It seems that in the early days of the semester the first words are more easily internalized when *der, das,* or *die* are omitted (possibly because the markers themselves constitute similar semantic units and begin with the same sound, thereby causing some confusion). At later stages—within the first six to eight hours of class—the definite article is presented as part of the noun without apparent difficulty. Some students have indicated that they do not listen to the sound of the definite article consciously, but rather know to attend to what follows; random sampling indicates that the definite article was indeed attended to by students; they demonstrate an ease in identifying the gender group of the noun in question.

Students are now called upon to point to the picture corresponding to the sounds the teacher calls out. This second step of the lesson gives clear-cut evidence of both reception and short-range retention having taken place. For the five- to seven-minute duration of this activity some half-dozen students (who want to show they can "figure out" what the teacher is saying) are called upon. Observations over the five-year period demonstrate that only rarely is a lexical item incorrectly pointed at. Reasons for this high success rate are simple. The eight sample items given earlier represent a carefully considered process that should be adhered to as each day's lexical sets are chosen. The nouns selected are neither generically (semantically) nor linguistically related; no two animals are presented, no two words begin with the same sound, and no transparent cognates (*Sofa, Garten, Haus*) occur. Intralingual homophones such as *Gabel* (fork) or *Teller* (plate) provoke some laughter when introduced, but they also give rise to mispronounced—and probably poorly-stored—German. As a consequence of the word-screening, several interfering mechanisms seem to have been short-circuited for the students even before they begin processing the vocabulary.

The participants remain attentive and eager to volunteer and continue their work during this period; their informal responses as they refer to their learning skills are extremely positive. This sense of success forms the bridge to the third phase of the introductory lesson, that of physical response techniques, as used by practitioners of the nineteenth century natural and direct methods and more recently by James Asher (1972).[4] Students observe the instructor as he or she performs and says a simple act, i.e., "*Ich stehe auf*," (I stand up) at normal conversational speed. The command is thereupon given for all to perform the same task, "*Steht auf!*" (Stand up). A series of five or six such motor acts develops into a ten to twelve minute activity involving the instructor, the entire group, and individual class members. Gradually the instructor's oral presentation of the act (involving little-attended first-person pronouns and markers) has been removed from major focus as students respond to singular and plural commands—a shift which itself is aided by the teacher's quick retention of some names to assure that a distinction between group and individual response is made. The motor activities further help to reduce tension about learning German, especially as the fourth part of the lesson gets underway. The by now universal heritage of the television program "Hogan's Heroes"—universal comprehension among teenagers of *ja, jawohl,* and *nein*—makes for the introduction of interrogative (inverted) word order. As a final motor act, the teacher has the students report back to the picture board; a rapid and very short (less than two minutes) reentry of the vocabulary begins as preparation for a yes/no game. Beginning with one-word rhetorical questions and affirming or denying their veracity, the teacher uses himself or herself as a model: "*Eule? Ja. Blume? Ja. Tisch? Nein; Eule. Tisch? Jawohl!*"

The class responds to the game's rules easily, for they are cued by this point in the lesson to an underlying aspect of the course—its problem-solving mode. As a consequence of the quick conveyance of the game rules, the one-word question easily becomes expanded to a full question, "*Ist das der Tisch?*" (Is that the table?) *Ja* and *Nein* are reaffirmed by the teacher's commentary; rejoinders such as "*Ja, gut, das ist der Tisch*" or "*Nein, das ist die Strassenbahn, das ist nicht der Tisch. Wo ist der Tisch?*" are continually brought into use.[5] The ten-minute sequence continues, and during this time the classroom *lingua franca* has begun to develop: word order, the cognate *ist*, the demonstrative *das*, the use of the definite articles, and even some beginning usage of *Wo?* and *Was?* ("Where?"/ "What?") all occur. During the game the air is filled with meaningful linguistic and paralinguistic clues (a preposition such as *unter* coupled with the appropriate gesture), as well as with such stock forms of expression as *gut, sehr gut,* and *hier* (good, very good, here). The student has participated in exercises that allow for involvement without the necessity to mouth unusual sounds (although certainly several try to) and formally "remember" what they've done. That in the case of German the first day's deep structures are of one with English also improves the students' feelings of successful comprehension and communication.[6]

Should time remain for what has been a rewarding experience for the class, the teacher can spend some time reworking motor commands. The teacher should not abruptly switch back to English as the bell rings, for reasons outlined earlier. It seems important for the students to come to expect that for their German teacher English is not for giving commands and directions that they are to heed.

Subsequent early lessons. Class activities of the second day usually begin with a short exhibit of a teacher's customary ability to forget the names of many students,[7] after which the use of German is exclusive. Typical second-lesson plans consist of the following:

1. Name identification through "*Ja/Nein*" game, formulaic greetings ("*Morgen!*" or "*Tag!*"), and traditional German hand-shaking.

2. Warm-up through group commands; teacher uses first-person verb forms to get activity started before shifting to exclusive use of second-person singular and plural command forms. Two new commands may be introduced.

3. Transition to "*Ja/Nein*" activity involving students' motor responses:

   T.: *Geh mal ans Fenster, Karl!*
   (Karl silently performs requested act, "goes to window.")

   T.: *Lina, ja oder nein: Hebt Karl die Hände, ja oder nein?*
   (Orally—or through head movement—Lina gives appropriate response.)

   T.: *Nimm Platz, Karl!*
   (Karl sits down.)

   T.: *Michael, steht Karl auf? Ja oder nein?*
   (Michael responds appropriately.)

4. Picture-board activities:

   a. review of previously-learned items with

   b. graduated introduction of new words, which are purposely posted and integrated into the older items;

   c. pointing activities by individuals;

   d. short "*Ja/Nein*" game.

5. Table items—replicas of pictures, and possibly one or two new items, are displayed on table; teacher simultaneously touches and identifies item. Students are called upon to touch an item called for by the teacher.

6. Teacher continues to use table items for about two to three minutes, continually repositioning them while stating what he or she is doing, i.e., "*Ich stelle . . .*," "*Ich lege . . .*," etc.; a student should be called upon for performance of a few similar actions if time permits.

7. As a closing activity, teacher points to large face of cardboard clock (hitherto set at three minutes before the end of class), saying "*drei Minuten*"; thereupon, teacher has students stand up while greeting students individually, shaking hands, and uttering such phrases as "*Wiedersehen*," "*Tschüss*," and trying to pinpoint some more names.

At the end of this second lesson the activities have helped the teacher to set the pace that both the teacher and the students should sustain. This is a difficult aspect for the teacher contemplating a five-class teaching assignment and the too-frequent variety of preparations one has, not to mention patrol duty and other professional duties one normally fulfills. Unfortunately, there is no resolution to be offered to the dilemma. One must expect that a nonverbal group of learners continually asked to participate silently with only occasional yes's and no's, can also be expected to let minds, eyes, and ears wander (which happens at schools with or without windows, with cars screeching past, and with ceaseless background noise). If the teacher's pacing is turgid, students will process less language than they are able; such a "winding down" syndrome occurs during the reentry of lexical items involving individuals. If it occurs during other sections of the lesson, the effectiveness of the comprehension technique is impaired by the large gaps of silence which invariably occur.

Should the instructor consider reducing the number of lexical items during the first lessons, several problems besides that of brisk pacing enter the picture. Among them is the learning rate. Because we do not know the variance in students' learning rates (they probably differ as much as does the students' ability to distinguish unusual or foreign sound patterns—which itself would vary from class to class and thus serve as a nonconstant), we cannot know by what absolute number we can reduce the twelve or so words to that numerical point where all the students will acquire the new words without too-frequent repetition of those words. The repetition without diversity would be stultifying, and could quite possibly lead to some kind of rejection of the learning mode. At Southwest we have found—as certainly has been discovered in thousands of schools every year—the number of lexical items that may be introduced should start at the higher end of the scale. Observation of a dozen sets of teenagers since 1973 indicates that ten to twelve lexical items, when combined with an aggregate number of already-learned words (all simultaneously displayed), is an attainable and still challenging goal.

An extended repetition of a new word by the teacher is of course impractical; one has never expected motivation to be sustained over any real period by such recourse. Brisk variation by the teacher of the words to be learned without learner pronunciation can continually interest students; and, at this point, avoids the disadvantageous exposure to the varieties of mispronunciation that may be simultaneously encoded by the student along with the correct sound pattern—thus resulting in a set of pronunciations that serve to complicate the retention (and later recall) processes needlessly. Further, student production of newly-encountered words can negatively interfere with retention rates (Carey and Lockhart, 1973)—producing learner distress observable in various affective responses (laughter, silence, and so on) (Tomkins, 1965).

Classwork employing picture-board and table items, command forms, and true–false activities continue during the first week as more vocabulary is introduced and reentered. The isolated nouns predominate, few verbs are used, and even fewer formula responses are introduced. (Paralinguistic phenomena continue to perform their explanatory service, playing a large role in comprehension training and in language teaching in general.) The only significant addition to the techniques used during this period is the introduction of a series of programmed picture books, accompanied by cassette tapes, *Natural Language Learning,* developed by Winitz, Reeds, and García (1975). This learning series is a four-volume, four-hour set which provides students an alternative means of (either individual or group) comprehension training. The texts are pictures (nothing is written), each of which is given in a group of three items to ensure problem solving. A word (on tape) is heard, and the student must choose from among the three pictures that item that he or she has heard. The following page shows the correct answer (which cannot be seen until the student turns to that page). Each of the lessons (there are eight, of 100 problems each) increments and varies new vocabulary and structure (third-person singular, connectives, transitive and intransitive sentences) during its half-hour length. Several copies of texts and tapes are available for take-home by students who wish to do so. These programmed materials provide students with a faster-paced glimpse into some of the structures they will learn during the early part of the course; they also unconsciously learn that even a limited number of lexical items (the texts contain about 120 words) can be manipulated into original sentences of modest length (the 120 words are given in over 400 sentences). The tapes offer the students another authentic voice speaking the target language, and specifically using words that are known.[8]

In later lessons during this time of nonverbal response several other teaching methods are introduced. Not only at Southwest but also elsewhere, as reported by Asher and by members of the Texas group (Woodruff, Swaffar),[9] there are activities such as "*Simon sagt*" (Simon says); charades; pantomimes (students performing statements made by the teacher); map activities; some arithmetic problems with yes/no responses; table games (an object is taken from the table and the teacher tries to recall what it is, with students giving "hot/cold" clues); and simple narration by the teacher of ordinary events (based on the vocabulary learned), followed by somewhat more extended accounts of famous tales— "*Rotkäppchen*" is easy—accompanied by appropriate pictures. Testing techniques used, besides pointing at correct items and yes/no responses, include concentration games where students must remember the position of two pictures (a pair) from among many others turned on their face sides down—several Ravensburg table games, *"Memory"* and *"Natur-Memory"* for example, can serve as models;[10] picture identification by grid/plotting [a student writes "B–7" for *Vogel* (bird)]; and sound identification (students give the grid number for a word with the same beginning sound as the clue given by the teacher). As a means of knowing what kind of recall patterns students are developing, as opposed to a testing format, it is possible to have students write from oral dictation their idea of the spelling of the word spoken. When given, words such as *Apfelsine, Vogel,* or *Baum* (orange, bird, tree) elicit many variations. One encounters, for example, "fogal," "bowm," "kowft," "aquaseema," "apple-zeena," and "rouft" (for *raucht*). This helps the teacher in planning several options, including the mandatory suggestion to reenter such items with renewed frequency. Fill-in items are also possible tools at this time. The teacher makes a simple statement which students complete: T.: *"Das Auto ist auf_____ ."* (This example is used to show that the activity allows the teacher the opportunity to note the use of grammatical markers: Does the student write the proper form of the dative definite article, albeit misspelled?)[11] These activities are used during the first four weeks of the class; at about that time (it has varied up to six weeks) more than one or two students begin voicing more meaningful responses than yes or no. These young people are anxious to display their abilities (some even try to do so during the very first lessons); this is of course not to be discouraged. A word such as *Strassenbahn* (tram) or *Glühbirne* (lightbulb) captures the imagination of many a new learner, and planning for this oral response begins to take over.

Early verbal responses. Approximately twenty lessons have taken place; some 200 lexical items have been taught. Among them should be the words necessary for comprehension of easy rhymes and songs (with pictures), as has been mentioned. (A facility for guitar or piano becomes a worthwhile time investment for the language teacher at this juncture.) Rote activities such as this help the teacher evaluate the productive skills that students display, although it does not necessarily aid in determining how creatively students will use their knowledge. This subjective judgment is not the only available means; through the pictures and table items we may elicit the fluency and creativity of different students somewhat more objectively. By this time in the course, the teacher's language at the picture board and the table has included the coaching and summarizing responses and questions [verbs such as *können, dürfen,* and *wollen* (can, may, want) occur in such statements as *"Wer kann uns zeigen, wo die kleine Birne liegt?"* ("Who can show us where the little pear is?")] that help formulate descriptions and locations of items. The teacher may allow students to respond orally if they care to at the same time they correctly identify the picture or object being sought. A very frequent early response is a locative phrase (*"auf dem Tisch," "neben dem Baum," "über dem Haus"*). Some students will be able to say the phrase quite effortlessly, others will make do with a one-word answer, while still others make pronunciation errors which are corrected through a rephrasing or paraphrasing of the item by the teacher (using the same structural form and making the necessary grammatical corrections, if any). Within two or three lessons, a gradual incrementing of the questions has taken place, and all students have had an opportunity to show their productive skills. As this occurs, the teacher has been continuing a reentry of the employed vocabulary in short and approval-giving remarks ["*Jawohl—der Hirsch ist unter dem Baum, unter dem grossen grünen Baum.*" ("Yes—the deer is under the green tree.")].

As a further check on how well or how unprepared students are to respond orally, another quick and simple device may be used: the cassette player (or, if one is not available, a tape recorder with a long microphone cord). Students pass the machine along after having said whatever it is they want to say in German. The teacher then has time to review the tape for many different aspects of language fluency—vocabulary, variety, structure—without slowing the tempo of the class activity (or having to take notes in front of the students). Usually, the tapes reflect a very wide range of lexical items used in declarative statements (high frequency) and interrogatives (low frequency). A smaller range of verbs and verb forms is used, reflecting the predominant usage of second- and third-person forms and the ability of the students to manipulate the nouns with much fewer verbs—as well as reflecting the large number of nouns taught. Of the sentence forms that occur, these are the most frequent:

> Subect–Verb–Object
> Subject–Verb–Prepositional Phrase
> Subject–Verb–Object–Prepositional Phrase
> Interrogative–Verb–Subject

If it can be determined that the students' speaking abilities as evidenced on the tape are better than 65 percent correct and fluent, our program at Southwest moves along with other early speaking activities (below). If the fluency of the students is weak—if an ease of response is not present, if there is no clarity to the statements—we continue with pre-speaking activities that require little oral response. In the past, Southwest students displayed their ability to respond to questions with little apparent temporal delay and with much fluency at a point between the fifth and eighth weeks of class. From the perspective of goals attained, we may say that the students have been repeatedly exposed to and understand the following:

1. A vocabulary of some 350–400 words
2. Structures
   a. Present tense of verbs and subject pronouns: strong emphasis on familiar commands, singular and plural; strong emphasis on present indicative forms, singular; some beginning recognition of plural forms "we" and "they"; infrequent usage of polite forms.
   b. Case markers: definite article forms for all genders and plurals

effortlessly recognized; some recognition of parallelism in use of indefinite articles and the negative *kein.*

c. Prepositions: strong usage of locative prepositions, *über, unter, neben, zwischen, auf, an, hinter, in, vor*; strong recognition and usage of *von* as substitute for genitive case forms; some recognition of *durch, für, ohne, um.*

d. Interrogatives: effortless identification of *wer, was, wo, wessen, womit, wieviel*; some recognition of *wann, was für, warum.*

e. Modals: good recognition of singular forms of *müssen, können, sollen, dürfen,* and *möchte*; misrecognition of forms of *wollen* for future continues.

f. Pronouns: strong recognition of subject pronouns and some singular and plural dative and accusative forms.

g. Possessive adjectives: good recognition of *mein, dein, sein, ihr* (her).

h. Reflexive pronouns: knowledge of singular forms *mich/mir, dich/dir* apparent, as a result of command exercises and motor activities training.

i. Word order: excellent recognition of declarative structure (Subject-Verb) and interrogative forms; limited recognition of inverted word form (Object–Verb–Subject).

3. Stock phrases

a. Students understand various expressions of greeting, farewell, rejoinders such as *wunderbar, gut,* etc., and are aware of teacher's use of fill words (*schon, aber, noch, doch, also, nun, naja*) without being able to completely understand them.

Students are able to demonstrate the following skills using this knowledge:

1. They attend the teacher with almost full comprehension, which is evidenced by:

a. Their ability to perform simple motor tasks in accordance with directions given them, of both short and extended length.

b. Their ability during the performance of these motor tasks to make distinctions of a somewhat sophisticated nature (such as distinguishing between sizes and colors of the same object and displaying little confusion when apprehending and successfully manipulating words of similar phonological quality (*Ast/Arzt, Birne/Biene*) (branch, doctor, pear, bee).

2. They demonstrate successful internalization of deep structure of the language by rapidly and effortlessly responding to directions involving (nonverbal) use of pointing or pantomiming and similar techniques.

3. They begin to generate some polysyllabic responses relating to verbal cues offered by the teacher:

a. Phonological accuracy of response is usually quite good (and certainly above average in quality).

    b. Morphological accuracy varies in quality and scope: definite article (nominative) markers are well-internalized; third person forms and command forms are uniformly well-reproduced; use of dative forms of the definite article is not yet apparent except in those few phrases (*auf dem Tisch, an der Wand*) ("on the table," "on the wall") that seem to have taken on formulaic quality; possessive adjectives are used without addition of the (feminine) endings.

4. Students have developed writing skills, although sound/letter correspondences for the German orthographic system have not been introduced.

5. Their comprehension training gives evidence of a transfer to reading skills (Reeds, Winitz, and García, 1977).

Student ability to generate meaningful responses with the limitations of the language used in class does not announce a shift in basic method or practice. Continued stress is placed on silent active acquisition of the language. The classroom teacher's temptation to formally reintroduce students to grammar already internalized must be overcome; students will continue to internalize more aspects of structure without this. In addition, there would probably be interference of their knowledge of similar English rules; these rules would be misapplied to the target language.

Should one argue that generalizations of the structures learned cannot take place if no formal invocation of grammar occurs, my insistence that we continue to be patient and not overload or short-circuit the student's successful acquisition is based on a five-year period of dealing with over 200 youngsters. It seems to me that Southwest students—and others—should be afforded the luxury of being taught surface grammar rules at a later time, rather than during the first six or so months of second-language learning. Surface grammar rules seem to force students to consciously manipulate material that they had previously (and successfully) unconsciously manipulated. Perhaps an example can illustrate the issue that giving the rule is to invite its own violation: If we assume that a group of students who have been exposed to verbs (modals and others) for forty hours are told that first-person forms end in *-e*, we may expect some misapplication of the rule to *ich kann* or *ich muss*. What on the one hand was gained for some pedagogical generalization has been lost in the confusion of a specific instance. That the correct information for these modals had already been internalized had probably been demonstrated. For the teacher to have to reenter the correct form and then attempt to aid in erasing the misapplied rule must be regarded as an inefficient exercise. (If my supposition is correct, there is only a very small group of "rules" of structure that do not have qualifiers attached to them; therefore, we harm the cause of rule-giving when we are forced to give immediately the exception(s) upon misapplication by a student. Furthermore, our interest in language teaching is not rule-teaching, but rather rule-governed language learning in the wider sense of learners understanding the bases upon which that specific target language is built. But this is not the place to investigate this long-standing argument.) The students are not yet—and they won't be for some time—mature or maturing speakers of German (nor readers, for that matter, of Brecht or Mann). It seems justifiable to expect that, as in the case of first-language learners, surface grammatical constraints be imposed *after* many hours of comprehension and many hours of speech production in the presence of and cooperation with models.[12]

At that time when the teacher has gathered sufficient evidence that the students are speaking and responding to questions with apparent verbal ease, some further fixing of pronunciation skills may be undertaken with the class. A variety of activities may be employed—songs, rhymes, animal sounds, and other mimetic strategies usually are frequent; in addition to one-on-one tutoring, some individualized language-laboratory activities might be investigated. Most experienced teachers are aware of the many avenues open to deal with this aspect of a first-level course, but it might be well to point out that most students will display good or better-than-average pronunciation skills as a consequence of the delay in oral response. Students, for instance, have not picked up and stored one another's errors; each seems to duplicate the patterns processed from the reliable model(s) of the first six weeks.

Homework assignments may also be given as a means of helping students "fix" common sentence patterns. The earliest assignments, albeit simple, offer a wide opportunity for the display of creative and mimetic generation of sentences. A standard assignment is to have students write seven to ten sentences of their own. Alternative options follow, such as directed sentences (which allow less flexibility) where students are given a series of questions orally which they write down, or nouns offered as subjects. Later on, after some improvement in student spelling is noted, some written questions are possible. Spelling activity, like surface grammar, seems to interfere with proper usage and pronunciation, and is therefore not stressed in the traditional manner. Assignments are checked and spelling is corrected for each student. Except for a few individuals, spelling abilities improve steadily during the second half of the first year without formal, in-class exercises. Before *Vogel* or *Badewanne* exist in their commonly-seen form, a period of adjustment to the language's orthography takes place over a two-semester sequence.

Other homework assignments are given that attempt to generate rule-governed speech. Multiple copies of tapes are available for take-home that contain questions, for example, that students answer orally. Pictures are distributed which students are to describe and possibly answer questions on. Many of the pictures are duplicates of the picture wall items, and because these are either of a "still-life" or of a limited activity, a student can reasonably be expected to follow the model of the teacher and refer to several background items (which had been previously learned in other contexts). A sample picture would be one of a garden, complete with patio, chairs, books, a fountain, plants and flowers, and people speaking. Pictures offer students a chance to unify the separately-learned lexical items and produce a synthesis of semantically-linked/linkable words into what for that individual is a novel generation of statements. The unique quality of each such presentation allows a healthy kind of competition in class as students speak.

During this same period of homework assignments, cognates—heretofore purposely ignored—must be dealt with. At Southwest, our experience has been that during the nonverbal stage such words as *Sofa, Auto, Stuhl,* and *Zigarette* interfere with pronunciation, and attempts at real production; students tend to fall back on their English pronunciation, and begin speaking these words and noncognates to the eventual detriment of their already-developing skills. Very few cognates are introduced, therefore, except those that are somehow unavoidable. Generally, cognates are not introduced during the early verbal stages; students are able to comprehend them during both periods, and for many purposes we prefer to emphasize the noncognate group.

Testing or evaluative techniques follow earlier activities, with supplemental exercises (multiple choice, oral translation, and cloze techniques) employed contemporaneously. Associative word games are also useful in measuring originality and the spontaneous generation of sentences or phrases (Sell, 1977).

Activities during the verbal period. During earlier stages, as students begin to refine simple oral skills, some attention is paid to the acquisition of abstractions (freedom, duty, etc.). Taking into account the earlier vocabulary, the program attempts to make it possible to develop the meaning of such nouns through a series of contextual pictures and ideas. Should, for instance, the word "prisoner" be part of the learned vocabulary, some easy remarks relating to the prisoner's condition of doing time (in idiomatic German, *er sitzt*) are understood and can be further expanded to show the release of the individual and the comparison to another (typical) free being, the bird (and the rapidly comprehended *vogelfrei*). The idea here is not new but for purposes of clarification bears repeating: One moves from specific circumstances to more generalized situations, and expands upon that by ready-at-hand examples, be they relative to local or larger issues (i.e., freedom for Soviet Jewry).

The use of tenses has made little apparent penetration to the student, as displayed by verbal responses. Although the teacher makes reference to past and future events, students in the Southwest program operate within a present-tense framework during the first level. Several students use *ich war* or *warst du* (I was, were you), but relatively few attempt a present-perfect tense formulation. Although this aspect might be seen as a weakness of the method, students display sufficient capability of operating in class activities without reference to the past (and with little reference to the future),[13] as they respond to questions and engage in other class activities. Certainly, to follow up on the objection that students must develop tense skills, the course could be structured so that past tenses may occur more, as is done in the University of Texas–Austin high school outline.[14] At present, usage of the present perfect remains part of later course work, although on the basis of the Woodruff lesson plans some investigation will be made into restructuring the Southwest program. Some valid objection to the use of the present perfect at an early stage of internalization is rooted in the fact that the varieties of participial forms as well as the use of two auxiliaries, *sein* and *haben* (to be and to have), where English uses one, may cause some puzzlement as students attempt to generate transformations and rules from a relatively small data base of verbs and forms that they are hearing.

Another issue that frequently appears in professional literature, student/ student talk, should be mentioned here. The same problems that exist elsewhere are encountered at Southwest; students are capable of relating basic ideas to one another in the target language, but they usually don't unless made to. Students who speak German to the teacher do not seem ready to overcome the various phenomena and social taboos of the high school milieu, and talk with their peers. During the preverbal period, the problem of exchanging information is negligible, of course. During the early stages of speaking, some activities (questions and answers, associative games, skits, etc.), create a semblance of student/student talk. Possibly as a consequence of defeat, it has been our experience that if our expectations are kept low in this area, they will usually be met. It is now our preference that communication between students be an occasional function or outgrowth of an activity. During this later period of oral response, students are still willing to take on the role of (younger) children learning a first language—to gain the teacher's approval. They remain much more hesitant to use bits of language to communicate with their friends; until such time as activities, devices, and lexical knowledge break down the social barriers of a classroom of teenagers, the task remains an elusive one. Of the several attempts made during the past five years to motivate students to speak to other students in German (including an annual two-week spring study trip/ family stay—which does get students to attempt to communicate with one another, if even for a limited time span), we are hopeful that increased implementation of many small-group activities during the twelfth to fourteenth week period, led by community volunteers who speak German, can further the usage of German.[15]

Continued comprehension training takes place during this stage of Level One, of course. Students are now capable of the following skills:

1. They comprehend a vocabulary of 600–800 words.
2. Their knowledge of structure improves:
   a. With increased knowledge of plural forms of present-tense verbs.
   b. With maintenance of good usage of the definite article markers (especially in the dative forms).
   c. Dative and accusative prepositions continue to be learned.
   d. More interrogatives are learned (*woher, was für,* etc.).
   e. Work on various modals (e.g., *mögen, sollen*) continues and a wider range of semantic use of modals is apparent.
   f. Pronouns and possessive adjectives are in constant use and give evidence—nonverbal and verbal—of being acquired.
   g. Word order in sentences is expanded to include some facility with modal transformation.
3. They are able to employ stock phrases (including items from rhymes or songs) as they appear.

The pre-Christmas period of Advent begins at about this point in the course, and, in addition to our devoting time to a sustained series of short cultural readings and related Christmas activities,[16] it is used as a time of intensive oral review emphasizing the modals *wollen* and *sollen* (want, should). (It may be recalled that earlier in the semester students made the improper identification of *wollen* as the future-tense verb; at this time many of the students are able to make the distinction between *werden* and *wollen* as a consequence of class-work.) Questions such as *"Was willst du vom Nikolaus?"* ("What do you want from Santa Claus?") and *"Was soll ich deiner Schwester kaufen?"* ("What should I buy for your sister?") coupled with follow-up interrogatives, attempt to continue the synthesizing activities of earlier class periods. Fixing of meanings of *wollen* and *sollen* occur. A *"Christkindlmarkt"* is usually set up by students in the third and fourth year class, and students from Level One spend two class periods shopping in German, and conversing as much as possible about the items on display. The post-Christmas period often serves as a time for some intensive questioning on holiday activities—which involves extensive discourse with perfect tense forms. Short narratives are introduced by the teacher (average length, fifteen to twenty sentences), and questions and practices concerning holiday activities are explored. Those students still uncomfortable with tense manipulations continue using present-tense verbs as they respond:

T.: *Was hast du von deinem Bruder bekommen?* ("What did you get from your brother?")
S.: *Ich habe eine schöne Bluse.* ("I have a nice blouse.")

There is some generalization made by students, because of the intensive use of such verbs as *besuchen, bekommen,* and *kaufen,* to make the necessary trans-formations to perfect tense form, but it is still too early for the students to be able to display a knowledge of the past tense system; their work at this point is more in keeping with item substitution drills more akin to the audio-lingual approach of the 1960s. For students who express some interest in learning about the past tense, as well as for others who the teacher feels might profit from it, there are individual packets which are given for in-class work coupled with motor activi-ties. Discussions between teacher and student during the physical response stage are strongly teacher-molded; students recognize the verb usage as some-thing they have heard, but are hesitant about responding.[17]

During the January–February period (fourteen to sixteen weeks), in addition to various short listening activities for purposes of acquisition, students begin a shift to another facet of the program that they encountered with the present-perfect: the use of individualized mini-units which deal with both culture and (formal) aspects of structure. Examples of such materials would be special work on modals, forms of address, possessives, pronouns, the use of a dictionary (what those items in parentheses mean), advertisements, spelling, cooking lessons, etc.[18] The materials are for students to complete and deal with during class sessions when the instructor uses part of the time to work with small groups, as well as with individuals. During this period, the individualized activities take about thirty minutes every other day. Vocabulary is still presented via the picture board, the table items, and even illustrations from books. This period is used to help students "catch up," whether that is a real or an imagined need, and it gives them a chance to synthesize much of what they have worked on for the first semester.

It is at this time that the program shifts materials, to a series of published audiovisual lessons, *Deutsch durch Audiovisuelle Methode (DDAV)*,[19] an older but quite serviceable series of fifty units (filmstrip and tapes) designed during the late 1950s and early 1960s (the St. Cloud materials). Units 1–4 of the first level of this series allow students to listen to new voices as they hear learned vocabulary; reenactment of the materials, with many additions and deletions, becomes part of class. Students are given uncaptioned picture books to help prepare for class enactments, skits, questions (of a descriptive nature), etc. By this time the students have been in German Level One for a period of fourteen to eighteen weeks, and the transition from a listening situation to a four-skills program has taken place. Students are given continued instruction in oral-delay activities for acquisition purposes. Classroom work during this, the last third of the school year, is based on a variety of selections from supplemental texts and materials, on intensive work of Units 5–11 of *Deutsch durch Audiovisuelle Methode,* and the constant reentry of materials that had been studied earlier. As many techniques and activities as can be thought of, oral and written, are used for individual, small-group, and large-group practice. It is our practice to introduce upcoming vocabulary in comprehension training sessions that take place much earlier than the time when frequent reference would be made to such items (new vocabulary in *DDAV* Unit 9 is brought in some weeks prior to Unit 9, for example), but such planning cannot always be the rule. One simply cannot hope to program student acquisition of language so perfectly that everything is ready when needed. When lexical items that arise out of our work do occur, we simply fall back on the traditional attempt to describe the item through learners' known language. The amount of vocabulary learned during this ten- to twelve-week period is probably about 300 to 400 words, and, compared with the earlier weeks of Level One, is a simple challenge. Major emphasis at this time is on assuring the students that speaking skills can be used in class in a variety of experiences which their earlier training in listening has made easier for them.

CONCLUSIONS

The previous pages have outlined the major activities and techniques of the Southwest German program as it developed during the period 1973–1978, giving the reader a present-tense view of Level One work. In the five years since inception of this method, we have reached some conclusions for our activities that may or may not be applicable in other situations on the high school or college level. Our experience has been that, by emphasizing comprehension training and severely limiting oral response, our students are able to learn and retain much structural and lexical information in a way that reduces those problems usually found among adolescent second-language learners in American high school classrooms. Retention of both vocabulary and structure remain high, for instance; pronunciation difficulties are reduced to very low levels. Students of varying academic backgrounds successfully participate in major parts of the course, something that will probably continue to be an important sidelight in language-teaching methodology in urban districts for some time to come.

Among the formal tenets that have verified themselves repeatedly during the five years, two must be mentioned especially: the avoidance of introducing thematically-linked words; and the nonlinear introduction and employment of structure. Whenever, for instance, items such as fork, knife, and spoon are taught as a grouping, the learner invariably displays some kind of delay or awkwardness in demonstrating acquisition of the information, be it through pointing or speaking or giving an immediate direct translation. It seems that the delay is an apparent consequence of memory search and rejection of the other two objects similarly classified at the same time that the word sought after was first learned. The delay, on the basis of our observations, does not occur when the items are learned separately during the course of days or weeks, rather than during the same session.

Comprehension-training activities and nonverbal responses comprise some 25 percent (up to eight weeks) of the Level One program. During the later stages of that period students begin to explore various tentative means of expressing themselves orally. At that point when the teacher is satisfied that the students are able to listen and respond to batteries of questions dealing with the learned vocabulary, we may say that the major contribution of listening comprehension is over. It continues to play a significant role for the remainder of the first two-thirds of the school year, however; although the students' perceived importance of the need to speak forces comprehension training off center-stage, as it were. Reentry activities during the period of weeks eight to thirteen reinforces the various items internalized before and during that period. Writing skills begin to stabilize and reach the accepted forms, for instance, and early reading activities play a role in shaping student work along these lines. The work of integrating and synthesizing the students' skills continues, with time taken for individual and group work, including a shift to the use of an audiovisual series of filmstrips. The students who are responding with well-molded statements cannot be turned away from speaking activities; they have had so much (real or perceived) success in dealing in German that some are often loathe to continue work on the picture board, which they now consider "Baby-Deutsch." It is possible to hypothesize that Southwest students—and others, too—require many more hours of silent attention to the language (and its attendant paralinguistic phenomena) to become excellent speakers of German. The assumption of recreating much the same aura of child language periods seems to this author unworkable at the high school level. Reasons for this include attitude and motivation; no matter how successful students perceive themselves to be in classes of comprehension training, it may be that, as happens at Southwest, students become disinterested in sessions of comprehension activities after that point when they find themselves capable of speaking meaningful sentences and uttering statements with honed skills. Obviously, more research—more exacting methods of research—is needed to determine if the assumption that listening activities must give way to speaking and listening activities in a high school classroom is valid.

For better or worse, ours is a verbal society; for youngsters in a milieu where talk became background noise for the television some time ago, participation in directed nonverbal activities for a sustained period of time requires discipline that more often than not youngsters do not employ. That they participate in the Southwest program now does not mean that they do so as easily as earlier students seem to have done four years ago. (Reasons for this are variable and unverifiable.) From the perspective of the German program, their willing and interested participation can be sustained if the students are given the opportunity to express themselves after the first quarter of the year. Students gradually move into a four-skills course after approximately eighteen weeks of listening and listening/speaking activities. Their knowledge of structure, our earlier-described list, is displayed throughout the first year, and after.

With respect to linear learning of structure, it is possible that the same phenomenon occurs during the traditional teaching of surface grammar as when grouped nouns are given to students. Consequently, the Southwest students rely on an approach that attempts to maintain the semblance of a natural situation. Acquisition of structure in this manner by pupils gives us adequate indications that there can exist vital elements of first-language learning in second-language situations that require extensive discussion and demonstration. Certainly the employment of this technique puts a heavy burden on the teacher who meets a class with specially developed skills in German or any other language without a textbook sequence to rely upon. The departure from the textbook as the foundation of the course is not so revolutionary when one recalls that in the history of (both formal and informal) language teaching books for whole classes are relatively recent developments; Comenius, Gouin, Palmer, and natural and direct methodists are notable figures and proponents who either could not or did not fall back upon the infamous "two-by-four" method of teaching (i.e., the book has two covers, the classroom has four walls) (Kelly,1969). Structure and textbooks seem often to be a hand-in-hand aspect for language teachers, and so any discussion of linear learning must account for the many arguments for and against the teaching of surface rules, as Kelly (1969) noted.[20] The program at Southwest demonstrates the need to use simple structure during the listening period, as, quite surely, textbook authors also attempt to do. The creativity and spontaneity that we try to foster without pattern drills and without production skills as a means of internalization is an attempt to avoid compounding learner difficulty. This is the case whether or not the discussion deals with cognates to be introduced or complex structures, the possibility of whose recombination and manipulation at so early a time in Level One would be either infrequent or largely theoretical. An excellent example of such a form would be that of an early 1960s audio-lingual text rejoinder (Spanish, ALM, Level One): "*Yo no sabría qué hacer si tuviera que hablar español todo el tiempo!*" ("I wouldn't know what to do if I had to speak Spanish all the time!") To our present way of thinking, back-learning and other strategies for having this sentence and many others from several sources reproduced without really being understood is of questionable value in very real terms of time and expenditure of effort.

Questions of how structure is to be taught are frequently connected to discussions of the quantity that must be taught in the space of a school year. Because the Southwest program is a relatively self-contained one (there is no junior high school program, for instance), our response to queries of coverage may not be applicable to other institutions where there are multiple sections taught by several teachers. The question of coverage of grammar has been debated for years and will continue to be discussed without universal resolution in our profession. For Southwest, we consider the work accomplished during the first year of a high school course realistic in terms of structures learned. If during the first year there are some German students whose learning rate is slower than desirable, there are several means used to ensure the student's success—and "catch-up"—in the following (third) semester. Our goal is to ensure well-prepared students within specifically stated parameters during the first year. The students are allowed, that is, a period of creative hypothesis-testing for as long as possible; they are attempting to express themselves in (for them) novel ways that form the basis of real communication. Students trained in comprehension activities, be they elementary picture pointing, intermediate questioning, or advanced discussion between the teacher and a native informant performing a simple science experiment, continualy must be shown that they can have insights into the language through meaningful activities. The students must be aware that their strengths, such as relaxed, creative sentence generation (whether simple or complex), can lead them into further active cooperation with the teacher and with one another.

Comprehension training cannot be portrayed as the panacea for the ills in modern foreign language classes. Its function is much more than as the transitional stage that it is usually assigned. It serves as an integral aspect of a system of language teaching—both inductive and deductive—that attempts to reduce to a minor role the use of production during the first year as a means of language acquisition.[21] The Southwest program is not so much a model, but more an example to show that cautiously thought-out and executed techniques of comprehension training can prove successful in the foreign language classroom where the variables of philosophy, teacher ability, and student needs remain paradoxically constant.

Notes

1.   The methods used, while not so universal as the cinematic "Hit 'em with all you've got," do owe much to the tradition of teaching as an eclectic activity. That in foreign language classes we keep rediscovering techniques used generations ago is well substantiated by Louis G. Kelly in his *Twenty-five centuries of language teaching* (1969). Many of the practices discussed and found in the Southwest High School German program—direct association, pictorial procedures, the use of German instead of English—may be traced to St. Augustine, Comenius, and Lamy (seventeenth century) respectively (cf. Kelly, 1969, pp. 10–23).

During the past five years many works have been consulted and utilized to establish the program; foremost among them are the following:

Asher, J. J. "The learning strategy of the total physical response: A review." *The Modern Language Journal, 50,* pp. 79–84, 1966.

————. "The total physical response approach to second language learning." *The Modern Language Journal, 53,* pp. 3–17, 1969.

————. "Children's first language as a model for second language learning." *The Modern Language Journal, 56,* pp. 133–139, 1972.

Ervin-Tripp, S. M. "Is second language learning like the first?" In E. Hatch (Ed.), *Second language acquisition.* Rowley, Mass.: Newbury House, 1978.

Fraser, C., Bellugi, U., and Brown, R. "Control of grammar in imitation, comprehension, and production." *Journal of Verbal Learning and Verbal Behavior, 2,* pp. 121–135, 1963.

Hatch, E. M. (Ed.) *Second language acquisition.* Rowley, Mass.: Newbury House, 1978.

Lenneberg, E. H. (Ed.) *New directions in the study of language.* Cambridge: M.I.T. Press, 1964.

McNeill, D. *The acquisition of language.* New York: Harper and Row, 1970.

Miller, G. "The magical number seven, plus or minus two." *Psychological Review, 63,* pp. 81–97, 1956.

Postovsky, V. A. "Effects of delay in oral practice at the beginning of second language learning." Ph.D. dissertation, U. of California at Berkeley, 1970. Also published in *The Modern Language Journal, 58,* pp. 229–239, 1974.

Sittler, E. *Die Logik des Hörens: besser Hören* = besser Lernen. Schriftenreihe des Pädagogischen Instituts Düsseldorf, Heft 26, Juni 1975.

Winitz, H. "Problem solving and the delaying of speech as strategies in the teaching of language." *Asha, 15,* pp. 583–586, 1973.

Winitz, H. *Comprehension and problem solving as strategies for language training.* The Hague: Mouton, 1975.

Winitz, H. and Reeds, J.A. "Rapid acquisition of a foreign language (German) by the avoidance of speaking." *International Review of Applied Linguistics, 11,* pp. 295–317, 1973.

2.   Among the many sources for children's literature, the following are easily accessible and useful:

Goertz, H. *Kinderlieder, Kinderreime.* Wien: Carl Ueberreuter, 1973.

Inter Nationes (Bonn-Bad Godesberg). "Wir Lernen Deutsch mit Kinderliedern." Institutions-programm 1972, Position II, 8 (Teil 1 u. 2).

McGuinn, R., and Steinmetz, D. (Eds.) *NFSG Songbook.* South San Francisco: Compile-A-Text Publishers, 1976.

Minnesota Univ., Foreign Language Curriculum Center. "Es weihnachtet sehr," Mini-Unit G–108, by M. R. Anderson.

3.   Ideal Corporation, New York: *ID 2000. Initial sounds in Spanish. (Initial sounds in French, ID 2020)* Also available in the Ideal series are other picture card boxes dealing with contrasts, spatial relationships, and logical sequence (*ID 2701, 2702, 2681–85*).

4.   Although Asher (1972, p. 133) refers to "as far back as 1938" in discussing earlier experiments regarding comprehension training, it seems that his views do not account for the varied historical background that makes active demonstration in the 1970s so often a rediscovery. In his discussion of mime and demonstration, Kelly (1969, p. 11) refers to a J. Levy writing on the natural method in 1978:

> "I have it from a very trustworthy authority that in some New England town a teacher of the 'Natural Method' gambols around the room to express the idea of *to run*. If this be the general case, school committees will no longer be called upon to deliver certificates of proficiency to teachers of languages: this duty will devolve on P. T. Barnum."

5.   Obviously, other truncated remarks and short sentences naturally flow from this first query, i.e., '*Wo ist denn der Tisch?*" "*Kannst du den Tisch nicht finden?*" Many remarks follow the modeling of parents speaking with their children; sentences are simplified and repetition is important.

6.   Some two years' experience with Level One Spanish students indicates that although the initial structures are not congruent, this technique is still successful.

7.   It is possible that this embarrassing lapse, which occurs universally, should help serve as proof that it is difficult to learn initially items/names in undifferentiated and semantically-linked groupings, and also that it is difficult to learn language in that manner (Underwood, 1966).

8.   In addition to commercially prepared tapes, several recordings by local informants have proven worthwhile in helping students adjust to other voices. In more advanced levels, several tapes from Inter Nationes are employed, as well as cassettes made by Southwest High School students on trips to Germany in 1976, 1977, 1978, and 1979.

9.   A series of papers and materials available through the Department of Germanic Languages at the University of Texas at Austin. Cf. "Lesson Plans, First Six Weeks," prepared by Dr. Margaret Woodruff. (The materials show a continued use of linear grammar introduction and little oral delay.)

10.   *Ravensburger Spiele* is a catalogue of games that can be adapted and used for all levels. It is available from Otto Maier Verlag, D–7980 Ravensburg, Markstrasse 22–26, Postfach 1860, West Germany.

11.   An example would be a student in Level One who used an incorrect definite article marker for dative, and immediately (in less than a second), with little frustration or hesitation, made the necessary change; we were fortunate to have "caught" this instance on videotape.

12.   A learner-initiated desire for linear grammar information is not thwarted. Typically, only a few class members will ask why the definite article transformations occur; the question is couched as "Why is *der Ball* sometimes *dem Ball*?" This query occurs when students seem to have internalized several numerous examples of the shift and begin formulating hypotheses. One often heard is "you change *der* to *dem* if you use a preposition." Thus, it seems that the questioner is seeking confirmation of an independently-arrived-at solution. Because by this time students are well aware that they cannot speak English in class, the questions occur at other times of the day and other places.

It is the author's belief that errors generated by such incorrect or half-correct hypotheses are not so great a disadvantage to the learner's progress. Such errors as a misplaced ending or article are essentially local in nature and do not affect global transmission and comprehension of the message conveyed, either by the teacher or at a later date by the student.

13.   Occasional use of *Morgen kommen wir nicht* and similar time expressions are used as alternatives to the future tense.

14.   Margaret Woodruff, "Comprehension and Communication, Fine: But What Do You Do About Grammar?," 1978. (Available from the author, University of Texas, Austin, Texas.)

15.   Here again the question of the use of different voices and the need for teacher creativity is apparent. The Southwest students have hosted visitors who taught a folk dance, talked about a science experiment, demonstrated the finer points of cooking Rotkohl, and generally helped students listen and occasionally answered questions.

16. "Es weihnachtet sehr," U. of Minnesota Mini-Unit G–108, and Susanne Ehrlich, *Weihnacht. Christmas in Germany.* Skokie, National Textbook, 1975.

17. During this time, the following is a typical conversation:

Teacher:	*Madeleine, geh mal ans Fenster und mach's auf!*
Student:	(performs action and sits down)
T:	*Gut, danke. Madeleine hat das Fenster aufgemacht. Was hat sie aufgemacht? Hat sie die Tür aufgemacht?*
Second Student:	*Nein, das Fenster.*
T:	*Ja, natürlich, das Fenster hat sie aufgemacht. Tim, geh auch ans Fenster und mach jetzt das Fenster zu, bitte.*
Third Student:	(performs task)
T:	*Gut, jetzt hat Tim das Fenster zugemacht. Hat er das Fenster aufgemacht, Leo?*
Leo:	*Nein.*
T:	*Richtig, das Fenster ist zu; Tim hat's zugemacht. Hat Leo das Fenster schon zugemacht, Michael?*
Michael:	*Nein, Tim was [sic] ans Fenster.*
T:	*Ja, Tim war am Fenster und hat das Fenster zugemacht. Und wer hat das Fenster aufgemacht? Carla?*
Carla:	*Madeleine öffnet das Fenster.*
T:	*Ja, Madeleine hat es aufgemacht und Tim—was hat Tim gemacht?*
Carla:	*Tim schliesst das Fenster.*

18. There is a wide range of mini-units available from the Foreign Language Curriculum Materials Center at the University of Minnesota, 224 Peik Hall, Minneapolis, Minnesota. In addition, several author-made units are used.

19. Presently available from Heinle and Heinle, 29 Lexington Rd., Concord, Mass. 01742.

20. Kelly (1969, pp. 226–227) writes: "The progress of the idea (grammatical analysis) can be traced from attacks on it, one of the first being that of Comenius, who restates very clearly the earlier objections of G. H. Cominius and Petrus Ramus:

"And the second grave error is that right from the very beginning of the course, youngsters are driven to the thorny complexities of language; I mean the entanglements of grammar. It is now the accepted method of the schools to begin from the form instead of the matter, i.e., from grammar, rather than from authors and dictionaries."

21. Kelly (1969, p. 310): "By 1967 J. B. Carroll had arrived at the position held by Erasmus, three hundred years before, that both deductive and inductive methods are to be used in teaching concepts, one reinforcing the other."

References

Adams, M. "Methodology for examining second language acquisition." In E. M. Hatch (Ed.), *Second language acquisition.* Rowley, Mass.: Newbury House, 1978.

Asher, J. J. "Children's first language as a model for second language learning." *The Modern Language Journal, 56,* pp. 133–139, 1972.

Carey, S. T., and Lockhart, R. S. "Encoding differences in recognition and recall." *Memory and Cognition, 1,* pp. 297–300, 1973.

Kelly, L. G. *25 centuries of language teaching.* Rowley, Mass.: Newbury House, 1969.

Lambert, W. E., and Tucker, G. R. *The bilingual education of children.* Rowley, Mass.: Newbury House, 1972.

Reeds, J. A., Winitz, H., and Garcia, P. A. "A test of reading following comprehension training." *International Review of Applied Linguistics, 15,* pp. 307–319, 1977.

Sell, R. "Early emphasis on speaking: An associative approach to foreign language learning." *Foreign Language Annals, 10,* pp. 103–113, 1977.

Tomkins, S. *Affect, cognition and personality. The negative effects.* Vol. 2. New York: Springer, 1965.

Underwood, B. J. *Experimental psychology.* New York: Appleton-Century-Crofts, 1966.

Winitz, H., and Reeds, J. *Comprehension and problem solving as strategies for language training.* The Hague: Mouton, 1975.

Winitz, H. Reeds, J. A., and Garcia, P. A. *Natural language learning.* Vols. 1–4. Kansas City, Mo.: General Linguistics Corporation, 1975.

Subject Index

Author Index

DATE DUE